The IDG Books *CyberBuck$* Advantage

We at IDG Books Worldwide created *CyberBuck$: Making Money Online* to meet your growing need for quick access to the most complete and accurate computer information available. Our books work the way you do: They focus on accomplishing specific tasks — not learning random functions. Our books are not long-winded manuals or dry reference tomes. In each book, expert authors tell you exactly what you can do with your new technology and software and how to evaluate its usefulness for your needs. Easy to follow, step-by-step sections; comprehensive coverage; and convenient access in language and design — it's all here.

The authors of IDG books are uniquely qualified to give you expert advice as well as to provide insightful tips and techniques not found anywhere else. Our authors maintain close contact with end users through feedback from articles, training sessions, e-mail exchanges, user group participation, and consulting work. Because our authors know the realities of daily computer use and are directly tied to the reader, our books have a strategic advantage.

Our authors have the experience to approach a topic in the most efficient manner, and we know that you, the reader, will benefit from a "one-on-one" relationship with the author. Our research shows that readers make computer book purchases because they want expert advice. Because readers want to benefit from the author's experience, the author's voice is always present in an IDG book.

In addition, the author is free to include or recommend useful software in an IDG book. The software that accompanies each book is not intended to be a casual filler but is linked to the content, theme, or procedures of the book. We know that you will benefit from the included software.

You will find what you need in this book whether you read it from cover to cover, section by section, or simply one topic at a time. As a computer user, you deserve a comprehensive resource of answers. We at IDG Books Worldwide are proud to deliver that resource with *CyberBuck$: Making Money Online*.

Brenda McLaughlin
Senior Vice President and Group Publisher
YouTellUs@idgbooks.com

D1401092

CyberBuck$:™
$ Making
Money Online

CyberBuck$: Making Money Online

Kim Komando

IDG Books Worldwide, Inc.
An International Data Group Company

Foster City, CA ◆ Chicago, IL ◆ Indianapolis, IN ◆ Southlake, TX

CyberBuck$™: Making Money Online

Published by
IDG Books Worldwide, Inc.
An International Data Group Company
919 E. Hillsdale Blvd.
Suite 400
Foster City, CA 94404
www.idgbooks.com (IDG Books Worldwide Web site)

Library of Congress Catalog Card No.: 96-77693

ISBN: 1-56884-718-1

Printed in the United States of America

10 9 8 7 6 5 4 3 2 1

IE/RY/QZ/ZW/IN

Distributed in the United States by IDG Books Worldwide, Inc.

Distributed by Macmillan Canada for Canada; by Contemporanea de Ediciones for Venezuela; by Distribuidora Cuspide for Argentina; by CITEC for Brazil; by Ediciones ZETA S.C.R. Ltda. for Peru; by Editorial Limusa SA for Mexico; by Transworld Publishers Limited in the United Kingdom and Europe; by Academic Bookshop for Egypt; by Levant Distributors S.A.R.L. for Lebanon; by Al Jassim for Saudi Arabia; by Simron Pty. Ltd. for South Africa; by Pustak Mahal for India; by The Computer Bookshop for India; by Toppan Company Ltd. for Japan; by Addison Wesley Publishing Company for Korea; by Longman Singapore Publishers Ltd. for Singapore, Malaysia, Thailand, and Indonesia; by Unalis Corporation for Taiwan; by WS Computer Publishing Company, Inc. for the Philippines; by WoodsLane Pty. Ltd. for Australia; by WoodsLane Enterprises Ltd. for New Zealand. Authorized Sales Agent: Anthony Rudkin Associates for the Middle East and North Africa.

For general information on IDG Books Worldwide's books in the U.S., please call our Consumer Customer Service department at 800-762-2974. For reseller information, including discounts and premium sales, please call our Reseller Customer Service department at 800-434-3422.

For information on where to purchase IDG Books Worldwide's books outside the U.S., please contact our International Sales department at 415-655-3172 or fax 415-655-3295.

For information on foreign language translations, please contact our Foreign & Subsidiary Rights department at 415-655-3021 or fax 415-655-3281.

For sales inquiries and special prices for bulk quantities, please contact our Sales department at 415-655-3200 or write to the address above.

For information on using IDG Books Worldwide's books in the classroom or for ordering examination copies, please contact our Educational Sales department at 800-434-2086 or fax 817-251-8174.

For authorization to photocopy items for corporate, personal, or educational use, please contact Copyright Clearance Center, 222 Rosewood Drive, Danvers, MA 01923, or fax 508-750-4470.

is a trademark under exclusive license to IDG Books Worldwide, Inc., from International Data Group, Inc.

About the Author

Kim Komando

Computer technology is nothing new to Kim Komando. When she first sat down at a computer at age 9, it was the beginning of what *Information Week* now calls a "one-person PC industry."

In 1985, Kim earned a computer systems bachelor of science degree from Arizona State University, which she financed by providing classes in computer hardware and software training. After college, she secured a position as an IBM marketing representative and later became a large-business systems account manager at AT&T, where she received various awards for her sales achievements. The next beneficiary of Kim's talents was Unisys Corporation, where, in 1991, she single-handedly closed the largest commercial deal with an $11 million sale to a Fortune 500 company.

While she was at Unisys, Kim began writing her weekly syndicated newspaper computer column and hosting radio and television programs. Her initial media success gave birth to The Komando Corporation.

Welcome to the world of IDG Books Worldwide.

IDG Books Worldwide, Inc., is a subsidiary of International Data Group, the world's largest publisher of computer-related information and the leading global provider of information services on information technology. IDG was founded more than 25 years ago and now employs more than 8,500 people worldwide. IDG publishes more than 270 computer publications in over 75 countries (see listing below). More than 90 million people read one or more IDG publications each month.

Launched in 1990, IDG Books Worldwide is today the #1 publisher of best-selling computer books in the United States. We are proud to have received eight awards from the Computer Press Association in recognition of editorial excellence and three from *Computer Currents'* First Annual Readers' Choice Awards. Our best-selling ...*For Dummies*® series has more than 25 million copies in print with translations in 30 languages. IDG Books Worldwide, through a joint venture with IDG's Hi-Tech Beijing, became the first U.S. publisher to publish a computer book in the People's Republic of China. In record time, IDG Books Worldwide has become the first choice for millions of readers around the world who want to learn how to better manage their businesses.

Our mission is simple: Every one of our books is designed to bring extra value and skill-building instructions to the reader. Our books are written by experts who understand and care about our readers. The knowledge base of our editorial staff comes from years of experience in publishing, education, and journalism — experience which we use to produce books for the '90s. In short, we care about books, so we attract the best people. We devote special attention to details such as audience, interior design, use of icons, and illustrations. And because we use an efficient process of authoring, editing, and desktop publishing our books electronically, we can spend more time ensuring superior content and spend less time on the technicalities of making books.

You can count on our commitment to deliver high-quality books at competitive prices on topics you want to read about. At IDG Books Worldwide, we continue in the IDG tradition of delivering quality for more than 25 years. You'll find no better book on a subject than one from IDG Books Worldwide.

John Kilcullen
President and CEO
IDG Books Worldwide, Inc.

IDG Books Worldwide, Inc., is a subsidiary of International Data Group, the world's largest publisher of computer-related information and the leading global provider of information services on information technology. International Data Group publishes over 276 computer publications in over 75 countries. Ninety million people read one or more International Data Group publications each month. International Data Group's publications include: **ARGENTINA:** Annuario de Informatica, Computerworld Argentina, PC World Argentina; **AUSTRALIA:** Australian Macworld, Client/Server Journal, Computer Living, Computerworld, Computerworld 100, Digital News, IT Casebook, Network World, On-line World Australia, PC World, Publishing Essentials, Reseller, WebMaster; **AUSTRIA:** Computerwelt Osterreich, Networks Austria, PC Tip; **BELARUS:** PC World Belarus; **BELGIUM:** Data News; **BRAZIL:** Annuário de Informática, Computerworld Brazil, Connections, Super Game Power, Macworld, PC Player, PC World Brazil, Publish Brazil, Reseller News; **BULGARIA:** Computerworld Bulgaria, Networkworld/Bulgaria, PC & MacWorld Bulgaria; **CANADA:** CIO Canada, Client/Server World, ComputerWorld Canada, InfoCanada, Network World Canada; **CHILE:** Computerworld Chile, PC World Chile; **COLOMBIA:** Computerworld Colombia, PC World Colombia; **COSTA RICA:** PC World Centro America; **THE CZECH AND SLOVAK REPUBLICS:** Computerworld Czechoslovakia, Elektronika Czechoslovakia, Macworld Czech Republic, PC World Czechoslovakia; **DENMARK:** Communications World, Computerworld Danmark, Macworld Danmark, PC Privat Danmark, PC World Danmark, PC World Danmark Supplements, TECH World; **DOMINICAN REPUBLIC:** PC World Republica Dominicana; **ECUADOR:** PC World Ecuador; **EGYPT:** Computerworld Middle East, PC World Middle East; **EL SALVADOR:** PC World Centro America; **FINLAND:** MikroPC, Tietoverkko, Tietoviikko; **FRANCE:** Distributique, Golden, Hebdo-Distributique, Info PC, Le Guide du Monde Informatique, Le Monde Informatique, Reseaux & Telecoms; **GERMANY:** Computer Partner, Computerwoche, Computerwoche Extra, Computerwoche Focus, I/M Information Management, Macwelt, PC Welt; **GREECE:** GamePro, Multimedia World; **GUATEMALA:** PC World Centro America; **HONDURAS:** PC World Centro America; **HONG KONG:** Computerworld Hong Kong, PCWorld Hong Kong, Publish in Asia; **HUNGARY:** ABCD CD-ROM, Computerworld Szamitastechnika, PC & Mac World Hungary, PC-X Magazine; **ICELAND:** Tolvuheimur/PC World Island; **INDIA:** Information Systems Computerworld, PC World India, Publish in Asia; **INDONESIA:** InfoKomputer PC World, Komputek Computerworld, Publish in Asia; **IRELAND:** ComputerScope, PC Live!; **ISRAEL:** People & Computers; **ITALY:** Computerworld Italia, Computerworld Italia Special Editions, Macworld Italia, Networking Italia, PC Shopping, PC World Italia, PC World/Walt Disney; **JAPAN:** DTP World, HP Open World Japan, Macworld Japan, Nikkei Personal Computing, Open World Japan, OS/2 World Japan, SunWorld Japan, Windows World Japan; **KENYA:** East African Computer News; **KOREA:** Hi-Tech Information/Computerworld, Macworld Korea, PC World Korea; **MACEDONIA:** PC World Macedonia; **MALAYSIA:** Computerworld Malaysia, PC World Malaysia, Publish in Asia; **MEXICO:** Computerworld Mexico, Macworld, PC World Mexico; **MYANMAR:** PC World Myanmar; **NETHERLANDS:** Computer! Totaal, LAN Magazine, LanWorld Buyers Guide, Macworld, Net Magazine, Totaal! Beurskrant; **NEW ZEALAND:** Absolute Beginner's Guide, Computer Buyer, Computer Industry Directory, Computerworld New Zealand, MTB, Network World, PC World New Zealand; **NICARAGUA:** PC World Centro America; **NIGERIA:** PC World Nigeria; **NORWAY:** Computerworld Norge, Computerworld Privat (Datamagasinet), CW Rapport Norge, IDG's KURSGUIDE, Macworld Norge, Multimediaworld, PC World Ekspress, PC World Nettverk, PC World Norge, PC World's Produktguide, Windows World Spesial; **PAKISTAN:** Computerworld Pakistan, PC World Pakistan; Panama: PC World Panama; **P. R. OF CHINA:** China Computer Users, China Computerworld, China Infoworld, China Telecom World Weekly, Computer & Communication, Electronic Design China, Electronics Today, Electronics Weekly, Game Camp, Game Soft, Network World China, PC World China, Popular Computer Weekly, Software Weekly, Software World, Telecom World; **PERU:** Computerworld Peru, PC World Profesional Peru, PC World Peru; **PHILIPPINES:** Computerworld Philippines, PC World Philippines, Publish in Asia; **POLAND:** Computerworld Poland, Computerworld Special Report, Macworld, Networld, PC World Komputer; **PORTUGAL:** Cerebro/PC World, Computerworld/Correio Informático, Dealer World Portugal, MacIn/PCIn, Multimedia World Portugal; **PUERTO RICO:** PC World Puerto Rico; **ROMANIA:** Computerworld Romania, PC World Romania, Telecom Romania; **RUSSIA:** Computerworld Russia, Mir PK, Sety; **SINGAPORE:** Computerworld Singapore, PC World Singapore, Publish in Asia; **SLOVENIA:** MONITOR; **SOUTH AFRICA:** Computing S.A., InfoWorld S.A., Network World S.A., Software World; **SPAIN:** Computerworld España, COMUNICACIONES WORLD, Dealer World, Macworld España, PC World España; **SWEDEN:** CAP&Design, Computer Sweden, Corporate Computing, MacWorld, Maxi Data, MikroDatorn, Nätverk & Kommunikation, PC/Aktiv, PC World, Windows World; **SWITZERLAND:** Computerworld Schweiz, Macworld Schweiz, PCtip; **TAIWAN:** Computerworld Taiwan, Macworld Taiwan, PC World Taiwan, Publish Taiwan, Windows World; **THAILAND:** Thai Computerworld, Publish in Asia; **TURKEY:** Computerworld Turkiye, MACWORLD Turkiye, PC WORLD Turkiye; **UKRAINE:** Computerworld Kiev, Computers & Software, Multimedia World Ukraine, PC World Ukraine; **UNITED KINGDOM:** Acorn User, Amiga Action, Amiga Computing, Appletalk, Computing, GamePro, Macworld, Network News, Parents and Computers, PC Advisor, PC Home, PSX Pro UK, The WEB; **UNITED STATES:** Cable in the Classroom, CD Review, CIO Magazine, Computerworld, Computerworld Client/Server Journal, Digital Video Magazine, DOS World, Federal Computer Week, GamePro, InfoWorld, I-Way, JavaWorld, Macworld, Multimedia World, Netscape World Online, Network World, PC Entertainment, PC World, Publish, SunWorld Online, SWATPro Magazine, Video Event, WebMaster; **URUGUAY:** PC World Uruguay; **VENEZUELA:** Computerworld Venezuela, PC World Venezuela; and **VIETNAM:** PC World Vietnam.

Dedication

For my mom and dad. I love you.

Acknowledgments

In this book, I tried to answer every question that anyone has ever asked me about my company's online marketing success through e-mail, on my talk-radio shows, during live online chats, and on the Kim Komando's Komputer Klinic online message boards. Consider this book an official Kim Komando "how to do business in cyberspace" brain dump.

Thank you to America Online for giving my company a chance way back when the online service had only a few hundred thousand members. I am appreciative of the millions of people who now visit my company's online areas on not only America Online, but also the Microsoft Network and the Internet. These folks are the real crux of my success.

I want to thank the entire staff of The Komando Corporation for waiting patiently at my office door before interrupting me while I finished typing whatever sentence I was working on in this book; Bruce Boyle, for programming the CD-ROM; John San Filippo, for sorting through the fodder and making sense of it all; all the online Komandos (everyone from Komando1 to Komando25 and those to come), for designing, maintaining, promoting, and programming the online areas; and Barry Young, for being my friend.

What would a Komando book be, of course, without dear Mother Komando providing constant reinforcement? I am so lucky to have such a great mom who is also a wonderful friend. (I swear, though, if she asks me one more time, "Did you type 'The End' yet?" things are going to get really bad for her.)

I also want to thank Greg "Get the Deal" Croy, Erik "Who Needs Sleep?" Dafforn, Rebecca "Make Those Authors Look Good" Whitney, Beth "The All-Knowing Computer Whiz" Slick, Melisa "Marketing Maven" Duffy, and the others at IDG Books Worldwide. As always, their assistance is invaluable.

Hey, Mom, get this: THE END!

This is just the beginning of your online success, however. So get started on your online road to riches. See you online!

(The publisher would like to give special thanks to Patrick J. McGovern, who made this book possible.)

Credits

Senior Vice President and Group Publisher
Brenda McLaughlin

Acquisitions Manager
Gregory Croy

Acquisitions Editor
Ellen Camm

Brand Manager
Melisa M. Duffy

Managing Editor
Andy Cummings

Administrative Assistant
Laura J. Moss

Editorial Assistant
Timothy Borek

Production Director
Beth Jenkins

Production Assistant
Jacalyn L. Pennywell

Supervisor of Project Coordination
Cindy L. Phipps

Supervisor of Page Layout
Kathie S. Schutte

Supervisor of Graphics and Design
Shelley Lea

Reprint/Blueline Coordination
Tony Augsburger
Patricia R. Reynolds
Theresa Sánchez-Baker

Media/Archive Coordination
Leslie Popplewell
Jason Marcuson
Melissa Stauffer

Senior Development Editor
Erik Dafforn

Editor
Rebecca Whitney

Technical Reviewer
Beth Slick

Project Coordinator
Valery Bourke

Graphics Coordination
Gina Scott
Angela F. Hunckler

Production Page Layout
E. Shawn Aylsworth
Cameron Booker
Todd Klemme
Jane Martin
Drew Moore
Mark Owens
Michael Sullivan

Proofreaders
Christine Sabooni
Michael Bolinger
Rachel Garvey
Nancy Price
Dwight Ramsey
Robert Springer
Carrie Voorhis
Karen York

Indexer
David Heiret

Contents at a Glance

Table of Contents

Chapter 10: Making Sure That Your Security Net Is in Place 211

Chapter 11: Tapping New Markets with Global Online Marketing 227

Chapter 12: Essential Ingredients for Your Online Area 243

Foreword

In 20 years of writing and editing for professional trade and business magazines in about as many different industries, I have come across many "experts" in their fields — brilliant people with educated minds, visionaries, technical scientists, specialists so finely attuned to their industries that I have marveled at their awesome knowledge. Marveled, yes. Understood? Rarely. Not without major brain strain. Isn't that a hoot?

Several years ago, as the founding executive editor of a magazine that covered online marketing, I was again "editorially challenged" to find an expert, this time in the online world. Could anyone out there clearly communicate how emerging online businesses could be applied to the needs of marketers? I spoke to strategists, visionaries, doctorates in computer science, programmers, software developers (okay, I was desperate!) and journalists who specialized in computer topics. When I finally narrowed my search to a handful of candidates, I was dismayed to find that, once again, all were at a loss when it came to speaking or writing about online marketing in *plain English*.

Then came an unexpected breakthrough — in the form of a 98-pound, blond dynamo named Kim Komando. Kim and I "met" in an e-mail introduction (naturally) by a mutual business colleague and friend. She was great! With credentials a mile long, her writing was at once educational, to the point, and easily understood. Readers adored her work and responded with notes of gratitude, relief, and cries of "More!"

Kim Komando is a computer genius, a teacher, and a *communicator*.

CyberBuck$: Making Money Online is a shining example of Komando at her best. As you read this latest offering and review the accompanying CD-ROM, you will see what I mean. *CyberBuck$* delivers on its promise to teach you all you need to know in order to market your products and business online. How's that for a nice change of pace?

I don't know about you, but I'm so tired of the hype and endless stream of "can't-miss educational opportunities" that claim to teach you how to make zillions of dollars by marketing your business online that I could (please pardon the expression) just puke. As though it's not arduous enough for ordinary business mortals to get up to speed in the "interactive age," we have to ascertain which so-called experts are for real and which are simply trying to cash in on our need to know.

Who can miss the blazing headlines in the business, entertainment, and media press regarding the latest online bonanzas? But that's just the point: The merging of business and entertainment and media is what online marketing is all about. Kim Komando is clear about that. Hence, *CyberBuck$: Making Money Online*.

Although the book is based in part on the author's solid knowledge of the technical aspects of computer architectures and online advancements, *CyberBuck$* conveys much-needed information in a way that we "mere marketing types" can understand. As you read *CyberBuck$*, you'll see what I mean. Lightbulbs in your head will flash all over the place! Not all of us are born to understand the inner workings of a machine before we can use it effectively. Nor do marketers need to be inundated by technical computer jargon before they can launch cost-effective, highly successful online marketing programs. After reading *CyberBuck$*, you'll feel empowered, not discouraged.

In my experience, what marketers want and desperately need in order to get their online marketing programs kick-started are *answers*. From the basic question of "What's the difference between the Internet and a service like America Online?" (which, let's face it, too many of us are embarrassed to ask) to the more complicated matters of motivating online buyers, acquiring necessary tools, handling online competition, choosing equipment, understanding marketing and buying cycles, interpreting customer profiles and demographics, integrating traditional advertising, managing the potential for "branding" and other image issues, devising online selling techniques — it's all here!

Read, learn from, and enjoy *CyberBuck$: Making Money Online* — and then get down to the business of online marketing!

Kathy St. Louis Ricciardi
Interactive marketing consultant

Introduction

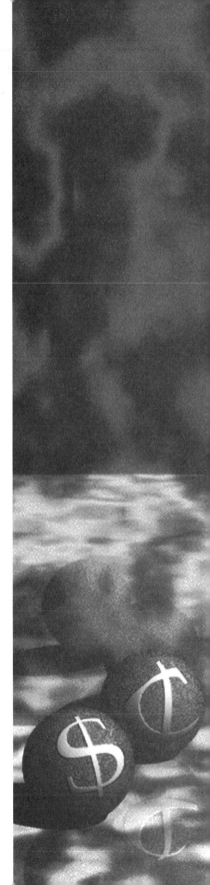

When someone uses the term "computer millionaire," you probably think instantly of Bill Gates. That's understandable. Dollarwise, there's a great deal to think about. Gates, however, is certainly not the only success story in the history of personal computing. For example, many people don't even realize that Gates had a partner when he started Microsoft. His name is Paul Allen, the current owner of the Portland Trailblazers professional basketball team, and he and Gates are still good friends. Although Allen's net worth is only about half his former partner's, he's still in the billionaire category.

Plenty of other people outside of Microsoft have become computer millionaires. Steve Jobs and Steve Wozniak, the founders of Apple Computer, are two examples. More recently, Marc Andreesen, the technowizard behind Netscape Communications, became an instant millionaire the first day his company began to offer public stock. The list goes on.

I have talked with and worked with many people who have made their fortunes in computers. Without exception, they all have one thing in common. None of them set out to get rich. None of them set out to own big companies. None of them set out to become household names. They all started out with a vision of what computers could do for themselves and for other people. Then they turned that vision into reality with hard work.

The explosion of the Internet and the commercial online services has been compared with the California Gold Rush of the 1800s, and rightly so, in many ways. The tremendous popularity of cyberspace has created a whole new world of opportunity for people with the vision, courage, and determination to "go for it."

Some Practical Advice

Almost daily, people send electronic junk mail to at least one of my numerous e-mail addresses, claiming that I can make, for example, $70,000 a week by spending just two hours a night on my modem. The U.S. Postal Service has been delivering this type of garbage to my regular mailbox for years. The only difference now is that it can be delivered through cyberspace in a matter of seconds.

I don't know who tomorrow's computer millionaires will be, but I can tell you who they *won't* be: people who view the online world as one giant get-rich-quick scheme. The technology may be new, but the work ethic is the same. Tomorrow's online industry giants will be the people who develop a solid, innovative plan and then work to see it through.

If you have checked a bookstore recently, you know that it has dozens of titles about making money in cyberspace. When I recently flipped through several books about cyberspace marketing, however, I couldn't find a single word to indicate that any of the authors of these books had ever made a single dime online, other than by telling *other people* how to do it. That's what sets this book apart from the others.

I started Kim Komando's Komputer Klinic on America Online in 1993 and have been successfully running that business ever since. Soon my company launched its Web site, and business has never been better. My point is that while the authors of other books have been busy writing about online success, I have been busy *doing* it. I am not trying to boast; it's simply the truth. This book is the only one I know of that was written by someone who is willing to "practice what you preach."

If you purchased *A Gazillion Ways to Make Money with Your Modem* or *Today's Top 10,000 Online Business Ideas,* you picked up the wrong book. In those books, you see plenty of examples of people who have achieved some level of success online, but I don't necessarily recommend that you try to copy any of those methods. The business that's right for someone else may not be right for you. The key to all major success is innovation — something that only you can provide for your business.

This book provides practical advice from someone who has been there. Most other books focus exclusively on the subject of being online; they ignore the business principles that have applied for years and years in the offline world and that still apply in the online world. This book is about online business, and I devote as much of it to the business part as I do to the online part. By the time you finish reading this book, you should have plenty of information you can apply to *any* type of business.

To continue the California Gold Rush analogy, you can consider this book your pickax, pack mule, and canteen — and perhaps a field guide for differentiating fool's gold from the real thing. My goal is to give you the basic tools you need in order to achieve online success. It's still up to you, however, to get out there and find that gold.

How This Book Is Organized

The 21 chapters in this book are divided into six parts and an appendix that tells you how to install the CD-ROM in the back of this book.

Part I: Doing Your Homework

The first two chapters in this book set the stage for what's to come. In Chapter 1, I set the pace by giving you my theory about the commercial online business environment; it's no different from those late-night television infomercials. I share the secret formula used in successful infomercials and show you how you can use it in your business online. I also tell you where the online services and the Internet came from and explain how you can use them to your advantage.

Chapter 2 talks about the type of equipment you need in order to get online. Need is a relative term, of course. If you're on a shoestring budget, you may not be able to afford what you really need. The chapter also tells you about some different ways to get by with less than you need, at least temporarily.

Part II: Online Marketing 101

Part II begins to get into the nuts and bolts of cyberspace marketing. Do you remember when I said, earlier in the Introduction, that you would probably find information in this book that you can apply to any business? Part II is where it all begins.

In Chapter 3, I introduce some generally accepted psychological principles that explain what motivates people in a broad sense, and then, drawing on my own experience, I describe what motivates people in an online buying situation.

After you have a general understanding of how to motivate your potential customers, you have to decide exactly whom you're most likely to motivate. In other words, you have to determine exactly who your customer is by developing a general profile of your typical customer. In Chapter 4, I talk about the study of demographics.

If you're going to sell, you obviously have to sell *something*, either a product or a service. In Chapter 5, I tell you how to sell products online, beginning with the basics of a product's life cycle and moving on to product development. This chapter presents some concepts for naming and packaging your products and, perhaps most important, gives you some sound advice about how to avoid potential legal problems.

Chapter 6 covers the other side of the selling game: selling services. This subject is much different from selling products, because you can't pick up a service in your hand and examine it for quality workmanship. A service business requires, by its nature, much more faith on the part of buyers; this chapter tells you how to overcome obstacles associated with this challenge.

I have yet to see an online business book that gives its readers any worthwhile advice about pricing products and services. Chapter 7, therefore, puts this book in a class by itself. Entire books have been written about pricing strategies, but this chapter truly does describe the basics you need to know for pricing your online goods and services.

Part III: Commercial Online Services and the Internet

By the time you get to Part III in the book, you should have a clear idea about the *who* and the *what* of online selling. The chapters in this part of the book talk about the *where* and the *how.*

Most other online-business books gloss over the commercial online services, not because they're not viable places to market your goods, but because the authors don't have any experience in that area. *This* author does — I got my start in online marketing with America Online. In Chapter 8, I share the information I have gathered over the years to help you decide whether a commercial online service is the right place to set up your cybershop.

The Internet offers some noteworthy advantages over commercial online services, the least of which is *not* a lower start-up cost. Chapter 9 takes a broad look at the World Wide Web in addition to the many other Internet services. In this chapter, I explain how the Internet differs from the online services as well as how it's the same.

One of the most common questions I hear from would-be cyber-entrepreneurs is, "How will I get paid?" Chapter 10 answers this question in great detail. It discusses not only the various ways in which you can collect your money but also the risks associated with each method.

You're probably thinking primarily about selling to people within the United States. Being online tears down any geographic limitations, however, and opens up an entire worldwide market. In Chapter 11, I give you tips for tapping in to those foreign markets.

No matter whether you're on the Internet or on a commercial online service, all good online sites have many things in common. Chapter 12 offers my short list of online-area essentials and sound advice about how to implement them. From good-looking text and graphics to increased functionality, this chapter covers it all.

Part IV: Advertising, Publicity, and Sponsorships

"If you build it, they will come." That line from the movie *Field of Dreams* has become quite famous. Unfortunately, that's not true in the area of online marketing. It's more like, "If you build it and tell all your friends and relatives about it and promote the heck out of it to the media and buy some well-placed advertising and always remember to keep your customers happy, they will come."

Advertising isn't cheap. A good advertising campaign pays for itself many times over; a bad one can bleed you dry. There are many, many ways to advertise your online business. There are far fewer *good* ways, however, to advertise your online business. Chapter 13 tells you how to distinguish the good from the bad in online advertising.

Chapter 14 covers the other side of promotion: publicity. Publicity means getting the word out to the media and, ultimately, the people, through such vehicles as press releases. The good news is that publicity is much cheaper than advertising. The bad news is that the work it involves is much more difficult. This chapter tells you how to make the most of the time you spend generating publicity.

However much fun and excitement you find in cyberspace, you have to realize that it's all still part of the larger real world. Chapter 15 tells you, therefore, exactly how to promote your online business in the offline world.

Part V: Keeping the Lines of Communication Open

If you do build it and they do come, your real challenge is to get them to come back a second, third, and fourth time. I'm talking about building customer loyalty, which is the focus of this part of the book.

Chapter 16 describes database marketing, or analyzing information you already know about your existing customers and using that analysis as the basis for additional marketing plans. All the big corporations do database marketing, and, thanks to computer technology, you can do the same thing from your home office.

So many online businesses are competing for your customers' attention that it's easy for your business to become a victim of the concept "out of sight, out of mind." From e-mail newsletters to free online information, Chapter 17 tells you how to put your name and your good reputation in front of your customers as much as possible.

Part VI: Must-Have Insider Knowledge

Every online business book has a list of online sites you can check for more resources, and Chapter 18 is my list. This list represents *the best* of the best. Set aside at least a few hours to explore all the valuable information these sites have to offer.

Chapter 19 contains all the information that you wish you didn't have to know. This chapter describes all the basics of the legal issues facing online marketers. Copyrights. Trademarks. Service marks. What's the difference? How are they the same?

Although Chapter 10 talks briefly about online security, it's a topic that's important enough to discuss in more detail in Chapter 20. I describe many of the different ways in which cybercriminals may try to infiltrate your business and, more important, present ways to prevent it from happening.

Finally, in Chapter 21, I wrap it all up, by giving you some of my opinions and best guesses about where this whole thing called cyberspace is headed. I may be right; I may be wrong. I can say one thing for sure about the future of online marketing: It will make some people very, very rich. And you can be one of those people.

Wow — you got a CD-ROM and a free home page too!

The appendix in this book contains the information you need in order to set up and use the *CyberBuck$* CD-ROM packaged in the back of this book. Here's a preview of some of the neat things on the CD-ROM:

- ✦ *CyberBuck$: The Book* so that you can search for items in the book easily and quickly rather than dog-ear the pages or look up topics in the index
- ✦ A free trial membership to America Online so that you can see firsthand the areas I mention in this book
- ✦ AT&T WorldNet Service software so that you can get an Internet account and surf the Web
- ✦ Preview and demonstration software from Network Music, Innovative Quality Software, iMALL, Inc., TuneUp.com, Ӕxpert, Inc., and Interactive Marketing Communications
- ✦ The information you need to get your *free* home page on the Internet
- ✦ Special pricing offers on my company's line of computer learning systems and SurfWatch, the parental-control software program

Icons and Fonts Used in This Book

This book has so many insider tips, tricks, and secrets to running an online business that it's easy for you to miss something. Because the folks at IDG Books Worldwide, Inc., are pretty smart cookies, they came up with a way to make sure that you don't overlook the important points:

Tip

When you see a Tip icon, you should read that paragraph not just once, but twice. Think of a Tip as a way for me to get in your face to tell you something you need to do.

Note

The Note icon indicates interesting information (something that I might tell you over a cup of coffee).

Warning

When you see this icon, picture me waving my arms in front you and saying, "Pay attention, or you could get into deep trouble!"

One more thing. When I mention a Web address I want you to visit, it's shown in a monospace font, like this: `http://www.komando.com`. This font makes it easier for you to pinpoint a Web address on the page.

Some Final Thoughts

With *CyberBuck$* in your hand, you have the information you need to get your online enterprise up and running. Now you just have to believe in yourself. You can do it. Heck, if I can, you can too! I want you to muster up all the enthusiasm you can to ensure your success. While you are doing all this, don't forget my dear mother's sage advice: "Put a smile on your face, and get your butt in gear!" Now go make some money!

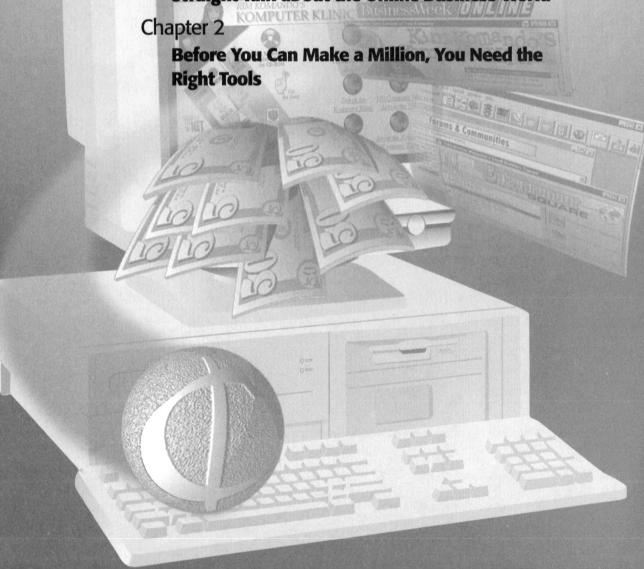

Part I

Doing Your Homework

CHAPTER 1

Straight Talk about the Online Business World

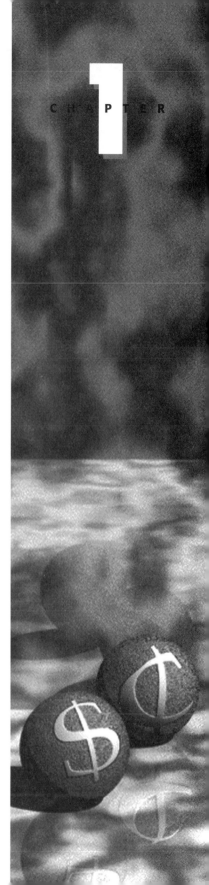

Right now, hundreds of thousands of businesses exist, and they fall into thousands of different categories — maybe even more. Consider all the products and services being purchased at this moment in a wide range of distribution channels. New businesses start up daily, adding to the mix, as do the innovative methods devised to market products and gain sales.

People are capable of great feats of creativity, especially when it concerns making money.

Ozzie and Harriet Are Dead

A good example of pure marketing ingenuity is infomercials — those 30-minute commercials you see on television during the late-night or early-morning hours. Some people call them "infocommercials," and others call them "tube trash." Who would have thought 15 years ago that you could sell cleaning mops, wrenches, how-to-make-love tapes, fishing lures, makeup, and pet-grooming aids on television?

You probably would have laughed at anyone who swore up and down that John and Jane Q. Public would sit on their couch and watch a half-hour commercial about a product. "Pick up the phone and order it by credit card? You must be kidding."

Consumers have done just that, though, and with purchasing power in the range of billions of dollars. I know firsthand: If you have ever suffered from insomnia, you may have seen me, between the bass fisherman and the balding remedies, in infomercials touting the benefits of computer training. My shows (infomercials are called "shows" in the television industry, to give them that Hollywood aura, I suppose) have aired throughout the United States, Australia, and other parts of the world. My products have been sold through home-shopping channels, retail outlets, credit-card inserts, and direct-mail catalogs. And, of course, my company sells products online.

Time after time, business associates and wanna-be millionaires call my company's offices for help in getting their products advertised on television. It looks easy enough to do: Tape a half-hour show and buy the airtime, and more than 90 million television-equipped homes are within your reach. If a product works, you get wealthy fast. If a product doesn't work, no one really knows. You test a show during a weekend, and those two-day results are good enough to tell you whether the show will ever be broadcast again.

What these hopeful (and otherwise sane) entrepreneurs don't understand when they call for help is that it's not as easy as it looks. No overnight millions are made. Producing an infomercial takes hard work and lots of contacts. But there's more — much more.

You have to present the right product to the right customer at the right time. You must have a high profit margin for the product, protect yourself from legal headaches, and know what constitutes an offer that's just too good to refuse. Money and a great product are, obviously, imperative too. It's a huge risk, though. Only one of ten infomercials may ever air again after that fateful testing weekend.

Tip

Successful infomercials, however, have a common secret formula. (Okay, maybe it's not so secret anymore.) You see it in action if you watch enough infomercials. In a nutshell, here's the formula:

✦ Present information to demonstrate what need the product fulfills for the consumer. Teach viewers a few things while they are watching, to give the infomercial educational value.

✦ Give the program some sort of entertainment factor, maybe in the presentation of the product or by featuring a celebrity.

✦ Show people (who are just like viewers at home) who have benefited from using the product.

✦ Give the credit-card-bearing audience a special bonus just for picking up the phone and ordering *now*.

The proper mix of these ingredients makes for a winning infomercial. But I'm talking about computers and making money with the technology that uses ordinary phone lines to connect PCs to other PCs throughout the globe. Here's my point: The total online commercial environment is no different from late-night infomercials.

"Sales" Is Your Middle Name

Anywhere a business sets up shop with a PC online is basically one big infomercial. Information is available, and a great deal of it. You try to make it entertaining, as much as possible. You have a product or service that satisfies a need, and you want the orders — and lots of them — *now*.

In much the same way as the "Buns of Steel" advertisement is on late-night television, you are online for one simple reason: To tell your potential online customers, tens of millions of people worldwide, that your company exists and then to ask for an order.

As you can see, online marketing is not some great enigma. It is merely the next generation in the tradition of developing a product and figuring out a way to make money with it. You still need customers to come cash in hand. You still need to give customers the right message that will make them act. And you still need to deal with competition.

Online marketing can mean many different things to many different people. I talk in this book about marketing online in all its various incarnations, and I promise to hit hardest on the techniques that offer you the best moneymaking potential. Because the area of online marketing is still relatively new, you don't have to be all that innovative if your goal is to be an online business owner full of position, power, and wealth.

Marketing your company online involves not only the presentation of information to gain orders and sales. The manner in which you can use the Internet and the online services to better your business prospects is limited only by your imagination. Want to save money in postage and faxes? Send e-mail instead. Want to save money taking orders? Have customers fill out online order forms or, better, follow the lead of Federal Express.

If you call FedEx to schedule a delivery, the human or computerized operator needs certain information from you, including a pickup address and a delivery address. FedEx has developed, over the years, a sophisticated software tracking program that enables the company to know, among other things, precisely where a package is located at any point in the delivery process.

FedEx put a modified version of its tracking software on its Internet World Wide Web site. Rather than pay 20 people $12 an hour, for example, to punch numbers into a computer, the company gets *you* to do it and saves money at the same time. (Ingenious.) Figure 1-1 shows the Federal Express Internet home page.

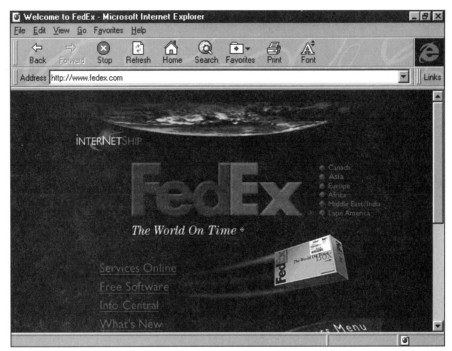

Figure 1-1: The Federal Express home page delivers the goods.

Pioneers in any industry struggle to find the right path, and, frankly, only a handful succeed. It definitely is much easier to grow and sustain a business, regardless of its focus or products, when you employ proven techniques. A dollar is a dollar, after all, and it buys the same amount of candy whether it was easy or difficult to obtain.

I have had years of online marketing experience and have reveled in the online hits — and suffered through the misses. During some months, my company's online areas have barely broken even. The summer season is the toughest, when online traffic drops to all-time lows. It makes sense: When the weather is nice, who wants to be holed up in a dark room, tapping on a computer keyboard? You don't, and neither do your customers. (Well, maybe a few of them do.)

The online "ups" for Kim Komando's Komputer Klinic on the Internet, America Online, and the Microsoft Network have been, fortunately, greater than the downs. Often, as many as 150,000 people a day visit our virtual storefronts. These tens of thousands come because we continually promote the areas online and offline as well as update the areas daily.

Tip

As a teaser of the great things to come throughout this book, let me share with you the secret online marketing formula: Establish a unique presence, present the call-to-action message, make customers come back time after time, and have them buy something along the way — all of which you learn more about throughout this book.

Competing with Goliath

It seems strange that even Bill Gates, the computer industry Microsoft mogul, didn't forecast the imminent online explosion. Rumor has it that he called a supersecret meeting and chastised his upper management team for not predicting the company's need to give consumers far and wide online access.

Having interviewed Bill Gates myself once, it makes me wonder how a man with such business acumen, insight, and power could *not* have seen it coming. Microsoft may be late for supper, but it is pushing to become a major Internet player at the table with its development tools, strategic partnerships, and Microsoft Network. When you have the company that Gates has, you can hire thousands of people at one time and get into the online business. (I guess that you get a chance to reclaim your insight too.)

In a November 1995 speech to about 7,500 people in Las Vegas at the COMDEX computer industry trade show, Gates said that he sees software and the Internet as equalizers for small businesses. "Small-business people will be able to connect to the online world on an equal basis to the bigger guys. The Internet is kind of like the gold rush: The excitement is incredible," Gates said. "Now, fortunately, this is a gold rush where there really is gold."

You don't have to be a Bill Gates, though, to participate in online riches. I started the Komputer Klinic on America Online (AOL) in the back bedroom of my home with one employee whose desk was my dining room table. It took only two months from the time I made my pitch to AOL about why it needed me on its service until the launch date of my area on the service (mid-October 1993). The Komputer Klinic had a few hundred thousand potential customers the first day. AOL grew and grew, as did the Klinic's online presence on the Internet and other commercial online services. It was a good thing.

Today the number of potential online customers worldwide is, much like a television buying audience, in the tens of millions. Online marketing is an incredible opportunity for small and large businesses alike. Anyone can do it, as long as the right formula is employed. The underlying moving force that has opened the door for online marketing, however, is the sheer growth the online community is experiencing. Never in history have so many people jumped so quickly on one bandwagon.

Imagine that it's 10 or 15 years ago and you own a retail store that took years to establish. Your store is stocked with a precise number of books, gadgets, museum replicas, and toys for upwardly mobile professionals. You hear the bell on your door jingle as someone passes through the front door. It's a well-dressed man in his mid-30s.

You ask, "May I help you?"

"Just looking," says the visitor, who seems to be taking a shelf-by-shelf mental inventory. Minutes later, he picks up your best-selling leather organizer, holds it up high so that you can see it from across the room, and says, "You'll soon be able to sell this and everything in this store with a computer. People all over the world will look at pictures of your products on their computer screen and buy them by typing their credit-card numbers." You would not have said out loud what you thought deep down — "This guy is nuts!"

New marketing channels take time for acceptance. In the early 1920s, for example, radio stations were trying to figure out how to make money. AT&T came up with the idea of toll stations, a concept much like phone booths. Any person with an inkling and the cash could stop by a "toll station" and broadcast a brief message on the radio.

AT&T tapped in to a big market and a big station (WEAF in New York) for its toll station test. The test was a flop. On August 28, 1922, after a month of no tollbooth sales, WEAF dropped the toll-station idea for generating sales. The radio marketers went back to the drawing board and came up with a way to sell minutes, not just seconds, on a radio station. But many skeptics thought that because people wouldn't buy seconds on the air, why would they be inclined to buy minutes?

WEAF decided to market advertising time in bulk minutes to qualified companies. Its first commercial was a 10-minute dissertation promising a better life in the Long Island suburbs. It worked. The station made more than $127,000 in home sales in three weeks. That was a great deal of money in the early 1920s. Today, just try to listen to the radio (other than public radio, of course) without hearing a commercial.

The online marketing arena is here, much like radio was in the early 1920s. The online industry has a long way to go, but you are lucky to be on the forefront of it because the number of online customers is growing like never before. And you, Mr. or Ms. Cyber-Entrepreneur, are in a great position — you weren't the first to tap in to this market.

If You Build It, How Many Will Come?

Let's look at some statistics. One survey released toward the end of 1995 indicated that within two years of the survey date, 77 percent of all businesses in the United States will have an online presence. Don't simply pass by this number: *77 of every 100 companies* will have something about themselves available to customers through a computer. About 38 percent of businesses indicated that they were already online, and another 39 percent said that they would be online within two years.

Another study showed that between the winter of 1994 and June 1995, the total number of subscribers to commercial online services jumped from around 5 million to more than 12 million. Picture twice the total population of Phoenix, Arizona, connecting to an online service in six months!

What's more, according to the same study, those 12 million subscribers represent only about two-thirds of the total number of personal computers equipped with modems. Another 6 million or so people already have the basic equipment they need in order to get online — they just haven't done it yet. (Maybe they are still just trying to figure out how to hook up their modem. Who knows? If you have ever tried to read a modem manual, you can relate.)

These numbers, however, do not account for all the new computer owners to come — the hundreds of thousands over the next few years who will, additionally, make a computer as common as a telephone. With the number of potential customers that high, it's easy to see why many businesspeople see dollar signs when they hear the mere mention of the word *online*.

It's difficult to pick up a magazine or newspaper without seeing some mention of a new Internet survey touting to be the best predictor to-date. No matter which survey you see, the common theme is that the increasing number of people tapping in to the online gold rush will continue, only maybe faster than we have seen until now. What could possibly account for such explosive growth? Using just one word, it's marketing. But the profit potential and low cost of entry help too.

America Online's Success Makes Way for Yours

We all should say thank you to America Online (AOL). Most of the recent online growth is due to the company's ingenious marketing efforts (and disk-manufacturing capabilities). AOL has flooded the marketplace with start-up disks by direct mail and packaged with magazines, books, software programs, and anything in between. The company's marketing invasion has gotten to the point that the punchline of many computer jokes involves finding things to do with its leftover start-up disks. Some people have even proposed converting the disks into coasters and giving away disk sets as gifts. In the spirit of recycling, my company offered to return leftover trial membership disks, which contained an outdated version of the AOL system software. AOL didn't want them, even though we had thousands of its disks lying around.

Don't get me wrong — AOL isn't the only one playing this marketing game. It's just playing harder than the other commercial online services and big-time Internet providers. In the past few months, disks from every major online service have turned up either in my mailbox or attached to a magazine. I even found one recently in the seat pocket on an airplane.

The AOL marketing plan wasn't just to hand out free disks left and right, though. The *brilliant* part was that the company developed strategic partnerships with other companies that would help spread the AOL religion. AOL went directly inside consumers' homes and minds in a big way. How? Who better than media personalities (such as myself), newspapers, magazines, organizations, talk shows, and television channels to tell the world about you?

Putting the offline in the online world

Okay, so it's clear that there's gold in these electronic hills. But it is important for you to know where your offline business fits in to the online world.

I can't think of one thing I can do online that I can't do offline and that someone else isn't doing offline. If I want to communicate with a friend in Chicago, for example, I can call or send a letter. If I want to make travel arrangements, I can contact a travel agent or call the airline. If I need information about a certain topic, I can drive down to the public library. If I want new software, I can go to the computer store and buy it.

What is different about the online world is not what we do, but *how* we do it. It would take three or four days for the U.S. Postal Service to deliver my letter to Chicago (assuming, of course, that a disgruntled postal worker didn't burn it under some Chicago bridge, as has happened in the past). With e-mail, I can get a letter there in seconds. I can spend a half-hour explaining my plans to a travel agent, or I can book everything online and see the lowest available fares in a matter of minutes. Finding information on just about anything is a snap online, especially compared with a trip to the library. And what could be easier than downloading new software directly into your own computer?

Being online doesn't let you do new things as much as it lets you do things in a new way. This concept is important as you mold your online marketing strategy. Look beyond your monitor to see what is happening with your products, and then tailor that vision for an online world.

AOL doesn't need as many expensive four-color magazine advertisements, direct mailers, and flashy television commercials as other companies trying to reach customers. It gets publicity, otherwise known as "free advertising," from every company and personality associated with its online service. Whenever MTV does an AOL promotion, it is often simulcast on nationwide television. I invite folks to visit the Komputer Klinic on AOL in my television segments, radio shows, magazine columns, and elsewhere. Imagine at least another thousand different people and companies doing the same thing with your product.

AOL taps in to a whole new audience without spending a dime in television time. Wait — it gets better. If your company strikes the right deal, AOL and others pay you a bounty fee for every person to whom you hand a disk who stays online for a certain period. That's why you see AOL disks every time you turn around: Creative moneymaking without much effort.

Like "Beautiful," "Online" Has Many Meanings

For some people, "online" means connecting to a major commercial online service, such as AOL or CompuServe. For others, online means having an Internet account with a local-access provider and dialing right in to the Internet. You may own or work for a company that offers direct Internet access without the need for a modem to get online. For a few diehards, online means dialing in to a local bulletin-board system (BBS) to exchange ideas about some common interest or topic.

All this discussion of what "online" means simply boils down to someone connecting a PC to someone else's computer system to do *some* thing. *That's* being online.

From a financial point of view, some definitions of the word *online* are obviously more lucrative than others. You can bet your life that AOL makes more money in a week, for example, than any BBS in your hometown makes in a year. And if you weren't interested in making some money, you probably would not have bought this book.

Go back to the commercial online services one more time. Just who am I talking about here? When someone says "online service," most people think of the "Big Three" (or, lately, the Big Two-and-a-Half): AOL, CompuServe, and Prodigy.

The Microsoft Network (MSN) started out as, a toe-to-toe competitor in the online services market but it hasn't exactly had an avalanche of customers. The Apple Computer service eWorld tried for years to make it — it shut down. Learn a lesson here. To succeed online, you still need, even with the resources of a multibillion-dollar company, a unique product with mass appeal.

Other online services are out there, and still more are popping up. GE Information Services, a unit of General Electric Co., has on the World Wide Web a service called GE BusinessPro that's designed for small businesses and home offices. It offers small businesses volume-buying plans, newsletters, business forms, information, and "all-you-can-eat" electronic-mail. The base cost is about $25 per month, assuming that you already have Internet access. If not, GE Information Services provides access for an additional charge.

The CompuServe service WOW! targets at-home consumer users. It features distinct online content tailored for adults and children, Internet access, e-mail, and multimedia sound and motion. The WOW! kids' view includes parental controls for both Internet access and mail delivery, along with the ability to deny access to chat rooms and electronic shopping.

@Home, a joint venture of Tele-Communications Inc. and Kleiner Perkins Caufield & Byers, is rolling out across the country with the intention of being the interactive cable online service of choice.

Who can forget the AT&T WorldNet splash that left that phone company over-whelmed by the response? I can tell you even more stories, but let me get to the point. All these services, big or small, have something of potential value to you: customers who have money to spend on your products or services.

In one sense, all online services are the same. They all let you connect to their com-puter systems to exchange messages, retrieve information, and conduct various types of business. And they all charge for these services. So what makes them different from one another?

All the services have some minor distinctions. If you compare AOL with CompuServe, for example, you can see that the two services have plenty in common (see Figure 1-2 and Figure 1-3): They're the two largest online services on the planet, they both have millions of members, and they both offer their members access to the Internet. The two services have many features in common, such as daily news and shareware downloads, yet they are very different.

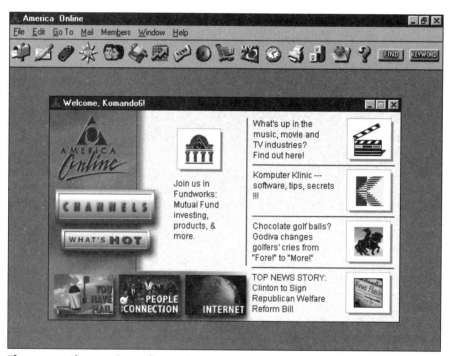

Figure 1-2: The America Online Welcome screen.

In terms of content, the AOL target market is the consumer — the home user. Maybe you have seen the commercial in which a man orders flowers, books airline tickets, and downloads some information about dinosaurs for his daughter, all in time to make the basketball game. The content on AOL is developed to appeal to this type of user — the average person dialing in from home.

Figure 1-3: The CompuServe Welcome screen.

CompuServe, on the other hand, started out primarily as a service for business users, and this area remains its stronghold. Sure, you can find some family-oriented content on CompuServe, but its main goal is to satisfy the needs of professional people.

Both AOL and CompuServe have similar interfaces in that they're both graphical (although you can also access CompuServe from a character-based terminal). The two systems organize their information much differently, however.

The bulk of CompuServe content is organized into *forums,* which are individual areas, each of which relates to a special area of interest (see Figure 1-4). In these forums, you can exchange messages with other users, find valuable information, and often download shareware and freeware files. Each forum is similar to a room, and you must completely leave one forum before you can enter another. This setup can make moving around in CompuServe seem somewhat cumbersome.

AOL content, on the other hand, is not as compartmentalized. AOL has forums too, but you can enter one forum in one window, enter another forum in another window, and jump back and forth between the two with just a click of your mouse. This capability makes moving around in AOL easier than moving around in CompuServe, but, with so many windows open on your screen, it's also easy to lose track of where you are (see Figure 1-5).

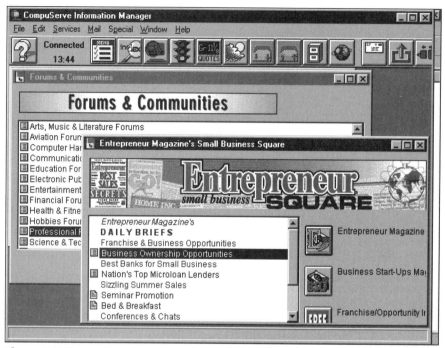

Figure 1-4: CompuServe forums can be confusing to muddle through.

The only way to tell which online service meets your personal needs is to try them all. Fortunately, a tryout doesn't cost you anything more than an investment of time. As I said, all the biggies hand out free trial memberships like candy. One danger exists, however: You may just find that you like two or three services equally, which can drive your monthly online bill sky-high.

Can You Start Your Own Online Service?

To an end user, an online service is merely a window on a computer screen and a monthly charge on a credit card. At the other end of the phone line, however, plenty of things are happening. This section looks behind the scenes so that you can see just what it takes to run a successful online service. If nothing else, reading this section should convince you that you can find many easier ways to make money online than by starting your own online service. (Leave that to the pioneers who want to weather the trail in the deepest of winter.)

Figure 1-5: America Online forums are easy to navigate but easy to get lost in too.

For starters, one company in Florida provides, according to its advertisement, all the software you need to "start your own online service, as full-featured as AOL, but at a size that's easy to handle." Big claim, eh? It's hard to say how long that company will be in business. I'm sure that it will have some takers on its offer; most people, I fear, will buy the package and be disappointed at the results as their new online service turns into America Offline or Can'tuServe.

It's easy to predict the disaster. Even if you have all the technology, you're still missing one important ingredient: content. You either have to spend countless hours developing your own or convince someone else that your service is worth providing content for. Go ahead — try to tell ABC News that your fledgling online service is the perfect place to call its online home and see how far you get.

I know that some of you won't believe that you can't do it, though. There's a diehard in every crowd. If you still want to start your own online service, the first thing you need is, obviously, one monster-size computer system. The AOL host system, for example, is housed on major mainframe computers that fill entire rooms. That's some major dollars right there — in the millions — and you're just getting started.

Next, you need a mountain of telecommunications equipment so that people from the outside world can "talk" to your monster-size computer. Equipment is only part of the telecommunications puzzle, however. You have to set up a network of local-access numbers around the country so that almost no one has to make a long-distance call in order to dial in. If you think that your phone bills are high now, wait until you have hundreds of high-speed lines throughout the country. CompuServe, for example, has almost 500 local-access numbers worldwide with about 50,000 dial-in ports.

Your monster computer can't do much, of course, without software. The cash-in-hand (or credit card in hand) public can't send any of its money your way if it doesn't have the software to connect to your monster computer. You need computer programmers (plenty of them, in fact) to make sure that everything works correctly at both ends of the modem connection. Prodigy has an entire team of programmers dedicated to the service, working in different shifts around the clock.

Next, you need lots of employees to run the thing — everything from high-level managers to file clerks. More than 5,000 employees are now on the payroll at AOL (rumor has it that more than half work in some technical-support capacity).

You have to consider system features and content. E-mail is a given, but not just e-mail on your own network. All online services now provide access to Internet e-mail. Virtually all the major players, in fact, offer access to several Internet services. This list shows the three most popular services and areas that people use on the Internet:

- ✦ **File Transfer Protocol, or FTP:** A method of *downloading,* or transferring, files from the Internet to your PC
- ✦ **Usenet newsgroups:** Electronic message boards on the Internet
- ✦ **The World Wide Web:** The graphical, clickable face of the Internet

The content you have to provide is a huge challenge. Although you develop some content yourself, you have to convince outside companies that it's to their benefit to develop content for your new service. Because many people believe that the online service market is already oversaturated, convincing companies can be a tough sell. Also, some online services sign up companies with exclusive arrangements: If you see the perfect information service on CompuServe that you want to have on your online service, you probably won't be able to get it. CompuServe likes to make companies agree to be on CompuServe and nowhere else.

Because online users just love to download free software, you have to figure out a way to stock your service with plenty of shareware and freeware too. Getting the files isn't too tough, especially considering that the concept of downloading files embraces the essence of shareware: Distribute at will. Still, downloading is only the first step in getting all the shareware and freeware your hard disk can handle. By far the most common question in the Komputer Klinic "Ask the Staff" area is, "I down-loaded a file — now what do I do to use the program?" This area gets about 175 of these inquiries per week. Ask yourself who will work your online tech-support desk. And what about toll-free telephone support?

Last but not least, you have to market your new service to the buying public. This area is big business, and, because the competition out there is fierce, you have to spend plenty. The AOL marketing budget — even considering all the publicity it continually gets — is, shall we say, a hefty chunk of change. It has to be in the multimillion-dollar range.

If you can pull it all off, of course, the rewards can be substantial. Combined 1994 earnings for AOL, CompuServe, and Prodigy were somewhere in the neighborhood of *half a billion dollars.* Just a year or so later, however, America Online revenue for the first three months of its 1996 fiscal year (ending March 31, 1996) rose to a record $312,340,000, an increase of more than 185 percent from $109,104,000 in the third quarter of fiscal 1995. See the trend?

How Does the Internet Fit into All This?

Now that I have (I hope!) convinced you not to waste your time and money starting another online service, I present you with an online service competitor and collabora-tor: the Internet. You can't open the newspaper or turn on the television these days without hearing something about the Internet. In the summer of 1995, it was reported that the television, radio, and print media mentioned "the Internet" more than 21,000 times. President Clinton got second billing, with only 18,000 mentions. But what is the Internet, really? And where did it come from? Why is it here, and why now? Let me briefly give you the condensed version.

In 1957, the U.S. Department of Defense formed the Advanced Research Projects Agency (ARPA) in response to the U.S.S.R.'s launch of Sputnik, the first artificial earth satellite. The purpose of ARPA was to establish the United States as the world leader in military science and technology.

In less than ten years, ARPA began to focus much of its efforts on developing a computer network that could withstand a major disaster. In other words, its developers wanted a network that could function even if one or more of the sites on the network were blown to smithereens. Thus was born ARPAnet in 1969, a network designed to interconnect military researchers around the country. The ARPAnet design was based on the assumption that the network was unreliable, and that, therefore, most of the work had to be done by the communicating computers. (This assumption is important, and I tell you why in a moment.)

ARPAnet was a great thing, but, unfortunately, it was available only for military research. About ten years later, another government agency, the National Science Foundation (NSF), formed NSFnet based on the same principles and technologies ARPAnet used. NSFnet was made available for any scholarly research. In the years since then, other similar networks were introduced, and (through mergers and interconnections) they grew collectively into what we now call the Internet.

Remember when I said that it was important that the design of ARPAnet was based on the assumption of an unreliable network? This design principle is what makes so many different services and different computers available over one network. Because the Internet itself doesn't do anything except carry information from one computer to another, the number of different services available on the Internet is limited only by the creativity of software developers. You can use just about any type of computer, from a Commodore to an Apple to a PC to a UNIX workstation, to connect to the Internet, as long as you have a modem and a live phone line.

Business on the Internet is relatively new, though. Because the Internet was originally developed as an educational tool, it was used almost exclusively by students and teachers at their respective universities. As both the number of services and the amount of available information grew, the demand for Internet access from people outside the academic world also grew. Anything that attracts the attention of a large segment of the American public also attracts the attention of American business — it's capitalism in action.

How do BBSs fit into the picture?

In your search for an online business, don't overlook local bulletin-board systems (BBSs). A BBS is similar to an online service, except on a much smaller scale. Usually, someone with a spare computer installs some BBS host software and connects the computer to a modem, allowing access to the public. Many BBS systems are started simply as a hobby and are free of any charges.

Other BBSs cater to a specific niche, and their owners (also called *system operators*, or *sysops*) can charge monthly or annual access fees. With the Internet growing by leaps and bounds, however, it's increasingly difficult to offer something on a BBS that isn't already out on the Net. Some types of BBSs remain popular: adult-entertainment BBSs, for example, and ones that have loads and loads of the latest shareware and freeware. For your purpose, however (making truckloads of money), BBSs are extremely small fish in a big, big sea.

Even that's changing, however. Many companies that develop BBS host software have realized that it's tough for their customers to compete with the Internet. Rather than fight the march of progress, these companies are developing enhancements that enable BBSs to become an integral part of the Internet. Rather than dial in to a local BBS, you can connect right over the Net. This capability creates a tremendous opportunity for sysops who already have an established BBS presence.

Today companies of all sizes are flocking to the Internet, and specifically to the World Wide Web. The Web puts a graphical face on the otherwise cryptic Internet and enables businesses to deliver information visually to millions of people around the world, 24 hours a day. Services such as video teleconferencing, cheap long-distance phone service, live audio and video broadcasts, and telemedicine all are in various stages of refinement too. No one can accurately predict where the Internet will be in a few years. Just know that you have to be there, whether it's for your business or pleasure. The sooner you do it, the better off you are.

Some CyberBuck$ Klues to Get You on Your Way

No matter how you get online, you have many ways to bring a business online — many right ways and many wrong ways. Where you bring your business to the online community and which method you use both depend on which type of business you're running. Still, a few basic principles apply to virtually any cyber-entrepreneur. This section presents a few just to get you in a *CyberBuck$* state of mind.

When fax machines exploded on the scene, everyone realized that putting fax numbers on business cards and other stationery was a good idea. Businesspeople are beginning to understand that the same realization is now true for e-mail addresses: People expect you to have an e-mail address these days. If you don't have one, potential customers may look at you with a little skepticism, especially if your business involves a technical field.

Tip

It won't be long until people expect to see your World Wide Web address along with your e-mail address. Take a look at those appliance and car commercials that have absolutely nothing to do with being online. At the bottom of the screen, however, the companies' respective Web addresses are displayed just so that interested Net surfers know where to go for information.

Being online is about being accessible. For you and your business to be accessible to the online community, you must have, use, and publicize your e-mail address.

While I'm on the subject of e-mail, it's important to realize that e-mail not only lets potential customers reach you but also lets *you reach them*. One example of reaching your customers by e-mail is publishing your own electronic newsletter for customers and potential customers. Whether you're doing business via an online service or on the Internet, a newsletter can be a valuable tool.

Have you ever noticed that when you buy something from a particular store, you end up on that store's mailing list? Businesses small and large keep their existing customers coming back for more by keeping them informed about sales, specials, and other events. Keeping in touch with existing customers is even more important when you're doing business online. Remember that you don't enjoy these types of benefits as a location advantage because, as far as consumers are concerned, every business in cyberspace is pretty much in the same place.

That's where a newsletter comes into play. I go into more detail about newsletters in Chapter 17. For now, just keep in mind that online communication is a two-way street.

But that's all public-relations stuff. How do you *conduct and market* your business online? That's the subject of this entire book, but I give you the short list here, just to get your wheels turning. Remember that much of *how* you conduct business online depends on *what kind of business* you're in.

At the simplest level, you can use the electronic version of classified advertising, which all the major online services have. Some charge for classified advertising, and others don't. If you're an Internet user, some Usenet newsgroups also accept classified advertising.

Tip

No matter where you run your ad, you should remember two important things about classified advertising:

✦ Make sure that you pick the best possible classification. Here's an example off the top of my head: If you run a computerized pet registry (not very likely, but stay with me on this), you're much better off advertising your service under Pets than under Computers.

✦ Make sure that you give all the information someone might want, including an accurate description of your product or service, the cost of the product or service, and (most important) how to contact you to buy your product or service.

Another way to promote your business online is to buy direct online advertising. For anywhere from $50 to more than $50,000 per month, depending on when and where you want your advertisement to pop up and on which company's home page, you can have a combo advertisement. The online ad shows your company's message and also puts Net surfers one mouse click away from your company's home page. The advertisement is a *link* to your home page. A couple of companies have developed free-to-the-public e-mail services paid for solely by advertising dollars. In exchange for a free e-mail account, consumers see your advertising message displayed in the header of their e-mail messages.

I have my personal favorites, of course: You can create your own forum or area on a commercial online service. If you have an AOL account and want to see an example of perhaps the best online forum in the entire galaxy (rivaled in significance only by the invention of disposable diapers and no-run pantyhose), check out the keyword KOMANDO. For your eye-browsing pleasure, it's also shown in Figure 1-6.

Okay, maybe my Komputer Klinic isn't quite as important as disposable diapers or no-run pantyhose, but I think that it is a good example of the different things you can do with an online forum. The Klinic has shareware and freeware available for downloading, useful news and information, answers to your PC questions, and, of course, a place to spend your money.

Figure 1-6: Perhaps the hottest area on America Online.

The Internet equivalent of an online forum is a home page on the World Wide Web. The graphical structure of the Web enables you to do virtually anything you can do from an online-service forum. And, frankly, it's much cheaper.

There are two sides to every coin, of course. Although establishing a presence on the World Wide Web is less expensive than doing so on an online service, being on the Web poses some unique challenges. For starters, because thousands and thousands of Web sites are out there (with more added daily), you have to work much harder to get customers to your site.

Tip

You also have to remember that every Web browser displays Web pages a little differently. If you design a Web page that looks great when it's viewed with Netscape Navigator, it might not look as good when it's viewed using the Internet gateway on AOL. When a potential customer from AOL comes along and sees that your page *looks* strange, he will assume that it *is* strange and is likely to move on to some other site. The bad news is that no universal solution now exists for this problem. One way around this problem is to tone down the graphics and artwork on your company's home page. The good news? It's always getting better, and, heck, you have this great book in your hands.

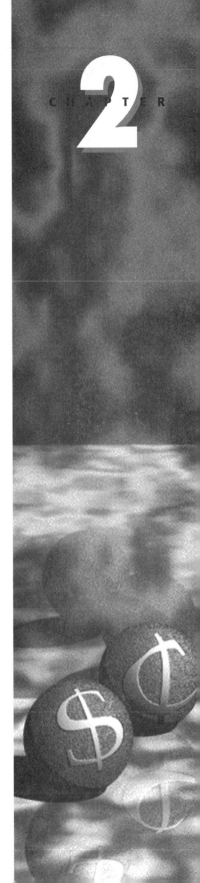

Before You Can Make a Million, You Need the Right Tools

"We don't like their sound, and guitar music is on the way out."

Decca Recording Company, in rejecting The Beatles, 1962

Just as you have to read the "Before You Get Started" section of any software user manual before you can get down to business, before you can begin making a gazillion dollars online, you have to take care of a few nitty-gritty details first. In other words, you have to have all your digital ducks lined up before you can make duck soup.

In this chapter, I describe the absolute essentials for putting yourself and your business online. I also tell you how to save money and get by without the extras, at least until your business starts booming and your bank account soars.

Even if you already have an online service account or an Internet account, read this chapter. I wrote it. You'll like it. Heck, you probably will pick up a few tidbits that you don't know about now.

Obviously, if I'm talking about making money with a computer, you have to have a computer. Can you use just any old computer? Yes and no.

First, let me make one distinction. All the major online services cater primarily to the two major computer platforms: Windows and Macintosh. You can connect to America Online, CompuServe, Prodigy, and all the others regardless of whether your computer says "Welcome to Macintosh" or plays the Windows welcome chimes.

On the other hand, although the Internet itself is made up of a bunch of minicomputers or mainframe computers or even personal computers that run an operating system called UNIX or Windows NT, you don't need a computer running UNIX or Windows NT to access the Internet. Because the Internet connects computers, you need a computer. The type of computer doesn't matter; you can use a Macintosh, an IBM-compatible, a Sun workstation, an Amiga, or some other model. I would bet my last dollar that no matter which type of computer you name, someone else out there is using it to connect to the Internet.

I believe that most people who want cybercucks and who are starting a business use Windows personal computers and that the rest are mostly Macintosh users. In fact, I'll even make my prediction more specific: A full 85 or 90 percent of you use a Windows machine, and the remainder are Mac aficionados. (My "prediction" is based on bona fide computer market surveys.) The following section continues with this assumption.

What Kind of Equipment Do I Need?

I discuss the DOS/Windows world first. You don't need an ultrafast PC to get online. Any old XT-class machine circa early 1980s with a working modem and a shareware communications program can connect to the Internet. But it probably won't let you use the features of the popular commercial online services.

Tip

As far as the Internet goes, you not only *want* to be on the World Wide Web — it's also an necessity. The Web is a graphical environment. If you talk about graphics on a PC, you're talking about Microsoft Windows. Virtually all *Web browsers* (the programs that enable you to navigate through the World Wide Web) and all programs that connect you to the online services run under Windows. If you truly plan to make a go of this online thing, you need Windows. If you're still stuck in DOS land, you have to make the switch. End of story.

You don't have to just run Windows; you have to run it well.

In business, time is money, and you don't want to waste your time staring at the Windows hurry-up-and-wait sign (the hourglass cursor). In addition to attractive still images and photographs, the Web can also deliver a wide range of other multimedia elements, including sounds and full-motion video. If you're trying to squeak by in this "faster is better" world with a 386 machine and 4MB (megabytes) of RAM, forget it.

Note

To get any level of respectable performance and access to the places you need for your online business, you must have at least a 486 DX2/66MHz with 8MB of RAM. Even a system such as this one is at the subentry level. A Pentium-based PC with 16MB of RAM is better. Maybe you can't afford this system yet, and that's okay for now, but you have to make a reasonably equipped computer a priority item. Your online business success depends on it.

Note

Our Mac friends are in the same boat. Sure, you may be able to get things rolling with a Mac IIcx or some other 030-based system. If you really want to keep the pace, however, you need a souped-up Quadra or an 040-based Performa. If you have the extra money (with prices being cut every day, it's not that much more), go for a PowerMac. The newest models offer easy CPU upgradability, which protects your investment for many years.

No matter which kind of computer you use, either a Mac or PC, as a cutting-edge cyber-entrepreneur, you have to be at least dead even with the technology curve, not behind it.

Monitors

To be able to see what you're doing, you need a monitor attached to your PC: SVGA 256-color, plain and simple. I know — it doesn't cost that much more to go to thousands or millions of colors.

Tip

I suggest that you stay with 256 colors, for two reasons:

✦ Virtually all the online content you find is designed for 256 colors because it's the lowest common denominator for displaying decent-quality graphics and photographic images.

✦ If you plan to develop any online content, you want to see it on your screen just as the rest of the world sees it on theirs. Again, that means 256 colors. Get extra VRAM for your personal viewing pleasure; just don't think that you need it for online marketing.

When you're choosing a monitor size, use the same rule you use for your PC's hard disk size, its amount of RAM and processing power, and your bank account: The bigger, the better.

Because you probably will be working with plenty of graphics and different windows, a larger monitor should help boost your productivity. You can get by with a 14-inch monitor, but I suggest that you get at least a 15- or 17-inch monitor, if you can afford it. The technical people in my office whine that my monitor is bigger than their TV sets at home. It measures 21 inches, but I've been checking out the 36-inch monitors. Just wait 'til they see that baby delivered!

Modems

The greatest computer system in the world won't get you very far into cyberspace, of course, without a modem. A *modem* (short for *mo*dulator-*dem*odulator) is a gadget that enables your computer to talk to, or exchange information with, another computer. The computer you connect to may be your friend's PC, a local BBS computer, a commercial online service's monster-size computer, or a computer designated to be a source of information on the Internet.

A modem's talk speed, or data-transfer rate, is measured in *bits per second,* or *bps,* which is simply the speed at which information travels from computer to computer. The data-transfer rate works much like the speedometer on a car: The higher the transfer rate, the faster the information moves between computers.

You need a modem, and not just any modem. You need a good one.

Before I continue, let me hit you with Komando's Rule of Modems: A top-of-the-line modem always costs around $500, but you can always get a good dependable modem for about $150.

I remember a few years ago, when I got my first 2400-bps modem. I could have picked up a 4800 bps modem for about $500, but I got mine for — you guessed it — about $150. When the 9600-bps modems came in at about $500 and bumped the 4800-bps modems down to the $150 range, I passed. Smart move, because it wasn't long before 14,400-bps modems popped in at $500 and pushed the 9600-bps modems down to around $150. Then — wham! — here came the 28,800-bps modems, and before I knew it, the 14,400-bps modems were at $150.

Now companies are producing 36,600-bps modems, and ISDN and data-cable modems are also becoming more popular, all in the range of $500 and more. Guess what? Yes, you can now buy 28,800-bps modems for around $150. If you're ever looking for a new modem, look for one that's about $150. Right now, that means a 28,800-bps modem.

You should watch out for one thing when you buy a 28,800-bps modem. One of the reasons it took 9600-bps modems so long to catch on is that no one could agree on a standard. You could communicate at 9600 bps, but only if the person at the other end had the same brand of modem. It wasn't very practical, to say the least.

Since then, modem companies have smartened up and adopted common standards that almost every manufacturer follows. The standards make sure that no matter which make and model of modem you have, the computer-to-computer communication is as fast and reliable as possible.

That brings me to the 28,800-bps modems. When the modem gods first looked down upon the earth and realized that they could make a 28,800-bps modem, they didn't have a standard to attach to it. One company, which shall remain nameless, tried to cash in and push its own standard, the V.FC standard. This company and some other modem manufacturers "assumed" (we all know what taking that word apart means) that V.FC would be the latest and greatest modem standard. Factories began churning out V.FC modems, and then something happened. The modem gods, in all their technological wisdom, quickly changed their minds (gods, like certain smart people, reserve this right). They decided that they liked another standard better: V.34. The big-time modem manufacturers immediately stopped the production of V.FC modems and began rolling out V.34 modems.

To you, all this means that you must be careful when you go modem shopping. Some V.FC modems that don't support the V.34 standard are still floating around on the market. All these numbers and letters may sound confusing, so just remember this: When you buy a 28,800-bps modem, make sure that the packaging mentions something about V.34 compatibility.

In addition to ensuring that the modem's communications are tried and true, another benefit of standardization is data compression. If two modems are using the same compression technology, they can provide you with an effective throughput that's much greater than the real throughput.

Okay, come on back. Here's what I mean. The V.34 modems can *compress* data, or shrink it, by as much as a 4:1 ratio. Even though the data is moving at only 28,800 bps, as much as four times that amount of uncompressed data is traveling over the phone line in any given period. That's the equivalent of more than 115,000 bps!

Usually, the process works without a hitch. Problems arise when you're using an older computer. After the data hits your modem and the modem uncompresses it, the data, in order to keep up the pace, has to move at 115,000 bps between your modem and your computer. Unfortunately, older serial ports (the things inside your PC to which your modem is connected) *can't* keep up that pace, and the data becomes bottle-necked. It's similar to driving down the 405 freeway from Los Angeles to Orange County on a Friday afternoon at 5:30 p.m.: Nothing moves.

A couple of modem quick fixes, however, are easier than driving in L.A. One option is to buy an internal modem rather than an external one. I generally like external modems better because you can tell a great deal from those blinking lights. I can also hook the same external modem to my desktop PC and to my notebook PC. With an internal modem, however, you're assured that it has everything it needs — right there on board — to get the job done.

If you want to stick with an external modem, all you have to do is replace your *I/O card* (the expansion card with all the ports on it) with one that supports the newer 16550AFN UART chips. Don't bother trying to pronounce it; just make sure that the serial card has it.

As you may gather, the key is the *UART chip,* which provides reliable information transfers. The chip becomes very important on an older, slower machine on which the computer itself is not capable of handling the incoming data quickly enough. The UART chip has a small amount of internal memory it can use to hold this data temporarily. Without the UART chip, most problems occur during the transfer of data (when you upload and download files).

On the Mac side, if you have a PowerMac or a late-model Quadra, you don't have a problem. On an older machine, you can still use a 28,800-bps modem; you just won't be able to realize the full benefits of the 4:1 data compression.

Have you heard enough about modems? I have just one more thing to say, and I'll drop the topic. When you go modem shopping, you're likely to be puzzled by the fact that modems which seem to have the same features can vary widely in price. If you're more comfortable spending a little extra money to get a name-brand piece of equipment, go for it. Between you and me, I have used cheap modems and I have used expensive modems. After I'm online, I have never been able to tell the difference between one and the other.

Phone lines

After you have your computer and your modem, you need one more important element to be able to connect with the rest of the world: a phone line. You can get by using your regular home number, but do you really want to?

Let's look at this from a technical standpoint first. Do you have call-waiting on your phone, a service in which a beep sounds to let you know that you have another incoming call? This signal also sounds if you're connected with your modem; the tone blocks the modem from hearing the other modem just long enough for them to disconnect. If you forget to disable call-waiting before a modem session, one incoming call will blow you out of the water, so to speak. When you're online, you will suddenly see a message such as "Connection terminated." How rude.

Tip

Fortunately, Bell companies provide a way for you to temporarily turn off call-waiting. The most common way is to dial *70 before dialing the number you want to call. Incoming callers then hear a busy signal or get kicked into your voice-mail system until that particular call ends. The command required to turn off call-waiting varies by telephone carrier. Contact your phone company and ask for the correct dialing sequence.

Because you're in business, remember that the tax man cometh. Are you planning to deduct those phone expenses on your tax return? Try breaking out the business-only expenses on your phone bill once, and see how much time you waste. (I have a hard enough time trying to read the hieroglyphics on my insurance bill.)

Now think about the logistics. How much do you use the phone for personal conversations? How much does your spouse or, in these politically correct times, your life partner use it? Even more important, how much does your teenage son or daughter use it? If you will be making *money* online, you will be spending lots of *time* online. If someone else in your home is on the phone gabbing about the neighbors or last night's date and you want to be online checking sales or traffic, you lose money. You'll cop an attitude too. When you add it all up, I think that you can see that one phone line just can't support all that traffic or, more important, be worth grief on the home front.

The good news is that in most houses equipped with modular phone jacks, getting a second line is a simple matter. You see, most newer homes are already wired with the necessary connections for a second line. One short visit from the phone company service crew and a hundred bucks or so later, your second line will be ready for action. My advice for that second line is not even to bother with extra goodies such as call-waiting. It's primarily a data line, and extra calling features just cause problems.

When you call to order your additional phone line, be sure to ask about any specials. For example, you always see specials advertised for additional home telephone lines just for teenagers. It makes total marketing sense. Teens live on the telephone, and a second line keeps the peace. Forgive me, Ma Bell, for I have sinned. When I started my company in my home that I occupied alone, I took advantage of a promotion for a discounted teenage line that came with no installation charges.

Sign-on software

So now you have all the hard stuff you need to get online. But what about the software? As I mentioned in Chapter 1, it's easy to find free startup kits for most of the major online services. It's so easy for you, in fact, that all you have to do is look on the CD-ROM in the back of this book. The CD includes a trial America Online account.

CD-ROM drives

While I'm thinking of it, I want to say a few words about (don't worry — it's not about modems) CD-ROM drives. For sure, you don't need a CD-ROM drive to get online. If you don't have one, however, I strongly recommend that you get one, even if you have no intention of getting into CD-ROM-based multimedia. When you're in business, you never seem to have enough time, and a CD-ROM drive saves you plenty of time.

I recently had to have an employee of mine install Microsoft Office on a Macintosh. Because we didn't have the CD-ROM version on hand, he had to spend an afternoon flipping 30 floppies in and out of the drive. If we had had the CD-ROM version, it would have taken only a couple of clicks of the mouse. I told him to think of the hours of floppy disk swapping as therapy. He didn't laugh.

As software programs become larger and more complex and CD-ROM manufacturing gets less expensive, it only makes sense for software developers to distribute their programs on CD-ROMs. It makes even more sense for *you* to install software from a CD-ROM. In addition to being faster, CD-ROMs are also much more durable than floppies. In short, they're just better.

Money Talks

After you have the software for the services you want to try, you need one more thing: a credit card. Even to sign on for a free trial membership, virtually all Internet providers and online services require a credit-card number. The reason is that if you go even one hour over your allotted free time, they have to be able to collect from you.

Some Internet providers and online services accept checking-account information rather than a credit-card number. Then every month they automatically zap enough money from your account to cover that month's charges. This method can be a hassle, especially if you forget to have enough money in your account on the due date. This situation is very possible, even if you're careful. You don't know until it happens exactly how much they will take. If you go crazy one month and spend 50 hours on America Online, you could have a major bill and a major problem.

Some Internet service providers let you mail a monthly check. They can do this because they usually charge a flat fee. If you forget to send your check, however, you may find yourself cut off from cyberspace. Having your online charges billed to your credit card just makes life much easier.

Warning

Other Internet providers will cut you a deal if you pay up front for a year's access to the Internet. Don't do it. There are so many Internet service providers that a shakeup is bound to occur. If your luck is anything like mine, the one Internet provider you pay in advance is the one that will close its doors. Even if it doesn't close up shop, how will you feel six months from now when it lowers its regular prices?

Tip

Some Internet providers try to confuse you by offering two kinds of accounts: a shell account or a SLIP (Serial Line Internet Protocol) or PPP (Point-to-Point Protocol) account. Although some technical differences exist, SLIP and PPP accounts are basically the same.

If you have a shell account, you can dial in to the Internet service provider's system by using any communications software you want, such as Procomm Plus or Zterm. Your communications software then acts as a "dumb terminal" from which you access and use programs that reside on the Internet service provider's computer. For example, you might dial in and run the Internet service provider's mail program to check your e-mail. With a shell account, everything you do is character-based — it has no graphical elements. Therefore, you cannot access the World Wide Web through a shell account.

On the other hand, a SLIP/PPP account gives you direct access to the Internet and all its services. After the dial-up connection is established, you use software running on your own computer to access various Internet services.

A SLIP/PPP account has two important advantages over a shell account:

✦ **You can choose the applications you want to use.** You may find that you like using Eudora for e-mail, for example. If something comes along later that you like better, however, you can switch over to the new program whenever you want. The Internet service provider doesn't determine which programs you use.

✦ **You have access to the World Wide Web.** I could give you a number for how many Web sites are available now, but that number would be much, much higher by the time you read this book. Let's just say that the World Wide Web is getting bigger and bigger every single day. Figure 2-1 is an example of a great spot to visit on the Web.

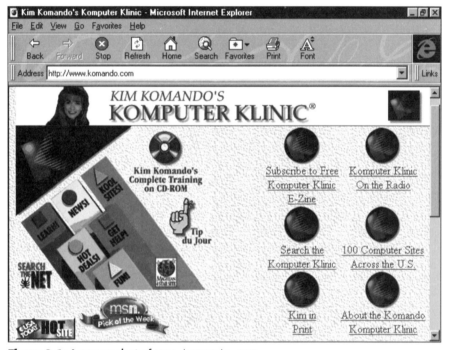

Figure 2-1: A screen shot of www.komando.com.

Bigger obviously means more popular. And more popular means more people. And more people means more potential customers. What's my point? For now, if you're thinking about doing business on the Internet, make sure that you have a SLIP or PPP account and begin learning the ins and outs of the World Wide Web.

The Online Internet Versus the "Real" Internet

I get this question all the time: What's the difference between having an Internet account with a local access provider and having an account on a major online service? A look at pricing tends to favor the Internet for all except the lightest users (the 10-to-20-hours-a-month type). With computers, however, price isn't always the top concern for the average American. After you get on the Internet, you can blow through ten hours in one or two days if you're not careful.

An online service offers you a neatly packaged set of features and services, all available through one easy-to-use interface. On the other hand, even the World Wide Web, clearly the easiest to use of all Internet services, is much more complicated and much more likely to confuse a first-time user than America Online, for example. If you get into such things as Gopher and FTP, the Internet suddenly becomes very cryptic. Add in all the various ways in which files can be encoded or compressed on the Internet, and the whole process can become intimidating for all except serious users.

This discussion brings up the issue of one interface versus many. If you log on to CompuServe, all the information you encounter is presented in a relatively standard interface, no matter which type of interface it is (see Figure 2-2). On the Internet, however, you're likely to have a separate application and therefore a separate interface for each Internet service. Chances are that if you have an Internet account, for example, you have, at minimum, an e-mail program, an FTP program, and a World Wide Web browser. Some Internet programs combine several services into a single interface, but the interface still depends on which program you use. More obscure services, such as Finger, usually aren't included.

The flip side is that, with tens of thousands of Usenet newsgroups, an ever-multiplying number of Web sites, FTP sites scattered around the globe, and more, the Internet offers much more content than any single commercial online service could ever hope for.

There's little you can do on an online service that you can't do somewhere on the Internet, and there's plenty the Internet offers that online services don't (which helps explain why all the major online services keep expanding their Internet capabilities). Again, the main thing that keeps average people away from the Internet is the lack of a standard, simple interface. And again, this situation is changing too.

As I said earlier in this chapter, having an Internet account is usually cheaper than having an account with a major online service.

So how do Internet service providers do it? How can they offer unlimited access for such a low cost compared to an online service? The answer is simple: Virtually all the information to which an Internet service provider connects you is supplied by someone else. An Internet service provider has to develop very little, if any, content of its own. All it needs, in a nutshell, is a computer system with a high-speed connection to the Internet and enough dial-in modems to reasonably accommodate its subscribers.

Figure 2-2: The opening screen for CompuServe Information Manager.

Should you use an online service connection to the Internet or just go for the Internet?

So you have the online services, and you have the Internet. And now all the online services are offering access to the Internet, and the Internet providers are offering access (for a fee, of course) to commercial online services. Is an online service really the way to go to get to the Internet? The answer is most likely no. If you're a heavy America Online user and you want to pop out to the World Wide Web every once in awhile to see what it's like, accessing the Internet through America Online may be a good idea.

For any extended use, however, the limitations of access through an online service go beyond their prohibitive pricing. With e-mail, for example, all the major commercial online services allow you to send e-mail to and receive it from other commercial online services as well as to and from the Internet — but with one important restriction: You generally can't send an e-mail message with a huge file or attachment to anyone outside the commercial online service on which the mail originates.

To you, this problem can be a real pain if you're involved with any sort of venture that includes sending large documents as attachments with your e-mail. You can't do it, so an online service is clearly not the way to go.

File transfers, or what online folks simply call *FTP,* offer another example. If you are using an online service's Internet gateway to download or FTP a file from the Internet, it's generally a two-step process. First, the file is transferred from the FTP site to the online service's computer. Then you download the file from the online service to your PC. That means extra time (and money) online. If you have a PPP account, the file goes directly from the FTP site to your computer, which cuts out the middleman, so to speak.

These are only a couple of examples. I could come up with more, but then maybe you would get bored and fall asleep. (Or, worse, *I* would fall asleep and not finish this chapter.) Here's the bottom line: If you're interested in the Internet, don't rely solely on an online service for Internet access. Get an Internet account.

When "free" is too good to be true

Let me talk for a moment about those free trial memberships to the online services and the Internet. They usually cover you for your first month for 15, 50, or maybe more hours. Go past the last minute of that last hour, however, and the meter begins ticking. Each service sets its own hourly rate, but you can figure around $3 per hour, give or take. If you're online 20 hours your first month, therefore, your 10-hour free trial membership will cost you about $30 or less. Be sure to check with the online services for any special pricing programs designed for heavy online users.

You have to be careful. People joke about having an online addiction, but it can happen. Don't think so? Check out at `http://www.hkstar.com/~joewoo/hazard. html`, the Web Addiction home page. At this site, you can find both tongue-in-cheek and serious information about this phenomenon. You can even get the e-mail address for the Internet-addiction support group.

Tip

Excess is especially tempting for new users. The first time you log on, you may want to check out the news-feeds that are only a few minutes old. Then you may go looking for awesome shareware — and find plenty of it. You don't just look at the descriptions, of course — you will probably download a couple of hours' worth. Then you have to send e-mail to all the friends whose e-mail addresses you have been saving for the past two years. After you get on the World Wide Web, you start out close to home. Then, two or three hours later, you find yourself connected to a tourist information center in Amsterdam or an art exhibit in China — and you have no idea how you got there. How long do you think it takes to filter through thousands of Usenet newsgroups to find the ones you like?

As a cyber-entrepreneur, you have to stay even more aware of this temptation because, in addition to all the fun and frolicking, you have to be online for business reasons. If you get careless, your next credit-card statement may come as quite a shock.

Cyberbucks: Tips to Hold on to Yours

At the beginning of this chapter, I mentioned that — after I told you about all the stuff you absolutely must have — I would talk about ways to get by for awhile without that stuff. In other words, I want to give you some tips about starting on a shoestring.

The first step to starting any venture on a tight budget is to see which resources you already have available. For example, do you have Internet access through your employer? More and more companies are adopting the "networked PC on every desk" philosophy. If your company is one of them, it can be a great starting point.

Don't get me wrong. I'm not suggesting that you spend your hours "on the clock" tending to your personal business. That's plain dishonest. But many employers don't object if you show up early or stay late to use your PC for personal stuff. My advice is to be up front about it and ask permission. That way, you avoid any potential problems down the road.

If you're an employer, it's difficult to watch every single minute that a member of your staff is online. You may as well set a policy about online use now because employees will use their online accounts for personal reasons anyway, even if it's just to send e-mail to a buddy.

Every employee of my company has, at minimum, an America Online account, an Internet account, and a Microsoft Network account. A few other staff members have these accounts in addition to a CompuServe account, a Prodigy account, or a Lexis/Nexis account.

My company's policy is that employees can use company accounts for personal reasons during lunch or at home as long as they don't abuse the privilege. Examples of abuse include downloading an excessive amount of shareware files, visiting the online chat areas with a corporate account, or being involved online in any manner whatsoever with anything of either a sexual or unethical nature. Laying down a few rules keeps your company's online charges from becoming overwhelming, which — at a few dollars per hour and even a few employees — adds up quickly.

Figure 2-3 is a sample employee Internet/online service account policy, written by Wes Morgan (morgan@engr.uky.edu) and Arlene H. Rinaldi (rinaldi@acc.fau.edu). You should always have your employees or contractors sign a document like this one.

Network Computing Policy

This organization is responsible for securing its network and computing systems in a reasonable and economically feasible degree against unauthorized access and/or abuse, while making them accessible for authorized and legitimate users. This responsibility includes informing users of expected standards of conduct and the punitive measures for not adhering to them. Any attempt to violate the provisions of this policy will result in disciplinary action in the form of temporary revocation of user accounts, regardless of the success or failure of the attempt. Permanent revocations can result from disciplinary actions taken by a panel judiciary board called upon to investigate network abuses.

The users of the network are responsible for respecting and adhering to local, state, federal, and international laws. Any attempt to break those laws through the use of the network may result in litigation against the offender by the proper authorities. If such an event should occur, this organization will fully comply with the authorities to provide any information necessary for the litigation process.

Section 1: General computing policy

After a user receives a user ID to be used to access the network and computer systems on that network, he or she is solely responsible for all actions taken while using that user ID. Therefore:

1.1 Applying for a user ID under false pretenses is a punishable disciplinary offense.

1.2 Sharing your user ID with any other person is prohibited. In the event that you do share your user ID with another person, you will be solely responsible for the actions that other person appropriated.

1.3 Deletion, examination, copying, or modification of files and/or data belonging to other users without their prior consent is prohibited.

1.4 Attempts to evade or change resource quotas are prohibited.

1.5 Continued impedance of other users through mass consumption of system resources, after receipt of a request to cease such activity, is prohibited.

1.6 Use of facilities and/or services for commercial purposes is prohibited.

1.7 Any unauthorized, deliberate action that damages or disrupts a computing system, alters its normal performance, or causes it to malfunction is a violation regardless of system location or time duration.

Section 2: Electronic-mail policy

Whenever you send electronic mail, your name and user ID are included in each mail message. You are responsible for all electronic mail originating from your user ID. Therefore:

2.1 Forgery (or attempted forgery) of electronic-mail messages is prohibited.

2.2 Attempts to read, delete, copy, or modify the electronic mail of other users are prohibited.

2.3 Attempts to send harassing, obscene, and/or other threatening e-mail to another user are prohibited.

2.4 Attempts to sending unsolicited junk mail, "for-profit" messages or chain letters are prohibited.

Section 3: Network security

As a user of the network, you may be allowed to access other networks (and/or the computer systems attached to those networks). Therefore:

3.1 Use of systems and/or networks in attempts to gain unauthorized access to remote systems is prohibited.

3.2 Use of systems and/or networks to connect to other systems, in evasion of the physical limitations of the remote system/local, is prohibited.

3.3 Decryption of system or user passwords is prohibited.

3.4 The copying of system files is prohibited.

3.5 The copying of copyrighted materials, such as third-party software, without the expressed written permission of the owner or the proper license, is prohibited.

3.6 Intentional attempts to "crash" network systems or programs are punishable disciplinary offenses.

3.7 Any attempts to secure a higher level of privilege on network systems are punishable disciplinary offenses.

3.8 The willful introduction of computer "viruses" or other disruptive or destructive programs into the organization network or into external networks is prohibited.

Signature: _____

User ID: _____   **Date:** _____

If you're a teacher or student at a college or university, you may have a couple of online options at your disposal. First, you may have access to Internet-linked computers on campus. If you do, chances are that access to those computers will cost you little or nothing. Second, many colleges and universities offer their students free dial-up Internet accounts. Keep in mind that some college- or university-provided accounts do not allow access to the entire Internet — just to certain portions. For example, you may be able to send e-mail but not surf the World Wide Web. Some people even continue to take a class every semester just so that they can keep their student Internet account. (I guess the fact that they're getting an education in there somewhere is just an additional benefit.)

In Chapter 1, I more or less dismissed the local BBS scene as not a large enough market for cyber-entrepreneur purposes. If you're starting out "lean and mean," however, a BBS can be a good entry point into cyberspace. More and more BBSs are offering Internet access, usually in the form of e-mail and Usenet newsgroups. You can use virtually any shareware communications package, and the cost to join a BBS is usually minimal, if any. If you can get things rolling with access to only e-mail and Usenet newsgroups, you may want to consider getting an account with your local BBS.

Do you have a friend or relative with online access? No one, no matter how close she is to you, will foot the bill to let you use a CompuServe account. Someone with a flat-rate Internet account, on the other hand, might be willing to let you tap in to her account now and then — as long as you don't interfere with her Net surfing.

Here's one last tight-budget tip. I mentioned in Chapter 1 that a couple of companies offer free consumer e-mail services. The idea is that the entire thing is paid for by advertisers whose advertisements you see in the headers of your e-mail messages. If you're considering an e-mail-based business, this one might be for you.

Note

I want to stress that all these tips for starting on a shoestring are only temporary measures. If you want to run with the big dogs, you can't play with the pups for long. Your goal should be to set up a full-blown online connection, as described at the beginning of this chapter.

Just to make sure that you have everything you need, here's a checklist of all the different online components I recommend in this chapter (remember that these are *minimum* requirements!):

◆ **Computer:** 486 DX2/66MHz with 8MB of RAM, running Windows 3.1 or (better) Windows 95 or a Macintosh Quadra with 8MB of RAM

◆ **Monitor:** SVGA, 256 colors

◆ **Modem:** 28,800 bps, V.34

◆ **Phone line:** Dedicated for business use

◆ **CD-ROM drive:** Optional but recommended

✦ **Online software:** Included on the CD-ROM in the back of this book is a free trial membership to America Online and the sign-up software for AT&T WorldNet Service

✦ **Payment method:** Credit card (checking account accepted by some services)

✦ **Self control:** Gotta have it, especially if you join an online service

Part II

Online Marketing 101

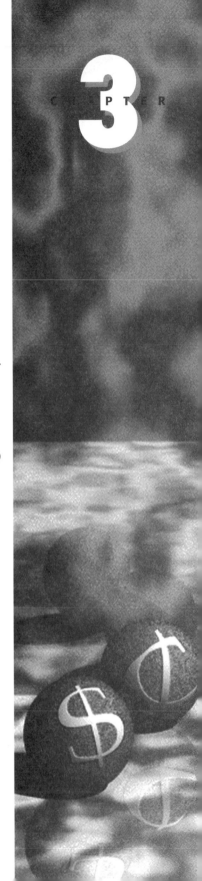

CHAPTER 3

Unlocking the Secrets of Your Customers' Buying Motivations

"Everything that can be invented has been invented."

Charles H. Duell, Commissioner, U.S. Office of Patents, 1899

When you look at the way most companies utilize their online presence, they treat the online environment as though it were one big infomercial. It's part information. It's part entertainment. But virtually any business area is truly one big commercial.

Every company online is selling *some*thing. A company may cleverly disguise its sales pitch, however, within valuable information. For example, visit a magazine's site online. You can read the latest issue, but don't be surprised by the "subscribe now" button at the site or a picture of an aspirin bottle in the middle of a story about the U.S. deficit.

Take this "big infomercial" idea a step further: Even people with a personal home page online are selling something — themselves. Infomercials are nothing more than the natural evolution of television marketing. Television commercials have been around, after all, since Elvis Presley made his celebrated appearance on "The Ed Sullivan Show." Online marketing is the next wave in the tradition of making your product or service available to consumers far and wide.

You must remember that being online doesn't enable you to do new things as much as it enables you to do things in a new way. Almost anything you can do offline you can do easier and quicker online. You may remember the examples I mentioned in Chapter 1 of using the online environment to communicate over long distances, book travel arrangements, and find information.

What I *didn't* tell you about in Chapter 1, though, are the devices, in rudimentary development stages, that you attach to your PC to have online sex. I don't elaborate on the science of "teledildonics," however. Use your imagination. I know that you're more interested in being online and using its distribution system as a new way to market and sell your products and services. I just threw in that tidbit to make sure that you were paying attention.

In Chapter 1, I also gave you an overview of different ways to conduct online marketing. No matter which method you choose, plenty of experts are out there to help you along the way. Be careful with self-proclaimed experts, however. Too many people know just enough to be dangerous, and they can cost you money and time along the way.

Even after you read this entire book, you may need help in certain areas. Just realize that marketing online expertise is within your reach. Programmers can create your cyber-environment. Certain advertising agencies specialize in online marketing to create the right message. Public relations folks help spread the word through online and offline news services, interviews, and feature articles. In short, no matter what your online marketing needs, someone out there specializes in just what you require.

Note

Before venturing into the online marketing arena, however, you must understand one point: In the larger picture of doing business, marketing online is not much different from any other type of marketing. "Online" implies a new *way* to do something, not necessarily something new to do.

Beware of Geeks Bearing Gifts

When you participate in online marketing, you have a product or service you showcase to a potential customer. It's your job to present your message in a way that makes the customer act. You want customers to act *now,* but you also have to be careful.

Note

Hard-sell, pushy sales techniques hardly work offline, and the odds are even lower online. You always have to remember that the marketing medium is on a computer screen. It's more difficult, therefore, to convey electronically the feelings of trust most consumers need in order to act.

Blatant hawking or downright fraud exists more on the Internet than on commercial online services. The commercial services have policies, online police who patrol the service, and members' terms of service that prohibit fraudulent behavior.

The Internet is pretty much out of anyone's control, but the situation is changing. Consumer advocacy groups and the U.S. government are cracking down on consumer fraud on the Internet. For example, a Massachusetts woman used to operate New Discoveries, a site on the World Wide Web that advertised a new treatment for AIDs. "In six weeks, you are HIV-negative," the ad said. "Even near-terminal patients can recover."

Visitors to the site were told to send $24 for a book that would reveal the cure, which was a solution made from wormwood, cloves, and black-walnut hulls. (***Note:*** No medical evidence substantiates this claim.) Customers could also dial a 900 number to get the information at a cost of $1.99 per minute.

At the time this book was written, New Discoveries was shut down because the state attorney general's office issued a temporary restraining order. If, after an investigation, New Discoveries is prosecuted for fraud, it can be ordered to pay penalties of as much as $5,000 for each count.

Check out `http://www.fraud.org` to find out what the bad guys are up to and how to stop them. You can report suspicious activity on the Internet, learn how to limit the use of your personal financial information, and get tips, alerts, and advice. Figure 3-1 shows the National Fraud Organization home page.

Another Internet site, Dr. Jeffrey Lant's Money Mall, is a good example of hard-sell marketing conveniently located at one Internet site (`http://www.worldprofit.com/lantmall.htm`).

At the Money Mall, you can "Learn the Closely Guarded Secrets of How to Buy Scrap Gold and Silver and Easily Earn $75,000 Every Year!" and "How to Fax Your Way to $10,000 Each Month and You Don't Even Need a Fax Machine!" Or how about this one: "How to Get Other People to Line Up and Obey Your Every Command." I don't know about you, but I have enough trouble getting my dog to do his thing outside the house.

It is interesting to read, however, what's on the bottom of almost every page in the Money Mall. "The Publisher posts all information on the Jeffrey Lant Money Mall in good faith, but cannot vouch for its accuracy. That is the responsibility of each individual advertiser. Advertisers purchasing positions on the Mall agree to make no false or exaggerated claims or knowingly provide data for posting they know to be incorrect or untrue. Further, they agree to protect and indemnify the publisher from any claims for libel, copyright violation, plagiarism or privacy and other suits or claims based on the content or subject matter of the information they provide."

Interestingly, most of the advertisers in the mall do not accept credit-card orders for their products. Some sites offer fax-back information lines in addition to toll and toll-free order telephone numbers. They also have order forms to fill in and send off to post office boxes far and wide.

Figure 3-1: The National Fraud Organization, whether you check it out online or offline, is designed to help stop Internet scams.

Wait — Don't Leave Yet!

All this brings me to my next point. After a potential customer leaves your virtual storefront, statistics show that you probably have lost the sale. It's not much different from someone changing channels while a television commercial is airing (albeit some commercials are better than regular programming). Just as in a real retail environment, after customers are gone, they're usually gone for good.

You have to create an online infomercial that makes a customer act. Let me take a moment to clarify what I mean by "act." In the ideal situation, the most desirable action is a sale. Because you want the person to buy something from you or at least *do* something on the spot, you have to present the information and your message in a clearly understood, entertaining, and attractive manner. The offer must not cross the fine line of being too good to refuse and unbelievable because anything that good simply cannot be true.

You also have to give customers one or more methods by which to act. Whether you implement secured credit-card transactions or rely on third-party payment systems, such as First Virtual Holding (see Figure 3-2), you have to give the public a means for spending its money *now*. Don't ever rely on an instruction such as, "To order this item, mail a check to XYZ." Believe me, the check will never get in the mail.

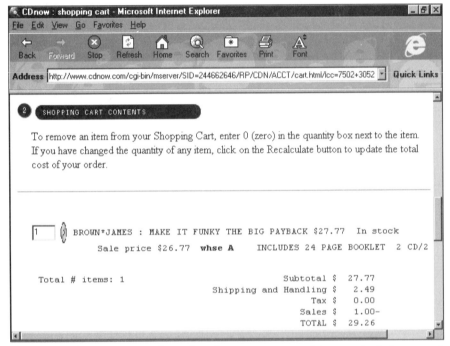

Figure 3-2: If you accept credit cards online, you can complete an order before a customer leaves your site.

In some instances, of course, the desired action is simply an inquiry. Suppose that you're a real estate broker and you decide to publish your listings on the World Wide Web. You have the greatest Web page stocked with four-color photos, floor plans, and ratings of local school districts, and you even promote the fact that you share commissions on co-brokered deals. It's your own little Multiple Listing Service book on the Internet.

Here's where the buck stops. No one will ever authorize you to charge $100,000 on his MasterCard to pay for a house he has seen only on his computer screen. What you want here is an inquiry. Again, you have to provide the public with a way to make that inquiry *now*.

In the example of a World Wide Web real estate office, you have to develop an online inquiry form that people can fill out and submit directly from their Web browser, as shown in Figure 3-3. The statement "If you're interested in this property, please call this number" just doesn't cut it. *You* have to do the calling.

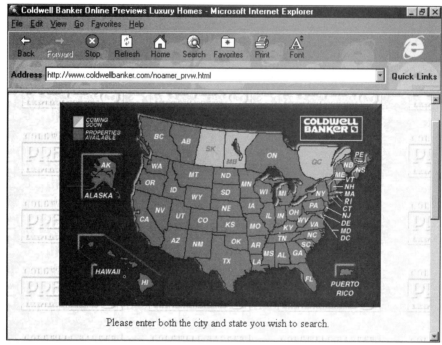

Figure 3-3: When an order cannot be paid for electronically, use an inquiry form.

So how do you motivate the buying (or inquiring) public? What can you say or do to make people take immediate action?

How about a little trip to the psychologist's office? More specifically, step back in time to the mid-1950s and visit a particular psychologist: Abraham Maslow.

Maslow and Madison Avenue

Abraham Maslow developed a long-standing and highly respected theory based on the idea that we all have needs (the difference between a desired state and the actual state) and motives (the inner movement that directs a person to satisfy a felt need). He believed that any person's needs could be categorized and arranged in five levels, from the basic needs of food and shelter to the highest human goal of self-actualization. (And remember that Maslow never met Madonna.)

This theory is usually represented graphically as a pyramid, as shown in Figure 3-4.

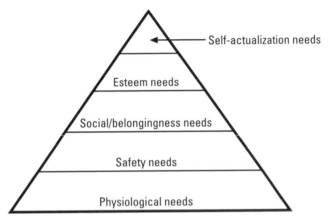

Figure 3-4: Maslow's pyramid of needs.

Tip

The lowest level on the pyramid represents our most primary needs. According to Maslow, a person will not, and in fact cannot, attempt to fulfill the needs of one level until she has fulfilled the needs of the preceding level. After a need is satisfied, it is no longer a motivator.

I know what you're thinking. "What the heck are you talking about, Komando? Needs? Motives? I want to market my business online."

Stay with me on this. Here's what Maslow's theory means. If you're starving to death, you will risk going out in grapefruit-size hail to find some food. After you find something to eat, you won't even think about finding a significant other with whom to share your food until you find a warm and safe cave. After you meet that special someone in the cave and share some raw meat, you're likely to fall in love.

Now things are looking good for you. You begin to feel sort of cocky, and your entire tribe looks up to you because of the risks you have taken. You have esteem, status, and a sense of importance. With your entire life in front of you, you can now try to figure out your true destiny. When you do, you will have become a self-actualized person, albeit still a caveperson. (In real life, of course, now is the time that a huge Tyrannosaurus rex shows up and has you for a snack, but I'll save that for a discussion of Murphy's Law.)

Maybe you don't like my cave story, so take a quick look at Maslow's theory in the context of today's offline marketing. It's all around you.

Starting at the bottom of Maslow's pyramid, the Tyson Foods slogan "Feeding you like family" and Campbell's "Soup is good food" are examples of messages aimed at satisfying your most basic physiological needs.

One level up in your quest for self-actualization, you find messages targeted to fulfill your safety needs. Two examples are the Metropolitan Life Insurance maxim "Get Met. It Pays" and the American Express slogan for traveler's checks: "Don't leave home without them."

After you have eaten and feel safe, the statements "Here's to good friends," from Lowenbrau beer, and "Reach out and touch someone," from AT&T, attempt to influence your purchasing decisions by stressing the innate human longing to be accepted socially by individuals and groups.

If you go up one more level (with just one more to go before reaching the top of the pyramid), slogans such as the Omega watch advertisement "Guaranteed to make a lasting impression" attempt to go after your sense of accomplishment, esteem, and achievement needs. Ditto for "Membership has its privileges."

Finally, you reach the pinnacle of the pyramid. You may not think that a car can help you become self-actualized, but Lexus apparently does. The car company's slogan "The Relentless Pursuit of Perfection" is geared toward the human craving to realize your utmost potential and fully use your talents. Even the U.S. government knows about Maslow. The Army promises to let you "Be all that you can be."

Maslow did an excellent job of explaining how people assess their needs and satisfy motivators. His theory holds a solid place in Marketing 101. But the theory has some problems.

For starters, people act and react differently to the same situation on different days. We *are* human, after all, and not capable of uniform responses to the same message. More important, when you really think about Maslow's pyramid, any product or service could be related to fulfilling one or more of the needs on the five levels.

Further knocking down the pyramid's foundation is the sheer barrage of different marketing messages sent to you in a wide spectrum of mediums. Everywhere you turn — television, radio, newspapers, magazines, billboards, buses, and even more places between — you see ads.

It seems that companies are finding more and more places to sneak in advertising messages too. One airline company executive recently told me that his airline was thinking about selling the outside space on its jets to advertisers for millions of dollars per plane. It's not the worst idea I have ever heard. Yet the clear-cut problem is the remote, but possible, public relations disaster. Imagine the television news coverage and newspaper nightmares if the only remains from a jet crash were the advertising company's logo on the rear rudder. Not a pretty picture.

The average American is exposed to more than 500 different advertisements daily. Because it's pure sensory overload, we unknowingly filter the messages. Maslow certainly didn't think about this possibility 40 years ago, but no one thought of selling advertising space on jets either.

Komando's Theory of Buy-Me-Now Needs

Maslow's needs, whether together or separately, are what motivate people. It's a solid premise on which to develop your online marketing plans. That's what you want to do — motivate people to buy your product or service, which brings me to Komando's Theory of Buy-Me-Now Needs. (I am sure that my theory is destined to make me eligible for a Nobel prize.)

My theory permits you to assess the needs of someone else: your potential customers. You have to see things the way your potential customers do. You have to consider that they have their filtering sensors up and, therefore, look at their needs and motivators a little differently. Furthermore, humans are complex, with needs and motivators that overlap. Like Maslow, I have broken down consumer needs into these five basic categories (for the purposes of this discussion, each need is equal to the other):

✦ Practical

✦ Pleasure

✦ Communication

✦ Idolization

✦ Benevolent

My theory also makes one major assumption: Whether you are offline or online and no matter what your business, you are selling something. Presenting the right message to make customers act becomes even more crucial to marketers as consumers demand higher levels of satisfaction. Now that you have seen Maslow's pyramid, I present Komando's pie chart of buy-me-now needs (see Figure 3-5).

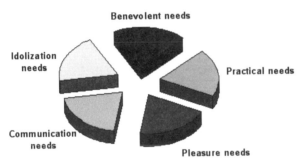

Figure 3-5: Komando's buy-me-now needs in one convenient pie chart.

Practical needs

Marketers must provide customers with something that's sensible in nature. In an attempt to target practical needs, marketers use such claims as "Save time," "Save money," and "It's so easy."

Satisfying today's practical needs can involve anything from getting airline tickets delivered in 24 hours to purchasing an ultrafast modem in order to travel the information superhighway at supersonic speeds. Your product performs some task, or helps perform some task, that customers want to accomplish. Your product or service doesn't offer the emotional benefits, however, that consumers get from other products.

Pleasure needs

Pleasure and entertainment needs are self-explanatory. They include anything from eating the middle from an Oreo cookie to romance and the other things we do to seek gratification. Everyone (with the possible exception of a few IRS agents) wants to have some fun. If you can help people have some fun, you stand to make lots and lots of money.

Communication needs

What do I mean by "communication needs"? I'm talking about the human desire to express ourselves and interact with others. I don't mean just verbal expressions either. The human desire for expression includes wanting to demonstrate that you are cool, rich, hip, thin, strong, or whatever other adjective you want to throw in there. Products in this category include what might be called "vanity" items. It makes no sense to wear a five-karat diamond if no one knows its value or the status it represents.

Idolization needs

Have you ever wondered why they chose Michael Jordan and not you to sell Hanes underwear? The reason is that everyone has certain idolization needs — the desire to relate to and connect with our "heroes." Don't take it personally, but I probably wouldn't buy underwear from you in a million years. (And I probably wouldn't wear Michael Jordan's underwear either.)

Benevolent needs

Last, and probably least, in the moneymaking pie are benevolent needs, which include our desires to be charitable and extend a helping hand to the world around us. I'm the first to admit that you probably won't make a fortune trying to satisfy anyone's benevolent needs. But you do have to recognize how these needs fit into the larger picture of where people are willing to spend their money.

By now you're probably like the woman on the Wendy's commercial who screams, "Where's the beef?" Okay, okay. Let's get into some real-life examples of online businesses that are attempting to meet the different needs from the Komando pie.

Komando's Theory of Buy-Me-Now Needs in Action Online

Whether you have an Internet account or an account with a commercial online service (if you don't have one or the other by now, you have pretty much missed the point), you have access to the World Wide Web. That's the reason that all the examples in this section are from Web-based enterprises. I cover each form of being online in detail later in this book, but I want every one of you to be able to log on and check out these examples for yourself. It's important that you know how to sell before you begin selling.

One more caveat: The Web is constantly changing. The same features that make it so easy to *start* doing business on the Web also make it easy to *stop* doing business on the Web. I tried to choose Web sites that look like they will be around for a while, but I can't guarantee that every one of them will be there when you log on.

Putting the "p" in "practical" in online selling

Let's look at some practical needs. The first place I want you to point your Web browser is to `http://www.icstrategies.com/penril/`. This site, the home page of an extremely fast modem offered by Penril Datability Networks, is a classic example of good online selling, as shown in Figure 3-6.

First, the product is a natural for the online community. You can't be online without a modem, and the page has an attractive design (that's a must). It's also simple. You have three options: Click the "What's the Big Deal?" button to learn more about the product, click the "Prove It" button to see some hard, cold statistics, or click the "I Gotta Have One" button to place an order. Customers with Netscape secured-transaction capabilities can place credit-card orders on the spot, which means that Penril can cash in on impulse buying. Everyone else can fax their orders. All in all, it's a nicely designed site.

If you want to look at something online that's practical and functional, check out The Grocery Club, at `http://rainer.bnt.com/~grocery/`. Granted, this site has limited geographic appeal (it caters only to the "lovely New River Valley of Virginia"), but what an idea! The Grocery Club home page is shown in Figure 3-7.

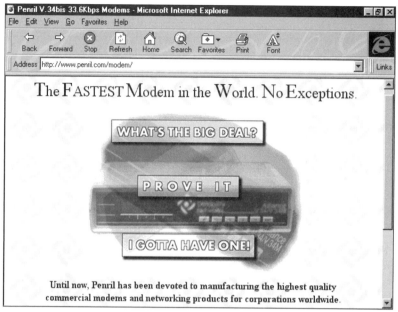

Figure 3-6: Selling modems online makes total sense.

Figure 3-7: Even buying groceries online is easy.

On my visit, I was able to cruise around the store, adding items of all kinds (from toilet paper to mustard) to my virtual shopping cart. All the while, a running total of my bill was displayed at the bottom of my screen, which is a handy feature when you're on a budget. When I went to the virtual checkout stand, I had the option to pay immediately with DigiCash (which I talk about in Chapter 10) or pay when I received my groceries. I also had the option to pick up the stuff at one of the company's stores or have it all delivered.

Keep in mind that this is just a demonstration of what grocery stores might be like in the future. Maybe, sometime soon, stores in your area will do the same thing. Then you never, ever, have to leave your computer. Oh, joy.

Even when you're on vacation, the traveling you do usually represents a practical need. Let me compare a couple of travel agencies that have established a presence on the World Wide Web.

If you point your Web browser to `http://www.interstar.com/advert/airfare.html`, you see what I consider a good example of a bad Web site. This site is the home of a travel outfit called 1-800-LOW-AIRFARE. (I once gave out a phone number like this one on my national talk-radio show, and some guy called in and asked me what to do with the extra letters.) Anyway, having three extra letters in a vanity phone number has nothing to do with the company's poor Web page. It's not much more than a boring billboard in cyberspace. You can't book reservations. You can't request more information. You can't even send e-mail to this group. Obviously, these folks need a copy of this book.

Hear me and hear me good. People go online to *interact* in an environment, not to look. They want to point and click to see more information. Unless you have absolutely the most amazing product since edible underwear, pasting a picture of your product on a home page with an 800 number just doesn't cut it. (I'm not saying that the pinup calendar girls don't get the traffic, but this book isn't about erotic connections.)

Compare the travel site in the preceding example to Aer Travel, located at `http://www.aertravel.com/browse/aer/`. Aer Travel seems to be a full-service travel agency, which is reflected in its home page (see Figure 3-8). The site contains plenty of information about the company's general services as well as special travel opportunities. Although you can't book a specific flight online, the page contains an online form on which you can supply all the information a travel agent might need in order to book a flight for you. Current Aer customers can choose to have their arrangements billed to their account profile that's set up with the company. Aer is an example of an online travel agency done right. Applause.

Everyone needs software, and everyone wants to save as much time and money as possible. Enter the online software superstore software.net, conveniently located at `http://software.net` (see Figure 3-9). According to one blurb on the software.net home page, "With more than 50,000 pages of news and reviews, and 16,000 products, we are committed to helping you find the right product at a guaranteed low price."

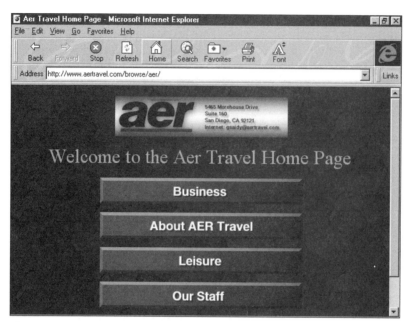

Figure 3-8: Go ahead — kiss the virtual Blarney Stone and book a trip.

Figure 3-9: It's difficult to find a person online who doesn't want more software.

You can not only shop for software at discount prices but also read reviews from major publications before you buy. If you do buy from software.net, you're talking instant gratification: You download your new software directly from software.net to your PC. This idea is new and exciting; software.net was the first company, in fact, authorized to sell Microsoft products online.

This outfit naturally caters more to businesses with high-speed, dedicated Internet connections. I have a nerd friend with a high-speed T1 line in his home, but he is the exception to the rule. For the rest of us, we could probably walk to a computer store in a neighboring county and buy Microsoft Office in less time than it would take to download it over a 14.4 Kbps or even 28.8 bps modem. As nonbusiness users move to higher-speed connections, this shopping method will become more feasible.

No matter what their age, girls (and boys) just want to have fun

Before I tell you about how to satisfy pleasure and entertainment needs online, I want to say a few words about what is called "adult online entertainment." Whether it excites you or disgusts you, you have to realize one important fact about online adult entertainment: It's very, very popular.

One fellow who runs an online classic-car exchange reports that his monthly "hit" count skyrocketed to more than 90,000 when he added a monthly pinup image to his site. See what one picture of one pretty woman can do for you? Another user had to shut down his online collection of nude images at the request of his Internet provider — not because the material was offensive but because it generated more than 5 million visits (or hits) in one 23-day period and the host system couldn't keep up.

Cyberspace is just like any other space. Sex sells. I'm not taking a stand one way or the other. You won't see sex at my company's site, although at a recent staff meeting we were talking about how to increase traffic and our Webmaster suggested a nude photo of me. I'm sorry to report that he's no longer with our growing company.

I just want you to be aware of what's out there on the Net. With that admonition, let's look at some pleasure-oriented sites.

What better way to sell subscriptions to a magazine such as *Playboy* than to provide a few online sneak peeks of its content? Check http://www.playboy.com to see what I mean or just sneak a peek at Figure 3-10.

If the magazine people were to put the entire magazine online, who would pay for a printed version? By putting just enough to give potential subscribers a clear picture (pun definitely intended) of what *Playboy* is all about, however, these folks have succeeded in creating a Web site that is appropriate for their particular business.

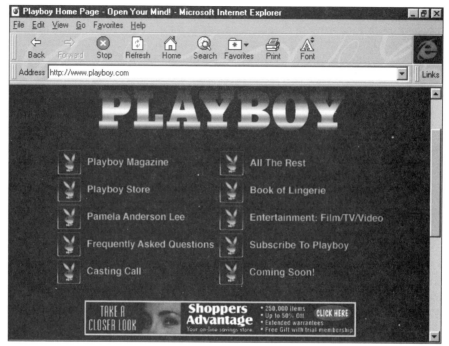

Figure 3-10: This site probably gets some heavy traffic!

The most important part of the site, at least for purposes of this discussion, is the ability to order your subscription online. Because the phrase "bill me later" is a standard option for magazine subscriptions, there's no need to worry about online payment methods.

You can't sell certain types of products and services online because they're simply offline things. That doesn't mean, however, that you shouldn't *market* them online. Virtual World is a great example.

Virtual World is a chain of virtual-reality theme parks. People like you and me can go to one of these parks to participate in interactive, multiplayer, 3-D virtual reality games. It's the video arcade of the future, and it all happens right there. Short of gift certificates, there's nothing that Virtual World can sell online.

Yet the appeal of Virtual World to Net surfers is as obvious as the nose on Karl Malden's face. It should also be obvious why the company has its own Web site. To see what I mean, point your browser to http://www.virtualworld.com/. It's a good example of a promotional Web site, as shown in Figure 3-11.

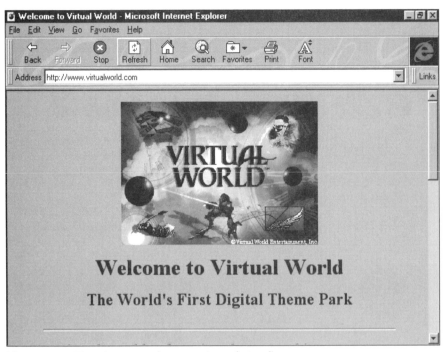

Figure 3-11: There's not much you can't market online.

Recently, *The Wall Street Journal* claimed that in order for online business to really take off, business operators will have to give online shoppers more incentive. With overhead costs for an online business as much as 50 percent lower than costs for a traditional business, online entrepreneurs are in a position to offer that incentive in the form of better pricing.

One business of this type mentioned in the article is an online music store called CDnow (see Figure 3-12). Its prices are competitive, and CDnow offers a variety of payment options, including credit-card transactions in Netscape Secure mode. Add to that more than 165,000 products and two-day delivery service, and you have what I call an ideal online business. You can check out CDnow at http://cdnow.com/.

American Whitewater Expeditions (http://www.aminews.com/ami/sites/American_WW/) is another example of an offline business with online potential. This site is an attractive and informative presentation of a truly exciting vacation opportunity. The inclusion of logos of accepted credit cards at the bottom of the page is an especially good idea. (Bring your life preserver and bring your Visa because they don't guarantee your safety and they don't take American Express.)

Figure 3-12: Buying music online is easy and fun.

The one area in which this page falls short is interactivity. In a broad sense, this page is no different from the 1-800-LOW-AIRFARE page I mentioned earlier in this chapter. The fact that it's more informative and interesting makes it more palatable, but I want to at least be able to request more information by e-mail.

Keyboard companions fulfill communication needs

Now look at some Web sites that help fulfill communication and interaction needs.

First, a trip to the PeachWeb Plantation (`http://plant.peachweb.com/`) demonstrates a good example of an online business that caters to our human need for communication. Have you ever checked out the chat areas on one of the online services, such as AOL? That's what the PeachWeb Plantation is all about. It's a gigantic chat service built around a Southern plantation theme, as shown in Figure 3-13. For only $7.95 a month (the price at the time this book was written, anyway), you can join and babble to your heart's content. You will be as happy as Scarlett O'Hara looking at Tara — before it burned to the ground, of course.

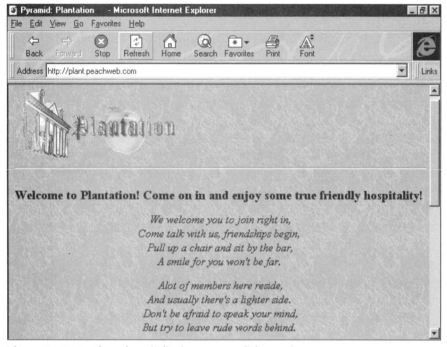

Figure 3-13: Southern hospitality is a mouse click away!

The PeachWeb Plantation has almost all the characteristics of a great online site. The interface is attractive and professional, the idea is clever, and the site is *extremely* interactive. The only low point I can see from looking at my cybersuccess checklist is that PeachWeb doesn't take credit cards: As a result, you can't subscribe online and get that instant gratification we all want so desperately.

Now go to another one of those "online marketing for an offline product" sites. I direct you to Reeves Import Motorcars, of Tampa, Florida. You can check it out at `http://www.bayanet.com/reeves/` on the World Wide Web and in Figure 3-14.

Sometimes a fine line exists between need and desire. If hiking and exploring are what you live for, you can probably make an argument that you *need* an off-road vehicle. On the other hand, it would be difficult to find anyone with a legitimate *need* for a Hummer, the civilian version of the vehicle that was so popular in the Desert Storm conflict.

Reeves claims to be the only Hummer dealership in the country with an exclusive Hummer test track (another word for obstacle course), and it has pictures on the Web to prove it. You can't help but be impressed when you see this beast cruising through a pool of water that rises up to its windows. Imagine working your way through traffic in this thing. This site doesn't list any prices, which I normally like to see, but the Hummer is definitely one of those "If you have to ask, you can't afford it" vehicles.

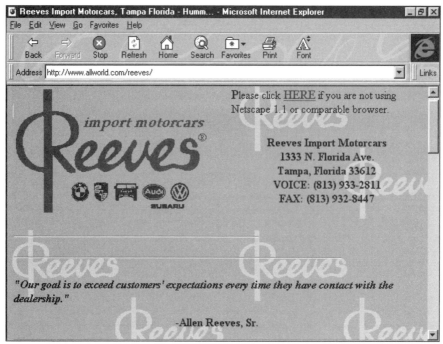

Figure 3-14: The Internet has truly something for everyone.

Are diamonds really a girl's best friend? I don't know, but they certainly help fulfill my communication needs — and, clearly, the bigger, the better. Thanks to American Diamond Exchange, shown in Figure 3-15, you can buy those precious little gems online, at `http://www.adexnet.com/main.htm`.

This site packs in lots of value-added service. Your first option is to go to the ADEX Education Center, where you can learn everything you need to know to make an informed purchase. You can visit the ADEX virtual showroom or its customer service center. If you're in the jewelry biz, you can even explore career and business opportunities. I especially like the Diamond Request Form, on which you can provide a detailed description of the jewelry you want, and American Diamond Exchange will then find it for you. Here's the clincher, of course: You can buy online with your credit card using Netscape Secure transactions. Good stuff.

I have to say one thing, however: If you plan to make a considerable purchase on the Internet, shop smart. Make sure that the company is legitimate by checking it out with the Better Business Bureau, the National Fraud Organization, and other consumer-conscious groups. Unless you have previously done business with the company, you may discover that a great deal on a home page may be nothing more than a scam.

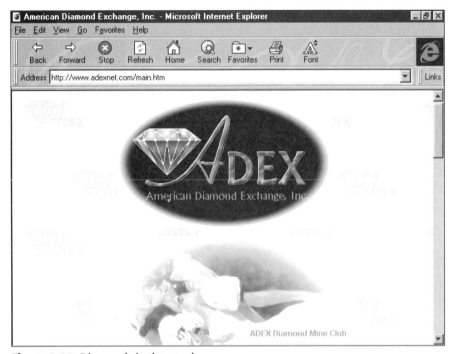

Figure 3-15: Diamonds in the rough.

Plastic surgeons can work miracles to correct many serious medical problems. With a full arsenal of breast jobs, nose jobs, and cheek jobs, however, they can also do wonders to fulfill our communication needs. Welcome to The Body Electric home page, whose cyberoffice is at `http://www.surgery.com/body/welcome.html` (see Figure 3-16).

At this site, you can find all sorts of valuable information about plastic surgery, broken down by specific body area. You can see "before and after" pictures, find general pricing information, and obtain a physician's referral.

Baby, I want to be a star!

Because both children and adults have idolization needs, your first stop on the Idolization Needs tour bus is Sail with the Stars. The company's home page, at `http://www.sailwithstars.com/`, is shown in Figure 3-17.

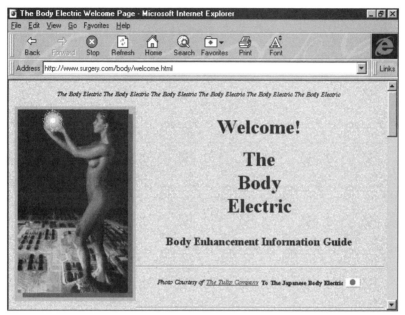

Figure 3-16: Enticing customers to "get plastic" and then not taking it.

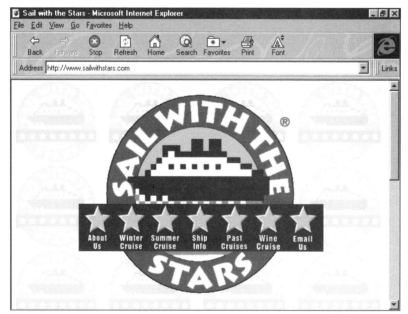

Figure 3-17: Hobnobbing with the stars.

This cruise service specializes in family cruises accompanied by youth stars. Past cruises have included Jonathan Taylor-Thomas, of "Home Improvement"; Jodie Sweetin, of "Full House"; Angela Watson, of "Step by Step"; and Tia and Tamera Mowry, of "Sister Sister."

This site is loaded with good information and an attractive form to fill out for additional details. One question I couldn't find the answer to was "How much moolah?"

Looking for Howard Stern underwear or a Jay Leno baseball cap? I don't know whether you can find these particular items at Movie Madness Merchandise, at `http://www.moviemadness.com`, but you can find truckloads of other star-related goodies. You can buy, in addition to merchandise, autographed photos of everyone from Don Adams to Stephanie Zimbalist and autographed cast photos from movies and TV shows ranging from *The Age of Innocence* to *Young Guns 2*.

This site has lots of merchandise. Best of all, it has lots of ways to order, including snail mail, an 800 number, fax, and — my personal favorite — online. Check it out in Figure 3-18.

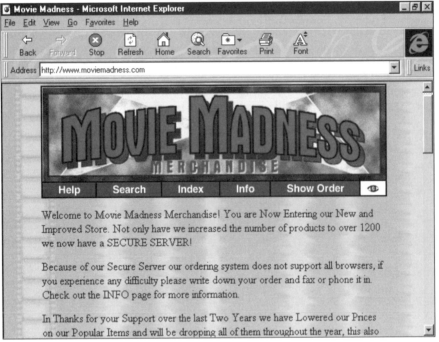

Figure 3-18: If you can't be a star, maybe some memorabilia can help you feel like one.

If you can't rub elbows with the stars, maybe you will be satisfied rubbing elbows with wax replicas of the stars. If you think that this opportunity might be just the thing for you, stop by the world-famous Hollywood Wax Museum the next time you're in the Los Angeles area. Still not convinced? Then visit the Wax Museum Web site first. You can find it at `http://www.ernestallen.com/TR/CA/HollywoodWaxMuseum/`.

This page isn't particularly impressive, but it does give you most of the information you need, such as the company's address and phone number. It has enough photos of exhibits to get you interested in going there. A site such as this one would benefit, however, from a "how to get there" online map, sort of like the maps folks sell on every street corner in Hollywood.

If you're not into Hollywood types, maybe sports is your thing. If you want authorized merchandise from your favorite NFL team, take a look at the AllSports.com Company Store, at `http://allsports.questtech.com/nfl/store.html`. It has a good selection of merchandise, and the prices seem reasonable. Unfortunately, I have to deduct major points for not providing an online ordering option or even a way to request more information.

Relying on the generosity of friends like you

The only type of need from Komando's list of buy-me-now needs that remains for me to discuss are benevolent needs. You probably won't make much money catering to these needs. In one sense, organizations that rely on contributions to sustain them-selves are still your competition, however, because you're all competing for the same online dollar. If a charity is near and dear to you, putting a link to its home page at your site adds some personality and a sense of humanity. I don't go into great detail about these types of sites, but the following list shows a few sites to check out. Make sure that you study them as closely as you studied the other sites in this chapter (even though they're charitable organizations, they're still *selling,* and some of them do an excellent job of it):

   ✦ Little Friends, at `http://204.243.112.2/cs/orphans/`

   ✦ Amnesty International, at `http://www.organic.com/Non.profits/Amnesty/` (see Figure 3-19)

   ✦ Save the Earth Foundation, at `http://www.commerce.com/save_earth/`

   ✦ Planet Peace, at `http://www.teleport.com/~amt/planetpeace/` (see Figure 3-20)

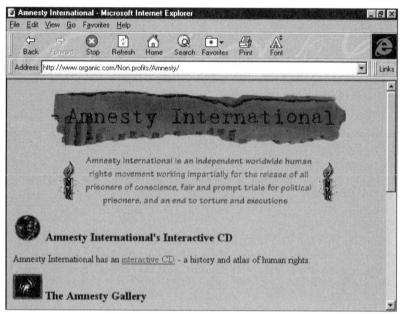

Figure 3-19: Helping support human rights online.

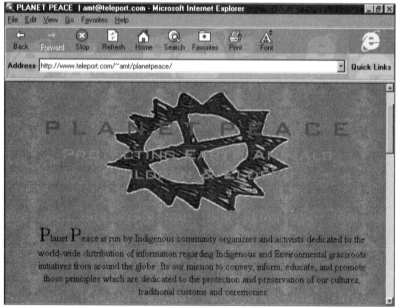

Figure 3-20: Looking for assistance to keep our world safe in the spirit of friendship.

Cutting to the Chase

What do all the words and pictures in this chapter mean? First, it means that there truly is no free lunch, even in cyberspace. Do you remember in Chapter 1 that I told you how I often get calls from people wanting to produce their own infomercials? All the things that make those wanna-bes stop dead in their tracks should have you thinking right now too.

If you're getting into an online business because you think that computers are cool, that online commerce is trendy, that you can make some fast money, or that you want something to brag about to your technoid friends, you had better think again. Computers are fun, but making money with one takes as much hard work as any other business does. Like my father always told me, you get out whatever you put in. It's that simple.

With that said, do you think that you can identify a public need you can satisfy through some online means? Can you motivate the buying public to accept your solution to that need over someone else's? And, most important, are you willing to bust your buns to make it all happen?

If you answered yes to all these questions, you have at least the cyber-entrepreneurial spirit. The tough part is putting it all together. That's what this book is all about. If you have the will and the desire, I can help you make it happen.

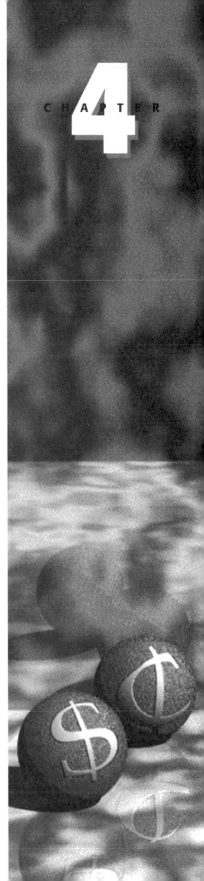

Getting to Know Your Customers

Whether you launch your online business in a spare bedroom or you have a big corporation behind your efforts, you must approach it as an entrepreneur: You have to be a little different. Take some risks. Don't be afraid of failure. Get creative. And yes, be a little crazy. It's perfectly acceptable.

Because people generally expect entrepreneurs to be ultraistic (that means radical, if you don't want to look it up), you have great latitude in your actions and decision-making. You don't have to be a stuffed shirt when you are an entrepreneur. The important thing is not to be feeble-witted — that may cost you your success.

I'm not saying that there are no absolutes to follow in your online business or in being an entrepreneur. Rules exist — and lots of them. The challenge lies in molding the rules to fit your particular online business. It's not that tough. Remember that online marketing isn't much different from offline traditional marketing. Even offline marketing rules change from product to product and then from marketplace to marketplace.

No matter what you are selling and where, you must remember this absolute: You have to figure out who will buy your product or service. In other words, who exactly is your customer? You can have *the* greatest product or service, but if the right people with the right purchasing power do not know about it, what good is it?

Tip

A smart marketer quickly learns how to pinpoint the individual in a household or within an organization who has the authority to make a purchasing decision. Without this knowledge, you may waste time selling the right product to the wrong person.

One online entrepreneur who sells personalized baby and children's gifts told me that one of her first orders was from a teenager, who obviously didn't have a credit card. The entrepreneur was so psyched to get an online order that she immediately painted the item before getting the necessary billing information. When she called the would-be buyer, the buyer said that she didn't know where the card was and would call back. You guessed it — the return call never came. This example is a minor one, but you can learn a big lesson from it. Make sure that you push your products on the people who have the power to purchase them. Or at least add to your Web page something like this: "Ask your parents for permission to use their credit card, and have the card ready when you call."

Looking beyond marketing online, you can see focused marketing every day. Consider these offline marketing examples. Gillette recently mailed out 400,000 razors to young men on their 18th birthday. Put many of your travel expenses on your American Express credit card and you probably will receive information about vacation packages. Evian water isn't sold in certain areas in which most consumers laugh at the thought of paying a few dollars for something they can turn on the tap and get for free.

Segmenting the Market

In marketing, targeting consumers with certain characteristics is called *segmentation.* Simply stated, it means dividing the total marketplace into groups that have the characteristics of consumers who will purchase your product or service.

You don't need huge computers crunching data all hours of the day or big marketing budgets to segment different markets and target customers. You merely have to be smart in your approach to get the right offer to the right person at the right time.

Suppose that you have a passion for expensive wines that come only from the finest vineyards in the south of France and the Napa Valley. You have studied wine for years and cultivated your palette, and now you want to turn this hobby into a profitable online venture. Who is your customer? It's not good enough to say, "My customer is someone who enjoys fine wine." I know that some people believe that a $2 bottle of hooch in a paper bag is a fine wine.

You have to identify what your potential customers have in common *in addition to* a need for your product. For example, do they know the difference in value between a $2 bottle of wine and a $200 bottle of wine, and are they willing to fork over the money?

Ask yourself some of these questions about what you plan to sell online:

✦ Will a particular age group be drawn to your product? If you're pushing a homemade cure for baldness, you don't want to waste time and money advertising in online areas frequented mostly by teenagers.

◆ Is your product intended for just one gender? You might be able to sell a boatload of Italian leather purses at a local flea market, but not if you go looking for customers in an online environment that caters to male interests.

◆ Can you speculate on some of your customers' other characteristics? If you sell parts and accessories for Porsche automobiles, for example, you can probably make a few intelligent guesses about your potential customers. Because they're probably well-educated and have higher-than-average incomes, you may be able to find customers in areas that don't necessarily have anything to do with Porsches but that nevertheless appeal to a more affluent crowd.

I don't mean to get personal, but did you brush your teeth this morning? About 99 percent of the population brushes its teeth every morning. Today it's a functional need. Because virtually everyone needs toothpaste, you naturally might ask, "Why segment the market?"

Okay, smarty-pants, which brand of toothpaste did you use? Topol removes smoking stains and freshens your breath. Perfect Smile promises to whiten your teeth. Close-Up gives you sex appeal. Crest helps prevent tooth decay. Colgate, Jr. lets kids see stars in its paste and reassures parents that their children have fluoride protection.

As you can see, even different brands of toothpaste are aimed at different consumers. You have to do the same with your online marketing. Even if your product is something that everyone with a PC needs, attempting to sell it to everyone with a PC will lead to failure. You have to know *what* your customers' characteristics are so that you can segment the market and tailor your message to your customers' needs. (The Komando pie chart in Chapter 3 shows graphically the customer needs you have to consider.)

A Behind-the-Scenes Look at Demographics

At this point in your *CyberBuck$* state of mind, you probably have *at least* one enterprise in mind that serves as the foundation for your new online enterprise. On second thought, maybe moneymaking ideas are buzzing around inside your head like a swarm of bees at a summer picnic.

If you're not yet jumping out of your chair with the greatest inspiration since a remote control for a TV set, however, don't sweat it. If your friends call you "crazy" whenever you tell them about your new online business, just put one tune in mind: Think of the song "Crazy," sung by Patsy Cline — it made millions.

For every objection that pops up in this stage of your online business, solutions exist. Trust me — the ideas and their time will come.

Speaking of ideas, for years I have carried a notebook wherever I go. My notebook is not the high-tech PC laptop you might expect from a computer guru like myself. It's a spiral-bound notebook, like the ones you can buy at any supermarket or stationery store for less than a dollar.

Inside this notebook I have written short notes about possible new ventures for my corporation. I call it my "Vision for a Mission" book. Granted, the title is a little corny, but the scribbles keep me on track and help me plan for the future.

Tip

Every entrepreneur needs a place to write down ideas, even ideas that initially seem crazy. Although you probably will need a fancy business plan for a few ideas later on, for now just write yourself notes that you keep in one place. This strategy is an important part of your online marketing success.

Some things you write in your notebook will be flat-out bad and have no market potential — not now or ever. More, however, will be "keepers." Interestingly, I wrote "Launch the Komputer Klinic on the Internet" about four years ago. Whenever I told my peers about this idea, all I heard was, "How could you ever find a customer on something that's inhabited only by the government and geeky programmers?" It just goes to show you. . . .

A strange thing happens with a personal Vision for a Mission notebook. As you begin writing down ideas, more ideas come.

If you already have a pocket organizer, use it as your notebook. I have tried using a PC notebook, but it's somewhat of a hassle to power up a laptop to record just one thing, especially when my inspiration comes at 2 a.m. I have tried the expensive leather-bound notebooks too, but my ideas don't get much better as the notebook's price increases.

From this moment forward, keep your personal Vision for a Mission book handy. Odds are that you will be bursting with ideas, and I want you to keep notes to yourself while you're reading this book.

Getting into a Customer's Mind

Beyond the "what" of customers, you have to consider the "where." Offline, the "where" is the geographic location of the highest potential number of customers with certain characteristics. Which city in the U.S. consumes the most bubble gum? Salt Lake City. If you're a dentist, you might find this little factoid helpful. In which city is the most prune juice sold? Miami (which might be one reason for its low sales of Ex-Lax).

Traditional marketers know their potential customers' facts and figures from studying the characteristics of current customers, keeping track of sales, and using this information in their promotional efforts. Knowing that Miami has an older population that likes prune juice, for example, a company that wants to increase sales might target a retirement area, such as Sun City, Arizona.

The online marketing "where" is a little different from the "what." You will be selling something online, and, of course, the "where" is still a geographic location. But suppose that you run an online restaurant-reservation service in Buffalo. How can you make a profit from people in other cities who visit your site? It's bound to happen.

Your online storefront might be available in the United States (on Prodigy, for example) or throughout the world (on America Online, CompuServe, and the Internet, for example). In the case of the restaurant service in Buffalo, you could sell buffalo chips and "Visit Buffalo" T-shirts to out-of-towners (although I'm not sure that customer demand would be all that high).

Because I'm talking about *online* marketing, your success formula must include (in addition to geographic location) another important variable: You must effectively promote your offerings to *where* potential customers are most likely to spend their time on their PCs. An online location isn't much different from a geographic location: It's a place that people with certain identifiable characteristics are more likely to frequent.

Tip

Figuring out your customers' attributes is the first place to begin when you're selling a product. Here's where one of the most important areas of market research, the study of demographics, comes into play. *Demographics* entails dividing potential markets into groups based on age, sex, income, occupation, household size, education, stages in the family life cycle, and other characteristics.

Consider a familiar example that is nothing more than demographic information collection in process. Every time you buy new software, a registration card is included in the package. The only information the software company needs for registration purposes consists of your name and address and the product's serial number. Yet most product registration cards include *at least* a handful of other questions about you, your computer, your habits, and your income.

My company is guilty of this practice. Self-addressed, stamped registration cards are packaged with our PC learning products, and the responses on the cards tell us a great deal about our customers. Among the questions on the customer feedback card is the demographic standard that says simply "Sex." We don't have to know whether a buyer is male or female in order to send a free program update when it becomes available — we just want to know who buys our products. (A good portion of respondents provide more personal responses, however, such as "three or four times a week." Go figure.)

These extra questions help marketers gather demographic information about their customers. What you may not know, though, is that many companies don't gather information for only their own use. Most registration cards also include a box to check if you don't want a company to "share" your personal information with other vendors. The term "share" is used rather loosely — it's more like "sell." Many companies compile information from their registration cards and sell it to other companies.

"Do you own a CD-ROM drive?" is now a common question on feedback cards, as is, "Are there children in your household?" Maybe the product you bought is on floppy disk and has nothing to do with children, but your answer is still important. Another company may come along next week, looking for a potential market for its new children's CD-ROM. If you answered Yes to both those questions, the company to whom you sent the card may well sell your name to the second company. If you answered No to one or both questions, your name isn't on the list.

In this case, the second company already knew the "who" — people with children and CD-ROM drives. What it didn't know was the "where," so it went to someone who had obtained the information directly from the horse's mouth.

If you're simply extending an existing business into cyberspace, you have an edge over someone starting from scratch. The reason is that you already have a customer base from which to draw. By now, you should know something about your customers. What you don't know, you can ask.

You can extract demographic information from your customers in a couple of ways. First, you can use the registration-card method I just described. Even if your product or service doesn't lend itself to any sort of actual registration, you can still include a postage-paid survey card in your packaging or billing. The key is to be polite and not intrusive.

Tip

If you maintain a customer database (which I strongly recommend, no matter what type of business you have), a telephone survey might be a good idea. It's probably a great idea, in fact. I realize that many people have a phobia about making these types of calls, but a phone survey has three advantages that can give you the most bang for the buck:

   ◆ It's cheaper than doing any sort of direct mailing.

   ◆ It's much faster than waiting for someone to return a reply card.

   ◆ Most important, it's much easier for customers. The easier you make it for customers to respond, the more inclined they are to help you out.

Give your customers an incentive to help you collect information. I suggest that you make it worth a customer's time to answer your questions. My company gives a free training CD-ROM (a $29.99 value) to customers who participate in our telemarketing survey. Always offer a giveaway or a chance to win something — anything — to respondents.

Getting into an Online Customer's Mind

Because you have to market your product or service over a specific medium, you need more than just information about people who buy products like yours. You have to know certain demographics about the people who use your chosen medium and match that information to the demographics of your target market.

Suppose that you have come up with a fabulous idea that keeps you awake at night and you know exactly who your customer is. You decide to market your idea on CompuServe.

Hold on! What if the demographics of the average CompuServe member don't match the demographics of your target market? You had better find another way to market your idea, that's what.

To illustrate this point, I present some demographic information from CompuServe (which was nice enough to provide these details).

According to the company's own research, only 17 percent of all CompuServe users are female. You already know, therefore, that CompuServe probably isn't the place to sell those Italian leather purses. Italian leather cowboy boots might work, though.

The average CompuServe user is about 41 years old. Furthermore, 57 percent are between 25 and 44 years old, and another 37 percent are older than 45. CompuServe is also probably not the place to sell Nirvana memorabilia. Based on these numbers, however, compilation CDs of '60s music may be the thing to sell.

In the area of education, 71 percent of CompuServe users have a four-year college degree. This number means that selling high-school-equivalency study aids on CompuServe probably won't make you the next Howard Hughes.

CompuServe folks are the marryin' types — that's for sure. About 70 percent of them are married. Are you thinking about online marketing for your new book *The Single Woman's Survival Guide*? I hope that you're not considering CompuServe. *Improving Your Relationship with Your Spouse* might not do too poorly, however.

As for kids, 49 percent don't have any children under 18. On the other hand, 51 percent have one or two children under 18. If your product appeals to one group or the other, you're looking at about half the online population of CompuServe as your potential customer, or about $1^1/_2$ to 2 million people located all over the globe.

Lots of numbers, eh? Here's something else to chew on. According to CompuServe's demographic profile, "Members overwhelmingly feel that technology is fun and are interested in reading, music, science and technology, physical fitness, and travel."

Tip

Consumer lifestyle and interests characteristics are used to *psychographically* segment a market. Demographic and geographic segmentation are a great start, but it's advantageous to get an even more definite picture of your potential customer. It enables you to tailor your product or service to how a customer would really use it.

Because online marketing isn't much different from traditional marketing, consider Chrysler. When it wanted to update its Dodge Ram pickup truck, the company sent designers across the country. Company representatives interviewed former Ram customers and collected lots of facts and figures. From these customer interviews, the automobile manufacturer determined that many Ram truck customers were construction contractors and workers who used the trucks as an office while at a construction site. In redesigning the Ram, Chrysler added new features to accommodate the designers' findings, such as an additional cigarette lighter for a cellular phone and enough space for a laptop computer.

What does all this mean? Should you take an ordinary product and change it to match an online audience? Of course, if it make sense. But trying to get The Monkees to reunite to record an album full of songs about getting married so that you can sell it on CompuServe might be a bad idea.

Like anything else, you can't just look at raw numbers and make a decision. You have to add a giant dose of common sense. Come up with similar numbers for your customers and see how they compare with the numbers for CompuServe in this section. If the results of the two profiles are similar, you may have found a good home for your new venture. If the results are as different as night and day, you had better keep looking.

Doing Research Online

Don't forget that your computer is more than a box you use to sell some stuff. It's an important tool you can use in almost every aspect of your business, including market and demographic research. Where can you go online for more information? This section checks out a few spots on the Internet as well as on some of the online services.

First, you can visit the Internet Business Center, at `http://tsunami.tig.com/cgi-bin/genobject/ibcindex`. It has all sorts of useful information, including the results of the third annual demographic survey of the World Wide Web by the Graphics and Visualization Laboratory (that sounds like an official outfit!). This particular survey revealed the following information about Internet users:

+ **Average age of all users:** 35.01 years

+ **Gender:** Male (82.0 percent), female (15.5 percent), "Rather not say!" (2.5 percent)

+ **Overall median income:** Between $50,000 and $60,000 U.S. dollars; estimated average income, $69,000

✦ **Three main ways to get on the Internet:** Local providers, 27.9 percent; national or commercial providers, 27.5 percent; educational providers, 26.5 percent

✦ **Geographical location:** United States, 80.6 percent; Europe, 9.8 percent; Canada and Mexico, 5.8 percent; all other major geographical locations represented, but in a smaller percentage

✦ **Marital status:** Married, 50.3 percent; single, 40.0 percent; divorced, 5.7 percent

✦ **Occupation:** Computer, 31.4 percent; educational, 23.7 percent; professional, 21.9 percent; management, 12.2 percent; "other," 10.8 percent

✦ **Use of online service:** "Do not subscribe to an online service," 39.0 percent; Prodigy, 37.0 percent; America Online, 30.0 percent; CompuServe, 21.1 percent (these three companies are the most dominant subscriber online services)

✦ **Share computer with another user:** 85.7 percent

This site has more than demographic information. Its links for sources of Internet business tools and news about Internet business are particularly useful for formulating your perfect-customer profile.

Next, try visiting AdMarket, a Web site jointly sponsored by *Hot Wired, Advertising Age,* and *Organic Online* (see Figure 4-1). It's located at `http://www.admarket.com/`.

Figure 4-1: *Advertising Age* is full of useful online marketing tips and current demographic information.

Yahoo! has an entire section devoted to demographics (see Figure 4-2). You can navigate through Yahoo! to get there or just go there directly, by pointing your browser to `http://www.yahoo.com/Computers/Internet/Statistics_and_Demographics/`.

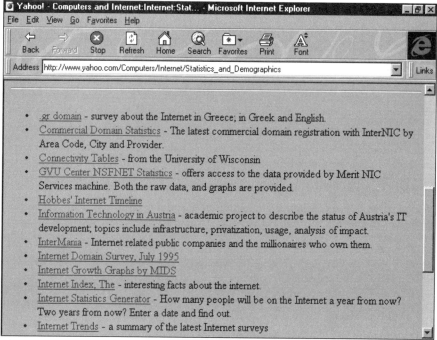

Figure 4-2: Yahoo! has an entire section devoted to the latest Internet statistics.

One demographic-related site that caught my eye is the Internet Statistics Generator, at `http://www.anamorph.com/docs/stats/stats.html`. This online calculator computes the size of the Web on any given future date, based on a statement quoted in a number of news sources in early 1995 that 27,000 sites were then on the Web and that the number doubled every 53 days. That number is difficult to believe, and it's even more difficult to believe that the Web can sustain that growth for an extended period. If it does, it means that on Christmas Day 1998, there will be 2,545,767,533,867 sites on the World Wide Web, which represents one Web site for about every 424.29 people on the planet. I don't think that's very likely. (Who in the world does the .29 represent?)

This same site offers another calculator to estimate the number of people who will have and use Internet access on any given date. According to this calculator (which seems to be based on a more reliable formula and on quantifiable research), on Christmas Day 1998, 247,648,105 Internet users will be out there surfing and shopping. That's a huge number of potential customers. The good news is that it represents only about 4.13 percent of the world's population.

If you're looking for demographic information with a broader appeal, you can even find the U.S. Census Bureau on the World Wide Web, at `http://www.census.gov/`. This site gives you instant electronic access to all sorts of demographic information collected by the U.S. government, as shown in Figure 4-3. (Incidentally, you can also find Census Bureau data on CompuServe, by typing GO CENDATA.)

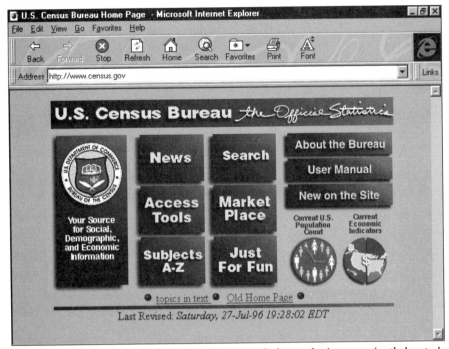

Figure 4-3: All the census information your taxes help pay for is conveniently located at the U.S. Census Bureau on the World Wide Web.

Tip

Another good government site is the FedWorld Information Network. (If you insist, you can dial directly into the FedWorld BBS system at 703-321-3339, which is a long-distance call for anyone outside that area code.) You can visit this site at `http://www.fedworld.gov/`. It's sort of a virtual clearinghouse for all sorts of government information, as shown in Figure 4-4. Tap in to government sites as often as you can. Your tax dollars paid for all this stuff, so you should try to make as much of these sites as you can.

Figure 4-4: When you need more facts and figures than a census can provide, point your browser to FedWorld.

You can also turn to your online service for demographic information. With its focus on business users, CompuServe has an especially large assortment of demographic data. It has free information in addition to pay services, such as Business Demographics, Neighborhood Demographics, and State-County Demographics. To find these free and pay-per-view services, simply type GO DEMOGRAPHICS. Here's a tip, though: So much free information is available that I would think long and hard before paying good money for information.

Looking Closely at What's Reported in the News

Every time a new study or survey comes out, it's usually summarized in a press release and distributed by any of a number of news wire services. If you have an account with a major online service, keeping track of the latest statistics is easy. The reason is that most online services carry all the news wire press releases.

As I was writing this chapter, for example, I logged on to America Online and went to Today's News. From there, I clicked Search News. For keywords, I entered SURVEY and INTERNET. I got quite a few hits this way, including three that were relevant to my research for this book.

In one hit, a joint survey conducted by CommerceNet and Nielsen Media Research claimed to be the most current comprehensive demographic of the Internet's users and applications. The study reports this information:

◆ Approximately 24 million people in the United States and Canada, representing about 11 percent of their combined population, use the Internet.

◆ World Wide Web users are ideal targets for business applications because they are typically more educated and have higher incomes than the rest of the population.

◆ More than 2 1/2 million people already have used the World Wide Web to make purchases.

◆ The U.S. and Canadian population as a whole spends as much time on the Internet every week as it does viewing rented videotapes.

◆ Sixty-six percent of the people who had accessed the Internet within 24 hours preceding their interview had done so from work, 44 percent had done so from home, and 8 percent had done so from school.

◆ Thirty-one percent of the people who access the Internet do so at least once a day.

◆ The average user spends about 5 1/2 hours online every week.

Another press release talked about the results of a survey taken by Yahoo!, by far one of the most popular sites on the Internet (hundreds of thousands of people use its search engine daily). This list shows some of the survey's key points:

◆ Users of the World Wide Web spend an average of 20 hours per week online.

◆ Fifty-five percent of respondents connect to the Web from home.

◆ Sixty percent of survey respondents subscribe to a commercial online service, but only 8 percent use that service to connect to the Web.

All these facts are interesting, but wait a second! One survey said that the average time spent online per week is 5 1/2 hours. The other said 20 hours. One poll says that 44 percent of users access the Net from home, and the other sets the figure at 55 percent. What's going on here?

Tip

Let me remind you of an old saying I always live by: "Don't believe half of what you read." Because polling isn't an exact science, you can't rely heavily on specific numbers. Instead, you must consider the trends those numbers reflect.

Because you don't know which of the two surveys just mentioned is accurate, what *do* you know from them? You know that about half of all Internet users access the Net from home, and that might be useful knowledge. You know also that the average Internet user spends between 5 and 20 hours online every week. That might be useful too. Users are primarily males in their mid-30s, and they are residents of the United States who make money as professionals in the computer or educational fields.

Tip

You should watch out for another thing when you're skimming news headlines and reading interpretations of various online surveys. Some news stories may come directly from the people who conducted the survey, but others may be just someone's interpretation of a survey. You can tell them apart by looking at the first line of the news item as it appears on your screen.

Press releases that are placed on the news wires by the originating companies and that are available on the commercial online services and the Internet look like this:

> NEW YORK — (BUSINESS WIRE) — CommerceNet and Nielsen Media Research today announced the results of the most comprehensive demographic survey to-date of the Internet's users and applications.

The Business Wire online news service places, for a fee, companies' press releases on the news wire services, in the hope that newspaper editors or journalists will use the press releases in a story. Another company, PRNewswire, does the same thing. Stories from Business Wire and PRNewswire are clearly press releases — full of hype (note the phrase "most comprehensive") directly from the company that made the news — not independent survey analyses written by research outfits, newspaper editors, or journalists.

Most online news services also carry newspaper columns distributed via news wire. The preceding press release from Business Wire, for example, looked like this when Reuters carried it:

> NEW YORK (Reuters) — There are about 24 million users of the Internet computer network in the United States and Canada, and most users typically are well-educated, and many have high incomes, according to a survey by Nielsen Media Research.

Unfortunately, most radio and television people and even newspaper reporters commenting on survey results are not necessarily the best-qualified computer experts. The "computer expert" at most radio and television stations and newspapers didn't start out that way. These folks were simply the people who were the first to have a PC in their home. Word spread, and suddenly the sports columnist became the computer columnist. The bottom line is "reader beware."

Knowing whom to trust

So you have surveys with conflicting results, and you have journalists who may or may not give you an accurate representation of those results. And you don't know which results used better methodology than the others.

Who can a would-be cyber-entrepreneur trying to segment a huge market and target the right customers with the right product turn to?

Me, of course. I have been around the online marketing block enough to know who buys and who doesn't. Here's my short list of probable characteristics for an average online customer:

✦ Male

✦ Between 25 and 45 years old

✦ Married

✦ College degree

✦ Above-average income

✦ Children, if any, are young

In addition, this person most definitely has access to at least one modem-equipped personal computer and knows how to use it. He also has some level of computer expertise, even if it's simply installing the software and getting his modem to work.

This last point is particularly important because it's the use of a personal computer that sets potential customers apart from the rest of the population. A marketing approach that works for the average consumer probably will not work with the average online consumer. You have to tailor or modify your product offering to match the consumer's needs or wants (in much the same way as an upscale gourmet market normally doesn't stock generic single-ply toilet tissue on its shelves).

Examining a few online successes based on demographics

Budding cyber-entrepreneurs who know that their customers have PCs and modems also know that computer-related products and services generally sell better online than do other types of products and services. Let's take a look at some people who have been successful in selling computer-related stuff online.

I'll begin this discussion by using myself as an example. As I mention in Chapter 1, I started the Komputer Klinic on America Online in the back bedroom of my home with one employee whose desk was my dining room table. I'm not about to give out any numbers, but, in the three years since then, I have to say that I have been very happy with the Klinic's success. Judging from the many comments I receive daily, people out there in cyberspace think that it's pretty cool too. If you want to stop by, go to keyword KOMANDO on America Online, or visit our sister site on the World Wide Web at http://www.komando.com, as shown in Figure 4-5.

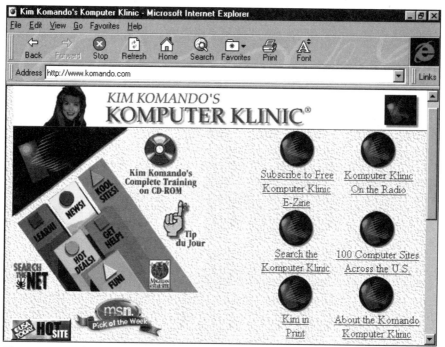

Figure 4-5: My favorite Internet destination.

If you live in a major metropolitan area, chances are that at least one free computer magazine caters to your area. These regional computer magazines are distributed at various pickup points where anyone can walk up and grab one. Most of these magazines, however, offer paid subscriptions for people who would rather walk to their mailbox than to their local computer store to get the magazine.

One publication of this type is *I/O* magazine, which is published in the Sacramento area (see Figure 4-6). You can find the Web version of the magazine at `http://www.mother.com/iomag`. Publisher Erin Smothers reports that the Web site is the magazine's number-one source of paid subscriptions to the printed version, averaging somewhere around 20 new subscribers per week. The beauty of this example is that even though the original product was designed for a regional audience, the information in the magazine appeals to any computer user. By establishing a presence on the Web, *I/O* can expand its subscriber base around the world.

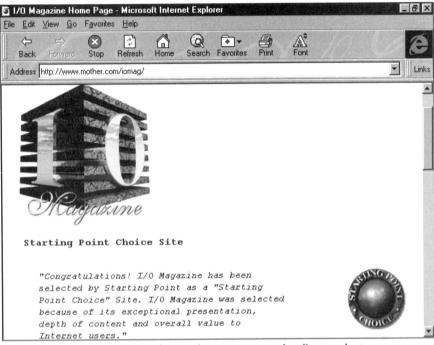

Figure 4-6: Computer-oriented magazines are a natural online product.

Standardized testing has its critics, but like it or not, a high score on an SAT test can go a long way toward getting your kids into a good college. Stanford Testing Systems develops and sells one of the leading SAT test-preparation software packages in the country, and it also sells SAT-related books (see Figure 4-7). Its Web site, at http://www.testprep.com/, has one great hook: It offers a free online SAT preparation course you can use whether or not you buy. The idea is, naturally, to promote the disk-based product, but the idea of "something for nothing" can create a strong pull for consumers.

Selling information can be a great idea because you generally don't have any physical inventory to worry about. If you have computer-related information to sell, you may have an online winner.

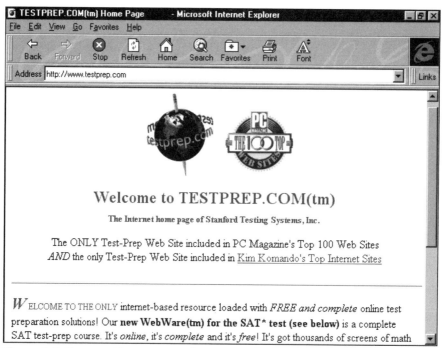

Figure 4-7: Parents with computers always want the best for their kids, especially when they can get something for nothing.

Robert Baker, of Baker Enterprises, is an excellent example of someone who has made his mark by selling information. Baker Enterprises, a one-person operation, publishes a news wire called New Product News, as shown in Figure 4-8. Baker compiles information about more than 25,000 companies and authors in the PC industry and their more than 73,000 products and then sells that information to various information distributors. On America Online (keyword NEW PRODUCTS), Baker's data makes up the PC Vendor Database. His information is also carried on Delphi in addition to a number of regional BBSs. He also licenses data to various companies that publish PC information on CD-ROM.

I'm not saying that selling computer-related stuff is the only way to make money online. Plenty of people sell products and services online that have absolutely nothing to do with computers. The trick is finding the *right* product or service.

Figure 4-8: Making use of free information is a proven formula for success.

Selling more than computer-related goodies

You might not be as successful selling magic thigh-reduction cream online as you might be selling sports memorabilia or car parts. (If your cream works, on the other hand, I would be happy to evaluate a bottle.) The good news is that plenty of *right* products and services are out there just waiting for you.

To give you an idea, here are a few examples of people who have been able to land the big fish without that computer hook.

Virtual Vineyards, located on the Web at http://www.virtualvin.com, is a classic example of what I'm talking about (see Figure 4-9). This outfit is a direct marketer of premium foods and wines over the Internet. It has been online since January 1995, but Robert Olson, the company's president, CEO, and chief propellerhead, claims that the company has been making money since the first day it went online.

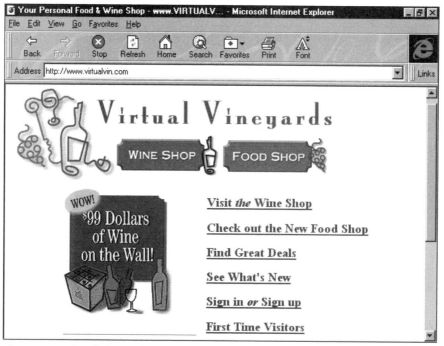

Figure 4-9: Virtual Vineyards is one fine wine.

"That the business exists and thrives is a matter of constant amazement to me," says Olson. "I mean, the products are good, and so are the people, but, still, that customers are willing to trust us to send them wines they've never heard of in exchange for good money just astounds me."

"Of course, *I* would do it," he adds, "but I thought I was a lunatic for trusting other people."

Olson attributes the success of Virtual Vineyards to the right combination of product quality and convenience. Virtual Vineyards gets bonus points from the Komando Evaluation Committee (me, basically) for offering a variety of ordering options, including credit cards, an 800 number, fax orders, e-mail orders, and CyberCash (a form of electronic-payment processing that I describe in Chapter 10).

Books and art also seem to do well online. One small operation that sells both is Ecopress. It has been using various Internet services to conduct business since 1993, but it just introduced its Web site in May 1995 (http://www.peak.org/~cbeatty/).

Chris Beatty, editor and art director, says that the Ecopress mission is to provide "books and art that enhance environmental awareness." Cyberspace has virtually no environmental impact, so it's the perfect marketplace for this sort of operation. Because Ecopress also markets its products though direct mail, bookstores, and outdoor-apparel and -supply stores, it is a good example of a traditional business that has extended itself into the online world (see Figure 4-10).

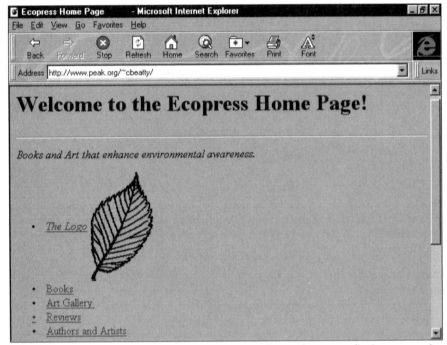

Figure 4-10: Specialty books and art to bring out the environmentalist in everyone!

For an example of a completely offline product that has met with reasonable success in the online market, you can travel to the heart of London's West End and visit the Vicarage Hotel, a small bed-and-breakfast establishment (see Figure 4-11). The hotel's presence on the Web began when an employee named Jim Rhodes decided to combine his job (working at the hotel) with his hobby (writing Web pages). You can look up the result at `http://wworks.com/hotels/vicarage/`.

Figure 4-11: Even though this London bed-and-breakfast doesn't accept electronic orders, it reigns online.

Rhodes reports that the hotel began receiving inquiries and bookings as the result of its Web page almost from day one. That response is especially amazing when you consider that the hotel doesn't accept any "plastic" payment — no American Express, no Visa, no MasterCard, no nothing. The hotel doesn't even own a fax machine. This nontechnical approach, of course, may be exactly what appeals to traveling Net surfers. The Vicarage offers a place where you can go to get away from all the technosensory overload you deal with every day.

Understanding that different online enterprises have common elements

One thing these examples have in common is that they all have a relatively universal appeal. Anyone in any location on this planet is just as likely as anyone else to buy from one of these places. But what if your brilliant idea has only local appeal, such as the Buffalo restaurant-reservation service I discussed earlier in this chapter? Are you out of luck? Hardly.

As I said, a commercial online service is no place for a product or service with only regional appeal. Those types of services are for large audiences, and they want everything they offer to appeal to a large audience, which is reflected in the high price you pay to advertise on one.

For only $240,000 annually, for example, America Online will develop and maintain an interactive marketing area on its service just for you. Throw in another $60,000, and it gives you a home page at its Web site. Even if you made $1 per restaurant reservation, you would have to process more than 800 reservations every day to break even with these numbers. I honestly don't think that Buffalo could even have enough good restaurants to support that level of activity.

On the other hand, for as little as $5 a month, you might be able to find space on a World Wide Web server for one page that describes your products or services. That's a cheap way to reach all the Internet users in your area, even if there aren't that many of them. That your cyberstore is also available to millions of other people outside your area is an additional bonus.

Tip

One word of advice, though. If you do go with some sort of regional business, make sure that the region is plainly identified on your home page. Users can get frustrated trying to connect to a site that is obviously regional and not know which region you serve. It's an even bigger pain to connect to a site that *isn't* obviously regional and become interested and then find out that it *is* regional.

By now, you should have begun to form in your mind a picture of your ideal customers. Don't be too concerned if they still look like Brad Pitt and Demi Moore. As you read through the next couple of chapters, they will begin to take on a more realistic form. Brad will age a little and maybe lose some hair off the top. Demi may pick up a few extra pounds and begin to look a little saggy. Before long, you will realize that your customer might be any average guy or gal on the street, your next-door neighbor, your mail carrier, or just about anyone else. That's why cyber-entrepreneurs are here: to sell *to the masses.* That's where the money is.

Making a Bundle by Selling Products Online

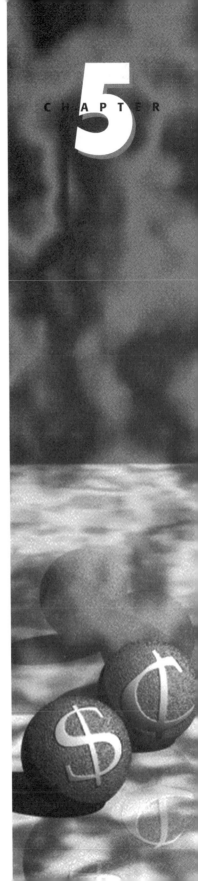

O n a fall day in 1991, I signed out for lunch at Unisys, where I sold multimillion-dollar computers, and walked into the KFYI AM (910) studios for a meeting with Mr. Fred Weber, the station's owner and general manager.

I had an idea. KFYI had talk-radio shows about local issues, politics, health, finance, gardening, car repair, real estate, and even astrology. Because not one show, however, focused on personal computers, I wondered, "Why not create a computer talk-radio show?" I don't know anything about talk-radio shows, other than that I listen to them. I do know a great deal, however, about personal computers. I have used a computer since I was 9 years old. I can talk about them without sounding like an engineer, and I learn quickly. I basically told Mr. Weber, "Teach me talk-radio, and you will have a hit."

I owe a great deal to KFYI because the station representatives and staff members gave me a chance. Today my talk-radio show is syndicated and heard in the United States, Australia, and Canada.

A big part of convincing radio stations to carry a syndicated talk-radio show is letting stations far and wide know about the show. My company has staff members whose only job is to call radio stations and send packages. It's difficult to give up control over a venture, especially when it's your baby. Every day, I also call stations and give them the pitch about why they need my show.

Most times, the program director (the guy or gal at a radio station who decides what listeners hear on their airwaves) simply responds at the end of the pitch by saying, "Send me a tape of the show and more information. Then follow up in a few weeks." Yes! I get my foot in the door, and that's all I need.

Sometimes, though, I never get a chance. The program director stops me midstream and says, "We have no room for another show. Check back in a month."

Then there are the "other" conversations. For example, I recently called a program director at a talk-radio station in Boston, which is a large market in the United States. I would rather not divulge the station's call letters, but suffice it to say that adding this station to our list of affiliates would be a very big deal.

When the program director answered his phone, I rattled off the same 60-second pitch I had given at least hundreds of times before.

"Not interested. Have a good day," he said. I moved fast, though, to intercept the pending dial tone, "I really hate to beg, but would you at least listen to a tape of the show if I send it? These packages cost me about $50, and I hate to waste money, but —"

"Well, all right, send the tape, and it better be good." He hung up the phone, and I sent the package to Mr. Congeniality.

A week later, I called him again, but not before I prepared myself for a "No, thank you." To my surprise, he wanted to talk about the weather, the talk-radio business, and my growing up in New Jersey. I almost fell off my chair when he said, "I love the show! You are as good as you said you are, and I spent all weekend reading your book. There's only one problem."

"Oh no," I thought. "He wants me to cut my long hair." (The program director at a San Francisco talk-radio station once asked me to do that, but I'll save that story for later.)

Mustering all the innocence of a child, I asked, "Problem? What might that be?" "Computers are a male gadget," he said. "They are, well, a fad."

I thought that he was joking! When I figured out that he really believed what he had said, I tried to use the obvious to convince him otherwise: "Look around your station, offices, schools, stores, banks, the newspaper, television. Personal computers are all around us. It's hard to find a newspaper classified ad for a job that doesn't require computer skills."

"A craze — that's all," he said.

The final weapons in my arsenal were statistics about the growth of the personal computer marketplace, the online service explosion, the Internet's becoming as common as the telephone, and the 200-odd million telephone calls consumers make to computer companies every year.

He wasn't impressed. "You have a great show, but not for Boston."

"What about the Massachusetts Institute of *Technology,* a few blocks from you? Boston College? Boston University? Even the Celtics have a Web page. The people and businesses in your area who depend on PCs? At least 35 percent of homes have one, and almost all businesses in Boston do."

He said, "It's a fad, but keep in touch. I like your enthusiasm."

Gee, thanks. I would have been better off blowing my $50 at a craps table in Las Vegas.

Everyone Has an Opinion

Opinions about the effectiveness and practicality of selling online run the gamut. Some marketers and business owners see online sales as a new, invaluable income stream that has the potential to rival the impact of television. These people are true online proponents whose profit-potential sermons rival religious evangelist techniques. Others aren't quite so sure, but here's my point: There's a skeptic in every crowd.

You can live without a PC, but do you want to?

In *Parade* magazine (the newspaper insert in some communities), someone recently asked the all-knowing Marilyn Savant whether he could get by, at this point, without having to learn anything about computers and the Internet. I shouldn't have been surprised, but I was, when Marilyn replied along the lines of "Absolutely not." She pointed out that many people also tried to avoid using both cars and television when those products were first introduced.

"The Internet will vanish"

Mark Stahlman, the president of the marketing company New Media Associates, predicted in early 1996 that the World Wide Web would all but vanish within a year. In other words, he implied that the Internet would go the way of the Pet Rock.

Stahlman reasoned that, considering the limited capabilities of the World Wide Web, which are mostly the result of low *bandwidth* (the amount of information that can be transmitted from computer to computer), advertisers simply can't manipulate the masses in the same way as they can manipulate other media, such as television and radio. Granted, it's more difficult to make a sale when all a consumer sees is a picture and some text on-screen. But vanish into thin air, Mr. Stahlman? Not likely.

Stahlman isn't alone in his opinion, however. A recent survey about online services, by Odyssey Homefront in San Francisco, claims that three of every ten people who own computers at home "still cannot name a single online service." Although most of us get free floppy disks that contain a trial online membership about every other week from one online service or another, many people have remained blissfully ignorant.

That's not three out of ten *Americans* — that's three out of ten people who *already own a computer*. A full 30 percent of your potential market doesn't have the slightest idea about how to get to you. By all estimates, they will someday, but not today.

I'm not trying to create a grim picture here. The good news is that your potential buying audience grows as your online business does. You have to pepper your dreams of wealth and riches, however, with a strong dose of reality. As I said in earlier chapters and am bound to say later, you won't get rich overnight by selling stuff online. Don't believe anyone who says that you will. Like any other business in any industry and at any point in history, cyber-entrepreneurship requires hard work, long hours, and plenty of dedication.

Selling Online Is Just Another Way to Sell Anything

Before I go into the "hows and whats" of selling products online, I want to talk about the other options John and Jane Q. Public have when they want to buy some hard goods that they can hold in their hands. Specifically, I want you to consider the advantages each option has over online selling so that you can adjust your online marketing strategy accordingly.

Reveling in retail sales

The most common way to get products is the good ol' retail purchase. You want something. You know which store sells it, or you can look one up in your *Yellow Pages*. You go to that store, choose your product, pick it up, and plunk down your cash, check, or credit card. It's that simple.

The advantage to buying retail is immediacy. Chances are, if you live in a reasonably populated area, you can go to the store and back in about half an hour. You get to use your new product in no time at all. It's virtually instant gratification.

Retail has a couple of downsides, though. First, you have to get dressed. (Nothing fancy, of course, but depending on your definition of "presentable," it could take some time.) You have to leave your comfort zone and go out to make your purchase because your purchase won't come to you. In addition, if price is a concern, it's not always easy or practical to check every store in town. You can quickly burn up more time and gas than it's worth. You can also spend hours on the telephone doing some price shopping (if you don't mind sitting on hold for what seems like hours while a store clerk looks up a price). Finally, you're limited by whatever your local retail merchant happens to have in stock. There's always a chance that the item you want is out of stock or, worse, that the merchant doesn't even carry the item you want. At that point, of course, you can place a "special order" and wait until it arrives at the store (and off you go again to pick up your purchase).

Shopping by mail

Catalog sales have been popular since, well, since before I was born, anyway. A catalog is great because it's similar to having an entire store packed into an easily portable book. A well-designed catalog is easy to use. You can see exactly what a merchant has to offer, and you can do so easily from any room in your house. Because you can normally order by phone at any time of day and have products delivered directly to your front door, catalog shopping is very convenient.

What's the downside of catalogs? First, even if the person taking the order is nice, nothing beats the instant gratification of having something you just bought. Even with the most efficient catalog operations (such as Sharper Image, L.L. Bean, or J.C. Penney), it usually takes a few days for the merchandise to make it from the warehouse to your door. Sometimes you can save time by choosing your merchandise at the local retail outlet, but that blows a good portion of the convenience factor.

Another drawback to catalog shopping is that you cannot pick up and touch an item before you buy. You have no way to check it for quality or craftsmanship. This factor can be important if you're not familiar with a particular product or brand.

Shopping in your underwear while you watch TV

The process of buying directly from television advertising has evolved quite a bit over the years. This sort of thing used to be limited to standard-length commercials for such products as the Popeil Pocket Fisherman or the Ronco record album *The Greatest Love Songs of 1973, as Performed by the Buffalo Philharmonic Orchestra.*

Then along came my personal favorite, the infomercial, which gave marketers a full 30 or 60 minutes to persuade the American public to buy their merchandise. The inevitable next step in this evolutionary chain was the Home Shopping Channel (HSC), which is one big, never-ending commercial complete with hosts and computerized order-taking systems with such adoring names as Tootie. HSC broadcasts telephone calls from people who have bought a featured product and who then describe how much they love it. Do you really think that they would let anyone on the air who says, "I bought that piece of crap, and it ruined my life"? But I digress.

No matter which television means of selling products you consider, direct marketing by television offers one important advantage: Customers always get to see (or hear, in the case of prerecorded music or product testimonials) a demonstration of the product. They get a much better idea, therefore, of exactly what they're spending their hard-earned money on. When customers have this information, they are more likely to order a product. A 30-day, money-back guarantee flashing on-screen doesn't hurt either. As someone sits there on the couch, she might think, "If I don't like it, I can always get my money back."

Understanding How Online Shopping Stacks Up

The question you have to ask yourself is, "With all these other options, why would someone buy online from me? Or, stated in a more proactive way, you have to give people a great reason or two (more is almost always better) that makes them buy online from you.

To get customers to want to buy from you, you first must address some shortcomings in these other purchasing options. In other words, what makes *your* online business so great?

Point-and-click convenience

For starters, you can offer much greater convenience over the traditional retail shopping experience. Shoppers only have to point and click on the item shown on their computer screen and then type their credit-card number and shipping address. They can shop 24 hours a day, 7 days a week. If you have an online catalog, you never have to worry about an item someone orders being out of stock. If you run out of something, you can simply remove that item from your online catalog until you get a new shipment.

Created especially for the shopper, and it saves you money

Although you cannot compete with a traditional catalog in terms of portability, an online catalog (at least a well-designed one) wins hands-down in functionality. You can build in interactive features that provide more detailed product information and offer other useful information and services that serve as additional benefits for your customers. Suppose that you sell T-shirts emblazoned with "Save the Whales" on the front. When someone buys a shirt, you can automatically offer that person a "Save the Whales" baseball cap too. You can provide interesting online information about whales, complete with photographs, video clips, and sounds. It's all about being innovative in your approach, which is to sell whale-related clothing.

Another downside to traditional catalogs is the initial capital investment. Because paper catalogs cost plenty to print, the larger the catalog, the higher the cost. Add some four-color photos, and watch the cost go up exponentially. These types of issues give catalog publishers a vested interest in keeping the information in their catalogs to a minimum. A thin line exists between not quite enough, just enough, and a little too much information in a printed catalog. Oh — you want to mail that catalog? You didn't say that. That will cost you addressing and postage charges too.

The cost associated with a few extra bits and bytes, on the other hand, is minimal.

You can afford to make your online product information rich and informative. No postage is involved in showing your online customers your wares — everything is on their screen. The more *quality* information you provide, the better off you are and the more sales you make.

Inspecting Some Offline Products with an Online Twist

All the snazzy online catalogs with their correct mix of information and products don't bring in any sales, of course, if they're filled with products no one wants. Your most important challenge is, by far, identifying a product that a good number of online consumers will want to buy from you. The reason you have to be so careful is that a product with a strong general appeal doesn't necessarily translate to a product with strong online appeal.

As an example, shoes can be, in a general sense, a great thing to sell. Just ask the folks at Florsheim or Nike. Everyone needs shoes, and they are available in a broad enough price range that virtually everyone can afford to buy shoes. It's easy to see why you probably wouldn't last long selling shoes online, but let me explain anyway. How would you ever try on the shoes? You might just say, "I know which size I need because I always take a size 8." I can assure you that most people can slap on a pair of size 8s that fit and a pair that they can't even squeeze a heel into.

A few product categories tend to do well online, and these are the areas on which I want you to concentrate your efforts. Remember the Vision for a Mission book I suggested that you create? If you didn't do it, go back to Chapter 4 and look in the section "A Behind-the-Scenes Look at Demographics." If you have already started your book, you get a gold star because it's time now to pull it out. The reason is that I want you to examine with me each of the categories and businesses I discuss in this section. When a reason that a particular online business is working strikes a chord with your own potential online business, write it down. If at all possible, visit the online business I mention so that you can see exactly what I'm talking about.

Hot, hot, hot! One-of-a-kind products

Behind door number one, a working category for online success is *specialty products,* the products that might be difficult to find at a local retail store or mall. These products include one-of-a-kind items, items sold in only certain geographic areas, or items for which the buying audience isn't large enough for mass distribution.

For example, The Internet Medical Products Guide, at `http://www.medicom.com`, illustrates two good points. Figure 5-1 shows the company's home page.

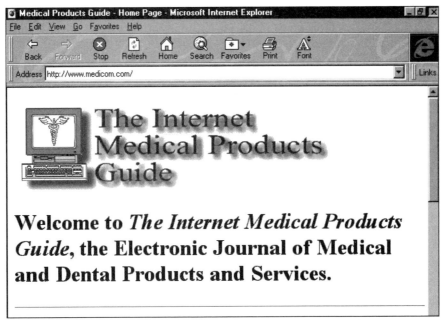

Figure 5-1: The Internet Medical Products Guide caters to doctors and hospital-equipment needs.

First, this site demonstrates that there's not much that can't be marketed online. Did you sew up your last patient only to discover that your micro-retractor was missing? No need to open him back up. You can find a new one at The Internet Medical Products Guide. Did you just discover that you're out of intravascular lung-membrane catheters? Not to worry. You can find them here.

The other good point this site brings out is that selling your own stuff isn't the only way to make money online. You can also promote other people's stuff. MEDICOM, the company that runs The Internet Medical Products Guide, doesn't sell any of these products. It just provides a cyberspace location from which other companies can promote their wares. If you can find a similar niche in which plenty of companies can participate but not too many are direct competitors, you might be able to do the same thing and make a chunk of change along the way. It's the standard get-rich formula: Make a little money from a large number of people.

Speaking of niche markets, consider Air Pix Aviation Photos. This one-man operation, run through the aviation forum on America Online (keyword AVIATION), is a good example of combining a personal interest and entrepreneurial spirit to make some money, as shown in Figure 5-2. Owner Marion Pyles has been doing aerial photography for more than 20 years. He really struck gold, however, at least in a small way, when he began producing and selling photographic business cards for pilots. Pyles still dabbles in other areas of aerial photography, but the bulk of his revenue is generated from these business cards.

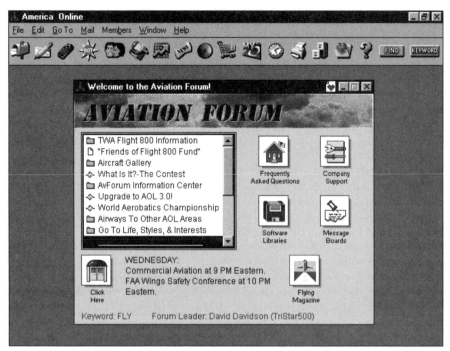

Figure 5-2: Hobbies for which you have a passion often open the door to the best online business for you.

At a number of online sites, shoppers can buy gourmet foods, fine wines, specialty coffees, unique items (such as toilet paper with Jesse Helms's face on it), and geographically specific items (such as fresh Seattle fish and Maine lobster). Successful sites owe much of their success to the fact that they offer products not commonly found in a local grocery store. Better yet, shoppers can order products online and have them delivered.

Computer-related products tend to do well, of course, in an online computer environment. After all, depending on exactly which computer product you're selling, whether it's a "Surf Naked on the Internet" T-shirt or training materials for the latest software products (both of which are available through, naturally, Kim Komando's Komputer Klinic), nearly 100 percent of the people you "encounter" online are prime candidates to purchase your product. Looking only at sheer numbers, computer products can make an excellent choice for online marketing. At the very least, you know that your customer is on a computer.

Knowledge is power, especially when you can make money by selling it

Information products, which are the things that can be delivered online, are also natural online business opportunities. They include any sort of information you can offer in a digital format. You can think of a commercial online service, such as America Online or CompuServe, as one big information product. It gathers up information providers (television networks, newspapers, magazines, radio stars, and organizations) and houses them in one convenient place for consumers.

At the other end of the spectrum is a man whose talent lay in writing humorous limericks (you know — "There once was a man from Nantucket. . . ."). That may not sound like much of a talent to you, but he turned it into an online gold mine. For a mere dollar a year, customers could put their name on his limerick e-mail list. This dollar gave them the assurance that every morning for a year when they woke up and checked their e-mail, a brand-new limerick from this guy would be waiting. By capitalizing on the concept of "If you could sell something for a dollar that everyone needs," this online poet reportedly had a six-figure annual income. And all he had to do was write one limerick a day and send some e-mail. "There once was a woman named Komando. . . ."

Examining the Online Product Life Cycle

I don't mean to sound like a Greek philosopher, but everything that happens in the universe follows some sort of cycle. Just as Mufasa explains to Simba the "circle of life" in the Disney hit movie *The Lion King,* you have to understand that your products all have their own circle of life. They move from infancy to childhood to adulthood to retirement to death. You have to recognize each stage and market accordingly.

Your online business follows a predictable cycle, in which it goes through these stages:

✦ **Introduction:** You put your product online (your "baby" is born).

✦ **Growth:** Shoppers see your product online (your "child" begins to grow).

✦ **Maturation:** Your product becomes stable (it reaches "middle age").

✦ **Decline:** Your product fades (it reaches "old age").

In this section, I explain each stage in-depth.

Putting your product online

In the *introductory stage,* you bring your product to market — your "baby" is being born. The most important part of this stage isn't necessarily the selling; it's the promoting. Because the product is new and unknown, your job is to provide information about it and its incredible features. Your number-one responsibility is to make the public and the press aware of your product. You might also want to target awareness toward distribution channels so that these channels can help sell your product too. The goal is to make your audience aware of your product so that they accept it.

To see an excellent example of a product that was handled well during its introductory stage, just think of Microsoft Windows. Although both Windows 95 and Windows 3.1 are fantastic products, the earliest versions of Windows weren't all that great. That didn't matter. Microsoft invested loads of effort and money into promoting Windows as a desktop standard. Unless you have lived in a cave for the past ten years, you know what the payoff was, for both Microsoft as a company and Bill Gates as its chairperson.

Figure 5-3: SurfWatch, a parental-control software program, is a great example of a company that introduced a product the right way, resulting in major profits for its developers.

Another good introductory example is SurfWatch, a parental-control and Internet-blocking software program. It keeps little Johnny (and even big Johnny) out of nasty areas on the Internet. When this product was introduced, the SurfWatch company focused its efforts on educating the public, the media, and government officials on all the sexual content on the Internet. It had the solution, of course. I did a television segment about the program, in fact, before the product was even finished. In less than a year, privately held SurfWatch created the Internet content-filtering market and was sold to Spyglass for about $12.6 million. Figure 5-3 shows the SurfWatch home page, at http://www.surfwatch.com.

I tell you everything you have to know (and then some) about advertising and promotion in Chapter 13. In the meantime, just be aware that in order to get the word out, you have to launch a broad and varied campaign.

Making sure that shoppers see your product

Assuming that you have a good product and that you did a good job up front of promoting it, your product then moves into the *growth stage.* During this period, sales begin to increase, your name becomes more recognized, and people begin looking specifically for you and your product. Word-of-mouth advertising makes your phones ring. Suddenly, you have competition because your success gets noticed by others with similar ideas and products.

Dozens of Internet-related products are now in this stage. All you have to do to find them is look in your local newspaper, favorite computer magazine, or a zillion different places online. Also in the computer marketplace, all-in-one devices (for example, a laser printer that doubles as a laser printer, fax machine, and copier) are in the growth stage. Looking outside the online world, sport utility vehicles and plain-paper fax machines are in the growth stage.

During this phase, you refine your entire operation. You learn exactly what works and what doesn't in terms of promotion, pricing, and customer service. You have to focus especially on the service aspect because few people will tolerate poor service for even the greatest product on the planet. On the other hand, prompt, courteous, intelligent service can, in the eyes of the public, make up for a great deal of other shortcomings.

Stabilizing your product

At some point your product matures. That is, it becomes about as popular as it ever will be, and then sales level off. You might think that this is the stage in which you can breathe easy, but it's not. On the contrary, your potential market is dwindling right before your eyes. You have a fair number of competitors taking profits from your company, and they slash prices to attract new buyers.

During this stage, you should begin planning for the future evolution of your product. Is there some way you can upgrade the product? Can you offer something even better? Can you add more value to your product? Can you change the size of the package or relabel the product for a different audience? Can you increase the number of users? Can you find new uses for the same product? Do other viable markets or industries exist that you haven't tapped? Have you tried the international market-place?

With the onset of color ink printers that offer a great price and near-laser-quality printouts, the market for home-user laser printers is dwindling. Laser-printer prices are plummeting. To add more perceived value to their laser printers, many manufac-turers now include a healthy share of software and discounts on everything, including long-distance calls. Printer manufacturers are also developing new products that include the all-in-one devices I mentioned earlier in this section.

Dealing with a fading product

The last stage in the product cycle, the *decline,* is inevitable. Sometimes this stage occurs because the market becomes saturated, but most often it's brought about by advances and innovations from competitors. CB radios were replaced by cellular telephones, and everyone knows what happened to the IBM Selectric typewriter. Twenty or so years ago, the Selectric was the envy of typists around the world. You either had one, or you had something else that wasn't "an IBM." The Selectric wasn't cheap either — it cost somewhere in the neighborhood of $600. Then computers with word processors suddenly appeared. You could hardly give away a Selectric. A Web site on the Internet shows what a Selectric competitor, the Remington Rand type-writer, looks like when it is dropped from a 10-story building. Death. To see for yourself, point your Web browser to `http://www.dropsquad.com/typeaftr.jpg`, or take a peek at Figure 5-4.

Although decline is inevitable, it doesn't mean doom. It just means that you must work diligently to ensure that your product line evolves with the marketplace so that you continue to meet the changing needs of the public. You may also have to drop some products in exchange for others, which simply places you back at the beginning of the cycle of a product's life.

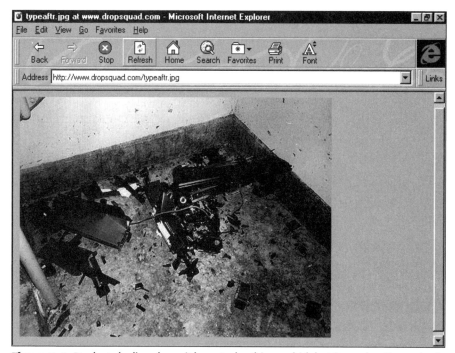

Figure 5-4: Product decline doesn't have to be this morbid, but it can be, if you don't see it coming.

Creating New Product-Development Strategies

If you want to be successful in selling your own product online (versus selling someone else's), you have to do plenty of work before you ever make that first sale — or before you even have a product to sell, for that matter. The first order of business is, obviously, creating a product to sell. Coming up with ideas is easy; coming up with *good* ideas is another thing altogether.

The answer you seek lies within

The best way to begin is by examining your own talents, skills, and interests. A standard rule for writers of both fiction and nonfiction is "Write about what you know." The Sunnybrook Home for Wanna-be Writers is filled with otherwise talented authors who failed to follow this simple and obvious guideline. This same rule applies to your online business. The ultimate online business is one in an area in which you have some expertise *and* a strong interest.

Tip

It isn't a matter of having either the skill or the interest in a field — you must have *both*.

The reason that you must have skill is clear: If you're an expert in a particular field, you know the ins and outs and can intelligently handle any unexpected problems that are likely to throw a novice for a loop. I can guarantee you that every ounce of experience you have will someday, somehow, prove beneficial to the success of your online business.

Interest is equally important for your long-term success. It's possible, for example, to make tons of money selling Herbalife nutritional supplements or Amway cleaning products. When you consider the number of people who try these types of companies compared to the number who succeed, however, things don't look so promising. It's not that these companies don't offer valid business opportunities. Some people have literally made their fortunes in various multilevel-marketing programs. The people who tried them and didn't make it, however, are the ones who discovered that peddling vitamins to your friends and neighbors isn't all that interesting — no matter how much potential money is involved. And you can lose many friends along the way.

Look at your competitors

Determining where your experience and interests lie is just the beginning. Choosing a product based solely on these two factors is no guarantee of success. The trick is to use them as a basis for finding a product that meets with mass-market acceptance.

So how do you tell the good from the bad from the ugly? The best and easiest way is to look around and see what your competitors and potential competitors are doing. It's not likely that you will have an idea so revolutionary that no one else is already involved in something similar. Even if you're the first to bring a particular product or type of product to the online arena, you can still learn from your offline counterparts.

For sure, you don't want to copy someone else. If you do, you have no clear-cut way to distinguish yourself from the others. Establishing that distinction is one of the most important parts of online marketing.

You have to do more than observe; you have to study. Remember that just because you see another company conducting its business in some unique way, it doesn't mean that it is necessarily successful at it. To whatever extent you can, you have to examine your would-be competitors over as long a period as possible. The idea is to see what changes and improvements they make during that time. In other words, you want to observe how vendors evolve with the changing marketplace.

When you look at other products in the marketplace, make sure that you don't look at them from your perspective as a competitor. Put yourself in the shoes of potential customers. Examine the other product objectively, and try to fill in the blank in this simple statement: Gee, this product is nice, but I wish that it _____.

If you can provide a product that meets the need you just identified, you may have a winner on your hands.

When I got into the computer training business, many companies were teaching people the basics of using popular software programs. The problem was that the trainers assumed that trainees knew "geekspeak," or the lingo and terms that were used. Not so. That's where my company has found its niche, whether it's in products, online marketing, television, radio, or print. Now The Komando Klinic is known worldwide for making computers easy and fun to use.

Look all around you

Product development goes beyond just looking at your competitors, however. Beyond that, you also have to look at the marketplace as a whole and determine where you and your competitors fit into the current business climate.

Could any current or predicted trends affect your business? If you plan to borrow money for your start-up, how do interest rates look these days? Is money tight? Are products out there that complement your product line? Can you survive (not live the way you do now) if no one buys anything from you for six months? These questions are just a few you must answer.

After you have identified exactly what your product is and where it fits in the "big picture," it's time to begin developing your physical product. Exactly what that means varies from product to product; I couldn't possibly fit into one book — or even a dozen books — everything you need to know about how to develop every possible product. If your product is a revolutionary, new software package, for example, you had better begin working on that code. If you hire a programmer, offer her a royalty rather than up-front cash. On the other hand, if you're developing some sort of mechanical device, you have to fine-tune the design on paper and begin looking for a manufacturer. For help with specific types of products, check out online resources, your public library, and your favorite bookstore. You can also check small-business networking groups as well as the Small Business Administration, available in almost every community.

Warning

The biggest mistake many start-ups make is having too much inventory. I get calls regularly from people who have a warehouse full of a product they can't move. While writing this paragraph, for example, I received a phone call from the chief operations officer of a public company who told me that he has 10,000 Windows training CD-ROMs he wants to sell for 30 cents more than his cost.

Inventory is money you don't have and have already spent. We produce only 100 CD-ROMs of a new product at one time, and the most we have produced at one time is 5,000. My advice: Create only what you could possibly need. It may cost you a little more because you don't get a discount or lower price, but you will sleep better at night.

At the beginning of this book, I talked about infomercials and how they're test-run in ten or so relatively small markets for one weekend, just to gauge public acceptance. This same basic idea applies for your product too. Before you take that last step of all-out commitment, you should try testing your product in the marketplace.

Again, exactly how you test-market your product depends on exactly what your product is. If you are selling a software product, releasing the first version as shareware can be a great way to go. Plenty of mainstream commercial software packages got their start as shareware on local BBSs. Two that come to mind are Procomm, a popular telecommunications program, and Eudora, the de facto standard Internet e-mail program.

Every once in a while, a company hits pay dirt with this "try it for free" concept. Netscape Communications took this approach with its Navigator software for browsing the World Wide Web and captured more than 70 percent of the Web browser market. (*That* paid off big!) When Netscape went public in late 1995, Marc Andreesan, the "computer geek" who designed the Navigator software, became an instant *billionaire*.

Netscape is the exception, though. You shouldn't expect to make one red cent when you're market testing your product, because that's not the idea. Your primary goal in test marketing is to gather information — useful information you can use to refine and redefine your operation before you begin mass-marketing your product. At this stage of the game, customer feedback is king. I might buy a few of those blue-light-special training CD-ROMs and sell them online and on the radio, but only after I test the waters. I don't want that guy's problem to be *my* problem.

Choosing a Name for Your Product

In some ways, the process of choosing the right name for a product is almost the same as voodoo. You can never really know beforehand what the public will like or won't like. You essentially put on funny makeup, dance around the campfire in some sort of obscure chant, and pray to the name gods for a winner.

Okay, maybe that's an exaggeration, but you get the picture. You just never know for sure.

What's in a name?

Good names are easy to remember. They are a snap to pronounce. You immediately recognize what they do. Their meaning is global.

One of my favorite product names is Microsoft Word. Word. That's it. One simple word says it all. There's no question about what this program does. Word is obviously a program for words. Its beauty is in its simplicity.

Simplicity is no guarantee for success, of course. Consider the ill-fated program Bob, which Microsoft introduced in mid-1995. Do you even remember Bob? Bob supposedly offered us the world's first "social computer interface," whatever that means.

Bob's name might be simple, but it doesn't tell you anything about the product. It doesn't help, of course, that the name was attached to a truly lame product. By no means did the program flop on name alone, but I don't think that the name helped much.

How about Orville Redenbacher's Butter Lite Microwave Popcorn? There's a mouthful (no pun intended). Yet this is a great product name; it tells you absolutely everything you need to know about the product:

✦ It's from Orville Redenbacher, whose name has become synonymous with good popcorn.

✦ It's butter-flavored.

✦ It's some sort of reduced-calorie version.

✦ You can cook it in your microwave oven.

How much more could you possibly want to know? How much more information can a name possibly give you?

Giving your product name an image

A product's name is, of course, only part (albeit one of the most important parts) of the larger concept of product identity. What image do you want to convey? How do you want people to *feel* about your product? I know a graphic designer who asked these two questions of every new client:

✦ If you had to give your business a color, which color would it be?

✦ If your business were an animal, which animal would it be?

At first these questions about your product may sound silly, but go ahead and try to answer them. I think that you just may learn something new about your product (or more accurately, your view of your product). A "brown" product, for example, would have a dramatically different personality from a "red" product. Likewise, a product described as a cheetah would be perceived much differently from one described as a Vietnamese potbellied pig.

The trick is to see the world as your potential customers see the world and have your product fit in where they want to see it fit in.

If you want to focus your product according to the wants and needs of your customers, the easiest way is to have them do it for you. What I'm talking about is some sort of contest. You can have customers come up with a product name, a logo, a theme for a promotional campaign — virtually any part of the product identification package that's missing. You would be surprised at how little you have to offer some people to get them to put their creative side to work. The best prize you can award, for their sake and yours, is probably a free unit of your product. As long as it's a good product, the contest winner is sure to tell his friends about your great stuff.

Tip

The best part is that you can conduct the entire contest through e-mail and online postings. That way, you can get the word out quickly, gather public input easily, and compile all the submissions into a simple database. The entire process can be a real snap. Just be careful about where you post any notices. Bad online manners can come back to haunt you — or at least result in your getting some online nasty-grams, or *flames*.

You should be sure to cover yourself legally. The last thing you want is a contest in which the person who provides the million-dollar-winning name comes back and wants more money after you were the one who made the product a success. It's a stretch, but you just never know. Consult a lawyer because you have to ensure that all entries are your property — title, interests, rights — lock, stock, and barrel.

You also have to post your contest rules online for everyone to see in clear view. The rules should include, at minimum, the legal gobbledy-gook in this list:

✦ The drawing will be held at the offices of (Your Company Name), and the decisions of (Your Company Name) are final in all matters relating to the contest.

✦ The odds of winning depend on the number of valid entries received.

✦ No substitution, cash equivalent, or transfer of prize(s) is permitted, except at sponsor's option for a prize of equal or greater value.

✦ Federal, state, and local taxes, where applicable, are the responsibility of the winner.

✦ Prize winners will be notified by e-mail and may be required to sign and return an affidavit of eligibility in addition to a Waiver of Liability and, where legal, a Publicity Release within a specified time, or else the prize will be forfeited and awarded to an alternative winner.

✦ Any undeliverable prizes will be forfeited and awarded to an alternative winner (or winners).

✦ Original entries will not be acknowledged, and (Your Company Name) owns all title, interests, and rights to each entry.

✦ By participating, entrants agree to the official rules and, if a winner, to the use of, where legal, their name(s) and/or likeness(es) and statement(s) for advertising and publicity purposes without any compensation whatsoever.

✦ Furthermore, entrants agree to release, discharge, and hold harmless (Your Company Name) as well as its respective affiliates, subsidiaries, franchises, advertising and promotion agencies, and its respective directors, officers, and employees, from all claims or damages arising from their participation in this contest and the acceptance and use of the prize.

✦ Contest is open to all people. Staff members of (Your Company Name) as well as the immediate families (spouse, parents, siblings, children and their spouses, or any other members of the household) of the above are ineligible.

✦ The names of winners of this contest will be posted in the (Your Company Name) area and can be obtained by sending a self-addressed, stamped envelope to: (Your Company Name and Street Address).

Packaging Your Product

One of the biggest advantages to online selling is lower overhead. The cost of running a cyberbusiness can be as much as 50 percent lower than running a traditional business that sells the same products, especially in the area of packaging.

Think about the products you normally buy from traditional retail outlets. Plenty of time, effort, and money goes into the packaging of these products. You can bet that Campbell's, for example, pays a seasoned graphic designer top dollar to come up with label designs for its new canned soups. On the other hand, considerably less money is spent on the packaging design for generic or "store brand" soups. That's one of the reasons stores can sell these products for less and still make a profit.

The whole point is that retail packaging must be designed to do more than just hold a product. It must be appealing and eye-catching. The ideal retail packaging jumps out across an aisle in the store and grabs you. It calls out, "Buy me, buy me!" Okay, okay. Packages don't talk, but you get the idea.

Don't be a fool and spend big bucks

When you're selling online, you have a tremendous advantage over the folks who sell the products that line retail shelves. The reason is that people will buy your product online without ever having seen its packaging. They're motivated by your expert online marketing (which you learn about from me), not by some fancy design on a label. That means savings for you.

No matter what you are selling, your packaging should be functional — and that's it. Anything you do with packaging beyond what's necessary to ensure the safe shipment of your product is a waste of money and bad for the environment. For example, I could sell my top-selling Internet training CD-ROM inside a large, expensive box that costs around $2 per box. Or I can simply leave the training CD-ROM in its clear, jewel case that costs about 25 cents apiece. I use the latter option. The shipping costs are lower, and I make more money. Why spend any more than you have to?

You do have to give some consideration to your online presentation, of course. If you're doing business by e-mail, you can use the absolute minimum amount of packaging. If you have an online catalog on the World Wide Web, however, chances are that you will want to display a picture of the packaged product. In this case, you probably will want to put a photograph of the product on the package. You don't have to pay tons of money for a top photographer. Just make sure that your photos don't look cheap.

You can get plenty of extra mileage from your product photos as publicity tools too.

Don't be a cheapskate and spend too little

Just as you never want to spend too much on packaging, you also should never spend too little. If you're selling jars of your mother's spaghetti sauce online, you have to make sure that your packaging protects your product all the way to its final destination. If you get a reputation for delivering dripping boxes of tomato sauce and broken glass, I can guarantee you that you won't remain in business for a long time, no matter how wonderful mama's recipe is.

Again, exactly how far you have to go with your packaging depends on your product. If you're selling some sort of computer component (which is probably a little more likely than spaghetti sauce), you may have to invest in some electrostatic bags. If you're selling some sort of perishable items, your packaging must keep those items fresh for as long as possible. Put yourself in the shoes of your customer one more time: What packaging do you need in order to ensure that the product she receives is the exact same product that leaves your shipping department (which may well be located on your kitchen table)?

Give online customers some instant gratification

One thing you lose with most online sales is the benefit of instant gratification. After an order is placed, it still takes time for the product to be shipped from your business to the customer. It's up to you to decide just how far you want to go to reduce the impact of this problem.

For example, CDnow, the Web-based music store at `http://www.cdnow.com`, offers next-day delivery on all its products. The store's owners apparently realize that people often hear a new song on the radio and decide that they want to get a copy *now*. They know that being able to run to the store and return with new music (and ready to rock) in just a few minutes can be strongly appealing. Someday, when bandwidth problems are solved, companies will be capable of delivering music on demand over the Internet. In the meantime, the best that companies such as CDnow can do is guarantee next-day delivery (see Figure 5-5).

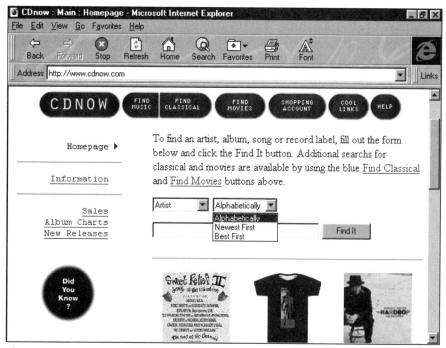

Figure 5-5: CDnow sells more than CDs.

Does your product have this same sort of immediacy? Only you can say for sure. If it does, you may want to consider the extra expense of next-day delivery.

Get the goods to the customer

No matter how fast you want your product to get to its destination, you still have to decide *who* will get it there. Today you have more options than ever. Here are just a few of the major names in the delivery business:

✦ U.S. Postal Service

✦ Federal Express

✦ United Parcel Service

✦ Airborne Express

The first thing you want to compare is, obviously, price. Figure out exactly what you're going to ship, and then contact each carrier to determine the cost to deliver that item within whatever time frame you think is best. Just keep in mind that price is only one consideration.

Do you expect many foreign orders? If so, you need a carrier that has a strong overseas network. Are you selling perishables? Then maybe you need a carrier who can provide refrigerated transport. If you plan to do a large volume of business with a particular carrier, most of them will let you set up an account so that you can pay your shipping charges monthly, as you do with any other bill. For each carrier, find out the answer to these questions:

✦ What are the requirements for a monthly account?

✦ Do you charge extra for picking up orders?

✦ Do you provide order tracking?

✦ In case of damage or nondelivery, do you insure each order, and for how much?

At the Komputer Klinic, we ship most of our products through the good old U.S. Postal Service. It costs much less than UPS, but we do use UPS for next-day deliveries.

Protecting Your Product and Yourself from Legal Nightmares

If you invent a new soft drink, you don't have to be a brain surgeon to realize that naming it Pepsi is probably not a good idea. The legal staff at the Pepsi-Cola Company will shut you down faster than you can say, "The choice of a new generation."

The thing to remember is that millions of products are out there. Just because you have never heard of a product with the name you chose doesn't mean that someone hasn't already used that name. If that someone used the name before you did, he or she or it has a right to use that name, and you're out of luck.

Choosing a name for a product is where the U.S. Patent and Trademark Office enters the picture. You can register your product name (among other things) with this agency so that anyone else who comes along knows that the name is already taken. Likewise, after you have chosen a product name, you (or your attorney, if you have the money) have to do some research to make sure that your product's name isn't already being used.

Your best starting point for this process is a government publication called *Basic Facts About Registering a Trademark*. This booklet gives you some great information in addition to all the forms you have to complete in order to register your trademark. It costs $2.50, and you have to ask for stock number 00300400680-3. Here's where to order:

Government Printing Office
Arco Plaza, Level C
505 South Flower Street
Los Angeles, CA 90071
Phone: 213-239-9844
Fax: 213-239-9848

If you still have questions about trademarks after you read this publication, you can call the U.S. Patent and Trademark Office directly, at 800-786-9199.

Perhaps you're wondering whether you can do your trademark research online. The answer is yes. CompuServe offers this type of search facility, and many sites on the World Wide Web host this type of research. Frankly, however, for purely monetary reasons, I advise against using these services. If you use any of them, they keep the meter running the entire time you're connected. On the other hand, all this same information is free at your public library.

A library trademark search used to mean poring over volumes and volumes of hardbound trademark books or fiddling with flimsy microfilm. Today, however, libraries in major metropolitan areas have all this information on CD-ROM and provide workstations in which you can do your research. After you get there, your search should go faster than if you had used an online service. Call your local public library for more details.

Although manufacturers, consumer groups, and government agencies have made a concentrated effort to provide consumer protection, it's still easy to find products online that aren't childproof or tamperproof. It's difficult, however, to find any product without any warning, limitation of liability, or legal mumbo-jumbo that says essentially one thing: You bought it from us, but use it at your own risk.

If you are selling a product, you should consult your lawyer and ensure that your product doesn't get you in trouble someday. You might need special warnings on your product (hair dryers, for example, have labels warning you not to use them in water). As with software programs, you may have to add to your packaging a flyer that limits liability. If your design is flawed, don't sell it. Ask your insurance agent about product liability insurance, and get a policy.

If you are selling a service, don't think that you are home-free. If you are selling any type of service, ask your insurance agent about errors-and-omissions (E&O) insurance. It can protect you from many things — namely, if you give incorrect advice and it hurts a client. I learned a great deal about E&O insurance from my accountant (that profession requires E&O insurance!). Be forewarned: E&O policies are expensive.

Some Final Examples

Earlier in this chapter, I mentioned that you may meet with success if you sell products online that are difficult or impossible to find locally. A good example is the Stash Tea Company (see Figure 5-6).

Figure 5-6: Stash Tea is piling up its stash of cash by being online.

Because Stash has been selling fine teas by mail order and other means since 1972, online selling was the next logical step. At the company's Web site (http://www.teleport.com/~tea/), you can find more than 80 exclusive blends of tea in addition to savory baked delicacies and tea accessories. The Stash site is also a great example of being able to provide extra information to online customers. Check out this site, and you will see that it's a virtual online tea encyclopedia.

Earlier in this chapter, I mentioned convenience as a major benefit of online shopping. That concept seems to be the main focus of Condom Country (http://www.condom.com). Although many of this company's products are available at the corner drugstore, this company saves its customers the hassle (and, for the timid, the embarrassment) of having to go out and shop for this item. Condom Country also offers a much wider selection than you're likely to find at the drugstore. Also, with online information such as "The History of the Condom" and "How to Use a Condom," this site holds true to the idea of giving customers more value-added information.

If you have any interest in magic, you probably already know that it can be tough to find a first-rate magic shop. Often, you get stuck going to some dinky novelty shop with one small section of low-quality items. Now, thanks to Magical Secrets: The Incredible Virtual Magic Shop, you don't have to search any farther than your computer screen, as shown in Figure 5-7. The Magical Secrets Web site is at `http://www.magical.com/secrets`.

James Biss, the owner of this one-person show, reports that although he started up Magical Secrets as a hobby with some tax write-off potential, "It has grown into a rather dynamic little business."

What made Biss decide to bring magic to the online world? "My understanding of Net demographics, that is, largely young males with disposable incomes (and time), seemed ideal for my product — magic tricks," says Biss. "Magic seems to be predominantly 'a guy thing.' The potential of the Web to reach these kinds of individuals around the planet was very tempting. The low barriers to entry made it a no-brainer!"

Figure 5-7: The owner of this Web site says that being online is "a no-brainer!"

What do all the products I have mentioned have in common? First, they all have a global appeal; they're not geographically limited. Someone in New York is just as likely to drink fine tea as is someone in New Zealand. Condoms? Well. . . .

Second, in terms of variety, these items aren't necessarily easy to find at local outlets. Depending on the size of the city, a local economy might not be able to support a specialty magic shop. When you multiply the handful of magic enthusiasts in each of these cities by the number of cities around the world, however, the numbers suddenly become very attractive.

Think this way, and you will be a success. You want to sell something to everyone who visits your online area. Good ideas take time. Be patient. Before you go to sleep at night, visualize your success. See your life the way you want it to be: the big house, fancy vacations, and cash in the back. I have done this for as long as I can remember. There is no such thing as an overnight million, but you can wake up with an idea or two. That's all you need — one good idea.

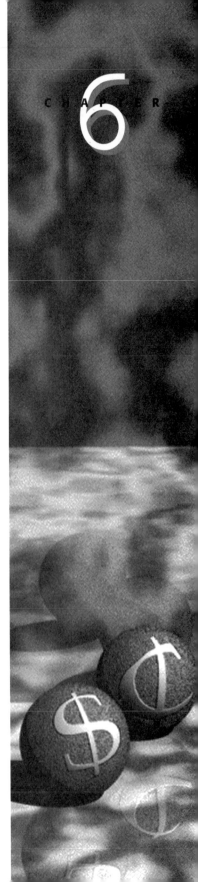

Selling Information and Services Online

From the time I entered grammar school and throughout high school, my father and I practiced a ritual. About 3 o'clock every afternoon, he picked me up from school on his way home from work. By 4 o'clock, we were having a bowl of soup together at the kitchen table. He and I exchanged stories about our respective days and decided what we should make for dinner for Mom. At the dinner table, I also learned about many of life's lessons.

I was probably about eight years old when my father held up *The Wall Street Journal* between us and asked, "What's different about this newspaper?" I remember his giving me that parental look of "What have I done wrong in raising this child?" as I replied, "There are no comics."

So he rephrased his question: "Why do you think that this newspaper has several long, narrow columns instead of stories all over the front page, like most papers?" I had no idea, but I knew that he would tell me.

My dad laid the front page of the *Journal* on the table and pointed out that it was organized into distinct sections. You could rest assured that the far left and right columns would take political or industry views, one column would describe what was inside the paper, one column would have different paragraphs all about one topic, and the middle column would always be an interesting story that wasn't really about hard-core business.

The reason for the columns was simple. People cramped into buses, airplanes, and subways on their way to work could fold the paper vertically, or by columns. By folding a newspaper in this way, you can read almost any story without ever turning a page.

To be able to explain the layout of the newspaper to me, my dad had to physically show me the paper. I wouldn't have understood the lesson otherwise.

With All Good Comes Some Bad

Accordingly, the online world is very much a visual medium. Rather than just tell your story, it's much better to show *and tell* it. To do so, you first must have products you *can* show. From just this point of view, Lladro fine statues would probably be easier to sell than dog food. Second, you must show those products online in the best way you can. Most successful online businesses are simply giant interactive catalogs. Your challenge is to find products that fit into the structure of a catalog you present on a computer screen.

That's not the only challenge you face when you decide to sell products online. Just like traditional retailers, you probably will have to tie up some money in inventory. You don't have to keep as much inventory on hand as a retail store, but you do need an ample amount to fulfill anticipated orders. If you develop a reputation for filling orders late — or, worse, not filling them at all — you're history, plain and simple. And what about your suppliers? Even if they're the ones who drop the ball, you're the one who ends up looking bad. After all, you, not the supplier, sold the buyer the goods.

You also have to worry about shipping your products, handling returns, and even fighting fraud. Our order-department manager recently took a phone call from the New Orleans police department. A few high school kids allegedly had gotten hold of stolen credit-card numbers and used the cards to order a bunch of products online. In the back of the abandoned house the kids were using as the shipping address, the police found lots of boxes, including one that contained our training products. My company lost money, and the police department kept the entire order as evidence.

Online selling isn't all sunshine, but don't get me wrong: You can build up a great business selling products online. Heck, I'm living proof of that. Just know that this sort of business is not without its own share of unique headaches.

Developing a Service Business

If you're in the business of selling information or some sort of service rather than a physical product — whether it's online or offline — you can eliminate many of these shortcomings. As an offline business example, think about your favorite pizza parlor and all the issues its owner must encounter daily, such as product quality, employees, deliveries, and equipment maintenance. The list goes on.

Now compare a pizza parlor owner's headaches to the stress your accountant faces. Being an accountant isn't easy work by any stretch (especially if Kim Komando is cracking the whip).

You have to keep up on tax-law changes and accounting standards. Not all clients pay their bills, or (seemingly worse) clients from hell want justification for every minute charged to an invoice. Tax season means long hours, of course. Ethics often come into play: What do you do if a client wants you to lie to an investment-banking firm about his financial prowess?

Sure, your PC helps with your business in general. It compiles client reports, estimates taxes, sends invoices, completes tax returns, tracks your time, calculates your client's books, and more. It should be clear, however, that the day-to-day hassles are more confined to specific types of problems. Being an accountant may not be easy, but running an *accounting business* is easier than running a pizza parlor (fewer things to go wrong!).

Now carry this line of thought over to an online example in which you decide to run an online information search-and-retrieval business. In this case, you can't really put anything in an online catalog. Your online business searches for information based on individual customer or business needs. After you find the information, you deliver it in an attractive report to whomever paid you to get the information in the first place.

Your online site might contain a compelling description of your services, a sample report of what you send customers, and maybe a few customer testimonials, but that's about it. No bells. No whistles. And you don't load up your online site with killer interactive applications with video and sound.

Because your Web site isn't a three-dimensional, multimedia experience, your basic online presence should be much easier to set up, at least from a logistic standpoint. Before you agree, let me delve a little deeper into how to run an online service business. (Maybe it's not your kind of "easy," after all.)

Looking at Offline Services with an Online Twist

However you look at it, if you're looking for a low cost of entry that's hot with opportunity, you're looking at the service business sector. This sector now represents about 75 percent of new jobs created and 75 percent of the total U.S. gross product. It sounds great, but before I continue, what do I mean by a service business?

Note

Like any business, a *service business* fulfills some need. When people buy something from you to satisfy that need, you get sales. Unlike a product-oriented business, a service business provides an intangible benefit to the consumer or user and usually involves the consumer or user in some way.

Consider Disney World. All its rides, attractions, and parades do one thing: provide the intangible benefit of fun and entertainment that is considered a service. (Walt Disney doesn't mind also selling a few hats, shirts, and trinkets along the way, but it is primarily a service business.)

Disney World is an example of just one type of service business. As with a hair salon or movie theater, the customer must go there to get the service. A pool service company and an overnight delivery service are examples of another type of service business, one that travels to a customer's location. A third type of service company, a hybrid of the first two types, involves the customer and the service company "meeting in the middle" (an Internet service provider or long-distance telephone carrier, for example).

Tip

So a service business may differ on where the service takes place, but all service businesses provide an intangible benefit. It's difficult to find any service business, though, that doesn't try to sell you something other than its primary services. Movie theaters sell popcorn. Overnight-delivery services sell extra insurance for your packages. Long-distance telephone carriers want you to order a special 800 number so that that your friends can call you for free.

Keep this "service 'em and sell 'em" idea in mind as you develop your online service business. After you fine-tune the service you are selling, think about which product you can sell along the way.

Technically speaking, virtually any service *can* be ordered online. The real question is whether the average consumer would *want* to order that service online.

Suppose that you prepare tax returns during tax season. You probably could do several tasks online: ask customers to fill out forms, have customers e-mail you all their financial information, and have them fax all their pertinent business forms to you. I would bet that you wouldn't get many takers, though.

This example reminds me of the time that Cathy Creno was writing a story about me for *The Arizona Republic.* The movie *The Net* was just hitting the theaters. (In case you missed it, the Internet plays a big role in fraud and mistaken identities.) Cathy asked me whether I resemble Sandra Bullock's character in the movie — that is, whether my entire existence consists of talking with friends and doing business by using my PC and my modem. I answered "no" and explained that I prefer talking on the phone or in person over using a keyboard. Cathy looked shocked and said, "You mean, you have *never* ordered a pizza online, like Sandra Bullock did in the movie?" No, I haven't. Frankly, it's still easier to do it by telephone, especially if you're like me and have to talk the operator into making the pizza the way you want it ("Use only half the normal amount of cheese and twice the tomato sauce. Oh, I have a coupon, and can you get it here in about 15 minutes, not 30?")

Tip

If you want to offer your service online, it must be one that makes sense in an online environment. I'm not saying that online pizza-ordering is a bad business; it will just take time for public acceptance. More important, service companies must consider the needs of their more demanding customers, like myself, who need more options than "Send me a medium cheese."

Sampling Some Internet Service Businesses

Let's take a peek at a few Web sites to consider in the online service business world.

Maybe you run a tiny software company with a fairly popular product. And maybe you're tired of answering stupid questions for free. Maybe you want to begin charging for technical-support calls. (The big software companies, after all, get as much as $25 per call.) You have one problem, however: You don't have the in-house capabilities and the expensive equipment to handle an inbound telephone technical-support operation. Maybe you should visit http://www.well.com/user/enet/faq.htm, the Entree.NET home page.

As a home page, this Web site is weak; I would expect more from a software company. The idea is interesting, however. This site apparently has all the equipment and facilities to have your company's customer-service calls routed through its operations. You still get the calls, but as they pass through Entree.NET, these folks keep the meter running, bill the caller's phone bill, and send you your cut.

Tip

This example demonstrates a great way to make additional revenue from existing customers without necessarily being there. I call it the "annuity fund approach." No matter which business you create, always look for a way to make some extra shekels by satisfying existing customer needs that require only minimal effort on your part.

Perhaps software is not your bag and you're in the advice-giving service business from 9 to 5. You can provide this service online too. Suppose that your children have trouble with bed-wetting, tantrums, and potty training. Don't call the Psychic Friends Network (yes, these types of service businesses are online too).

Why not try psychology? Parenting Solutions, at http://www.chesulwind.com/parents/ on the World Wide Web, is run by a group of child psychologists from Columbia University (see Figure 6-1). In exchange for $20, these folks will help you solve a variety of problems. Best of all, payment is on the honor system. If you're not satisfied with the results (perhaps you're just a cheapskate or get a cheap thrill from cheating others out of money), you don't have to pay.

If you consider yourself an expert desktop publisher, it shouldn't be too difficult to transfer your traditional print-design skills to the budding online arena. When you begin looking at some Web-design services, you see that many of them have their grass roots in advertising or print-catalog layout and design and desktop publishing.

One publishing site I found on the Web is Desktop Miracles, as shown in Figure 6-2. Go to http://www.desktopmiracles.com/ to see what it looks like. These folks offer all sorts of print and electronic media production services. If you look at the biography of company president Barry Kerrigan, however, you see that virtually his entire background revolves around desktop publishing and electronic typesetting.

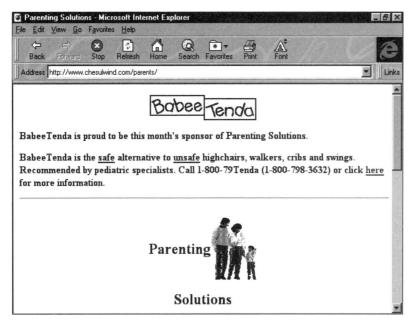

Figure 6-1: Need some help raising your kids? It's just a mouse click and an Internet connection away. You may be able to help others too, by offering your expert advice in a particular area.

Figure 6-2: Electronic desktop publishing offers success for many cyber-entrepreneurs.

I think that you get the point — I can see it in your eyes. In Chapter 5, I discussed some successful online ventures whose products had little or nothing to do with being online. That's fine — I'm sure that plenty of similar opportunities are out there, just waiting to be discovered. If you can tailor your product specifically to the online audience, however, your chances for success are that much better. It's common sense.

Delivering Information and Services Online

Being able to sell your offline services online is great. The true golden egg, however, is a service that can be ordered online *and* that can be delivered online. It's faster and, often, more profitable.

Virtually all services that can be delivered online can be broadly categorized as *information services*. I already talked about online information search-and-retrieval possibilities. Writing is another service that's an online natural. Every once in a while, I hire a freelance copywriter to help out with a particular project. I don't need to meet these people, as long as I know that they can write, which I can determine by looking at some writing samples. We can usually work out all the details via AOL e-mail, including work-for-hire agreements and submission of the finished work. My point is that it's easy to deliver information services online, no matter what the particular information might be.

Thomson MarketEdge, located on the Web at `http://www.marketedge.com`, bills itself as the Internet's most comprehensive financial information service for the personal investor (see Figure 6-3). For less than $10 a month, "MarketEdge provides you with the most complete financial information covering stocks, bonds, and mutual funds anywhere on the Internet." The introduction on this site goes on to say that "the *only* investment tool you'll need to make the right investment decisions is right at your fingertips."

This site demonstrates Business 101 in action. That is, any business consists of only three basic steps:

1. Materials (information, knowledge, Space Mountain, pizza dough, or whatever) are brought into the business.

2. Some sort of value (statistical analysis, sound advice, fun, or mozzarella, for example) is added to those materials.

3. The finished product (an investment report, finished tax return, great experience, superdeluxe with double anchovies) is sold to the customer.

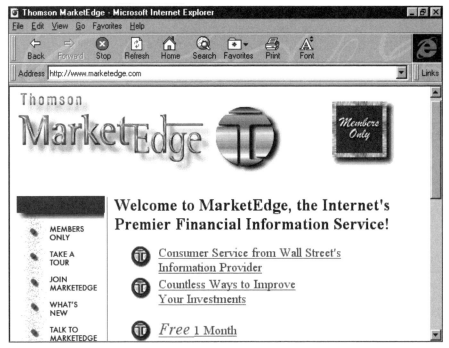

Figure 6-3: Repackaging and delivering free and specialized information for a profit can be a profitable online venture.

For a business to be successful, the price that's charged in step 3 must be higher than the expenses incurred in steps 1 and 2. I discuss the pricing of your online products in detail in Chapter 7.

For now, let's get back to MarketEdge. In its Stock Research Center, it offers the following information:

✦ Company reports

✦ Current stock quotes

✦ Current month's top-performing stocks

✦ Price charts from as long as two years ago

✦ A screening utility which lets you locate companies that meet your wants and needs

✦ Analytical reports on various stocks

✦ Unique content from the company's own experts

The interesting thing you must realize is that most of the information in this list is available elsewhere for free. Does this mean that MarketEdge is some sort of ripoff? Not by a long shot. When I said *free,* I didn't factor in the time element. Don't forget that time is money; it takes on even more value when you are your own boss. Sure, you could save the financial sections from two years' worth of newspapers, and you could call and order annual reports from companies that interest you (and wait days or weeks for them to arrive). You could also calculate this month's top performers and then plow through *Investor's Digest, The Wall Street Journal,* and *Barron's* for stock forecasts and investing tips. Just to make sure that all your bases are covered, you could also tune in to "Wall Street Week" and the CNN financial news.

The truth is, unfortunately, that it would probably take you months to compile all this information. And all that time translates to a double loss of income. You would lose all the money you could have personally earned while you wasted your time on this endeavor *and* all the income your investments could have earned if you had had all this information three months earlier.

Tip

My point here is that if you can repackage "public domain" information in a way that adds significantly more value for some potential customer base, you stand to make quite a bit of money.

When it comes to providing information, one of that greatest aspects of the computer is that it can customize information for a particular user. As a result, a number of custom news services have sprung up on both the Internet and the commercial online services, such as America Online (keyword NEWS PROFILES).

An Internet news service I find particularly interesting is Rex, which is a good name because it's simple to say. This site, at `http://daptyx.aimnet.com`, is an example of an Internet home page address that hardly rolls off your tongue (see Figure 6-4). Go ahead — try to say it three times fast. Then again, no matter how difficult it is to remember the address for your Internet home page, *any* home page is better than no home page.

With typical custom news services, you indicate which topics are of particular interest to you. Then, usually on a daily basis, the computer uses key words to search various news sources and look for articles that are likely to be of interest to you. With some services, you can view your custom cybernewspaper online; with others, you receive the information in separate stories by e-mail.

At this point, Rex isn't much different from the others. Rex takes the process of gathering information a giant dinosaur step forward, however. Every time you read an article from your Rex newspaper, you have the opportunity to rate it in terms of your interest level. Rex then uses your daily input to further refine the search criteria it uses to gather your custom information. You get more information that focuses on your individual needs now, *and,* as your needs and interests change, Rex adapts to keep pace without your ever having to reconfigure your preferences manually. Rex is one smart dinosaur.

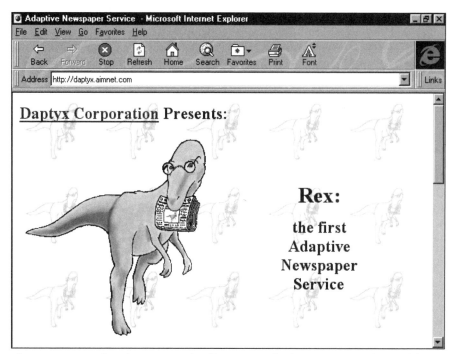

Figure 6-4: Rex takes the process of online newsgathering a giant step forward, by keeping track of your likes and dislikes.

At the time I wrote this book, subscription prices began at a meager $10 per month (cheaper than most daily newspaper subscriptions), with a free 14-day trial period.

Rex drives home another important point for would-be information and service providers: automation. Low-cost custom news services such as this one are possible because the computers do the work. Twenty years ago, only the richest of the rich would have been able to afford a comparable service because all the work would have had to be done manually.

You may think that $2,000 or $3,000 or more for a computer is plenty of money — and it is. When you consider all that your computer can do for you, however, you begin to realize that it would be a bargain at twice the price. If you paid a live, breathing, payroll-tax-eating employee to do all that work manually, you would end up spending the entire cost of your computer in one month on salary and overhead expenses for that employee.

Tip

The bottom line: Make your computer do as much work as possible so that you can spend more time making money that enables you in turn to spend more time doing what you really like to do — shop, spend time with your family, vacation, skydive — whatever.

Handling Problems with Services and Information

Just as with any business, of course, you must overcome a few obstacles as you travel the services-and-information road to success. If it were easy to be a millionaire, everyone would be jetting around like Donald Trump.

First of all, when you are selling a service, your "product" is an intangible one. No one will ever notice your product on a neighbor's coffee table and ask, "Gee, where did you get that?" People can't pick up your product and examine it. In a touchy-feely world, you're clearly at a disadvantage.

Warning

Service-oriented businesses can't appeal to a consumer's sense of sight, hearing, smell, taste, or touch. It's difficult for buyers to judge the quality of a service up front because they are buying only a promise until they receive the service and find out for themselves. Services usually last for only a certain time, unless you can figure out a way to have consumers come back time after time for more.

All this means that you have an acute need to demonstrate your services, or at least demonstrate your knowledge of your particular field. In the two preceding examples, it's easy for the two companies (MarketEdge and Rex) to demonstrate their services; they can simply offer a free trial account. After the trial period runs out, you either pay up or they cancel your ticket. That's pretty simple. If you can offer your customers a free trial period, do it.

Not all services, unfortunately, fit so nicely into the "easy to demonstrate" category. Suppose that you run a computer-repair business that you promote on a World Wide Web home page. This type of service is obviously a good match for the online environment, at least at the local level. Just as obvious, however, is that you can't go out and perform free repair services to demonstrate your skills. People, kindhearted as they might be, would quickly begin to take unfair advantage of your offer. You would soon be up to your eyeballs in work, which is a good thing. You would also be up to your eyeballs in debt because you would be doing all that work for free. That's a bad thing.

Proving That You Know Your Stuff

So how can you demonstrate this type of service? One way is to simply demonstrate your knowledge and expertise in your chosen field by offering free information about your field. Using the example of the computer-repair business, your Web site could include a "Ten Tips for Troubleshooting Your PC" page. You could even offer a free booklet through an online order form. This sort of thing establishes you as an expert. It offers the additional benefit of not having to repeatedly answer common (and often stupid) questions.

Another way to "demonstrate" your service is through customer testimonials. If you have satisfied customers, chances are that most of them would be willing to let you use their words to promote your business. If you have received letters of thanks or praise, you already have all the material you need in order to create a Customer Testimonials page on your Web site. Just remember to get a customer's written and expressed permission to use the testimonial *before* you publish it.

Another potential drawback you face is that services generally focus on a more narrow base of potential customers than do products. Just compare the market for toothpaste to the market for massage therapy. (Personally, I would rather wear a full plate of dentures than give up my massage therapist, but I don't think that I represent the norm here.) Compare the market for high-speed modems to the market for modem repair. In all my years in computing, I have never had a modem bite the dust. They generally become obsolete before they ever give out.

Target marketing is essential to your success. I discuss specific marketing strategies in Chapter 8 and Chapter 9, but, for now, just remember that the narrower your market, the greater your challenge in finding and connecting with that market.

Coming up with ideas is easy; coming up with *great* ideas is another thing altogether. I cannot (and neither can anyone else) tell you which service business is the best one for you, but I can certainly help you sort through the possibilities and come up with a winner. If you have read Chapter 5, some of what I say in this section may sound familiar, but it bears repeating.

Searching Your Soul to Come Up with the Ultimate Online Business

Business development always begins with self-examination. You have to be honest with yourself, and it helps if you have no distractions when you come face-to-face with strengths and limitations.

If you have kids, perhaps you can do this exercise when they are asleep or get up a little earlier before they wake up. Turn off all the brain clutter in your life. (It's easier than it sounds.) Forget about the bills, the IRS, your stupid manager, and the refrigerator that's on the blink again. Turn off the radio (unless I am on the air) and the television (again, unless I'm on it). The goal is to clear your mind, if only for 15 minutes. It can be the most important 15 minutes you spend on your future.

When you're ready, haul out the Vision for a Mission notebook you created in Chapter 4 and answer these questions:

✦ What are your talents, skills, and interests? (Everyone has unique talents — they're just in different areas.)

✦ What kind of background do you have that will help propel your online business?

✦ What do you like to do?

✦ Are there one or two things that you know a great deal about?

I know that you may be whining, "But I don't know anything about anything." Okay, maybe you're right, but I would bet that you *do* know something because you were smart enough to buy this book. Believe in yourself. No one better can.

Tip

What are your strengths? Your weaknesses? Service-oriented business often require more "people skills" than product-oriented ones. Do you have what it takes to communicate effectively and professionally with your clients and, almost more important, your potential clients? The goal is to work toward answering this question: If you were given every opportunity in the world, what type of service could you perform? It takes time to reach the answer. After you do, though, trust me — you will feel a sense of enthusiasm that you have never felt in your life.

If you need some inspiration, the World Wide Web offers many examples of service-based businesses and expertise in particular fields. Just type **service** on any of the Internet search pages, such as http://www.yahoo.com or http://www.excite.com. Hundreds of businesses started by people like you will appear for your browsing pleasure, as shown in Figure 6-5.

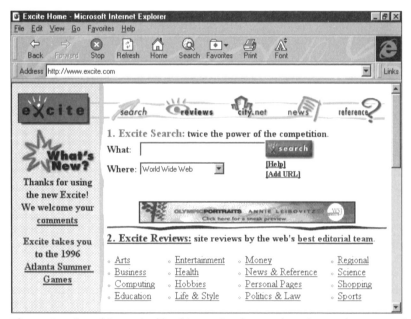

Figure 6-5: Searching a site like this one for the word *service* on the Internet brings up thousands of sites.

You're bound to get discouraged. It happens to everyone — even *I* feel low from time to time. When a black cloud covers you, I want you to look at all the various Internet service providers and World Wide Web page developers out there. Three or four years ago, no one had ever heard of the Web. No one on the planet can rightly post a sign that claims "In business on the Web since 1942." Because it's all brand-new, there's plenty of room for your business.

Plenty of people are making plenty of bucks providing different Web services — designing, hosting, developing, promoting, and whatever else. In a service business, the one thing that can often substitute for experience is money. If you don't quite know what you're doing, you simply hire someone who does. Criticized for his lack of formal education, Henry Ford responded that he had plenty of well-educated employees who could answer any question he might need answered.

The key here is financial resources. You either need lots of money *or* lots of experience. I'll go out on a limb here and guess that you don't have lots of money. You must, therefore, develop some sort of service with which you have lots of experience.

Chapter 5 discussed the need for having an interest in a particular field. With a service business, you have to be particularly careful. Maybe you're a repair technician for a major computer retailer and you feel burned out by your job. Because you long to branch out on your own, leave the corporate rat race, and become your own boss, you decide to open your own computer repair business.

That's fine, but what if the work involved in repairing computers is part of what you're burned out on in the first place? Becoming self-employed might relieve some of your short-term job stress, but in the long run you probably won't find much more fulfillment in your new business than you did with your old job.

The trick in this instance is to develop a business idea that builds on your current skills and expertise without necessarily duplicating your old job duties.

Making a Reality Check

No matter what the particular field, all service businesses are based on meeting needs in a personal way. If you are selling your advice and expertise, *you* are the product. Consider your local automobile-repair shop, which is a service business. Its owner wouldn't stay in business long if she prescribed a complete transmission overhaul for every customer who came in with a problem. Unlike product sales, in which every customer typically receives the same thing, an auto mechanic provides a unique service to each individual customer based on his need.

That you have the skills to provide a particular service is no guarantee that anyone on the planet needs the help your skills provide. As I was walking the aisles at a recent trade show, for example, I saw a guy whom one vendor had employed to draw people to its booth. This fellow billed himself as "The Original Butt Sketch." (I'll bet that his parents are proud.)

The service that sketcher provides is to draw full-body sketches of interested passers-by — with the model facing backward! This guy is a one-trick pony — either butts or nothing.

I can't be too critical of the butt-sketch guy because he seemed to be moderately successful doing his thing for parties and conventions. I can assure you, however, that he would never survive by providing this type of service to individual customers. Furthermore, I'm confident that there's no room in his geographic market for two butt-sketch artists.

I hope that you didn't miss my point here. When you're developing a service-oriented business plan, the consideration of what the market *needs* is just as important as what you have to *offer*. Before you quit your day job to become "The Original Online Butt Sketch Artist," you have to ask yourself whether people or businesses out there need an online butt-sketch artist. My guess is no.

Putting It All Together

So how do you identify the types or services that people need and will pay for? The best way is to look at your potential customers to see exactly what they're doing and how they're doing it. Don't just look at specific tasks, though. Just as important, you have to look at your customers' objectives in completing those tasks.

From there, you have two options. You can offer a service that helps your customers complete those same tasks in a more productive and efficient manner, or you can offer a service that provides a whole new means to achieve those same objectives in a more economical or beneficial way.

If all this sounds like mumbo-jumbo, just return to the computer-repair business for a simple example. Perhaps you observe that all the repair shops in your area perform only carry-in work (a customer must physically bring a damaged computer to the repair shop). As part of your business plan, you want to eliminate the customer's inconvenience of having to lug in a PC.

One option is to offer pickup and delivery service, either for free or at a price associated with a minimum repair charge. This price keeps the general process essentially the same — getting the machine fixed. It's just that you, rather than your customer, are doing the legwork. The other option is to offer a mobile repair business, or a repair shop on wheels, if you will. In this example, the old process is replaced by a new process in which computers are repaired at the customer's location. Either way, you provide to your customers the intangible benefit of saving time and aggravation.

Both these options solve the initial problem, and each has its own strong points and weak points. It's up to you to decide which approach is more appropriate for your particular market and for your talents, skills, knowledge, and motivation.

Getting your goods into the hands of customers

The development phase for a service business is dramatically different from that for a product-oriented business. If you are selling products, you must put a great deal of thought into producing or acquiring your product (or both). In a service business, the focus shifts to delivery: Exactly how will you provide your service to your customer?

If yours is some sort of information service that can be delivered online, most of the issues you have to address are related to computers:

✦ Will you provide your service via the World Wide Web?

✦ By using e-mail?

✦ Over a commercial online service?

✦ Do you have special programming needs? If so, who will do the programming?

✦ How will you get paid for your services?

All these questions are important, and you have to answer them now. You should consider these issues as key components, in fact, that make up your overall service business.

If you're developing an offline service you plan to market online, the issues you face are more logistic in nature. It's easy to take orders and answer inquires by using such methods as e-mail. The tough part is figuring out just how to fulfill your end of the deal after those online orders come through.

Knowing how to get paid for offline services is no mystery. You simply establish one or more of the traditional means of payment: cash, check, or credit card. When it comes to getting paid for online services (or products, for that matter), I'm a firm believer that the credit card is king. The great part about a service business is that, assuming that you do a good job, you're likely to get plenty of repeat business.

If you do get repeat business, it's feasible (and advisable) to establish an account for each customer. You can maintain a customer's credit-card number on file and issue a new debit for each transaction without the person having to resubmit his credit-card and billing information. It saves everyone time and reduces any transmission-security risks. In addition, you make more money because customers don't have to remember to order from you. It happens automatically.

In Chapter 10, I tell you in greater detail how to get paid for your goods electronically, but now it's time for another Komando story.

When my company was setting up our system on America Online for processing online orders, we couldn't find an off-the-shelf program that does it all — sign on to the service, download order files, put orders in an existing customer database, process orders, integrate with the inventory control database, print packing slips, and other tasks.

Order collection isn't as complicated as order processing. Starting with the collection, here's how it works: To be able to read information about a product, customers point-and-click on a product name displayed in the electronic mall. People who want to buy a product just enter their credit-card number, expiration date, name on the card, mailing address, and daytime phone number. Figure 6-6 shows the Komputer Klinic shopping mall on America Online.

You can receive orders in different ways, but the easiest method is to have just one — you hope! — big file that contains all daily orders sent to you (every 24 hours at a preset time) over the computer network that holds the mall.

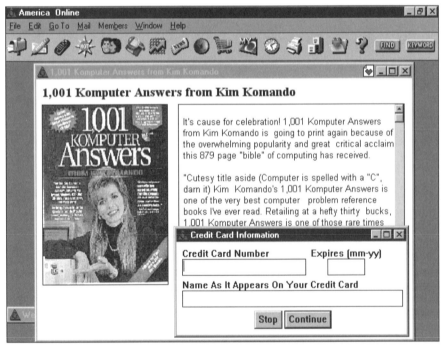

Figure 6-6: The Komando mall on America Online makes buying any of its products as easy as typing your credit-card number.

The file contains each element that comprises the order: customer name, address, and products ordered, for example. You don't have to reenter the information; every necessary detail is already in computer format. The challenge comes in making the order file in its present form compatible with your existing order-entry system. The Komputer Klinic's in-house system analyst and team of programmers spent four months fine-tuning a solid link between our online order system and our existing order-entry system.

The Klinic's programmers customized the Microsoft Access database program so that it takes just a few clicks of a mouse button to process an order. The result is office automation at its finest. Every morning, a member of my staff retrieves the online order file from the network and starts up the Access-based program. Then the employee goes and makes coffee while Access takes over and performs these tasks:

✦ Processes orders and checks for repeat customer names so that the main customer database has no duplicates

✦ Puts in a "to call" file the names of customers who ordered two or more products in one day

✦ Uses the IC Verify program to authorize credit-card orders and places the authorization code in the customer's record

✦ Puts "declines" (invalid card numbers) in another, separate "to call" file

✦ Prints packing slips for orders that have been approved

✦ Depletes on-hand inventory

The order-processing program performs all these tasks and then date- and time-stamps every step. (There's nothing like having the information you need in order to handle customer-satisfaction calls — it's incredible!)

You can find out more about IC Verify from your merchant banker (the company which provides the account that enables you to process credit-card orders), or just point your Web browser to http://www.icverify.com. Figure 6-7 shows the IC Verify home page on the Internet.

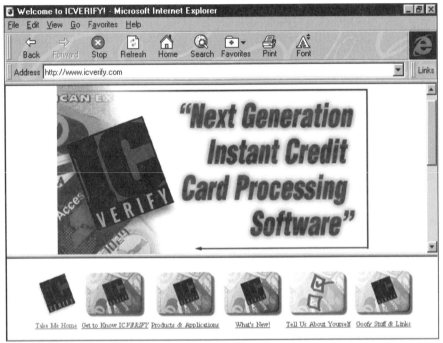

Figure 6-7: This company publishes software that processes electronic credit-card transactions.

Adding up profits quickly: fixed fees

If you're in the business of providing an automated-information service such as Rex or MarketEdge (refer to the section "Delivering Information and Services Online," earlier in this chapter), your best bet is to do as they do and charge a flat monthly subscription fee. Again, this fee makes things easy for both you and your customers. Flat-rate subscriptions make it simple to estimate future income based on your current number of customers.

Another option is to charge a per-use fee. The commercial online services provide a limited example of this concept. After you burn up your "free" hours for the month, the meter begins ticking. At the end of the month, you pay for exactly what you use — no more and no less. As another example, CompuServe charges extra to access its trademark database. If your customers are likely to use different types of services at different times, each with its own pricing structure, this is obviously the way to go.

One last word about credit cards, and it applies for products and services alike: If you're expecting a high volume of transactions, make sure that your credit-card fulfillment system is automated too. If your online business isn't on some sort of server that can handle this system for you, do it on your PC. As I mentioned in the preceding section, many credit-card companies can provide you with PC-based software to automate this process so that you don't have to spend endless hours keying numbers into that little pad on your keyboard. Worse, you don't want to spend hours on the telephone with a credit-card processor, getting authorization for every order you take.

Protecting your assets

To some extent, naming your service is no different from naming your product (refer to Chapter 5). To refresh your memory, I suggest that you don't waste your money doing research online that you can do for free at your public library.

In a service business, you must address one other naming issue. Because the chances are that your company name and your service name are the same, you probably will have to apply locally for a fictitious business-name permit. This permit gives you the right to use that particular name in your particular locality and puts other new businesses on notice that the name is already being used. Unlike with trademark registration, which can cost several hundred dollars, you can usually obtain a fictitious business permit for about $20 or $30.

If your service is in the advice-giving business, ask your insurance agent about errors-and-omissions policies. With these policies, you buy insurance that covers you in case you give someone bad advice and they sue you over it. You have to protect yourself and your company from any potential lawsuits.

You need a lawyer also to help you set up a corporation. You want to be sure that if someone does sue you over bad advice, he cannot get to your personal assets.

In closing, you can use online means to promote virtually any offline service. The question is whether it's appropriate to do so. The more closely your business relates to the online culture, the better your chances for success.

On the other hand, make sure that you don't sell cyberspace short. A friend of mine recently told me about a Denver-based (of all places) scuba diving instructor who gets the majority of his new business from his Web page. Go figure.

When it comes to online services, if you can find any sort of information that lots of people need, you have a potential market. Large-scale topics, such as stock information and general news, are probably overwhelming for aspiring cyber-entrepreneurs. Plenty of opportunity is out there, however. How about pay-as-you-go troubleshooting for a software program in which you're an expert? Perhaps you have a green thumb and can offer a Gardening Tip of the Day for a low annual subscription ($2 or $3). My experience is that the smallest ideas (at least the ones that start out small) are the ones that end up making the biggest money.

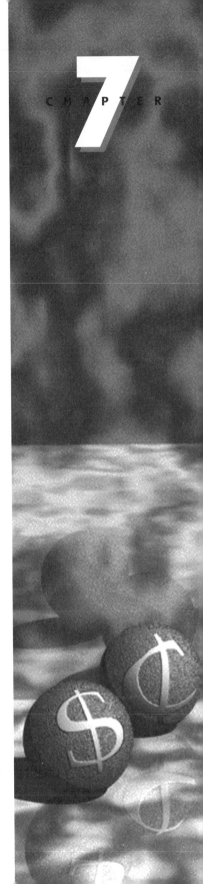

Pricing Your Online Products and Services

Hey, you! Yeah, you there, reading this book! Want to get a jump-start on building your Internet skills by using Kim Komando's Internet Training CD-ROM? Some people have paid $39.99 for it, and others have paid $24.99. Because you are reading this book (not in the aisle of some bookstore, I hope, to which I say, "Stop being a cheapo and just buy it"), I have a special deal.

To get the skills you need in order to compete immediately, call 1-800-KOMANDO, and be sure to tell the operator that you are a "promotion code 2001 customer." Specifying this code enables you to purchase Kim Komando's Internet Training CD-ROM for just $15.99 (plus shipping and handling, of course).

You might be thinking that I ripped off the customers who paid more than double the price I just mentioned. No, I have not, and let me explain. I hit you with a great many facts in this section, so pay attention.

Things Your Economics Teacher Never Told You

The price any business charges for a product or service depends on many factors. If you sell a product, hard costs are associated with putting that product together and packaging it. Service businesses must package their goods too (for example, in the description of a business on its Web page, within printed marketing materials, or by giving out freebies designed to build a client base).

Television, magazine, radio, newspaper, online, direct mail, and other advertisements cost money, and these marketing and sales costs must be built-in to the pricing formula. You don't want to pay for the ads; you want each one of your customers to pay for them as they buy your products or services.

Tip

Don't forget that your prices must leave some money for *you* after you pay for overhead, credit-card-processing fees, reserves for returns, insurance, taxes, toll-free telephone lines, shipping, and other expenses.

What about pricing variables? Manufacturing costs fluctuate with quantity. Make more goods, and it will cost you less per item to produce each one. That also means, however, that you will have more money tied up in inventory. That's not good.

The old supply-and-demand theory applies in any industry. When supply goes down and demand is high, price goes up. Always avoid any products, therefore, that require an endangered flower which only blooms in the rain forests every May.

If one of your suppliers goes out of business (or your rain forest dries up), you may need another (read: more expensive) supplier to help fulfill orders. Even after you work the numbers, a price that works in one market doesn't mean immediate success in another market. It's a bummer when you find that the perfect price which lets you make money is too high for the average consumer.

For example, my company's bottom line would benefit if I could sell the Internet Training CD-ROM for $179.99 and still maintain its current sales volume. It's a safe guess that no one would buy it. On the other hand, you may think that sales would blow out the door if I lowered the price of the training CD-ROM to $4.95. It costs less than $1 to press a CD-ROM, which leaves me roughly $4 to pay expenses. I would still make some money by lowering the price, but the underlying problem is not just that my company's margin would suffer severely — I probably would lose sales to boot. How many times have you thought, "If it costs only $5, it can't be any good"?

Coming up with the perfect price for your cyberbusiness's products or services involves more than crunching numbers in a spreadsheet. Pricing is the one area that, unfortunately, would-be entrepreneurs often overlook, whether their businesses are online or offline. More often than not, the entire development of their pricing strategy involves little more than a moment to take a "wild guess" at what the right price should be.

You must have more than a gut feeling about the perfect price to charge for a product or service. You also must do the calculations and competitive research to substantiate your feelings. The price you charge for any product or service ultimately determines how much money you make or lose.

If you charge the "right" price, you will be successful. If your price strays too far in either direction, high or low, your chances are mighty slim. It seems appropriate, therefore, to look briefly at how to price your online products or services. Most of what I tell you in this chapter applies to *all* businesses, including your new cyberbusiness.

Understanding What Pricing Is All About

Before delving deeply into pricing, look at these two important formulas (I realize that you may have seen them already, but they're here just to be on the safe side):

$$\text{Total revenue} = \text{Price per unit} \times \text{Quantity sold}$$

$$\text{Profits} = \text{Revenue} - \text{Expenses}$$

Take a moment to study these formulas. Your ability to sustain and grow your online enterprise depends on it.

What exactly is price, anyway? Yes, I'm asking you. You have seen thousands of price tags in your life, on everything from toilet paper to your first home. Now think about *your* definition of price. You don't have to write it down; I simply want you to come up with a few words to describe the word *price*. Come on, think about it. Got it? Don't lose it.

Before I get to the definition, let me turn to my trusty dictionary. It lists the first definition of *price* as "the amount of money asked or given for something; cost; charge." That's probably close to the definition you came up with. Price means cash, but it means so much more. Thank goodness, though, the dictionary lists something else.

The second dictionary definition is equally important. It says that price is "the value or worth of something." At the time I wrote this chapter, the big hoopla was that *Madonna* had not been added to the listing of new words for the next edition of the dictionary. Oh, dear. The folks who produce the dictionary might have better spent their time revamping their definition of *price*.

My dictionary doesn't mention that price is dynamic (it moves). Furthermore, the words *price* and *cash* are not synonymous in a barter situation. Suppose that you design an Internet Web page for a client (your lawyer) in exchange for your cyberbusiness's free incorporation papers. I recommend that, with a new business, you barter as much as possible to keep costs low and profits high.

Tip

Although my company is quite profitable, I still cut barter deals (just not as often anymore). I figured out early on that I could have online staff members and not pay them a salary. (This setup is great!) My company employs folks from Altus, Oklahoma; from Boston, Massachusetts; and even from as far as Australia. They answer e-mail, manage the company libraries, post new articles, and work the message boards.

These folks work hard in exchange for a free online account and, ahem, the glory. Their photo and a little story about them are posted in the About section of our online site, as shown in Figure 7-1.

Figure 7-1: You can find wonderful people who will help maintain your online site and forgo a salary in exchange for a free online account.

As you look at your hard costs of setting up an online business, stretch your imagination. If an expense (or two or three) on a spreadsheet is cutting into your profits, think of another way to get the same job done. Odds are that you can set up a win-win scenario that doesn't take cash.

Getting back to price, though, you can charge whatever you want for whatever you're selling. After all, you are the pricing guru in charge.

You could buy standard floppy disks pretty cheaply, for about 25 cents apiece, and then sell them in your Internet mall for $20 apiece. I would bet that somewhere in the world you could find a sucker or two willing to give you $20 for a blank floppy disk. On the other hand, if the buying public at large doesn't, as a whole, perceive an appropriate value or worth in the price tag you have slapped on your product, don't quit your day job. You'll be out of business before you can say "Rip-off."

By now, I'll bet that your definition of price has changed, so let me present you with the official Kim Komando definition of *price:*

> The fair value, either in cash or in services, someone is willing to give you in exchange for something you have that he or she wants or needs.

You must have a solid definition of *price* before you can begin to sell your products or services. That's *my* point. Now I give you George Bernard Shaw's attempt to illustrate a point about pricing to his friends at a restaurant. This wonderful story goes something like this:

> He asked a waitress whether she would have sex with him for $1 million. She immediately replied, "Yes."
>
> He asked her whether she would have sex with him for $100,000. She hesitated and said, "I guess so."
>
> He then asked whether she would have sex with him for $10,000. She said, "I don't know; maybe."
>
> He then asked whether she would have sex with him for $1,000. She said, "I don't know."
>
> He quickly asked, "Would you have sex with me for $100?" She said, "Hey!"
>
> He immediately asked, "Would you have sex with me for $10?"
>
> She said, "What kind of girl do you think I am?" He said, "We've already established that. Now we're merely haggling over price."

My purpose in telling you this story is not to help you fix your social life. I tell it only to illustrate that all customers have in mind how much they are willing to pay for goods or services and that finding that limit can sometimes be tricky.

Knowing What the Law Says about Pricing

Plenty of laws on the books at both the state and federal levels relate to pricing. Many of them were enacted around the time of the Great Depression, when big business was a relatively new phenomenon. To be honest, most of these laws were designed to keep big businesses from taking unfair advantage of "the little guy."

Because the chances are good that you're starting out as the little guy, these laws may not have a major effect on how you set your initial pricing. Nonetheless, this information is important, for two reasons.

First, the whole idea of your venture is to make it a success. Simply stated, you want to make money and lots of it. That means that you're probably not planning on being the little guy forever. If you learn a few things now about what is expected of you when you become a major player, you will be prepared when it finally happens.

Second, depending on exactly which type of business you're involved in, you may already be facing some major players. You should know which pricing laws are in place to protect you from your larger competitors. In case you think that these older laws aren't taken seriously anymore, you should know that a number of lawsuits are pending against Wal-Mart for alleged violations of these same laws.

Note

The specific area of law that applies to the Wal-Mart suits is known collectively as *unfair-trade laws.* These laws are enacted at the state level to make sure that companies don't sell their products and services way below cost just to drive their competition out of business. In the first case brought against Wal-Mart, in 1993, the company was found guilty of selling health-and-beauty products below cost just to push out three locally owned drugstores.

Whether or not you're guilty of this type of violation depends in large part on your intention in setting a particular price. If it's mid-July, for example, and you have a large inventory of ski caps sitting around from last winter, you're well within your right to sell them below cost just to get rid of them. On the other hand, if it's the height of ski season and you sell the ski caps below cost just to gain an unfair advantage over a competitor, you're probably in violation of the law.

The lesson here is simple. From a legal standpoint, you can't sell below cost and absorb the inevitable losses just to drive your competition out of business. If you believe that someone has taken this type of action against you, I suggest that you consult your attorney.

Tip

The legal profession is a competitive business. Pick up the yellow pages and you see pages and pages of lawyers who specialize in various areas. You can find lawyers who charge much less than $100 to more than $500 per hour for their services. Don't cut corners on legal fees or think that you will just read an agreement in which you obligate your company all by your lonesome. Here's my rule of thumb: Expect whatever contract you sign to be the only thing that helps you win a lawsuit, if the occasion arises.

As a new enterprise, you have room to negotiate. Always ask for a "new client discount." Specify that you want the lawyer to be a long-term business associate and that you know how difficult it is to find a good, honest lawyer. Explain that cash is a little tight — after all, you're just starting your business. Explain also that you want the lawyer to work with you. This is no time to be proud.

You know, from the largest firms to the sole practitioners, I have never had a lawyer turn me down. I normally request — and, more important, get — a 25 percent discount per hour for the first three months I use that particular lawyer. When you're paying $100 or $200 per hour, the savings add up quickly. After you find a lawyer you can work with, keep him. A good lawyer is hard to come by.

Setting Your Price Objectives

No matter what you're selling, you are obviously in business to make a profit. You can start up one of a million businesses, but there are only two ways to structure sales so that you make money at it.

You can sell lots and lots of your product at *volume-driven pricing,* or for a relatively low per-unit profit. Or you can sell a lower number or amount of your product at a greater per-unit profit, called *profit-driven pricing.*

Earlier in this book, I talked briefly about a Hummer car dealership. To refresh your memory, a Hummer is the civilian version of the all-terrain assault vehicle that was instrumental in Desert Storm. The price of one of these monsters starts at about $40,000, but they usually sell for about $70,000, after you throw in all the goodies and options. Figure 7-2 shows the Web site for a Hummer dealership located at `http://nowscape.com/a/hummer.htm`.

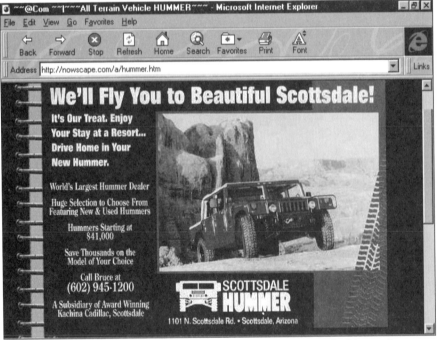

Figure 7-2: Big-ticket items, such as the Hummer, follow the profit-driven price strategy.

Suppose that you're driving down the street and you come across the Miracle Mile of Cars, or whatever they call it in your hometown. It's the area of town in which all the car dealers seem to have set up shop. On one side of the road, you see the Hummer dealer; across the street, you see the Saturn dealer.

Because the Hummer is truly an amazing vehicle, you stop at that dealer first to give the Hummer a test drive. Sure enough, it's wonderful. But because you almost choke on your bubble gum when the salesperson tells you its price, you immediately make a beeline for the Saturn dealer.

At the Saturn dealer, you find a moderately priced, quality-built car that can do everything you want your vehicle to do. You close the deal, and soon you're on your way in your new Saturn. As you pull away from the lot and look across the street at the Hummer dealer, you can't help but feel a tiny bit of jealousy. "It would be great," you think, "to be a Hummer dealer." After all, the Hummer dealer obviously makes more money than the Saturn dealer, right? Not necessarily.

The Hummer dealer is a good example of profit-driven pricing, and the Saturn dealer offers a lesson in volume-driven pricing (see Figure 7-3). Because many more people in this country can afford a Saturn than can afford a Hummer, a much larger potential customer base exists for a Saturn than for a Hummer. Ultimately, the Saturn dealer is likely to sell many more vehicles than the Hummer dealer. After all, in this example, *you* opted for the Saturn. On the Internet, drop by `http://www.saturncars.com`.

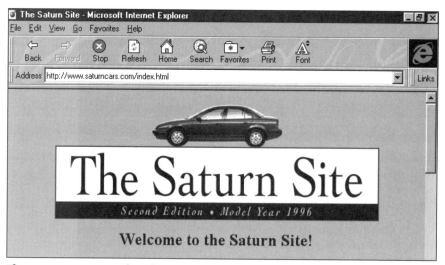

Figure 7-3: Saturn employs the volume-driven price strategy.

So who is making more money here? Because I don't know the markup on either type of vehicle, I'll just make up a few figures to illustrate my point.

Suppose that because of the Hummer's high price, the Hummer dealer sells only two vehicles per week. If the profit on each vehicle is $10,000, the weekly profit is $20,000.

Now suppose that the Saturn dealer makes only $1,000 profit on each sale. Because of the Saturn's lower pricing and better perceived value, however, the dealer sells 25 vehicles every week. That number puts the weekly profits for that dealership at $25,000 per week. In other words, in terms of profit in this example, you are better off owning a Saturn dealership than a Hummer dealership.

You may be wondering how all this applies to your new cyberbusiness. My point in this example is that pricing isn't just a guessing game. You must determine where you fit into "the big picture":

✦ Do you have an exclusive product with a small potential online market composed of people willing to pay a premium price? If you offer extremely specialized research services with few competitors, for example, you can probably charge a premium price and enjoy a handsome profit on your work.

✦ Or do you plan to offer a mass-market product that already has some online competition? If you plan to take a stab at selling pop music CDs online, for example, you already have some stiff competition. BMG, Blockbuster Music, Tower Records, and many more companies have a strong presence on commercial online services and Internet sites, on which you can sample some tunes, win prizes, and place orders.

In this example, you must price your CDs very aggressively (less than $10 U.S.) and, therefore, you must sell them by the virtual truckload to make any substantial money.

Get hold of some vintage albums, though, and you might do well. I did a quick search at Yahoo! using the words *rare* and *album*. Only seven sites appeared; of those, the one that's worth a peek is Scott Neuman's Forever Vinyl, as shown in Figure 7-4 (at `http://www.exit109.com/~sneuman/`).

It's difficult to say exactly how Scott is doing in the album-collection business because he still sells cars for a living. His pricing formula is simple: "I'm always looking for rare and collectible vinyl for resale. I'm not paying retail. But I will pay fair wholesale up to 20 percent off retail, depending on condition and value. I pay promptly and in U.S. dollars."

Scott makes it clear that, in exchange for his effort and time spent looking at your rare albums and buying them from you, he's going to make money. If you have an album worth $100 at a retail store, he will pay you as much as $80 for it, assuming that the album is in mint condition. This amount leaves a $20 profit that Scott will get when he sells the album, and it's much more of a profit per order than he would get with pop-music CDs. (But Scott won't be selling truckloads of original Beatles albums either.)

Figure 7-4: Find an angle that makes your products or services unique, and then you can charge more for them.

Tip

It's up to you to determine whether a volume-driven or profit-driven pricing strategy, or something in between, is more appropriate for your business. Don't be afraid to try different prices with your customers. Because your business is online, it's easy to change prices on the fly. Just be sure that you have done your homework (I teach you how to do that, in the rest of this chapter).

Using a Break-Even Analysis

The ditch alongside the road to success is lined with many businesses that have, for many different reasons, crashed and burned. One common mistake future business titans make in the area of pricing is not considering how much it truly costs to run a business.

Suppose that you invent the SuperWidget, a unique and wonderful device that virtually every person on the online planet cannot live without. You do some market analysis and study the pricing for similar (but, of course, clearly inferior) products and then determine that $5 is the right price to charge. You then launch your online business, and SuperWidgets begin to sell quite well.

Then, after months of shipping SuperWidgets, you discover that you're losing money! After additional research, you discover that when you add all your costs (rent, salaries, shipping, equipment, insurance — the whole enchilada), you're spending *$6* to manufacture each $5 SuperWidget.

Your knee-jerk reaction is probably to raise the SuperWidget price to $7. But what if the market won't support a $7 price tag for a SuperWidget? What if, your expenses aside, $5 really is the right price for a SuperWidget? Are you doomed? Not necessarily. You have to perform a break-even analysis to determine exactly where you stand. Don't worry — you don't have to be a CPA in order to do the analysis. Just have a calculator and some paper handy or put your PC with a spreadsheet program within reach.

Tip

The key to understanding a break-even analysis is realizing that some of your expenses are relatively fixed — your rent, for example. Suppose that you spend $500 a month on rent and that you sell 500 SuperWidgets per month. Your rent is costing you $1 per SuperWidget sold.

If you can boost SuperWidget sales to 1,000 per month, the cost of your rent will be only 50 cents per SuperWidget sold. That would lower your total manufacturing cost from $6 to $5.50 per SuperWidget. Got that? You merely factor into a formula your fixed costs so that you know precisely how much money it takes per order to make money.

Note

The purpose of a break-even analysis is to tell you how many units you must sell at a given price just to break even. After you have this information, you can then make intelligent decisions about whether to raise prices, increase production, or take some other action.

This process may sound confusing, but it really isn't. Here are some simple steps to help you determine your own break-even point:

1. Add up your total fixed expenses, including any expense that remains relatively constant every month, such as some of the items I mentioned earlier in this section — rent, salaries, insurance, office supplies, telephone, and online accounts, for example. Be sure to count your own salary among your fixed expenses. At least in the beginning, if you're still not making boatloads of profit, you're still making a living.

2. Determine your variable costs per unit. A major component of this figure will most likely be materials. For example, it may take $2 worth of materials to build a SuperWidget, no matter how many of them you build.

3. Determine the price you currently charge or plan to charge.

4. Subtract the variable cost from the price.

5. Divide the fixed costs by the number you calculated in step 4. This is the number of units you have to sell each month just to break even.

Don't worry if these steps don't completely make sense. In the following example, make these assumptions:

✦ Your fixed expenses are $10,000 per month.

✦ Your per-unit variable expenses are $3 per unit.

✦ Your selling price is $7 per unit.

Applying the formula I just discussed, subtract $3 from $7 to get a result of $4. Then divide $10,000 by $4. That result is 2,500. To break even with these expenses and this pricing structure, therefore, you must sell 2,500 units every month (and then some, so that you can earn a living). If you cannot, you must make some adjustments — raise your price, figure out ways to cut expenses, or both.

Granted, doing a break-even analysis isn't much fun. And because you have to sell stuff and build your online area, who has the time? *You* had better have the time, that's who! In addition to knowing precisely what it will take to make some money, you have something else — a goal. You have a target number that is realistic.

Write down this number in your Vision for a Mission book (if you don't know what that is, refer to Chapter 4). Post it on your forehead. Make it your meditation mantra. I don't care. Put it anywhere that you won't lose it, and keep it close to your heart. I have all my sales goals underneath the blotter on my desk along with a little piece of motivation that says, "What are you doing right now to take your company public?" That's my ultimate goal, which is possible only after my sales goals are met.

If you're not up to the job of making a spreadsheet from scratch, look for help no farther than on your computer. It's a good idea, in fact, to begin automating certain tasks (such as paying bills and tracking receivables) and keeping records of your business from the beginning.

Although a spreadsheet program is good enough to crunch some numbers and a word-processing program can turn out formatted invoices, if you're going to be in business, run your company as a business. Rather than use a few different software programs to manage basic accounting and business-management tasks, get a program that does it all — keeps records, warns you when your checking-account balance is low, creates a budget for you, reminds you to pay the bills, generates instant invoices, and more.

The Komputer Klinic accounting department uses QuickBooks Pro, from Intuit. My brother-in-law swears by DacEasy for his construction business. A friend who runs a recording studio is hooked on Microsoft Money. Just find a program you like, and then make it work for you (see Figure 7-5).

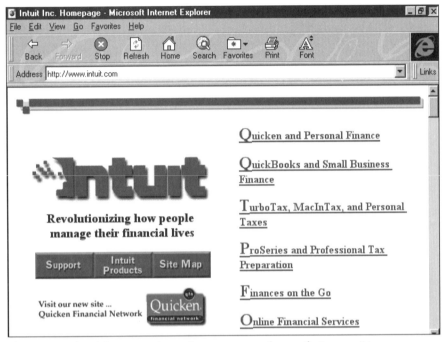

Figure 7-5: The right accounting software program is one that you put to use.

Tip

Every business works differently and needs different things. Ask your friends which programs they use for financial and business management. Then go ask your accountant which one she uses. You can save money on your accounting fees, and on your taxes, if you use the same software program as your CPA. For example, rather than have the Klinic's CPA keep track of our financial records (to the tune of $75 per hour), my employees and I do it ourselves, using QuickBooks Pro. But the CPA reviews our QuickBooks data files monthly just to make sure that everything is on track.

Don't Forget the Competition

After you have done all the calculating and the figuring, one other factor is just as important, if not more so: your competition. No matter how great your pricing structure looks on paper, you will have a tough time making any money if the guy or gal just down the Infobahn is selling the same product or service as you for a lower price.

Now is the time to put one of those Internet search engines to use to hunt down your competitors, as shown in Figure 7-6. Go to one of the Internet search standards:

✦ **Yahoo!:** `http://www.yahoo.com`

✦ **Lycos:** `http://www.lycos.com`

✦ **AltaVista:** `http://www.altavista.com`

✦ **DejaNews:** `http://www.dejanews.com`

✦ **WebCrawler:** `http://www.webcrawler.com`

Figure 7-6: The Internet search engines provide lots of information about your competitors that you can use to win the game!

On the commercial online services, check out the Directory of Services or use the Find command. On AOL, when you use the keyword FIND, you see the box shown in Figure 7-7. You can use the directories in all the online services by using specific search phrases. If you have the next great online desktop publishing service, for example, use the search phrase "desktop publishing." Many listings will appear on-screen, and you can tell by their description whether they're up your alley. See what you can find. Your goal is to snoop: Be *your* customer, and experience your competitor's stores. Then experience your store, even if, for now, it's only in your mind.

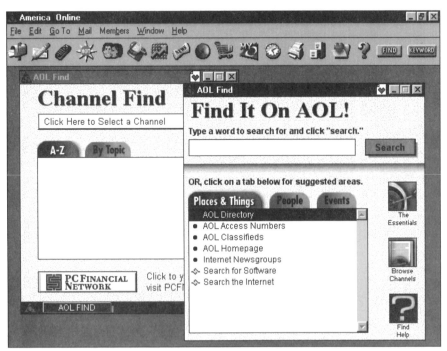

Figure 7-7: Online services have directories to help users find things. Use these directories to snoop on your competition!

Your findings are important stuff I want you to keep in your Vision for a Mission book. Haul it out. This is no time to be lazy. I know — you just got comfortable with a drink and this book. If you want to be financially comfortable the rest of your life, get up and start keeping notes about your competition in your Vision for a Mission book.

Tip

As you start looking at your online competition, begin with the obvious. Locate sites that market something exactly like your product or service. I realize that your idea is probably unique, but I am sure that, in this great big online world, someone out there has "kinda almost" the same business as yours. Even if it's a stretch, check out the site.

There's more involved in uncovering possible competitors, though. Will your product or service replace one that is already available? Consider the dent that e-mail has made on the U.S. Postal Service's revenues. The goal of both e-mail and the postal service is the same: Send a written form of communication. Sending e-mail is much easier, faster, and cheaper, however, than sending it by the good old-fashioned lick-the-stamp mail. E-mail as we know it will soon be replaced by something else. It's bound to happen. I'm betting that when video e-mail becomes available, it will edge out its competitors.

The final type of competitor you want to find is another type of product or service that can cut into your revenue. The idea behind this suggestion is simple: People have only so much money to spend after all the bills are paid. Given a choice, for example, would your online customer play your online multiuser game for a flat fee per month or buy the newest CD for entertainment? By knowing customers' demographics and profiles, you can figure out what else they spend their money on. You have to coerce them to spend their money with you (more about that in the rest of this book).

No matter the type of competitor, find out how much your competition is charging and then the exact product or service for which it charges that price. Look for other pricing clues. Does the competitor have a trial offer? A minimum order or length of subscription? This process sounds like a great deal of work because it is. Nothing comes easy, and don't believe anyone who tells you otherwise.

As best you can, try to determine whether your competitor is successful at what it's doing. Read the online profile of the company's owners and see whether they still have real jobs. That's one sure sign that the online business isn't making enough for its owners to be financially independent.

Subscribe to your competitors' mailing lists. Place an order online with them. I order my competitors' products all the time. I often call their toll-free numbers to get the inside scoop on new products and ventures they have coming down the pike. You want to know as much as possible about your competitors so that you can beat them. Think of it as a game. Knowledge is power, and you will learn more about how to use it throughout this book.

While you're snooping, write down in your Vision for a Mission book (refer to Chapter 4) what's good and what's bad about the whole experience. The idea is not to be a total copycat when you create your online business (you can get into legal trouble that way). You have to make your online business better — so much better, in fact, that no similarity exists between the two. Give the bad an overhaul, or don't use it at all.

The important thing to remember is that you don't necessarily have to offer absolutely the lowest prices in cyberspace. Just as in the real world, cybershoppers take into consideration such factors as service and convenience. You do have to at least be in the same ballpark with your would-be rivals, however.

If you want to see big-time rivals competing in full online color, sign on to America Online and use the keyword MUSIC, as shown in Figure 7-8. You can go to specific forums for record labels, music television stations, music news wires, magazines, and, of course, online music stores. You can also find links to Internet World Wide Web music sites.

Figure 7-8: Music-oriented sites are in head-to-head competition online.

Here's my customer story. I wanted to buy a particular CD, but I couldn't remember the group who sang it and I knew only parts of the song. Naturally (and probably much like you would do), I called a local music store. I posed my query to the clerk, who responded, "Like, hey, dude, I was born in the '70s. I can't help you." Gee, thanks. I called another store. "I don't know. I just work here." Yes, and that's precisely why I called you. At that point, I did what I should have done in the first place. I put away the yellow pages and signed on to America Online.

I bypassed the Grateful Dead forum and entered the Blockbuster Music store. I thought that the Cowboy Junkies may have sung the song I was looking for. Scrolling through the *C*s, I found that group's listings. (After you locate an artist or group, you can see different album covers, look at the song titles, and, best of all, sample the album's music.)

In the music forum, you can download a 20- to 30-second sample of a few songs from an album. This way, you can try before you buy as well as verify that it's the song you're looking for. It's not hard to do: You simply point and click on the music sound clip you want and watch the file be transferred from America Online to your PC or Mac.

After downloading a few music sound bytes, however, I realized that the Cowboy Junkies wasn't the group I wanted. To my surprise, the Blockbuster store had no way to search for a particular song or artist. Shame on them.

I then entered the online Tower Records store and found the Tower Tune Finder. It lets you search for music by category, artist, record label, album title, or words in a song title. I typed a few words of the song that I could hear playing in my head. In a few seconds, the listing appeared on my screen. Success!

Unlike the Blockbuster store, Tower had no album covers or sound samples — just a dialog box with information about when the album was released and a listing of the songs on the album. I could buy the album online on either CD (for $9.99) or cassette (for $4.44), plus shipping and handling.

So at least two major music companies are online, and both have their good and bad sides. Your competition, if you have any, will have good and bad sides too. It's up to you to figure them out and invest some time researching what your new cyber-business should offer. If you ever listen to my talk show and hear the 1989 tune "The Future's So Bright, I Gotta Wear Shades" by Timbuk3, you will know where it came from (the online Tower Records store).

Part III

Commercial Online Services and the Internet

Marketing Your Product or Service on the Largest Commercial Online Service

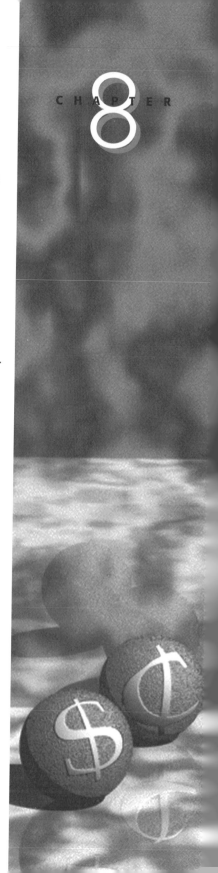

It's 7 o'clock Saturday morning. In 6 ½ minutes and one more cup of coffee, I will be on the air from coast to coast in the United States and throughout other countries. Closing the door to the studio in which I will sit for the next two hours, I hear the sweet refrain of the show's screener: "The Kim Komando Show. Please hold." "The Kim Komando Show. Please hold." "The Kim Komando Show. Please hold." "Thanks for holding. What city are you calling from? Your age? What's your question for Kim this morning?"

A 67-year-old woman from Augusta, Georgia, wants to know how to set up her business on the Web. A 13-year-old boy in Seattle, Washington, asks what it takes to sell Internet access. A 38-year-old former operating room nurse in Los Angeles seeks my opinion on the possibility of making money with a medical-expert witness-referral business on the Internet. A 42-year-old computer-repair technician in Charleston, South Carolina, wonders whether it's worth the time and money to learn how to fix Internet servers.

I can help ease Windows 95 challenges with simple answers, solve the debate over buying a Mac or a PC, tell parents how to keep their kids away from the smut that's available online, and even make computer widowers feel better. But it would be a real shocker to complete an episode of my syndicated talk-radio show and not have at least a handful of Internet-specific calls like the ones I just mentioned.

Callers who ask an Internet-related question or who call my show simply to discuss the topic are usually more computer literate than the average user. They are generally not afraid of technology and are aware of its far-reaching impact on their professional and personal lives. They have heard the Internet hype and understand that propaganda always has some element of truth.

With so much emphasis on the Internet, it's easy to overlook the commercial online services, such as America Online (AOL), Microsoft Network (MSN), and CompuServe, when you're looking for your own place in cyberspace. Although setting up shop on the Internet is usually less expensive and doesn't involve the corporate red tape associated with an online service, don't overlook the online services. In particular, don't skip past the largest online service, America Online (or AOL, as those of us in the industry call it). After all, that's exactly where I got my start — with Kim Komando's Komputer Klinic on AOL.

It was tough for a while to tell which company had the largest online service market. One claimed to have the most U.S. users, one claimed to have the most users worldwide, and another claimed to have the most installations in American homes. AOL, because of its wondrous marketing efforts, however (which I discussed earlier in this book — if you missed it, reread Parts I and II because there's no telling what else you missed), managed toward the end of 1995 and throughout 1996 to come out on top in all these categories. It's safe to say that the future will yield the same results too. AOL claimed, in fact, to be larger than Prodigy and CompuServe combined. The other two companies, of course, disputed these figures. Nonetheless, because AOL is the largest online service, it is a logical choice to illustrate the opportunities that are available through the online services. As I have said in various ways, if you want to play with the big dogs, you can't sit on the porch.

The Lowdown on America Online

So who is America Online? Straight from the horse's mouth (a recent AOL press release), "America Online is the nation's fastest-growing provider of online services with the most active subscriber base. AOL offers its subscribers a wide variety of services, including electronic mail, conferencing, software, computing support, interactive magazines and newspapers and online classes, as well as easy and affordable access to services of the Internet. Founded in 1985, AOL has established strategic alliances with dozens of companies, including Time-Warner, ABC, Knight-Ridder, Tribune, Hachette, IBM, and Apple Computer."

Okay, the company is not small potatoes. After you're the king of the hill, though, where do you go to keep growing?

You go conquer new lands, of course! To help accomplish this task, AOL has formed the New Ventures Division, whose purpose is to guide AOL into four new areas: International, Local Affiliates, Enterprise Solutions, and Software Products. In the following section, I take a closer look at what each one of these areas is all about, to help you decide where the opportunity for your cyberbusiness exists on AOL.

AOL at Home and Abroad

America Online. Get it? Until recently, AOL was available only in the United States. It only makes sense, therefore, that after AOL had established a solid foundation, expanding the service outside the United States was a top priority for the company.

In 1995 AOL announced a joint venture with Bertelsmann AG to establish an online presence in western Europe. It didn't take long for AOL to get up and running with separate content in the United Kingdom, France, and Japan. AOL is also now available in Canada, with content aimed specifically at Canadian members. AOL is increasingly getting into target marketing, which, as you already know, is crucial to online business success.

The goal is to make each country's version of AOL seem indigenous to that country while offering all members, no matter where they call home, access to the entire content of AOL. It's incredible: AOL continues to establish service in each country individually and then interconnects them.

From sea to shining sea, AOL looks the same

If you have ever been on AOL and used its Web browser, you have an idea of how this process works. A member in France, for example, connects to the French version of AOL, but he can switch over to the German version, for example, in much the same way that current AOL users switch over to the Web browser (see Figure 8-1).

Use the keyword INTERNATIONAL to check out the AOL international offerings, as shown in Figure 8-2. (Some computer things make total sense.) This keyword takes you to the International Channel, where you can find the latest news and information about other countries as well as Web links to other countries. At the time this book was written, Canada, Germany, Japan, France, and Great Britain had areas. You should note that all the information AOL presents in these areas is in English. This service has no native-language content (yet, anyway).

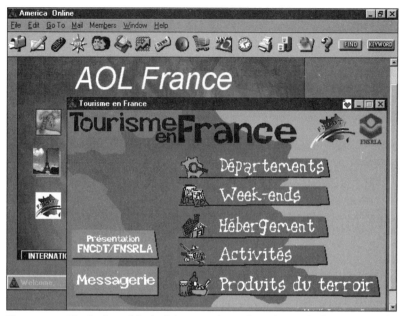

Figure 8-1: The look and feel of the French version of AOL is the same as the American version.

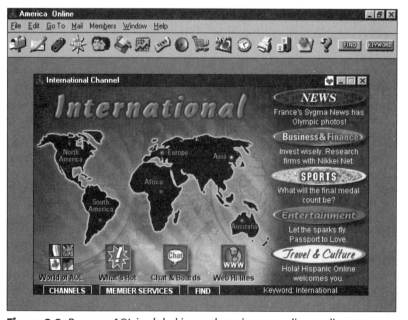

Figure 8-2: Because AOL is global in reach, so is your online audience.

Use the keyword INTERNATIONAL CAFE, and you're off to the International Cafe (not to be confused with the International Channel). The Cafe is a collection of foreign-language message boards and live chat areas (see Figure 8-3). You have the opportunity to communicate with speakers of Spanish, French, German, Italian, and Japanese in their native languages. You don't have to know the language — but it does help.

Figure 8-3: On AOL, you can chat, leave messages, and interact with people from all around the globe in their native tongue.

The International Cafe message boards (see Figure 8-4) are a great place to get insider marketing information for either your online or offline business. In the Spanish area, for example, one AOL member asked: "We want to use an iguana as a symbol for a children's health service in Latin American countries. Is there anything about an iguana symbol that might clash with language, religious, or cultural beliefs?" It's a great question to ask before spending any time on marketing efforts.

Among the numerous responses the member got was this one: "Depends on what it's to symbolize. Would you use a chicken for the same thing? Reason I mention it is that we used to eat iguanas; kept them tied up in the yard until they were butchered for food." In other words, find a new symbol.

Figure 8-4: The message boards in the International Cafe are a great source of country-specific information.

Think about it. The AOL member who asked the question could have spent hours researching the answer or paid an advertising and marketing company thousands to look into it. Instead, the answer appeared online for free!

Note

In addition to accessing country-specific offerings, you can access the entire content of AOL from several countries, including Armenia, Bermuda, Brazil, Bulgaria, Chile, Colombia, the Czech Republic, Greece, Italy, Lithuania, Malaysia, Mexico, New Zealand, the Philippines, Poland, Russia, Taiwan, and a slew of others. When you operate a cyberbusiness, you must remember that the world is truly getting smaller.

Home sweet home for AOL: America

As for selling any of your products internationally, remember that the bulk of your customers on AOL are, for now, from the United States. During the first quarter of 1996, for example, the AOL Komputer Klinic forum received 99.6 percent of its visitors from the United States and 0.4 percent from other countries. That's a small percentage of international visitors. That number was just 0.1 percent during the last quarter of 1995, however, so the international audience is, clearly, increasing steadily in tune with AOL expanding its global reach.

Your cyberbusiness, however, might just have something that sells better in the international marketplace than my computer-training products do. I just can't imagine what that product or service might be, unless you're in the blue-jeans recycling business. If you are, expect your foreign traffic to increase, but only if you promote your area properly online and offline.

The Regional Slant: Digital Cities

AOL initially put daily newspapers from throughout the country online, right there front and center for every member to see. People could read their hometown news online and also check out other newspapers. What a great idea!

Suppose that *The Orlando Sentinel* front-page story is an exclusive interview with the mayor of Orlando, Florida. The mayor wants additional taxes to pay for more freeways going in and out of Walt Disney World. I sign on to AOL and see the promotional text "Orlando Mayor Taxes Residents to Pay for Mickey's Freeways! Click here for more!"

I don't mean to be rude, but I really don't care about what the mayor of Orlando does. (I live in Arizona.) It doesn't affect my life that Orlando's taxes might increase. Even though I like Mickey Mouse, I'm still not going to click that button.

AOL forgot the cardinal rule of marketing: Present the right information to the right people at the right time.

The company moved quickly to change this situation, by developing a program called Digital City. This online area centers on one particular city. When you use the keyword DIGITAL CITY, you see a map of the United States divided into seven regions: Northwest, West, Midwest, Southwest, Northeast, Mid-Atlantic, and South, as shown in Figure 8-5. Click on the West region, for example, and you're presented with a list of cities that includes San Francisco, San José, Los Angeles, San Diego, and Phoenix. Click on a city, and you're whisked to an area that seamlessly provides a mix of AOL-developed content and World Wide Web links that relate to that particular city. Clicking on a Web link automatically switches you to the AOL browser and brings up that Web page.

The AOL goal is to build a sense of local community in addition to areas for local commerce and connectivity in major cities across the country. The content for each city-area includes news, entertainment, sports, and information about local events. You then have an opportunity to target-market specific geographic areas in which your customers might be located.

Figure 8-5: Digital City provides AOL with a way to target interests for its members by geographic area.

AOL says that the Digital City environment is ideal for commerce. Specifically, the Marketplace section provides an online area in which members can do business with local businesses. Washington, D.C., was one of the first Digital Cities to appear on AOL (see Figure 8-6). (Test sites should be up and running by the time you read this book.) I haven't yet seen any pricing information for participation at the local level, but it will be interesting to see how this area stacks up pricewise against the World Wide Web for local and regional businesses.

Each city has areas in which you can post your own free classified advertising and read ads other people have posted. You can shop in specific areas for automobiles, general merchandise, and employment opportunities. The Digital City concept is just getting off the ground, but it should prove to be a great way to combine the power of online advertising with the focus of regional print advertising. Because the Digital City concept is new, it provides an opportunity for your cyberbusiness.

This alphabetical list shows the 20 geographic areas of highest AOL member concentration (if you live in one of these areas, you may want to give some thought to the Digital City program):

Atlanta	Miami/Fort Lauderdale
Boston	Minneapolis/St. Paul
Chicago	New York
Cleveland	Philadelphia
Dallas/Fort Worth	Portland
Denver	Sacramento
Detroit	San Diego
Hartford/New Haven	San Francisco/San José/Oakland
Houston	Seattle/Tacoma
Los Angeles	Washington, DC

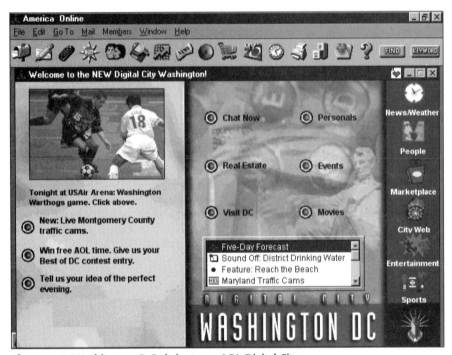

Figure 8-6: Washington, D.C., is just one AOL Digital City.

AOL and Business

With the CompuServe focus on the business world, its peak hours of use are during the day. Because AOL is targeted more toward consumers, however, it gets its heaviest use during evening hours. For this reason, plenty of AOL resources go largely unused during regular business hours. The purpose of the AOL Enterprise Solutions group is to convert those idle resources into productive resources by developing more extensive services for business users. Think of your local movie theater's Tuesday discount night, a day of the week when people generally don't go out, and you get the winning idea behind Enterprise Solutions (and virtually every video store in existence).

With all that money and all those computer resources, it only makes sense for AOL to get into the software business. And that's exactly what it's doing through, for example, NaviSoft, a company AOL acquired in 1995. The pre-AOL NaviSoft won the prestigious 1995 Seybold Award for Product Excellence for its World Wide Web-related software. The NaviSoft product line provides personal publishing capabilities to the AOL and Global Network Navigator brands. By leveraging its membership base, technology platform, and AOLnet (AOL's own telecommunications network), the AOL goal is to create a third-party developers' community.

So What?

Maybe you're thinking, "So what? Why should I care about what AOL has done in the past and has planned for the future?"

Suppose that you go on a blind date (don't you just hate those?) and the person is what your friends said he or she was — both pleasant and attractive. Is that enough to establish a long-term relationship? Not unless you are totally shallow. You would, understandably, want to know more. Is your date working toward a Ph.D., or did he or she just get fired from a floor-mopping job at Burger King? Is your date fit and healthy — or have some sort of incurable disease? Is the person financially sound? Did he or she just file bankruptcy? Is the person resigned to a lifelong commitment of psychotherapy? Does your potential mate smoke or take drugs? Is the person addicted to The Kim Komando talk-radio show? (That last one isn't a bad thing, but do you see my point?)

Tip

Before you make a potentially major commitment, such as which (if any) online service to do business on, you have to know more than just what that service can do for you. You have to know what it plans to do to keep its business viable so that you have the best chances of keeping *your* business viable. Simply stated, you have to move with the tide.

In addition, in the example of AOL, knowing where it's going helps you to see some potential opportunities that may be waiting down the road. Set up shop on AOL, for example, and you know that you can soon offer your goods and services to a large international marketplace. At the other end of the spectrum, it's now possible to put a regional spin on your AOL content.

I have one more point in all this discussion: By knowing as much as you can about any online service with which you may want to do business, whether it's AOL or one of the other giants, you get a clear idea of exactly who the company is trying to target as its ideal audience. Marketing on AOL is different from marketing on the Internet and the World Wide Web, where it's pretty much every person for himself (and, increasingly, herself). By now you should know who your target market is, so it shouldn't be much of a stretch to compare your target market with the target market of any particular online service. If it turns out that your target market and the target market of the online service make a good match, you have a much better chance of success with an online service.

Oh, No — More Demographics!

Do you remember reading about how important demographics are? I know that they're not the most exciting topic on the planet, but they are important. Eat your vegetables, and you will grow up to be big and strong. Know your demographics so that your financial statement can grow big and strong. This section looks at some information taken from a telephone survey to see what AOL has to offer in the area of demographics.

For starters, about 80 percent of all AOL users are male. I guess that it's safe to assume that the other 20 percent are female, but these days, you never know.

In any given month, a full 20 percent of members don't even log on one time. When you look at the total number of AOL members, therefore, you can automatically lop off 20 percent to come up with the number of people who have some sort of opportunity to see your stuff. Of the group that actually connects to the service, only 40 percent or so are online for more than five hours in a month. The other 60 percent is probably just checking for e-mail, and there's not much of a chance that they will see your content either. Don't be discouraged, though. With millions of members, even these numbers can be attractive to the right business.

One thing AOL offers that most of the other online services don't is the ability to set up multiple users under one account. You can log on under one name; your spouse can log on under another; and your child yet another — but all online time is billed to the same account. The survey showed that about 40 percent of primary members had secondary members in their households — your potential audience goes up again.

Compared to national averages, AOL members aren't the marryin' kind. At roughly 63 percent, the percentage of married members is about 10 points below the rest of the population. The good news, however, is that they seem to have plenty of money. More than half the AOL households report incomes between $50,000 and $125,000. That's double the national average! And that's lots more money to spend on your products and services. In addition, less than 10 percent are in the range of less than $25,000 per year.

As you can see in Table 8-1, the age breakdown on AOL runs close to the national population average until you get to the over-55 group.

Table 8-1	The AOL Age Breakdown	
Age	**AOL members**	**U.S. population**
18 to 34	37 percent	41 percent
35 to 44	34 percent	22 percent
45 to 54	21 percent	14 percent
Over 55	8 percent	23 percent

Here's the rundown on home ownership, education, and employment. About 70 percent of AOL members own their homes, compared with about 65 percent nationwide (no big difference there). Most have attended college, however, and two-thirds have received some sort of degree; the national figure is only 20 percent. Eighty percent of primary members are employed full time, as are 66 percent of their spouses. That's a large number of DINKs (*double income, no kids*) and DICKs *double income, couple of kids*). Breaking down that number even more, 46 percent hold executive/management or professional positions, 16 percent have technical careers, 9 percent are involved in sales, and 22 percent are self-employed.

One category you should spend some time reviewing is computing. On AOL, 75 percent of users are using Windows, 22 percent are Mac users, and another 3 percent consider themselves DOS users. Twenty-two percent for Mac users is higher than the market average of about 10 percent, but, because AOL started out as a Mac-oriented service, this number isn't too surprising.

A hefty 28 percent of all AOL members have two computers in their home. Sixty-three percent have 9,600 bps modems or higher, and 48 percent use 14,400 bps modems. Overall, 66 percent of AOL members own a CD-ROM drive, with a slightly higher number (71 percent) for those who indicate that they also have children. Of those CD-ROM owners, more than half have owned a CD-ROM drive longer than one year. When you add up all the numbers, it seems as though AOL has some sophisticated users.

Don't forget — I'm just using AOL as an example because I have plenty of experience on that service. This is the type of information you want to get from any online service, however, before you consider setting up shop on it.

Tip

A good way to get recent demographics from any online service is to call and ask for an advertising *media package*. A good way to get your hands on one of these packages is to make a phone call to the service's advertising department. Pretend that you want to buy advertising on the service or within one of the service's printed publications. Heck, you may even want to buy advertising after studying the information the online service sends you. Inside a media package, you get the service's marketing propaganda, including all the recent demographics you need in order to decide whether your potential customers match the online service's customers.

Getting a Piece of the Online Action

So what kind of deals does AOL strike? Let's look at the Greenhouse program. As a small start-up, the only place you can go on AOL to get a named forum — unless you own Times Mirror or just won at PowerBall — is the Greenhouse (see Figure 8-7).

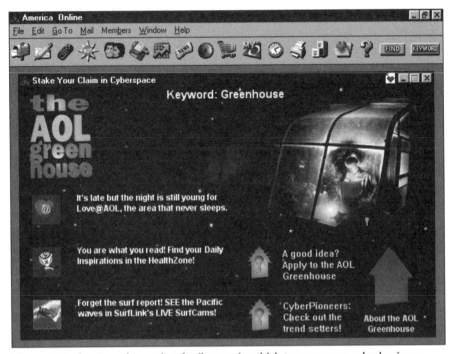

Figure 8-7: The Greenhouse is a fertile area in which to grow your cyberbusiness.

The Greenhouse program was designed specifically for entrepreneurs such as yourself to create online content and new interactive services. AOL chooses, from submitted applications, a handful of "creative, entrepreneurial online crusaders" to offer new services tailored specifically for AOL and the Internet. In exchange, the company provides those crusaders with access to several million AOL members, online promotion, participation in the AOL Web site and other Internet initiatives, production support, and maybe even seed money to help you get started.

"We're excited about this program," says Ted Leonsis, the president of AOL Services Company. "The magic of this medium is the ability for entrepreneurs to create compelling new content and help build an interactive community. We are looking forward to working with a new breed of content and service providers to provide fun, creative and, most of all, compelling content to our member community."

As you may have guessed from its name, the purpose of Greenhouse is to offer a "fertile proving ground for sowing the seeds of innovative new content that we recognize often comes from the small, unknown entities." If you think that you might have what it takes to be a Greenhouse crusader, take this short test, based on information from AOL:

- ✦ Are you a true crusader — dynamic, passionate, and creative?

- ✦ Does new media run through your veins?

- ✦ Do you live online?

- ✦ Do you know what works online and (more important) what doesn't?

- ✦ Are you way ahead of the technology curve?

- ✦ Do you have a unique point of view that you can communicate with a mixture of power, elegance, and humor?

- ✦ Are you an expert in the needs, expectations, and mind-set of a specific segment of people, and can you deliver exactly what those people are looking for?

- ✦ Are you an entrepreneur who can build a successful enterprise, branching across multiple media and generating multiple income streams?

If you answered yes to all these questions, AOL wants to hear from you. To learn more about Greenhouse and download an application form, just connect to AOL and use the keyword GREENHOUSE.

Here are some examples of folks who have already set up shop in the Greenhouse:

- ✦ **ParaScope:** The latest in conspiracy theory, UFOs, paranormal experiences, and other such stuff (see Figure 8-8)

- ✦ **SurfLink:** For avid surfers and fans of other extreme sports

- ✦ **Follywood:** A movie-oriented area with a wacky and irreverent slant

- ✦ **KidzBiz:** An interactive activity center for children of all ages, as shown in Figure 8-9.

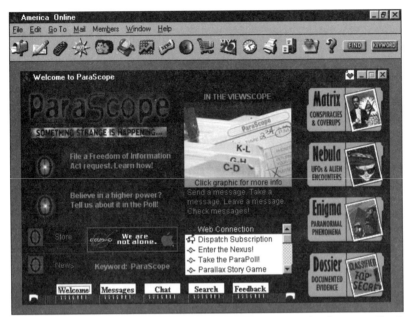

Figure 8-8: One cyber-entrepreneur got AOL to help him develop an online business that focuses on UFOs and the paranormal.

Figure 8-9: Online businesses targeted toward children can make you a winner.

Building Your Area (or, Don't Forget the Hard Work)

All this sounds great. But how do you learn to build your own area on AOL? The answer is that AOL teaches you, for free.

After you get the green light from AOL, you follow a standard set of steps to the final launch of your new area. The amount of time required for each step varies depending on the individual area's requirements. You usually can be online within 45 days after you and AOL agree on an acceptable format and supply the company with the necessary artwork. Here's the way it goes down:

1. AOL receives a mock-up of your area. You don't have to provide a whiz-bang computer-generated mock-up. A simple pencil drawing along with a flowchart work just fine.

2. AOL and you agree on a format (the look and feel of your area).

3. AOL begins making your artwork based on any artwork it receives from you, such as your logos or branding.

Note

AOL has some specific requirements for artwork. Some are aesthetic and subject to interpretation; others are technical and completely inflexible. Believe me — it frowns on content providers who don't get it right the first time.

4. Your responsibilities and training requirements are refined and put on a schedule. You or someone in your company goes to AOL University to learn about forum management, programming, and promotions.

5. The AOL art department begins to convert all art to the online art format.

6. If it hasn't already done so, AOL assigns a producer, who is your point of contact.

Note

A good producer is crucial to your success. Luckily, AOL hires talented people, many of whom have worked in some aspect of the entertainment industry.

7. Format deadlines are finalized and an official launch date set.

8. Both you and the AOL folks begin a full-blown effort to produce forms, message boards, libraries, shopping, and other areas that comprise your online forum.

9. Your test-only menu is placed in a hidden area for you to view. Adjustments are made to the area as the tweaking begins.

10. Both you and AOL review converted artwork, and the artwork is placed in the online form that will comprise your forum.

11. Testing of everything is completed.

12. Launch. Have a party. Send out your press releases. Invite your friends. And say good-bye to your free time! It's time to make lots of money.

You may be thinking that this process looks like a hassle. After all, you could set up a page on the World Wide Web in a day or two. Although you can set up a page that quickly, I guarantee that it's impossible to set up a *good* page in anything less than a few weeks or one month. That estimate assumes a minimum amount of sophistication and a maximum amount of expertise. No matter which way you go, getting your business online takes plenty of dedication and work.

Spreading the Good Word about Your Online Area

Having a great area on AOL doesn't do you much good if no one knows about it. After you establish an official presence on AOL, you can promote your new business in plenty of ways. You may want to consider promoting it, for example, through live, online events in which you "chat" with AOL members from around the country and the world.

Tip

Live events are popular with members. They drive members into your area and sometimes deliver the extra benefit of press coverage and the resulting high-visibility promotion. But the success of a live event depends on online promotion. Sometimes AOL supplements online promotion with off-screen press efforts to build large audiences for special events. My weekly appearance is on the news wire, for example. I try to make live appearances on AOL at least twice a month for one reason: My online traffic increases tenfold. AOL promotes online appearances in its Center Stage area (keyword AOL LIVE), as shown in Figure 8-10.

If you're an AOL member, chances are that you have seen a plug for my Komputer Klinic on the In the Spotlight screen. This screen is the first one you see when you log on. It's a great way to put your entire area just one mouse click away from many, many members. In addition to promoting magazines, chats, contests, and other areas, AOL uses this screen to present members with all sorts of important information. Members then have a good reason to take note of what's on this screen every time they connect.

AOL and all the online services offer many more ways to promote your online business, from listings in special directories to advertising in members-only magazines. There's no shortage of ways to promote your business. Keep in mind, however, that some of these methods cost money — money you may or may not have (yet, anyway).

The information in this section is an example of how just one commercial online service handles its content. Each service has different opportunities and pricing structures. CompuServe, for example, offers a product "mall" in which you can set up shop. Because this option is quite expensive, however (a minimum of $50,000 plus 2 percent of your sales each year), you must do well online to make this option worthwhile. Wait on this one until you get plenty of sales rolling in.

Figure 8-10: Live chats are a wonderful promotional vehicle no matter where your cyberbusiness is located.

The thing to remember is that in order to be a success with your own area on a commercial online service, you must be willing and able to make a substantial commitment of both time and money. Most important of all, however, is that you must have an *outstanding* product.

The Low-Cost Alternative: Online Classified Advertising

If building an online area doesn't appeal to you, you have an alternative: Go the classified-advertising route. Classified advertisements on an online service work in much the same way as the classifieds in any major newspaper.

The key difference between AOL and most anywhere else you can run a classified ad is that AOL lets you run them for free. (I like that!)

AOL offers the following classified areas:

✦ Business

✦ Collectibles

✦ Computers

✦ Employment

✦ General

✦ Habitats

✦ People

✦ Vehicles

Figure 8-11 shows the AOL classified-ads area.

If you had $950 lying around, for example, you could have taken advantage of this recent posting:

> For sale: Just inspected and serviced Mitsubishi 21-inch SVGA color monitor (with warranty). If you have always wanted a huge color monitor, this is for you. Will deliver in Washington metro area.

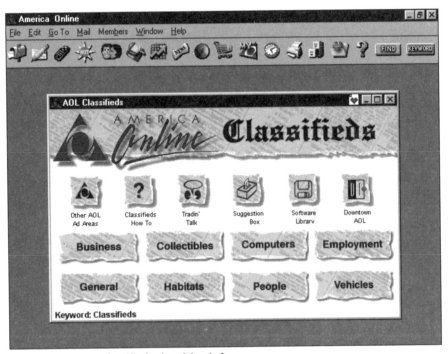

Figure 8-11: AOL classified advertising is free.

Looking for wheels? You could have jumped on this deal:

> 1985 Cadillac Seville. Yellow with brown "convertible look" top and brown-and-chrome wheel on trunk. This car is sharp! Interior in excellent condition; runs great; all options, including leather. Florida car with no rust. 114K miles, $3900. Must sell now.

Is your credit less than perfect? One classified advertisement on AOL begins this way:

> Bad credit? Can't get a credit card? Turned down for a loan? Gone bankrupt?

Warning

A word to the wise: Be careful when you respond to any classified advertisement. Many get-rich-quick scams and blind ads are purely bogus. If it sounds too good to be true, remember that it probably is.

Suppose that you're selling something that doesn't happen to fit neatly into any of these categories. That's okay. Keep in mind that several AOL forums also accept relevant classified advertising.

Warning

Before posting your message, always double-check to see whether the online classified advertising (outside the main AOL Classifieds area) is free. The *Chicago Tribune,* for example, puts its newspaper's classified section online, as shown in Figure 8-12. If you want your advertisement to appear online, you first must buy an advertisement in the *Tribune.*

Some of the following forums may be relevant to your online classified-advertising strategy:

✦ Aviation

✦ *Chicago Tribune*

✦ Christianity Online

✦ Downtown AOL

✦ Geoworks

✦ Military City Online

✦ *New York Times*

✦ Real Estate Center

✦ Photography Club

✦ *San José Mercury News*

✦ TPR Student Access Online

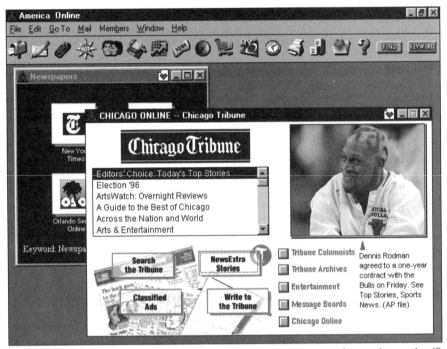

Figure 8-12: Many online areas, such as the `Chicago Tribune`, make you buy a classified advertisement in the newspaper before it automatically appears online.

Regardless of whether an ad is free, you cannot just post anything you want. You have to follow a couple of guidelines:

✦ Post an ad only in the appropriate folder. It's a good bet that just about anyone on AOL, for example, has some interest in computer equipment. But that doesn't mean that you can put an ad for computer equipment anywhere you want. It has to go in the computer section.

   Believe me, the AOL folks and forum managers take this stuff seriously. A while back, an employee of ours apparently posted an ad in the wrong spot. The nasty-gram that was posted in return said, in part, "As you may not be aware of the protocol of Classifieds Online, I'm sending you this courtesy note. Ads that are posted in the wrong folder are considered off-topic and are reluctantly deleted to maintain folder topic integrity."

✦ A member may post a maximum of three different ads for three different items per folder per day in all folders in the AOL classifieds.

✦ Post to the ad folders only ads offering merchandise or services wanted or for sale. Non-ad discussion postings should be posted to the Tradin' Talk area, which has been designated for that purpose.

Exactly how long your classified ad stays posted depends entirely on how much activity is in the folder in which you posted it. The reason is that the system is set up to accept a maximum of only 500 postings per area.

Every morning, all except the last 300 postings are dropped off, to make room for as many as 200 more that day. In low-traffic areas, therefore, your ad might remain posted for weeks. AOL estimates that if you post in a busy area, however, your ad probably will show up for two to four days. You have no guarantees, of course.

Automatic deletion of advertisements is a major drawback compared with paid classified advertising. If you post in a popular area, your message may be dropped off before many people on AOL have a chance to see it.

In contrast, on CompuServe you pay a small fee for classified advertising (which is simply added to your monthly bill), but your ad is guaranteed to run for a specific period. It all boils down to the old adage "you get what you pay for." Figure 8-13 shows the CompuServe Classified Advertising area (GO CLASSIFIEDS).

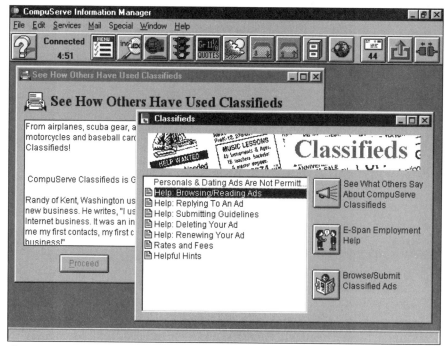

Figure 8-13: CompuServe offers its members an area in which to post classified advertising, but, unlike the AOL classified area, it's not free.

The cost of listing an ad in the CompuServe classifieds area depends on the length of the message and how long you want to post it (note the two-line minimum per ad):

+ **7 days (1 week):** $1.00 per line
+ **14 days (2 weeks):** $1.50 per line
+ **56 days (8 weeks):** $5.20 per line
+ **182 days (26 weeks):** $14.30 per line

In Chapter 13, I discuss more thoroughly the ups and downs of classified advertising.

The Bottom Line

Is a commercial online service the right place for your cyberbusiness? Only you can say for sure. If you think that you have a killer product or service that millions of people just can't live without, the answer may be yes. If you need or want help in setting up your site and are willing to trade certain restrictions and additional promotion for it, the commercial online services provide demographically appealing audiences. Rather than let your site get lost in a crowd on the Internet, an online service (although it delivers fewer customers) can help your site stand out. For more information, I suggest that you contact your online service of choice directly. Don't get discouraged if you get the runaround: You're dealing with big companies, and persistence pays off. I'm evidence of that.

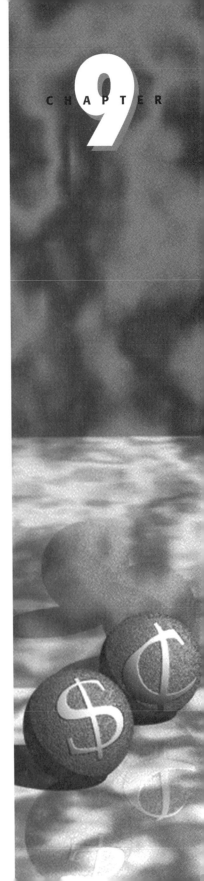

The Fast Track to Internet Success

Commercial online services can offer a great opportunity for the right person with the right product. You're probably tired of hearing this, but I *did* get my start on America Online, and I have no regrets. On the other hand, I think that you can tell from reading Chapter 8 that the commercial online services are not for everyone (just as I wouldn't be caught dead in a pair of army boots).

If you think that you fall into that "not for me" category, you're probably saying to yourself, "What about the Internet?" Even if you do set up shop on a commercial online service, does it mean that you should bypass establishing a presence on the Internet? Absolutely not. The more places customers have access to your products or services, the more potential sales you have.

So what about the Internet? Doing business on the Internet is different from doing business on America Online or CompuServe in many ways — some better, some worse. First, let's look at some of the advantages because, as some people in my life often ask, "What color is the sky in your world, Kim?" The answer: It's always blue.

Staking Your Claim

Like shopping for high fashions at a discount store, the Internet can be *extremely* attractive to businesses operating on a shoe-string budget. If you're clever enough to come up with a business you can operate exclusively through e-mail, such as the guy who came up with the "limerick of the day" I mention in Chapter 5, your online expenses may be next to nothing. Even if you decide to go all out and stake your claim on the World Wide Web, you can easily get away with less than a hundred dollars a month — as long as you're ready, willing, and able to take the "Home Improvement" route to Web design and do most of it yourself.

Because no one owns the Internet, no one can tell you what you can and cannot do — unless, of course, you break some sort of law. For the most part, though, you're free on the Internet to give your online presence exactly the look and feel you want. It is the ultimate entrepreneurial dream.

The Internet also offers a much larger audience (read that as "potential base of customers who have money to spend on your products or services") than do the commercial online services. The Internet population's numbers change faster than Dennis Rodman's hair color, but, as I write, more people have Internet accounts than are members of the top two online services combined.

In addition, all those America Online, CompuServe, Prodigy, and Microsoft Network members have access to the Internet. All those people can then spend their money in your cybershop. It's one gigantic market, and it's getting larger every single day.

Watching Out for Snakes before Setting Up Camp

The Internet sounds great, doesn't it? Not so fast, my friend. Although you may well end up doing business on the Internet, you still must be aware of the proverbial downside. What's the price (remember that word from Chapter 7?) for all these advantages?

For starters, remember that because commercial online services are multibillion-dollar businesses that depend on new members for continued growth, their reputation is important to them. If AOL gets a reputation for having too many busy signals or continually having certain services out of working order, cybersurfers will look elsewhere. In turn, the AOL bottom line will take a hit. The big online services have an *extremely* vested interest in keeping their systems, technical-support operations, and connections in tiptop shape — and they have the money to do it.

If you are setting up shop on the Internet, on the other hand, you probably connect to it through a local Internet service provider (ISP). I'm not trying to imply anything negative about local ISPs (some great ones are out there, and I have done business with some myself), but no matter whether an ISP's commitment to quality is as high as one of the commercial-service big guys, I can guarantee you that none of them has even close to the financial resources of one of those big guys.

If something goes wrong at your ISP in a major way, it could mean extended trouble for the company, and that translates into extended trouble for you. If your ISP forgets to pay its electric bill or its payment gets lost in the mail, for example, you will go ballistic when your customers cannot get to your Web page.

When you set up shop on an online service, your customers usually dial in to the system by using a dedicated phone number. (I say "usually" because you can also connect to some services via the Internet itself.) That means a direct link from the customer to your place of business.

When someone connects to your Internet site, however, and depending on the customer's physical proximity to your site, all the information that goes back and forth between you and your customer gets bounced through a few different computer systems along the way. If any sort of accident happens along the stretch of the information superhighway that connects you to a particular customer, you're out of luck until the problem is corrected. There's nothing much you or your ISP can do about it.

Warning

Whereas the goal of an online service is to provide you with a place in cyberspace to do business, the ISP's only major concern is to make sure that you have a connection to the Internet. Beyond that, you're pretty much on your own.

Whom do you call if all your graphics suddenly go to hell in a handbasket? What if you experience a security breach? Did you just discover that your design skills make a kitty litter package look like fine art? Interested in accepting credit cards? It's a snap when you're on an online service. The Internet is a whole different ball of wax, though. If you decide to "surf naked on the Internet," chances are that no one will be there to share your wave — or that no one will be close by to help when you wipe out.

Okay, I have given you fair and dutiful warning and have therefore fulfilled my obligation to you, my student. In English, that means that I hope I never have to say, "I told you so," but I just may have to anyway.

I'm sure that right now you're saying, "Yeah, right. I don't care what she says. I'm the super-mega-awesome Internet guru in my circle of friends, and I will do what I want. I *will* have my Web page up and making money in no time flat. I'll show her!"

Good for you. You should do what you want. I just want to help you do it as intelligently as possible. With that said, let me talk a little about the hot Internet topic for both today and tomorrow: the World Wide Web.

Webmastering 101

Later in this book, I go into more detail about how you can get absolutely the best performance from your Web site. For now, I just want to touch on some Web basics.

It has been said that the true power of the Web lies in the fact that it makes it easy and affordable for almost anyone to publish information to a global audience. It has also been said that that's the *worst* aspect of the Web. Greater access to the masses means loads of "not so hot" Web sites. The Web has done for electronic publishing what desktop publishing did for the printed page: Give everyone with a PC the idea that he's an instant graphic designer (even me, but I learned better).

Designing your site

In a cyberworld full of all these mediocre efforts, it's *very* important that your Web page stand out — in a good way, that is. If you have the skills to produce a top-notch Web page, more power to ya. If not, I urge you to hire someone who does. I think that my company has a great site at www.komando.com, but I'm not ashamed to admit that I didn't do a speck of the HTML coding.

Note

HTML, or *h*yper*t*ext *m*arkup *l*anguage, is the language of the Internet that sets up the way text and graphics appear on-screen. HTML, which is much like desktop publishing, isn't difficult to use. I did a few of the designs at the Komando Web site, but I owe it all to the expert designers I hired to do the job right and who responded to my subtle cracks of the whip.

Even if you hire a professional designer, you should still know some of the basics, just so that you can check a designer's work. The last thing you want is to spend your money on a Web page that doesn't work, for whatever reason.

Putting up a great Web site is a matter of walking a very fine line. On one side of the line, you want a site that is as attractive, interactive, and fun as possible. The simple truth, however, is that most people connect to your site by using a modem. Even the fastest modems on the market can seem sluggish if you try to stuff too many graphics and other elements on your Web page.

Maybe someday all of us will have in our homes and offices a high-speed T1 connection. With this type of connection, users can download, for example, a 2MB file in a few seconds rather than the ten minutes it takes using a 28.8 Kbps connection.

But you want to make money *now,* don't you? An experienced Web page designer can create a site that makes you say "Wow!" not only because it looks great but also because it doesn't take forever and a day to download each page.

If your entire Web site consists of one single page, coming up with a good design is as easy as coming up with a good design for a brochure or any other printed piece. The thing that sets the Web apart from any printed piece is *hyperlinks,* or the elements that enable you to jump from one information point to another with no stops between.

Organizing your site

Planning the way your information will be organized is even more important than having a nice-looking design. I know from talking to Web surfers around the country that they're more than willing to accept an average-looking site that's functional and easy to use. Yet many beginners all but overlook this area of Web development. In this process of *information mapping,* you simply figure out which information your customer is likely to need at any given point and then provide a hyperlink to that information right where she needs it.

Imagine that you're looking at a screenful of information about hang gliding. As you read through the information on-screen, you see a reference to the origins of hang gliding. You notice that the word *history* is displayed in a different color (it's a hyperlink). Because you have always wondered who first jumped off a cliff while clinging to an overgrown kite (oh, that brave pioneer), you place your mouse on the word *history* and click. In just a sec, you're connected to a computer that's sitting in Australia. (The different color is your clue that the word *history* is a launching pad.) In other words, despite not knowing how to get to the second computer, with a single point-and-click you have navigated halfway around the world and logged in to another computer system. The *USA Today* home page demonstrates information mapping at its finest, as shown in Figure 9-1.

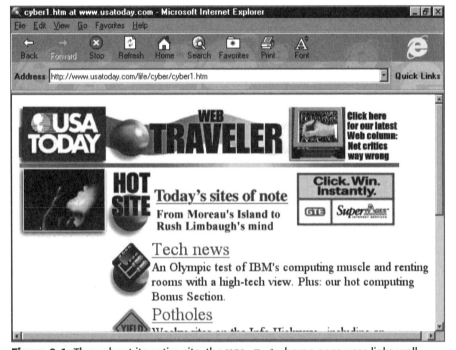

Figure 9-1: Throughout its entire site, the USA Today home page uses links well.

Again, you're walking a fine line. If you don't put enough hyperlinks on your Web pages, customers will give up because your site will be too difficult to navigate. On the other hand, if you add too many hyperlinks to your pages, customers are likely to become lost in your cybermaze and, again, give up because it's too confusing.

Tip

Remember that 99.9 percent of the general population is lazy. Rather than spend time learning, they take the easy road. The adventurous few give the learning process some time — they stumble and groan until they understand. More people, however, will leave your Web page and save face with their friends by telling them that nothing interested them. Word-of-mouth advertising will continue as they tell their friends, family members, business associates, and peers. You will have lost another customer and possibly more. This situation affects your earnings.

The best way to achieve balance when it comes to linking your pages is to provide only the hyperlinks that seem essential at any point — plus one more. That one extra link should take your customers to a complete, hyperlinked directory of your site, and that link should be on virtually every page of your site. Then, if your customers decide that they really want to leap from one side of your cyberstore to another, they can do it in just a couple of mouse clicks.

The most important thing to remember is that your customers are probably not much different from you. Do you like graphics that take two or three minutes to download? Do you want truckloads of bells and whistles that don't add anything except frustration to your online experience?

Snooping around for ideas

Tip

The best and easiest way to come up with great ideas for your site is to go surfin' yourself. Don't feel guilty about spending hours on the Internet looking around. You're working. See what works for *you* — and what doesn't. If you think that some feature is hot, chances are that your customers will too. If you come across what you think is the worst Web site in the history of computerdom, most of your customers are likely to agree on that as well.

Many self-appointed Internet Web-page rating organizations review sites, maintain top ten and bottom ten lists, and choose great sites of the day or week. Yahoo! does it; Magellan does it; *USA Today* does it; and the Microsoft Network does it. As you might expect, Kim Komando's Komputer Klinic does too. If you're new to the World Wide Web, these lists can be helpful. Use one of these sites to start your surfing. They can save you time by helping you differentiate the good from the bad and the ugly. Figure 9-2 shows a frequently updated page of picks from the Microsoft Network.

Tip

The great thing about checking out other sites — whether they're related to your business or not — is that you can see not only *what* they do but also *how* they do it: Just choose the View Source option from your Web browser menu bar, and you can see all the HTML code that makes up the page you're viewing. This slick trick is especially helpful if you are designing your own Web page. Figure 9-3 shows how easy it is to check out the HTML code behind a Web page.

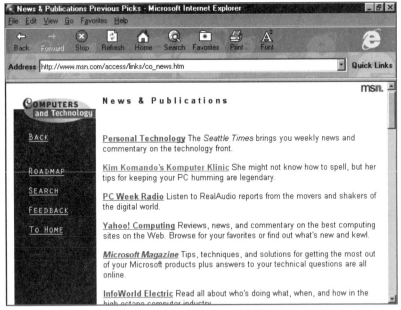

Figure 9-2: Save time finding great Internet Web sites by checking out online reviews, top ten lists, and picks of the day or week.

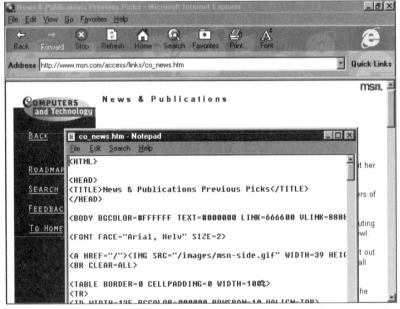

Figure 9-3: After you find a Web page you like, you can view the HTML code that made it possible.

Avoiding pitfalls

One other disadvantage of the Web that you have to be aware of is that not all Web browsers are created equal. HTML coding is standard, but the way your browser interprets that code is largely up to the programmer who designed your site. Although Web pages look somewhat similar from browser to browser, they do not look exactly the same. A Web page viewed on Netscape Navigator for Windows, in fact, doesn't even look exactly the same as the identical page viewed on the Mac version of Navigator.

So how do you handle this mishmash of Web browsers? Right now, it's all a numbers game. Netscape Navigator has roughly a 75 percent lock on the market. (Microsoft Internet Explorer is a distant second, and all others trail behind it.) If you develop a Web site that looks right when viewed through Navigator, therefore, you're guaranteed to please about 75 percent of your potential customers.

Just because a page looks different on different browsers doesn't mean that the page can't look good on all of them. As you develop your site, try viewing it using as many different browsers as you can get your hands on. (Most browsers are available for downloading.) That way, you can accommodate the widest possible customer base — which means, of course, more money in your pocket.

Ten Simple Steps to Determine Where to Begin

Setting up a Web site is certainly a little complicated, but that doesn't mean that it has to be difficult. The key is to develop (and follow, of course) a detailed plan from the beginning. To make the entire process as easy as possible, I offer you Komando's Ten Steps for Easy Web Site Development.

1. Figure out where you stand now

If you're lost, a map showing your destination can be a great help — but only if you already know where you are. If you don't have a clue where you're starting, the best map in the world doesn't do you much good. The same concept applies to developing a Web site. Before you get started putting together that awesome home page, you have to look at which resources you have available.

If you have an existing business that you're simply expanding on the Web, your first step is to look at which other printed information materials (brochures, flyers, catalogs, or whatever) you're already using.

At this point, you're looking for two things. First, from a design standpoint, the look of your Web site should be compatible with the look of your printed materials. The two elements don't have to be identical, but they should complement each other. Look for any distinctive design elements on your printed materials, and think about how you can port those elements to cyberspace.

The other reason to look at your printed materials is to find information that can be adapted to your Web site. Do you have a great brochure that tells everything there is to tell about your company? If so, it shouldn't take much effort to convert that information to your company FAQ (a file of *f*requently *a*sked *q*uestions, which I discuss later in this book). There's no sense in reinventing the wheel.

Now is also the time to decide how much of this information conversion you will do yourself. Plenty of excellent books on the market teach HTML coding, so you may be able to do much of it yourself. As I mentioned earlier in this chapter, however, you also must give some thought to those two important areas of graphic design and information mapping.

If these aren't your strong suits, do you have any friends who are skilled in these areas? I don't want you to become the person everyone avoids because you're always asking for favors, but most friends are usually willing to lend a *small* helping hand if you're reasonable about your expectations.

The bottom line for the first step is this: Decide which resources you have available *now*. Take out your Vision for a Mission book, and begin making lists (refer to Chapter 4). Write down everything you have in the resource department.

Tip

My company hires university students to help design and build Internet Web pages. Students will work for you for peanuts because you can help them get college credits for on-the-job training. Contact your local university, and tell the folks there that you have an opportunity for computer science majors to get real-life skills. You will be surprised by all the qualified applicants who walk through your door.

2. Decide where to stick your site

Setting up your own Web server (the computer that serves up your Web pages to the rest of the Internet) used to mean a major investment in a pricey UNIX-based computer system. Today, however, Web server software is available for your Mac or Windows-based computer. Dollarwise, you could probably get your own server up and running for just a few thousand dollars. But would you really want to?

Forget about dollars for a second. Instead, examine the amount of effort required to set up your own server. First, you must learn how to administer whichever software package you decide to use. The people who develop these packages try to make things as simple as possible, but there's no way around the fact that this stuff is complicated. If your financial survival depends on keeping your Web site in tip-top shape, you had better be an expert. (And that, I'm afraid, doesn't happen overnight.)

Just how do you propose to connect your server to the Internet? With high-speed T1 service priced at $1,000 or more per month, you probably will have to settle for something less. Whichever type of service you decide on, I can guarantee that working it all out with your phone company can turn more than a few hairs gray. Where will you put the whole thing, anyway? In your back bedroom?

Now compare all this trouble and expense to a connection through an Internet service provider. When you put your Web site up on an ISP server, all you have to worry about is that the ISP is a stable company. You maintain the files that make up your Web site, and all the computer geek stuff is handled by experts in the field — at a reasonable price. If you spend any more than a *maximum* of $100 a month for Internet service, you're probably getting ripped off. An ISP can offer you the use of a much better system than you can possibly afford yourself and save you plenty of both time and money in the process. Unless you're a propellerhead, an ISP is probably the way to go.

3. Find a good ISP

If you look through the yellow pages for a car dealer or a gardener, you're likely to see slogans such as "Serving Our Community More Than 20 Years" or "Established in 1962." If you're doing a blind search (in other words, you don't know anything about the potential vendors), statements such as these tell you that these places probably have a good track record, or else they wouldn't have lasted that long.

Unfortunately, you can't rely on these types of statements when you're looking for an ISP. Because all this Web stuff is still pretty new, an ISP that has been around even three or four years is considered an old-timer. Your best bet is to ask around and try to learn from the experience of others. The biggest isn't always the best — but the little guy may have to cut corners to keep afloat. The good news is that, as long as you use your own domain name (as described in the following list), you can change your ISP without changing your Web address.

No matter which ISP you choose, it should at least offer these basic services:

✦ **World Wide Web publishing:** Making this service available sounds like a no-brainer, and to a large extent it is. But just having the capability to serve up Web pages isn't enough; you have to consider how fast the ISP can serve up those pages. Any ISP worth considering has a T1 connection, and many established companies use T3 lines, which are even faster. The faster you can serve up your Web pages, the faster your customers can spend their money.

✦ **Domain name service:** A *domain name* is a company's Internet name, such as komando.com. The company's Web address incorporates that domain name into something like www.komando.com. When you set up your Web site, you can use the ISP domain name for your Web address, which makes it look something like www.komando.com/~users/yourcompany. Or you can spend about $100 and register your own domain name with *InterNIC,* the organization that keeps track of all domain names. After your domain name is registered, your Web address is simply www.yourcompany.com, which gives you these three advantages:

It looks like you have your own server. Image is always important, and no one ever has to know that you're using an ISP.

Your Web address never changes, no matter which ISP you use. If you get bad service from one, it's not all that tough to switch.

Your address is shorter and easier to remember. Compare `http://www.komando.com/~users/yourcompany` to `http://www.yourcompany.com`.

✦ **E-mail:** It goes without saying that you need at least one e-mail account to handle inquiries from, and messages to, your Web users.

✦ **FTP site:** *FTP* is short for File Transfer Protocol, the Internet service that lets you upload and download files from around the world. Your ISP should be able to provide you with a place to make downloadable files accessible to your customers. You may want to offer a complete catalog in Adobe Acrobat format, for example. Although this sort of FTP service isn't essential, you probably will find it handy as you explore new ways to enhance your site.

4. Register your domain name

The success of your online business probably won't be determined by whether you have your own domain name, but, as I mentioned in the preceding section, it's a good idea. The sooner, the better. Domain names are registered strictly on a first come, first served basis. One well-known computer columnist (no, not me) registered `mcdonalds.com` a while back and then used that address as a bargaining chip to get the company to donate to a favorite charity in exchange for giving McDonald's the right to use `mcdonalds.com`. The longer you wait, the more likely it is that someone else will register the name you want.

The good news is that registering your domain name doesn't cost that much. InterNIC charges $50 a year, and you pay for the first two years when you register ($100 up front). This registration process is something your ISP can handle for you, and many don't even charge you more than the $100 that goes to InterNIC. If anyone wants to charge you more than about $150, you're getting ripped off.

5. Determine your services

Knowing that you want a Web page is fine and good. Now you have to think about exactly what you will do with it. Will you sell products online or merely invite inquiries? Do you plan to take credit-card payments over the Web? Then you have to think about file encryption (which I describe in Chapter 10). Will you offer free information online? In which format?

Again, you can get plenty of good ideas just poking around other sites. Just to get you going in the right direction, it probably isn't a bad idea to start out at one of the major search engines. You can check sites, such as AltaVista, that attempt to index every single page on the World Wide Web, (go to `http://www.altavista.digital.com`). A search on AltaVista, however, usually produces many more "hits" than you would ever care to see (see Figure 9-4). Other search engines, such as Yahoo! (at `http://www.yahoo.com`), are more selective in their listings and are often more useful.

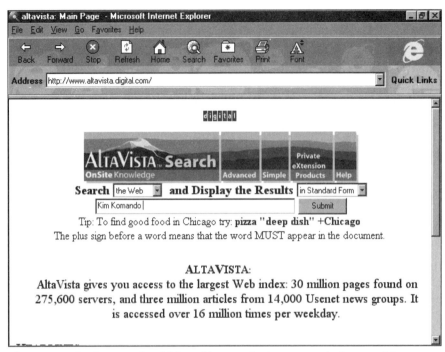

Figure 9-4: AltaVista searches high and low on the Internet and often provides more information than you would ever care to know.

6. Find some links

One of the best features of hyperlinks, as I mentioned earlier in this chapter, is that they enable you to provide your customers with services in addition to what's on your site. Suppose that you're selling sporting goods online. It's easy to add a few links that instantly transport your customers to the latest sports scores. With the right links, your site can become an information hub for your customers. While you're out there putting those search engines through their paces, make sure that you look for links that are appropriate for your target audience.

Warning

Be careful about just how you create those links. Adding a link to a particular page usually isn't a problem, but linking to a particular image or file on someone else's page can create legal problems. Providing a link to the page that contains the popular *Dilbert* comic strip, for example, is perfectly acceptable. One bright fellow, however, got the brilliant idea of embedding a link to just the Dilbert graphics file within his own Web page. This link gave users the impression that the comic strip was actually on his page. Dilbert's attorneys put an end to that in a hurry.

As you set up the links on your Web page, share and share alike. Find sites you like, and also find ones that offer you a reciprocal link (you link your Web page to another Web page, and it in turn links its page to yours). A reciprocal link is a terrific way to increase exposure and build traffic to your site.

7. Find a great designer

Unfortunately, finding a good Web designer can be even more difficult than finding a good ISP. Before 1994, most people probably thought that the World Wide Web was some old Japanese movie about giant spiders. Even the most experienced Web designers, therefore, have been plying their trade for only a couple of years — tops.

If you use a great designer, don't forget rule number one: Designers do their best work when you're specific about your needs. The less specific you are at the outset, the longer the process takes (and the more the price increases).

The thing to remember is that you don't want to be the guinea pig. Find someone who already has at least a few pages up on the Web. For every new Web site on the Internet, there has been at least a handful of problems that no one expected. An experienced Web designer knows how to deal with those problems.

Log on to a potential designer's Web site. (If he doesn't have his own site, what does that tell you?) From there, you should be able to connect to actual client sites.

This step is a good idea for two reasons. First, you get to experience firsthand the designer's work to see how it looks, feels, and functions in the real world. Second, whatever site you're looking at probably includes some way to contact its owner. Don't be afraid to send a short e-mail message to the company, asking whether it was satisfied with its designer. Even a lack of response may be a favorable commentary because most people are usually much more eager to share their bad customer-service stories than their good ones.

Finally, ask the Web designer which ISPs she prefers and why. Also make sure that the ISP supports all the latest programs, such as Java and QuickTime. CompuServe, for example, doesn't yet support CGI on its customers' home pages.

8. Prepare for what's to come

In some ways, publishing on the Web is similar to producing printed literature; in other ways, however, it can be very different. The process of producing a brochure, for example, has a beginning, a middle, and an end. After your printing house delivers your brochures, it's all over. On the other hand, Web publishing has a beginning — and then it just goes on forever! Your Web site is a living, breathing thing — virtually speaking, anyway. You must keep it updated with current information, new services, and site enhancements.

Who will be responsible for this ongoing maintenance? Depending on just how sophisticated your site is, you may be able to do it yourself or you may have to pay someone to do it for you. In any event, don't wait until after you have changed every price in your catalog to decide on these issues. Get your ducks lined up now.

9. Publish your Web site

After you finish developing your Web site, getting it online should be a piece of cake. Your ISP sets aside a special directory to hold your files. All you do is FTP (or upload) the files from your PC into the directory, and away you go. For more information about FTP, refer to the section "Find a good ISP," the third step in this process. You can update your site instantly by simply FTPing a new file to replace the outdated one.

Tip

The greatest Web site in the world doesn't do you much good, of course, if no one visits it. The most important part of *publishing* your Web site is *publicizing* it. Make sure that you register your Web address with as many Internet search engines as possible. Plenty of them are out there, and the more places a customer can find your name, the more likely she is to become your customer.

Tip

Rather than blow an entire afternoon tracking down different search engines, check out a site called Submit It (at `http://www.submit-it.com`). It lets you register with almost all the major search engines in one fell swoop (see Figure 9-5).

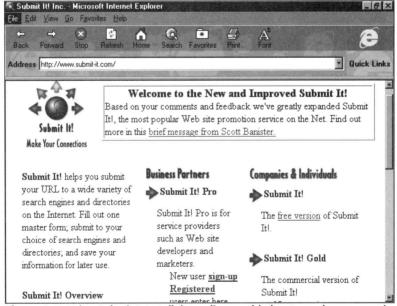

Figure 9-5: Using Submit It to tell the online world about your home page is a real time-saver, but you also have to tell the offline world.

Warning

One common misconception is that having your business listed on sites such as Yahoo! is all you have to do to promote your cyberbusiness. Wrong! Registering with search engines is just the beginning. Start putting your Web address on your stationery, business cards, and brochures. (After all, no one would ever search for Pet Rocks unless they knew that such a thing already existed.)

Any printed piece that has your address and phone number on it should also list your Web address. After all, you didn't go to all this trouble to have customers *not* find out about it. Let the world know about your Web site in any way you can. (Don't worry — I give you more in-depth scoop on publicity in Chapter 14.)

10. Keep the ball rolling

As I said in step 8, after you get your Web page up and running, it's a perpetual project. If you took my advice in the eighth step, in the section "Prepare for what's to come," you already know *how* to keep your site updated. The question now is *what* types of things you will use to update it.

First and foremost, you want to keep all the information about your company current. Have prices changed? Do you have a new toll-free number? Have you modified your return policy? Any information that affects your customers should be current at all times. This step shouldn't take a great deal of effort.

You should be on the lookout for any new services you can offer to your customers. These services can be as complicated as an MPEG video that visually demonstrates some important process or as simple as a new hyperlink to some interesting Web site you just discovered. Surveys show that Net surfers quickly become bored with stale sites and move on. In other words, bored customers are the same as no customers.

What Else Is on the Net?

Plenty of other services are on the Internet, including Gopher, listservs, and Usenet newsgroups. Gopher is basically an information-retrieval service. Before the World Wide Web exploded on the scene, many people around the world were trying to develop ways to create Gopher-based virtual shopping malls. When the Web showed up with its flashy graphics and multimedia potential, however, the business world quickly lost interest in poor ol' Gopher.

As for listservs and newsgroups, you can't really use these services to conduct business online. If you're careful, however, and listen to the advice I give you in Chapter 14, you can use these services to promote your business. The trick is to get your message out without offending anyone. For now, just be aware that I will help you utilize the resources on the Internet to their maximum potential.

A Few More Tips

In this section, I discuss a few more random tips to help ensure your success on the Internet.

Graphics: How much is too much?

There's no doubt about it: Graphics add pizzazz to your Web pages. Viewing even the most beautiful work of art, however, can be frustrating when the image takes two or three minutes to appear on-screen. Maybe someday all your customers will have lightning-fast, dedicated Internet connections, but for now you're stuck with customers who are probably using 14.4 Kbps and 28.8 Kbps modems. Keep that in mind when you're deciding how much graphical content to include on your Web page.

Tip

One thing you must realize is that the resolution on your monitor (or anyone else's, for that matter) is 72 dpi, or *dots per inch*. If you're creating a graphic element for screen display only, any higher level of resolution is a waste of your disk space and a waste of your customers' time. Bumping that image up to just 100 dpi increases the time it takes to draw on a customer's screen by about 40 percent. When you're developing graphics, be considerate of your customers.

The hi-resolution alternative

Sometimes you may want to distribute high-resolution versions of your screen images. If so, the standard format is JPEG (pronounced "JAY-peg"). The reason that JPEG is such a popular format is that it's a compressed format. For example, an image larger than a megabyte in some other uncompressed format will probably take up less than 100K saved as a JPEG. That difference saves your customers lots of downloading time. The bottom line: Save your high-res images in JPEG format.

Note

Even for commercial printing jobs, it's unlikely that you will ever need an image with a resolution greater than 225 dpi. If you save an image at 300 dpi, for example, it takes up a third more disk space than a 225 dpi version, and it doesn't benefit you in any way.

A room and a view

The World Wide Web is a graphical environment. I know — you're saying, "No kidding, Sherlock." But the reason I mention it now is that it's something to consider when you're in the market for a new monitor.

If you're on a tight budget, you're probably looking at buying a 14-inch monitor. If you check prices, however, you can see that 15-inch monitors don't cost that much more these days. That one extra diagonal inch can make a big difference in your viewable area.

Unfortunately, a big imbalance exists between screen size and price. Moving up from a 15-inch monitor to a 17-inch monitor can double or even triple the price. Go from a 17-inch to a 20-inch monitor, and you're likely to double the price again. You have to decide how much the added convenience and efficiency of a larger screen is worth in dollars and sense, but I would think about at least a 15-inch monitor rather than the 14-inch model.

The speediest Web pages

Most people like to see some graphics. They're what make the Web so fun and exciting. Some people like to cut through the bull, however, and get straight to the information they want without seeing a single image. For these people, you may want to consider an alternative home page that has no graphics. This process shouldn't take much effort because you can simply cut out the graphics from a copy of your standard home page. Many people will appreciate this option. Figure 9-6 shows you what my company's home page looks like when the text-only option is selected.

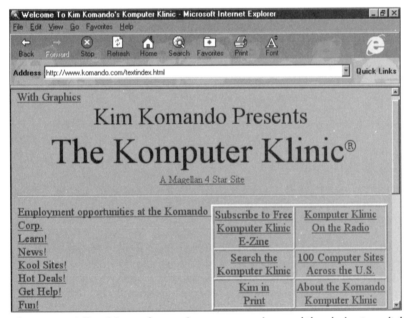

Figure 9-6: Offer visitors whose primary concern is speed the choice to switch to text-only mode when they view your home page.

The e-mail connection

Because many of your customers will come to you by way of a commercial online service, you have to know how to send e-mail to people on those services. Table 9-1 can help you with Internet e-mail addressing.

Table 9-1 Internet Address Formats		
Company	Address	Example
America Online	screenname@aol.com	KimKomando@aol.com (if you ever want to drop me a note, this is the address to use)
CompuServe	CompuServeID@ compuserve.com	12345.5555@compuserve.com (the comma in the CompuServe ID changes to a period)
Delphi Internet Services	username@delphi.com	joesmith@delphi.com
GEnie	username@genie.geis.com	donjuan@genie.geis.com
MCI Mail	numerical address@ mcimail.com	5551212@mcimail.com
Prodigy	userID@prodigy.com	KimK99A@prodigy.com

Don't be a Blackbeard

When you're starting a business on a shoestring, pirated software (illegal copies of commercial programs) can be awfully tempting. If you're headed down this path, make a quick U-turn.

In addition to robbing you of valuable technical-support resources, pirated software jeopardizes your entire business. You probably think that it's unlikely you will ever get caught, and you may be right. But what if you do get caught? Federal agents who raid a business take every piece of computer-related-anything that they can get their hands on. Even if you're eventually let off the hook, you might never see that equipment again.

Think about how much money you have invested in computer equipment. Blowing it all over some bootlegged software is just plain dumb.

Because you've got personality

Whether you set up shop in cyberspace or on the corner of First and Main, your business should reflect your unique personality — that's what gives any business its character. On the Internet, it might be as easy as dedicating a Web page to your favorite hobby, even if it has nothing to do with your business. It shows that you're not a one-dimensional person. In addition, you get that ever-prized foot traffic from people who share your interest. In short, make your business really yours.

Software on a shoestring

Pirated software brings me around to another one of my favorite topics: shareware. Sure, it's not likely that you will ever find the shareware equivalent of Photoshop or Quark Xpress. But most major software categories have shareware alternatives to the big commercial titles. If money is tight, a shareware program might be just what you need to get things going without resorting to illegal software.

Tip

If you spend any time at all online, you can hardly move without tripping over some sort of shareware. On the Web, just do a Yahoo! search for *shareware*. Most of the major online services have tons of it too. I know that you can find some great stuff in my Komputer Klinic on America Online (keyword KOMANDO). When it comes time to choose software, don't rule out shareware.

Web resources

Looking for online resources to help you develop your Web pages ? Check out these sites:

✦ **The Web Developer's Virtual Library:** `http://www.stars.com/` (see Figure 9-7)

✦ **HTML Grinder:** `http://www.matterform.com/grinder/`

✦ **Creating Net Sites:** `http://home.mcom.com/home/how-to-create-web-services.html`

✦ **Yahoo!:** Search for *Beginners' guides*

Offline commerce

The focus of this book is online commerce, but the Web can be a useful tool for promoting offline businesses too. If you run any sort of traditional business, either in conjunction with your online business or something completely different, make sure that you promote it on your Web page.

Figure 9-7: The Internet is loaded with helpful resources for developing your home page.

Tip

Go to Yahoo!, for example, and do a search for *restaurants*. No one (except for maybe Max Headroom) has ever eaten online, yet the Web has no shortage of eateries. The thing to remember is that your cybercustomers are living, breathing consumers who (hopefully) have lives away from their computers. Don't miss this great chance to promote your other ventures.

Tip

P.S.: Don't forget that you got a free Web page just because you bought this book. Instructions for creating it are in the appendix and on the CD-ROM in the back of this book.

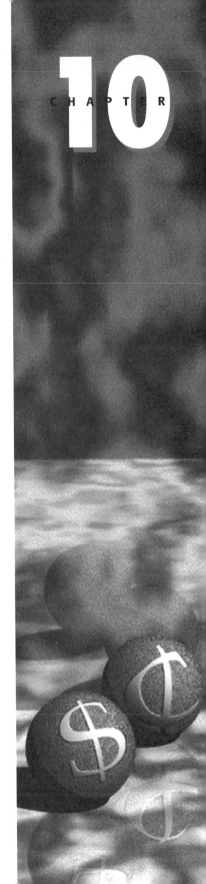

Making Sure That Your Security Net Is in Place

Go to the circus and you just may find a trapeze artist willing to work without a net. Every once in a while, some nut makes his mark by jumping his (choose one: motorcycle, car, truck, snowmobile) (choose one: on, under, through, over, from) some (choose one: pile of cars, skyscraper, raging inferno, canyon). If you search hard enough in Hollywood, you might even find someone willing to make a multimillion-dollar movie with me in the leading role. If you do, let me know.

All these people are willing to risk their careers — and, in fact, their lives — for a little fame and fortune. My guess, however, is that you're not willing to live quite as dangerously as you embark on your cyberjourney to wealth and well-being, so I take some time in this chapter to talk about Internet security.

Notice that I said "Internet security." If you're doing business on an online service, you're working in a closed system in which security is much easier to manage. Believe me, the big guys, such as CompuServe and America Online, take security seriously — so that you don't have much to worry about.

The Internet, however, is more similar to the wild, wild West: Anything goes. If you decide to set up your own Web server, you have to either become a security expert or hire one. Even if your cyberstore resides on the server of a local ISP, you have to be aware of the ISP's potential vulnerabilities and how you can act to help control security on your Web site.

So What Can Go Wrong?

Internet security is a hot topic these days. Of all the various issues that fall under the umbrella of security, the security of online financial transactions is *the* biggest concern. If someone sends you her credit-card number by e-mail, that information may have to hop through several sites along the way.

Consumers are afraid that at one of those "cyber pit stops," some clever hacker may intercept that information and use it for illegal purposes. For that reason, companies around the world are working on a variety of technologies to eliminate that concern. After all, three things influence people to buy most products or services: sex, greed, and fear. Guess which category security is in? That's right (it's not Pamela Anderson Lee's photo in a bathing suit) — fear.

The funny thing is that, of all the security issues to address in cyberspace, e-mail interception is the least likely to be a problem. It's true that your e-mail, in order to get to its ultimate destination, may have to bounce through a few sites along the way. These relay points are called *routers*. Not just anyone with an Internet server can be a router, however.

Note

The Internet community recognizes that hosting a router is an important and trusted function. Only institutions that meet the highest possible standards of trust can act as routers. Frankly, the possibility of a cyberthug on the Internet intercepting your credit-card number is little to none.

That's not to say, however, that a theft of any sort can never happen. You may remember Kevin D. Mitnick, the ill-famed hacker who, on Christmas Day 1994, broke into the computer system of the preeminent computer security expert Tsutomu Shimomura. Mitnick electronically swiped 20,000 credit-card numbers from the Internet service Netcom On-Line Communication Services, Inc. Soon after the theft was discovered, Warren Kaplan (the executive vice president of Netcom) was quoted in the *Wall Street Journal:* "We absolutely didn't know that the files had been taken. Mitnick is so shrewd, it was difficult to uncover. This guy is the Dillinger of cyberspace."

Christopher Schanot, a 19-year-old hacker from St. Louis, allegedly broke into national computer networks and obtained passwords to military computers, TRW (the credit-reporting service), and Sprint. While waiting for his trial, Schanot was released to his parents' care under 24-hour house arrest, with orders not to even *talk* about computers. His father said, "There are monsters out there looking for young, vulnerable kids to abuse for their own ends."

Despite these well-publicized incidents, the truth is that you have a greater risk of an unscrupulous restaurant waiter swiping your credit-card number from a receipt than of having it ripped off as it passes through the gates of the Infobahn.

Whether or not Internet security *should* be a public concern is not the point. The fact remains that it *is* a public concern. Because your customers worry about Internet security, it is now *your* concern. I discuss different secured-transaction measures later in this chapter, but first I explain what can really go wrong.

What follows requires you to sit up and pay attention. Follow me with these thoughts — they are important.

If information in transit is not a major concern, it stands to reason that information *not* in transit is the real concern. I'm talking about information that's on your computer or on a customer's computer. Although information that's in transit is similar to the proverbial moving target, information that's sitting still is just a sitting duck.

Note

You don't have much control, if any, over the security of your customer's system. Nonetheless, you should be aware of what can go on at that end. For one thing, most online commerce systems use some sort of *encryption* technique (a way of encoding information so that it's useless to anyone who may intercept it along the way).

Encryption offers protection, however, only while the data is in transit. What about securing the data before it's transmitted? Recent studies have shown that it's possible to create a program that sits undetected on a user's computer and waits for her to type a bank account or credit-card number. These programs know what to watch for. When they realize that you're entering credit-card numbers, they record them and send them to the programs' creators — before the information is ever encrypted! The likelihood of this scheme happening is another story, however (logistically, how does a cyberthief get the program that gathers the private information on the customer's computer?).

As you might expect, the Internet contains a culture that's dedicated to hacking. I interviewed a hacker on my talk-radio show who was, at the time, being pursued for stealing credit-card numbers. He told me that he did it for fun and used the credit-card numbers just to see if he could. Yahoo! devotes an entire section to hacker sites on the Internet, as shown in Figure 10-1.

Pouring a Bad Cup of Java

Java is a programming language you can use to write programs that run on the World Wide Web. The great thing about a Java program is that a developer doesn't have to write a DOS version, a Windows 3.1 version, a Windows 95 version, a Mac version, and an Amiga version.

Any Java-enabled Web browser, such as Netscape Navigator, can run the Java program, no matter which type of computer you have or on which platform it runs. The Java application code is simply transmitted to the browser, and suddenly your computer has new, powerful capabilities (even if only temporarily). Figure 10-2 shows an example of a good cup of Java — a puzzle in which you can move the pieces and solve in real-time online.

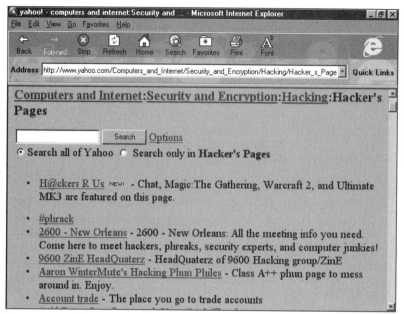

Figure 10-1: The Internet is loaded with information and programs for hackers.

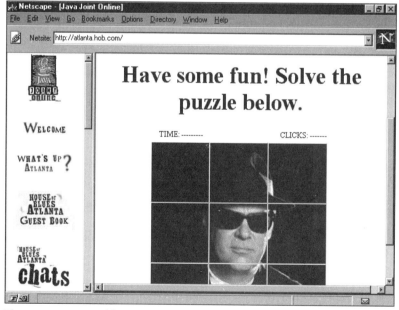

Figure 10-2: Java adds new capabilities to Web pages and opens the door for possible security breaches along the way.

That sounds great, doesn't it? The problem is that, as Java code is sent to your computer, your computer has no way to tell whether the program will do something undesirable. It's possible, therefore, to write a Java program that, when accessed, wreaks all sorts of havoc on a customer's computer system.

Of course, you would never put a program like that on your Web page, would you? What if someone does it for you? Now I have to begin talking about security at the other end of the line — your end.

Warning

A favorite secretive technique of computer criminals is called *spoofing*, or pretending to be someone else online. I'm not talking about going into a chat room and telling everyone that you look like Tom Cruise or Nicole Kidman or even that you *are* that person. Spoofing is pretending that you're a system administrator in order to gain unauthorized access to a secure system. It's scary to think about, but it's technically possible for a cybercriminal to spoof his way into taking over your entire storefront, at least temporarily.

It's not that difficult to do. Armed with the right information, a person could call up an ISP that's not on the ball and tell someone there a story: "Hello, I'm a new employee at XYZ Company, and I lost my password. I would hate for my boss to find out. Heck, I could even lose my job. Could you do me a huge favor and give the password to me?"

Again, this situation isn't all that likely to happen. Some hacker, however, may still attempt to gain unauthorized access to sensitive or confidential data on your system, whether it's your own system or the ISP's.

The bogus new-employee phone call example I just gave really happened to my company. The person got the password, and we didn't figure out what had happened until a few menu items suddenly disappeared. We were able to track where the problem originated by looking at records detailing who accessed what and when. That's not the only way a person can gain access to your system, however, and it's certainly not the worst thing that can happen.

An Ounce of Prevention. . .

It goes without saying that the best way to manage a security breach is to keep it from happening in the first place. What can you do?

The first step is to make sure that your system is as secure as it can be. When I say "your system," I mean whatever system you're doing business on, whether it's your computer system or your ISP's.

Tip

Your first line of defense is a reliable *firewall*, which is a combination of hardware and software that controls access to a computer system. Suppose that the only means of remote access to your computer is by using a modem that's attached to it. Simply turning off the modem is a firewall in its simplest form.

If you're involved with online commerce, you want the entire world, of course, to have access to your system around the clock. Although this access is great for customers, it's easy to see the problem it creates for security.

Your system is vulnerable to attack 24 hours a day, seven days a week. You have no reason to cut corners. Unless you're a phenomenally talented hacker, don't even consider building your own firewall. Just like brain surgery, this is one area you should trust to the experts. Unfortunately, a good firewall can cost as much as brain surgery. Just don't be surprised when you get the bill.

As you might expect, information about firewalls is available on the Internet. For timely information, check out the Computer Incident Advisory Capability (CIAC) Web page, at `http://www.alw.nih.gov/Security/CIAC-Notes.html` (see Figure 10-3).

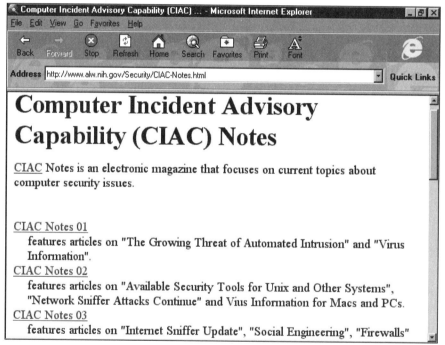

Figure 10-3: The CIAC is a great source of information about security breaches and prevention techniques.

After you have made sure that your system as a whole is secure, you can also take steps to ensure that your data is secure. If you receive encrypted information, such as credit-card numbers, over the Internet, you should leave the information encrypted until you can move it to an offline system. If you decrypt credit-card numbers on a system that's vulnerable to hackers, you might discover that all the trouble you went through for encryption is pointless.

Tip

A hacker may get the numbers anyway. If you decrypt the numbers on a remote PC with no direct connection to the Internet, for example, you eliminate your risk of a security breach.

Tip

After the server that contains your Web page and the information are both secure, look to your internal operations. Change passwords often, and use a mixture of letters, numbers, and other characters (such as the & sign) to create them.

You also must limit access to sensitive information within your company. When computers are networked within an office, limiting this access is tough, but not terribly difficult, to do. Ask yourself these questions:

✦ Who will decrypt the credit-card numbers?

✦ Who else knows the code?

✦ Which computers in your office have access to the code?

✦ Most important, how well do you know the people (or just the person) in charge of doing the job, and can you trust them?

Make one mistake, and your credit-card processing days may be over. No bank is likely to give you merchant account privileges again. (Some bank might do so, if you place a large enough deposit, in case you screw up again.)

. . .And a Pound of Cure

How can you tell whether you have been attacked? And more important, what should you do?

First, make sure that you review the activities on your system daily so that you know what's normal (and also to track what is and is not working). The best way to tell whether you have been attacked is to monitor your system constantly for *any* (I repeat — *any*) suspicious or unusual activity. Keep these questions in mind:

✦ Have you noticed an unexplained increase or decrease in traffic through your site?

✦ Are you suddenly using up considerably more disk space?

✦ When you look at the daily activity reports and hits from your Web site, do you notice any unusual activity or patterns?

If you answered yes to any of these questions, a good explanation probably exists. You should still check them all out, however. If you're on someone else's server, report any strange happenings to the system administrator or Webmaster.

If you're on your own system and you don't know how to proceed, contact CERT (Computer Emergency Response Team). The sole purpose of this nonprofit, around-the-clock organization, sponsored by various members of the Internet community, is to address security issues and concerns (see Figure 10-4). CERT works with the Internet community to facilitate its response to computer-security events involving Internet hosts, to take proactive steps to raise the Internet community's awareness of computer-security issues, and to conduct research targeted at improving the security of existing systems.

You can reach CERT by phone at 412-268-7090, by fax at 412-268-6989, or by e-mail at cert@cert.org. For some valuable information, I suggest that you visit its Web site, at http://www.cert.org.

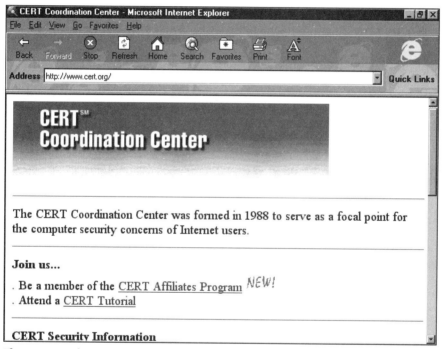

Figure 10-4: The Computer Emergency Response Team (CERT) addresses Internet security issues.

Note

Incidentally, you may wonder what kind of security breach can be indicated by using up too much disk space. Excessive disk usage on your system may mean that a hacker has set up a *warez* site, a hidden directory in which he puts all sorts of illegal software (or other things — you just never know). He then tells others in his hacker network how to access the site. In other words, you unwittingly become a clearinghouse for bootlegged software or worse — not a good idea.

So What's This Encryption Thing?

In its simplest form, *encryption* is the process of encoding information so that unauthorized people cannot read it. In a simple encryption scheme, for example, the letter *b* is substituted for *a, c* for *b, d* for *c,* and so on. If I write *npofz* using that simple technique, you know that I'm talking about *money*.

Computers can, unfortunately, figure out stuff like this much faster than people can. Because even a much more sophisticated encryption scheme is no problem for the right computer, the encryption wizards have come up with a little bonus: keys. In a key scenario, an encrypted message consists of both a message and its key. If you don't know the key, you have no way to figure out the message. The only problem with this technique is that if an encryption program uses a universal key, a person who has that key can decrypt any message generated by that software.

The encryption wizards then went back to the drawing board and came up with the idea of public and private keys. In this scenario, every user has both a public and a private key. If you want to send me a message, I send you my public key so that you can use it to encrypt the message to me. After a message is encrypted with my public key, only my private key can decrypt it. Virtually all modern encryption schemes, including the ones I describe in the following section, are founded on this basic model.

The PGP (Pretty Good Privacy) program is a highly secure public key encryption software program, originally written by Philip Zimmermann. Over the past few years, PGP has gained thousands of adherent supporters from all over the globe and has become a de facto standard for encryption of e-mail on the Internet (see Figure 10-5). Be aware, however, that the U.S. government has expressed concerns about PGP's encryption capability. Because the PGP program works so well, it is officially considered a munition under U.S. export laws. You can drop by the company's Web page, at `http://www.ifi.uio.no/pgp/`.

101 Ways to Spend Your Money

So you want to take payments over the Internet, eh? You might not have 101 ways to do it, but the number of possibilities is getting higher all the time. In this section, I give you the rundown on several of the most popular ways to handle cyberdollars.

Prearranged accounts

One of the most low-tech, yet most effective, ways to control secure commerce is to have each of your customers establish a separate account with you. First, they provide you with their credit-card number, address, and other information by fax or mail. Then, when they place an order with you, you already have the information you need in order to get paid for the purchase. No opportunity exists for credit-card fraud because you ship products to only a standard billing address.

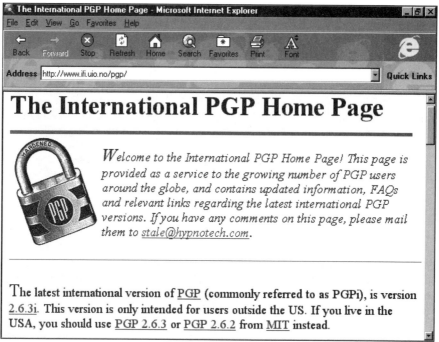

Figure 10-5: One of the many areas on the Internet dedicated to PGP, a program so powerful that even the U.S. government has taken notice.

The downside of this setup is that you must maintain account information for every one of your customers. Even with the most sophisticated database program, that process can take plenty of time, trouble, and money. In terms of effort to keep things going smoothly, a prearranged account clearly ranks at the bottom of the pack.

Encrypted forms

Another way to get paid over the Internet is to create standard online forms and transmit customers' input to your site in an encrypted format. Two common protocols are used for this purpose:

✦ **Secured Sockets Layers (SSL):** Developed by the ever popular Netscape Communications Corporation. Because Netscape has about a 75 percent share of the Web browser market, it should be no surprise to learn that its security scheme is the most popular. For the latest information about SSL and other security issues, visit the Netscape Web site at http://home.netscape.com/info/security-doc.html.

✦ **Secure HTTP (S/HTTP):** Developed through the joint efforts of a number of organizations, including the NCSA (National Center for Supercomputing Applications). Information about this protocol is also available on the Web: Just point your browser to the Web site of Enterprise Integration Technologies, another codeveloper of S/HTTP (http://www.eit.com/creations/s-http/).

The thing to remember about either of these encryption methods is that they provide only point-to-point security using encryption. You have no control over what happens before or after the data is encrypted.

First Virtual Holdings

The First Virtual Holdings company bills itself as "the first virtual bank in cyberspace." I'm not so sure that I would call it a bank, but it has enjoyed considerable success by introducing a simple three-party system to Internet commerce (see Figure 10-6). The third party (First Virtual) acts as the authentication source.

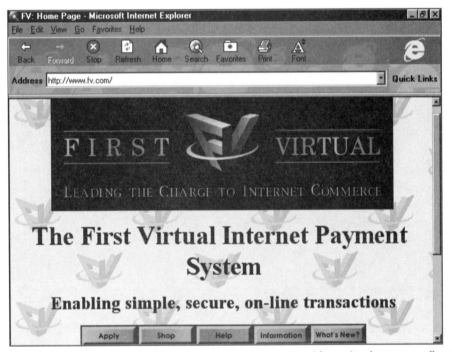

Figure 10-6: The First Virtual Internet Payment System provides a simple way to sell stuff over the Internet. No special hardware, software, or encryption is required — all you need is ordinary e-mail.

Here's how it works. First, you sign up your business as a vendor that accepts First Virtual accounts for payment. When a consumer who has opened a First Virtual account stops by your virtual store to purchase some real products, she gives you her First Virtual account number.

You submit the bill to First Virtual for payment in much the same way as you submit payment for a credit-card bill. Before First Virtual pays you, however, it sends an e-mail confirmation to the consumer. This way, everyone is assured that an authorized account user made the purchase.

Contact First Virtual Holding on the Web at `http://www.fv.com/`.

DigiCash

Another way to collect payment on the Internet is through a company called DigiCash (see Figure 10-7). Much like First Virtual Holdings, DigiCash provides security by introducing a third party into the transaction. In this case, however, the third party doesn't get involved until after the transaction has been made. For this reason, you're likely to get your real dollars more quickly.

Figure 10-7: The first DigiCash product was a road-toll system developed for the Dutch government. Now the company is using its patented technologies to secure Internet transactions.

First, you must sign up as a DigiCash merchant. Then your customers simply purchase *digital coupons* from DigiCash and spend them, just as though they were real money, at your cyberstore. These coupons are based on a technology the company calls a *blind digital signature:* Every coupon is both unique and anonymous — much like real money.

After you accept these coupons for payment, you redeem them for payment from DigiCash. DigiCash coupons have two great features:

✦ They're almost impossible to counterfeit.

✦ You can verify their authenticity as you receive them.

To contact DigiCash, point your Web browser to `http://www.digicash.com`.

CyberCash

The CyberCash company, at `http://www.cybercash.com`, takes another approach to online commerce. In this model, each customer has a *virtual wallet* that contains all his credit cards. When a consumer wants to buy something using this method, he can choose which credit card to use for the purchase, just as in real life (see Figure 10-8).

Figure 10-8: CyberCash works with virtually all credit-card-processing institutions to instantaneously process payments made by credit card, electronic check, or electronic coin.

Here's how a CyberCash transaction works:

1. A customer cruises your virtual aisles and chooses merchandise along the way.

2. When he finishes, he clicks the Pay button to launch his CyberCash wallet and then decides which credit card from the wallet to use.

3. Your server receives the packet, strips off the order, and forwards to the CyberCash server the encrypted payment information, digitally signed and encrypted with your private key. Because the credit-card information stays encrypted, you don't know anything about the credit card that is used, and the customer gains an additional level of safety.

4. The CyberCash server receives the packet and automatically moves it to an offline system behind its firewall. CyberCash then forwards the transaction to your bank, just as it does with any other credit-card authorization.

5. Your bank gets approval for the transaction; again, just like any other credit-card transaction.

6. CyberCash sends you an approval code, and the transaction is completed.

These steps may sound like a great deal of work to do to get a payment authorized, but the computers are doing all the work — and they do it fast. This entire process takes only about 20 seconds.

NetCheque

I have discussed in this chapter a number of ways to spend your money using your credit cards. What if you want to write a virtual check instead? NetCheque offers one possible answer. Without going into the gory technical details, what separates this service from the others is that a NetCheque transaction pulls the payment directly from your checking account rather than from a credit card (see Figure 10-9).

To find out more about this service, check out `http://gost.isi.edu/info/NetCheque/`.

What's a Would-Be Cybermillionaire to Do?

Aside from the do-it-yourself encrypted forms, all these payment methods represent one common problem: In every instance, your customer needs to have set up some sort of account somewhere in advance. Maybe someday the number of online shoppers will be so high that you will be able to offer a couple of these payment options and make a killing. Or maybe someday the online commerce world will adopt some standards so that you don't have so many options from which to choose.

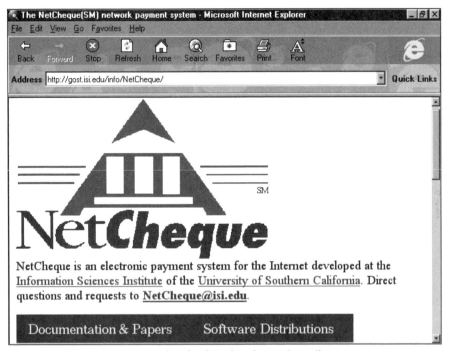

Figure 10-9: NetCheque puts the check in the electronic mail.

In the meantime, you have to make some money. None of the Internet transaction-processing companies seems to have an overwhelming market share. Which way you decide to go is up to you. For my money, encrypted forms of security seem to be the best bet. Head to head, they may not seem as secure as some other techniques, but — done properly — they're secure enough.

The most important thing is that encrypted forms of security make the entire online shopping experience easier for your cybercustomers. The easier you make the experience for them, the more likely they are to spend more of their money.

I don't mean to discourage you from any of these other payment options. You should check out every one of them before you make a decision, if for no other reason than to ensure that you're making the correct decision. With the Internet evolving daily, keeping on top of new payment methods is essential if you want to stay on top. Just as your Web page is never really finished, neither is your education. You may have noticed that this chapter doesn't have my usual flair for humor. Security and getting paid is serious stuff, and you must protect your business with the same vigilance you would use in protecting your children as they walk across the street.

Remember that no matter which online payment method you choose, folks still aren't as comfortable giving their credit-card number to a computer as they are giving it to a server in a restaurant. For this reason, you should either obtain a toll-free order hotline number for customers to call or set up on your Web page a form that lists your products. Have customers fill out the form — name, address, daytime phone number, and products they want to order. After completing the form, customers can click a Send button on your Web page so that you receive the order by way of e-mail. (The downside is that you have to call them to take the order by phone.) Figure 10-10 shows the form the Komputer Klinic used before I found a more secure way to accept orders over the Internet.

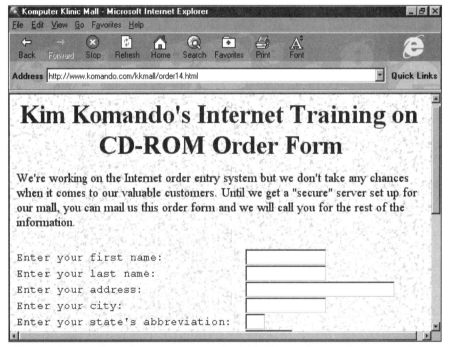

Figure 10-10: Until you have a secure method of taking orders on the Internet, have customers complete a form that they then send to you by e-mail.

The Komputer Klinic's online sales results show that for every order taken online, nine more will come by phone. People are more comfortable giving an order to a live human being. They believe that it's safer than giving it to a computer. If you don't have a toll-free number listed on your Web page, you lose potential sales. It's that simple.

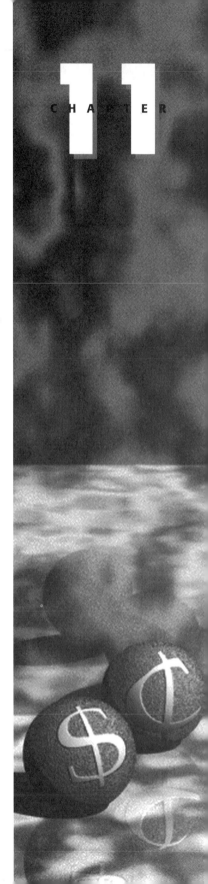

Tapping New Markets with Global Online Marketing

You probably will call me obsessive if I share this story, but that's the chance I take. I believe that you, my loyal reader looking to me for online entrepreneurial advice, ought to know about one of my flaws, although I don't think that I really have any flaws, that said, here's one possible imperfection my loved ones have brought to my attention.

First, understand that I work very hard. No matter how smart I work, though, merely keeping up demands working (more often than not) seven days a week, including national holidays. It's rare for me not to be in my office before 7:30 in the morning or to leave before 7:30 in the evening. But I still get my share of exercise, and I always make time to call my mother every day. My basic problem has nothing to do with taking care of my health and family. The personal challenge I face is learning how to relax.

You see, my definition of relaxing involves going online. There — I said it. You know, saying it didn't make me feel any better (or worse, for that matter). Many evenings, you can find me watching a movie, sipping a glass of wine, and tapping on a computer keyboard. I get online and go where I don't seem to have time to go during the day. I visit fun sites, competitors' pages, and newsgroups (all G-rated, I might add).

I am doing my homework, but it's not really work. I consider it a game to uncover things online that I didn't already know about, such as reading a mystery novel. Best of all, I can still watch a movie while surfing because of the delay between the time I type an Internet Web page address and the time it finally shows up on-screen.

When I first began marketing my talk-radio show, I spent many late nights visiting radio station Web pages. I was looking for the stations' program schedules, in the hope of finding a two-hour slot I considered perfect for my show.

When I found a match, I shot off an e-mail message to the station's management as an introduction to my show. I must have sent about 100 e-mail messages to radio stations that first month. I got some hate mail back. I got some leads. I got one sale — the network that currently airs my show throughout Australia (see Figure 11-1).

Figure 11-1: The Kim Komando Show is heard not only throughout the United States and Canada but also in Australia (the result of just one e-mail message).

One of the most amazing aspects of putting a business online is that you have an almost unlimited market. Suddenly you can branch out in geographic areas that weren't so easily possible until the online explosion occurred. An equally important consideration is that you can use online marketing to promote a local business just as successfully as you can promote one with customers the world over. Even better, after you're online, you already have most of the resources in place to grow your business from a small, local contender to a worldwide player.

To this point, you probably have thought of your new cyberbusiness only in terms of the U.S. market — and that makes sense. You know the market. You know the people. You buy mostly products geared toward satisfying American needs and wants. Because the United States has by far the largest number of online users in the world, this country represents the largest possible online market share to take advantage of your knowledge.

Nonetheless, millions and millions of online users are in foreign countries. You shouldn't automatically rule out this market segment — it's huge and untapped.

Granted, international sales are not appropriate for every business, especially those with a specific regional slant. A New York City taxicab company wouldn't do much business by asking people in Guam to call for a ride; on the other hand, you may have a business in New Mexico that sells authentic Native American goods. Even though the latter example definitely has a regional slant, people from around the world might be interested in acquiring its products. Even hiking trails and University of New Mexico class schedules may be of interest to someone who is thinking of moving to New Mexico. Many businesses don't do international business, however, because they simply cannot afford to promote themselves overseas. When you're online, the cost generally remains the same, whether you attempt to reach a local audience or a global one.

I spoke recently, for example, with a publisher of special-education materials who is in the process of developing the company's Web site. Because this company, Academic Communication Associates (ACA), gets virtually all its orders from catalog sales, it spends a great deal of time and money each year controlling inventory and laying out, printing, and mailing catalogs to potential customers who may not buy even one item.

This type of promotion and marketing isn't cheap by any means. To control the largest expense (printing costs), the company must be careful about how many catalogs it prints and to whom it sends them. The cost of sending foreign mail makes sending catalogs around the world prohibitive.

On the other hand, after ACA has its home page up and running, it will be able to reach customers around the world without mailing a single catalog. The company, which is putting together its Web site in phases, plans eventually to have a complete catalog and online system.

So Who Exactly Is Out There?

No one can say for sure how many people are online, for two reasons. First, no one can possibly track the number of multiple users of one account. Maybe you let Aunt

Betty use your America Online account once in awhile because she really doesn't need a full account of her own. That's two online users represented by one online account.

Likewise, no one can track the number of people with multiple accounts. I have a handful of Internet e-mail addresses, five public AOL addresses, and a private AOL address. I have a friend who, because of his involvement in all types of different ventures, has something like ten e-mail addresses, each for a different purpose.

As you can see, even if you could count the total number of online accounts on the entire planet, you wouldn't necessarily get an accurate user count. But you can learn something about the foreign market by looking at survey results.

One of the most interesting surveys is the annual World Wide Web Users' Survey, conducted each year by the Graphics, Visualization, and Usability Center (GVU), at the Georgia Institute of Technology. The results of its latest survey are available at `http://www.cc.gatech.edu/gvu/user_surveys/`, but I recap in this section the current survey results for international users. Of the 11,700 people who responded to the latest survey, about 2,500 live outside the United States (they represent 80 different countries).

Note

First, international users make up about 30 percent of the online population. When I'm coming up with a marketing strategy, I like to think of population percentages as the number of people in one room. If you picture 100 people in a room, in this survey, 30 of them are from different countries. See their faces. Visualize each of the 100 people going to their local McDonald's for a Happy Meal. The people in the room are different in many ways, but are more alike than you might imagine.

The number of people in the room will likely increase, however. Next year, rather than 70 people from the United States, 65 might be from the United States and the remaining 35 from other countries. The reason is that the Internet is enjoying a much higher growth rate overseas. No one will catch up to the United States any time soon, of course, but this growth rate does show you that, as time goes by, foreign markets will become increasingly lucrative for marketers such as you and me (see Figure 11-2).

Demographically (there's that word again) speaking, foreign users aren't all that different from United States users. About 90 percent are male, and more than 40 percent have incomes higher than $40,000. Here's one interesting point to ponder: The highest incomes are reported in Asia, where a full 20 percent claim incomes higher than $100,000.

Here's another noteworthy tidbit. Overall, foreign users spend plenty of work hours on their computers (an average of 30 hours a week). In contrast, foreign countries don't seem to have the resident gamesters we have in the United States. On average, international users spend very little computer time on recreational purposes.

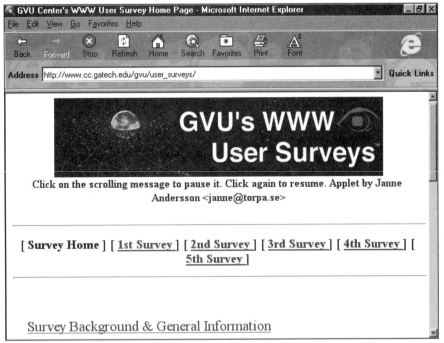

Figure 11-2: The Web-user surveys at the Graphics, Visualization, & Usability (GVU) Center are a free public-service effort. Keep up-to-date with global Internet user demographics so that you can better target-market their needs.

Why should you care about what people in other countries do in their spare time? If you're planning to go after a foreign market, this information tells you that you probably will be better off with a business-related product than with a consumer product (a multiuser interactive game, for example).

What else? It seems that many foreign users aren't the marryin' kind. On average, only 40 percent are married, with the figure down to 34 percent in Europe alone. As you may have already guessed, therefore, not as many users abroad have dependent children. Peddling global tips for keeping a marriage alive and raising children, therefore, might not be the best idea.

In the area of education, more than 90 percent of all international users are college educated, and 40 percent have at least a master's degree. As for careers, the two biggies abroad are education and computers. Depending on the exact area, computer careers account for anywhere from 30 percent to more than 50 percent of the online community. As I just mentioned, overall income levels are quite high for online marketing purposes.

As you can see, the demographics for foreign users don't exactly match up with the demographics for users in the United States, but they're relatively close. That's one great aspect of international online marketing: If you look at any country or region as a whole, it looks much different from the United States. The average citizen of Houston, for example, is probably different from the average citizen of Bogota, Colombia. Yet computer users from around the world seem to be pretty much the same — they're a breed unto themselves.

Marketing Globally with Local Appeal

If you want to go after an international market, you must not only know a little about the people, of course, but also remain sensitive to regional customs, language, and other considerations. Plenty of major American companies with huge marketing budgets have blown it overseas, at least temporarily, because they didn't do their homework in their proposed markets. Check out a few examples taken from *American Demographics* magazine:

✦ Braniff Airlines came up with a catchy slogan to promote its new upholstery: "Fly in leather," The Spanish translation was, unfortunately, "Fly naked." Sex may sell, but it didn't help Braniff.

✦ Coors translated its slogan "Turn it loose" into Spanish, where it was read as "Suffer from diarrhea."

✦ For years, chicken king Frank Perdue used the slogan "It takes a tough man to make a tender chicken." The Spanish version, however, doesn't quite get the point across: "It takes a sexually stimulated man to make a chicken affectionate." Can you imagine Perdue in a huge boardroom with his management team and having a heart-to-heart chat about this matter? There's Frank, plastering his face across the country and the world and telling people to trust him. He grows the best chickens. Whatever could his management team say to him? "We had no idea," wouldn't cut it with Frank. But I digress.

✦ The Chevy Nova was popular in the United States for many years, but it never sold well in Spanish-speaking countries. "No va" means "It doesn't go" in Spanish. So much for consumer confidence.

✦ Neither Pepsi nor Coke had much luck the first time they tested the Chinese market. The Pepsi slogan "Pepsi brings you back to life" translates to "Pepsi brings your ancestors back from the grave." Yikes! Coke used a different tactic. It tried to come up with Chinese letters that would be pronounced as "Coca-Cola." What it actually spelled in Chinese was "Bite the wax tadpole." (Sounds like something a surfer might say.)

✦ Biting a tadpole is one thing, but consider Clairol's luck. When it introduced its Mist Stick curling iron in Germany, no one in the company realized that, in Germany, "mist" is slang for "manure." (Need I say more on this one?)

✦ When Gerber began selling baby food in Africa, the company used the same basic packaging it uses everywhere else, with the cute little baby on its label. What Gerber didn't know is that many people in Africa can't read. It's a common African packaging practice, therefore, to include a picture of a jar's contents on its label. What would you think that a jar with a baby on the label contains? That's precisely what many Africans thought too.

There's no doubt about it — all these stories are funny. And, unfortunately, all of them are true. They all cost their respective companies plenty of money. The lesson to be learned is that if you expect to enjoy any sort of success in foreign markets, you *must* make sure that you fully understand that market.

More social and legal issues exist than I could possibly cover in this chapter, and they all vary from country to country and from region to region. The one place I suggest that you check is a directory called International Business Resources, on the Web at `http://ciber.bus.msu.edu/busres.htm` (see Figure 11-3).

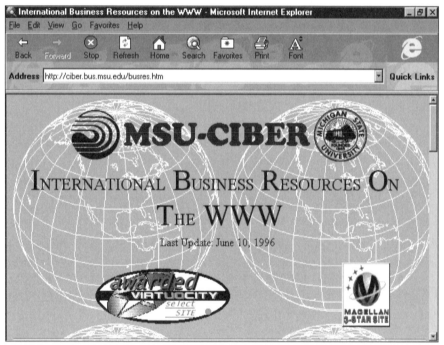

Figure 11-3: The Michigan State University Center for International Business Education and Research (CIBER) is a terrific source for one-stop international business information.

I want you to read the following section so that I can give you Komando's International Online Marketing 101 course. It can help you build the foundation for your international online business, no matter what it is or which countries it reaches.

Developing Your International Strategy

It may sound obvious, but the first step in developing a successful international strategy is to ask yourself one simple question: Is my product or service appropriate for an international audience? Don't be in a hurry to say "No way." Think about it. Remember the 30 percent of Internet users from other countries that I discussed earlier in this chapter? Can you picture any of those 30-odd people being enticed to purchase a product or service you sell? If your honest answer is no, don't simply skip ahead to Chapter 12. Maybe you haven't thought of all the angles. Continue reading this chapter to get the knowledge you need in order to market internationally someday because that day indeed may come.

I would bet that the guys who started up Yahoo! never imagined that they would have a complete Japanese version that works much like the English version does (see Figure 11-4). Check out the Japanese Yahoo! at `http://www.yahoo.co.jp/`.

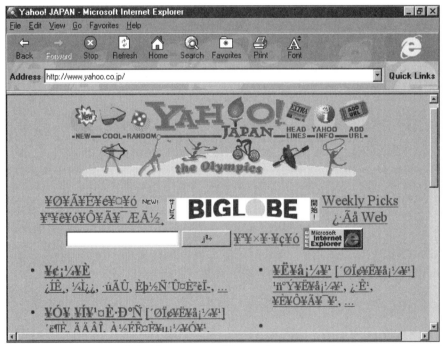

Figure 11-4: From one little idea — categorizing Web pages — Yahoo! has gained much global success.

If the Yahoo! folks went after this market, it's a good bet that you ought to at least think about it too. Rumor has it that at least five other foreign-language versions of Yahoo! are still to come. Yahoo! won't say what the languages are, but I can make one sure bet that at least one version will be in Spanish.

With so many different countries on seven continents, which foreign countries offer the most online marketing potential? It's difficult to say. The answer depends on exactly what you are selling. To get some help, point your Web browser to `http://www.stat-usa.gov/itabems.html` (see Figure 11-5).

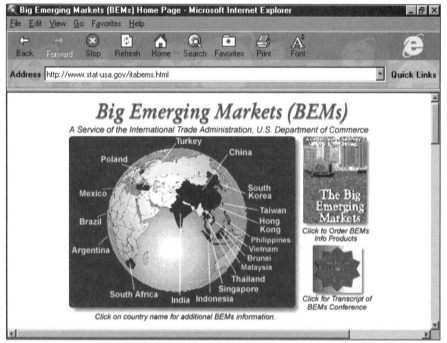

Figure 11-5: Markets that hold the greatest potential for dramatic increases in U.S. exports are not traditional trading partners in Europe and Japan. Rather, the greatest commercial opportunities are in the ten big emerging markets (or BEMs).

This site, the home of Big Emerging Markets on the Internet, is brought to you by the United States Department of Commerce. From here, if you click on China, for example, you can read the following:

> CHINA: The Biggest of The BEMs!!! The Chinese Economic Area (CEA), which includes China, Hong Kong, and Taiwan, is the biggest of the emerging markets worldwide. The CEA is the seventh largest economy in the world, with a combined GNP of $809.8 billion for 1993, and it constitutes the third largest trading partner for the United States — the fourth largest export market and third largest supplier. The CEA, which holds the world's largest combined foreign-exchange reserves, has the largest number and highest total dollar value of planned infrastructure projects (energy, transportation, telecommunications, and environment) in the world (more than $500 billion is planned for infrastructure-related equipment, technologies, and expertise during the next six years).

Finding a country to market to online is no easy decision. Afterward, the next place to establish your international-fortunes quest is by answering one obvious question: Do foreign businesspeople or consumers really need or want whatever you are selling? Used blue jeans, for example, are undoubtedly a hot item overseas. Specifically, Levi Strauss brands are on the most-wanted list.

While I was in Amsterdam recently for a speaking engagement, a woman at a restaurant offered me $175 in U.S. dollars for the pair of Levi's 501s I was wearing. (In case you're wondering, I did sell them to her after dinner. They were my favorite pair, but I never turn down a quick profit.)

Looking on the Internet, a search at Yahoo! produced only two sites selling used blue jeans. One link didn't work, but the other one did: I landed at Green for Jeans, at `http://www.green4jeans.com/`. I would bet that this site could get much more green if it made an international version of its Web page. Maybe no one there ever thought of it, or (quite possibly) maybe someone is working on it. Another factor is that not all currency is the color green. A typical Web surfer from Asia or Europe might not understand that this particular American company buys and sells used jeans.

As you contemplate making your products available throughout the world, you must consider adapting your message for the market. Bicycles in the United States are recreational items, whereas in many other countries they are a means of transportation. How will you market your product for its intended use in a particular country?

The next most important question to ask is whether you're pursuing only English-speaking markets or whether you want to widen your potential market to non-English-speaking countries. This question is important for a number of reasons. You obviously want to communicate your message in a country's native tongue. (This point should be obvious based on the examples of company slogans I mentioned earlier in this chapter, in the section "Marketing Globally with Local Appeal."

When it comes to international commerce, many marketers overlook the areas of packaging and documentation. How would you feel if you popped open the box on your new laser printer and discovered that the instructions were written in French or Japanese? Depending on your market, you may have to invest time and money in alternative packaging and documentation for your international customers.

Residents of another country may also speak different dialects. If you are planning to sell an online research report about U.S. government policies in Russia, for example, you may have to produce 13 different versions for each dialect.

You have to be especially careful if you're selling any sort of electrical device. The power supply (120-volt alternating current) is standard in all parts of the United States, but it varies abroad. If you manufacture an electrical device, are you willing to go back to the drawing board to create a foreign-market version?

You can't automatically assume that a good value in the United States is a good value in a foreign country. Different countries subsidize different industries within those countries, which can make prices unusually high or low. To promote domestic manufacturing, some countries may also impose seemingly unreasonable taxes and tariffs on your products. In addition, larger corporations often base their foreign-market prices on the economy in those countries.

Many people who live near the Mexican border, for example, routinely travel south to purchase their prescriptions at Mexican pharmacies, for savings of 50 percent or more. When you set your prices, you have to look at what prices are like in that market *and* which extra expenses you will incur in delivering your product to that country.

Getting paid for your worldly goods

That brings me to the all-important topic of how to get paid for goods or services you sell online and, more important, at what price? If you take credit-card orders, you're set. Visa, MasterCard, American Express, and Discover cards are an international standard.

Like Americans, people all over the world carry and use credit cards daily. The same Visa card works in Bohemia and in Boston (assuming, of course, that the card isn't over its credit limit). For your business, this compatibility makes it easy to accept credit-card orders from other countries. An example of a great international site is the Interflora International Flower Ordering Service. You can check it out at `http://www.fleurop.nl/`. This truly multilingual site (English, French, German, Spanish, Dutch) has dynamic images of flower bouquets for ordering and delivery in 18 countries (see Figure 11-6). This site is set up for secure credit-card transactions.

Most credit-card companies determine the *exchange rate,* the price of one nation's currency in terms of another nation's currency. Because exchange rates fluctuate, another country's currency can become more valuable or less valuable than U.S. currency. To avoid the hassles of working with currency conversions, ensure that credit-card companies give you the amounts for orders in U.S. dollars; double-check with the company that supplies your company's merchant account. Because policies vary, do your homework first or else you will lose potential profits later.

Figure 11-6: It's easy to order flowers on the Internet in many languages. You can pay for your flowers by using the international payment method: a major credit card.

Delivering the goods to foreign lands

After you get paid, do you have any idea who will deliver your product to your foreign customers? Even if you already have investigated all the appropriate business and marketing matters, logistical concerns still exist. Can freight carriers deliver your products to remote corners of the world? At a reasonable cost?

We use good ol' U.S. Postal Service airmail to ship our online international orders because it's the cheapest route. We haven't had any problems, as long as customers understand that it can take as much as two weeks for delivery. We charge a flat shipping-and-handling fee of $9 on all international orders.

Tip

If a foreign customer wants an international order shipped via Federal Express, Airborne, UPS, or another shipping company, we certainly can ship it that way, but only if the customer provides the account number used with the shipping company. Even then, to cover the cost of our time, we add $3 to the total amount charged for the order. Don't ever forget that time is money and that your customers have to pay for yours.

Covering all the payment angles

Even if you have credit-card processing under control, not every customer has a credit card. What about foreign customers who pay by check or money order? Have I got a story for you.

I popped my head into my company's order department just last week to say hello to everyone. Gazing through the glass to a supervisor's office, I noticed several checks and bank printouts lying on his desk. The look on the office manager's face was bad. Having worked with her for several years, I can recognize a "What the hell am I going to tell Kim?" face when I see it.

I walked into the office to see what the problem was. The problem was bad, and the office manager's look was right on target. Accounting had a problem, and the office manager was trying to get to the bottom of it. On the supervisor's desk was one pile of orders from Canada; another pile was from Australia. Still another stack was a pile of orders from as far away as Norway.

The amount that the bank said was deposited didn't match the amount that the order department said was processed. It wasn't the bank's fault, and no glitch had occurred in the order database. It was our fault.

Not one order operator had told customers who live outside the United States that our company accepts only U.S. funds. A customer in Canada, for example, who sent us a bank check for an order for one of our books did precisely what we had said to do: Send a check in the amount of $32.90. We then deposited the check and waited for it to clear before shipping the order. The bank credited the $32.90 check as a deposit for only $23.90. But why?

Exchange rates. We were losing $9 one order at a time. Glancing at the pile, I tried not to be too upset. At least by that point we were waiting for a check to clear before shipping the order.

Both employees were surprised that I didn't go ballistic. Instead, I took a deep breath and simply asked, "What are we going to do to ensure that this never happens again, and who will be responsible to see that it doesn't?" Both employees agreed to come up with a plan that included immediately retraining the operators who took the orders and the people who processed those orders, double-checking the policies and prices posted in our online shopping malls, and putting it all in writing for my approval. They were still working at 8 o'clock that evening so that the training could begin first thing the following day. (Now *that's* dedication.)

What about Exporting to Foreign Countries?

Selling products online internationally is a great idea, but what about offline sales? A recent survey reported that 90 percent of U.S. companies don't export products simply because they don't know where to begin. If you are selling internationally online, you may as well consider selling internationally offline too.

When you export a product, you basically sell to people located in other countries who sell them for you. Your best bet is to track down a company that already exports to the country in which you want to market.

To learn more about these companies and exporting in general, make your first stop the U.S. Department of Commerce. Off the Internet, you can visit one of almost 70 district offices located throughout the country and get excellent advice for selling to more than 60 different countries. Consult your local white pages for the office nearest you. In addition, the Department of Commerce has a toll-free hotline (800-872-8723). Call and ask for information to be mailed or faxed to you. Be patient if you use the phone number — you have to wade through lots of menus and options.

A useful publication for new exporters is *A Basic Guide to Exporting,* available for $16.50 from the Department of Commerce National Technical Information Service (stock number PB95-109799). To order, call NTIS at 703-487-4650.

On the Internet, look for the International Trade Administration. It's on the Web at `http://www.ita.doc.gov/` (see Figure 11-7).

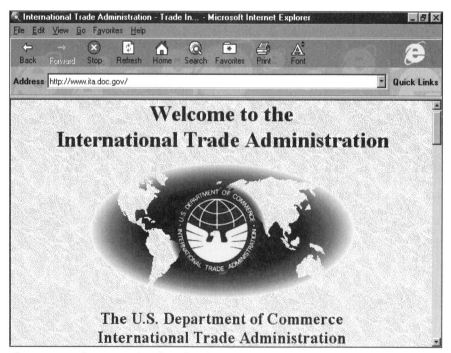

Figure 11-7: The International Trade Administration provides industry and country analysis for new-to-export and new-to-market businesses.

It's your one-stop shop for all government international information and exporting resources (go to `http://www.ita.doc.gov/how_to_export/ned.html`). After you get there, make sure that you check out the National Export Directory. It provides information about federal, local, and state resources that are useful for exporters at every level of export development. These resources are particularly useful, however, for people seeking new-to-export sources.

As I mentioned at the beginning of this chapter, international marketing isn't for every business. Plenty of questions must be answered and obstacles overcome. If you have made it this far and still have an interest in penetrating foreign markets, you just may have the right stuff to do so.

A Few Words about International Promotion

I discuss online promotions in detail in Chapter 14, but I want to make a couple of points in this section that are appropriate for online international marketers.

Obviously, you can't sell to foreign markets if you don't promote your business to foreign markets. If you're doing business on the Internet, you can go a couple of ways. The first possibility is to offer an alternative-language version of your home page — just a simple button that says, for example, "Click here for Spanish version." One click, and a potential customer sees your entire site in his native language.

Japan Air Systems (JAS), for example, enables you to check the airliner's flights and fares in English. In the middle of its Web page is a small button that says "Japanese Version." Check it out for yourself at `http://www.jas.co.jp/e_jashom.htm`. (Try to pronounce that address three times fast while you're looking at Figure 11-8.)

At the time this book was written, the JAS B777 was scheduled to take to the skies in April 1997. To commemorate its 25th anniversary, JAS invites the public to send, over the Internet, design schemes based on its corporate rainbow colors. The airline is giving away a prize — 2 million yen (not $2 million). The company obviously knows about exchange rates: It must make its point that the prize is in yen at least ten times per page. (At the time this book was written, 2 million yen was the equivalent of a little more than $19,000.)

Don't be worried if you don't know a particular country's language that well. You probably can find some sort of translation company to help out. If you point your Web browser to `http://www.languagesolution.com/`, for example, you find The Language Solution, a Florida company that does translating. This site is also an excellent example of a company that adapted a relatively nontechnical service (foreign-language translation) to an online environment.

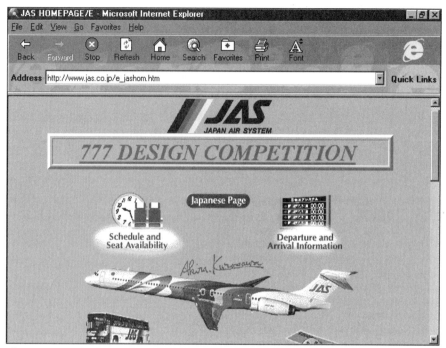

Figure 11-8: The button marked Japanese Page in the middle of the Japan Air Systems site changes the page from English to Japanese.

For another example of marketing online to visitors who speak a foreign language, check out the Dexim Industries home page, at `http://gurukul.ucc.american.edu/uiwww/us7015a/dexim/dexim.html`. The company sells top-quality sports cutlery (hunting knives) to both English-speaking and Spanish-speaking customers. Click the Spanish Version button to see the entire site in Spanish. Click the Versión en Inglés button to go back to the English version.

With more than 20,000 Usenet newsgroups on the Internet, a few are undoubtedly based in whichever country in which you're interested. (In Chapter 14, I talk more about getting publicity in newsgroups.)

You can also reach foreign customers on the commercial online services. In Chapter 8, for example, I described areas on America Online in which you can reach Canadian, German, French, Japanese, British, Spanish, and Italian customers. Most online services have areas similar to these.

In many ways, selling to foreign markets is no different from selling in the United States. Yet, in many ways, it's much different. The key to success in the international marketplace is being able to distinguish between the differences and similarities and adjust your plan accordingly. I would write more about this subject, but I'm off to relax — I have some online international markets to explore.

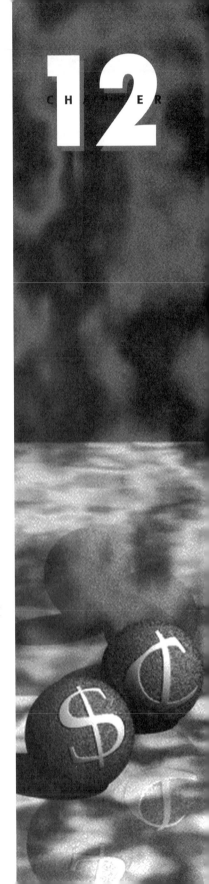

Essential Ingredients for Your Online Area

I hope that by now you have done your fair share of exploring the Internet and the commercial online services. If you haven't, you had better put this book down for a while (not too long, though — I'll miss you). Fire up your commercial online service or Internet Web browser. Go surfing and have some fun! Explore unknown lands! Point and click to your little heart's desire! Start out with the cool picks at Yahoo! (`http://www.yahoo.com`) and the *USA Today* online areas (`http://www.usatoday.com`). If you're using a commercial online service, check out its new area listings, usually listed under "What's Hot."

Keep following the links, and venture into unknown areas with no final resting place in mind. This exercise isn't all fun and games, though. I want you to pay particular attention to your first impression of the different sites at which you land in cyberspace. Keep track of the areas in which you spend the longest time nosing around.

You may be saying, "I can't put this book down — it's great, and I have to learn how to make some money online. What gives?" I'm so glad you asked.

Romping Around Online

Let me explain what makes the good online areas good and the bad areas bad. As you surf the Net, I'm sure that you will discover along the Infobahn some stops that strike your fancy (the home pages and online forums you tell your friends about, bring up at the dinner table with your family, or use in conversation to impress that hot date).

In addition to notable sites, you probably found other Web sites that made you wonder whether intelligent life truly exists, either in or out of cyberspace. You have to recognize the differences between the good and the ugly *and* understand the ways in which they are the same. This understanding will help you when you design your own online area.

Note

What makes people snub their nose at online areas? Often, the reasons are obvious: Certain online areas oppose personal standards of acceptable behavior, conduct, ethics, and moral values. Social causes and advocacy groups that are beyond "border-line controversial" are generally not included in a commercial online service's product offerings. You can find those groups on the Internet, however, because (as I have stated elsewhere in this book) on the Net, anything goes.

An Internet support network for neo-Nazi skinheads, for example, offends most people's standards of conduct and moral values. Notice that I specifically said "most people" — any particular cause always has a certain number of followers, or so it seems. No matter how well-designed a neo-Nazi site is, however, I would not visit it. I oppose those groups' beliefs, have no interest in their activities, don't want to be associated with them, and, well, you get the point. And I am not alone.

The second reason people ignore Web sites, other than offensive content (I leave it to you to define "offensive" for yourself) is that it's confusing or incomplete. Too many online areas apparently began with a good idea but failed to deliver. Maybe it's my marketing blood, but these incomplete online areas strike a deep chord in me. The proprietor tried (you can tell by looking at the screen), but something got lost in the translation from the creator's mind to the customer's screen.

The reasons for the failure of online businesses must be as numerous as the number of products and services available worldwide. Maybe the online area provides too much information or even too little information to entice sales. Perhaps the online area was selling wine before its time and the market didn't see the value in the offer. Or maybe the business was simply selling crap.

Speaking of crap, drop by `http://www.poop.com`. One clever entrepreneur has set up shop online to market — you guessed it. The folks at this site call it "endangered feces," otherwise known as coprolites or fossilized dinosaur droppings (see Figure 12-1). But I digress.

The history of personal computing is filled with good ideas that failed to deliver profits for its creators. Look at Microsoft Bob, a program that ran under Windows and claimed to offer the world's first "social interface" for personal computers. The basic idea was good — create an interface so simple and intuitive that any idiot on the planet could start up programs, find out the current time, and use a PC.

Figure 12-1: Poop.com proves that there isn't much you can't sell on the Internet.

Who knows how much money Microsoft spent making Bob and then trying to convince computer users that Bob was their friend? Bob turned out to be, unfortunately, a major PC memory and resource hog. The program was *too* simple for all except the most inexperienced users. Bob's need for plenty of system resources kept those inexperienced users from buying in to the concept of Bob. Users preferred making a few mistakes over waiting for Bob to catch up and show the result of where they pointed and clicked. You can't really blame them.

Whenever you offer a new product or service, you're gambling. No matter how much research you do or how good your mother thinks your ideas are, the chance always exists that the buying public will not want to spend money on whatever you are peddling.

I know this sad fact firsthand. For a while, the most commonly asked question on my talk-radio show, in my newspaper column, and online was, "What is the best type of personal computer to buy?"

From all the phone calls, letters, and e-mail messages I received, I got an idea. The members of my staff liked it. My mom said that she would buy it (but only if I gave her a discount). I even went on the air one Saturday before we created the product and asked every listener who called my show to give the product a thumbs-up or a thumbs-down. PCs were selling at an unprecedented rate, and all indications said that we should produce it — so we did. Guess what I have sitting in my company warehouse? Oh, about 1,000 copies of the audiotape *10 Easy Steps to Buying the Right Computer*.

With any physical product, such as Bob or Komputer Klinic training products, you stand to lose plenty of money if it's a flop. To bring a product to market, you spend money on product development, manufacturing, printing, product design, packaging, marketing, and many more tasks. If your service business fails, you lose some money, but not quite as much, especially if that service is entirely online-accessible.

Note

The great thing about a Web site or online area is that if you don't quite get it right the first time, it's not tough to make improvements. In a matter of minutes, you can move things around, change your offer, and modify your product. Unlike a static product, an online area is a living, breathing entity that you can change and update almost at will.

Even if you already have your company online, you should read this chapter carefully to make sure that you're getting absolutely the most bang for your cyberbuck. I would bet that you're not taking full advantage of the medium, but I could be wrong. (I was wrong once — those boxes in the warehouse prove it.)

Using the Medium

No matter what your product is, selling boils down to communication — sending the "right" message from you to your would-be customers. Whenever you want to communicate with someone, the first matter you have to consider is which communication medium you plan to use and the effect it has on how you communicate.

If you plan to publish a printed catalog, for example, you face a completely different set of issues and opportunities than if you decide to use direct telephone solicitation to sell your product: You would never attempt to influence your customers by printing a telephone script in your catalog (that would be stupid), for example, and you would never have to worry about photographs if all your orders were taken over the phone (your customers have already bought the product by the time it's shipped).

Likewise, you can offer all sorts of features and activities online that you can't provide by using any other medium. The key to the entire online experience, however, is interactivity.

Before I talk about what the heck interactivity really means to your ability to make money online, think about traditional advertising. It's nothing new — town criers hawked products in the streets long before Benjamin Franklin's *Gazette* even had ads on its front page. Today companies send their messages in newspapers, magazines, mailboxes, on television, and on radio. It's difficult, in fact, to go anywhere without seeing some type of advertisement for something.

Sending the Right Advertising Message

What makes an advertising message different, wherever it appears, depends on the advertisement's goals. Whereas most traditional ads were placed to simply generate direct sales, today's advertising goals are much higher.

Advertisements now do one of or a combination of three things: They remind, inform, and persuade customers of your company and your products or services. Your online advertisements and communications with your customers must achieve these three objectives too. Because your advertisements are online, however, your messages can do much more than merely stare a potential customer in the face. Your messages can jump out and bite them in the, ahem, face.

No such thing as an interactive magazine advertisement or direct-mail piece even exists. Even the scratch-and-sniff perfume ads and Publisher's Clearing House million-dollar giveaways are a one-way street. You act, but the advertiser doesn't really know whether you scowled at the smell or really believed that your name might be the winner they seek.

With an online area, however, you have a unique opportunity to connect with your customers by taking advantage of its primary inherent characteristic: interactivity. The communication is two-way because an exchange is possible.

Tip

Always remember the advertising R.I.P. rule: *R*emind, *i*nform, and *p*ersuade your customers. Otherwise, your company might R.I.P. another way (rest in peace).

Collecting Information in Online Guest Books

One of the simplest yet most effective ways to let your customers interact and know that you care about what they think is to ask them, and the easiest way to ask is to offer online customer surveys.

Surveys also serve an important purpose for you. Sure, they show that you care about your customers' thoughts and feelings — that's important. As long as you make an effort to word your surveys properly, however, you can collect important information about your customers — information that you can use later to keep those customers coming back for more. You can remind them about your company and your products and services. Equally as important, depending on the information you ask and receive in return, you can use customer feedback to fine-tune your messages to better satisfy their needs and wants.

The worst thing you can do in a survey is ask an open-ended question, such as "What do you think about such-and-such?" Remember how long it took your grade-school teacher to grade essay questions on a test, but how easily and quickly that teacher could grade multiple-choice questions? The same principle applies here.

Tip

If you let your customers ramble on, it's almost impossible for you to collect any meaningful information from your surveys. Instead, offer multiple-choice questions or the ever-popular "rate each statement on a scale from 1 to 10" sort of questions.

I can only imagine what a nightmare it would be for Domino's Pizza in Gainesville, Florida, to come up with any survey information that makes sense if it didn't include questions other than "What do we do well?" This site gets a gold star for asking customers for feedback (check it out at `http://dominos.gator.net/`) and giving possible answers to questions such as these:

✦ How often do you eat pizza?

✦ How do you rate our prices?

✦ How do you rate our service?

✦ How do you rate our cheesy bread?

By providing possible answers to customers, every response from every customer is in the exact same format. You can then easily tally the results of your survey, store it in a database program, and, more important, reach conclusions based on the results.

One type of survey that has extremely friendly packaging is an electronic guest book, as shown in Figure 12-2. If you have ever been to a wedding or any other large social event, you probably have signed a guest book (it's the thing to do). Because members of the general public already sign guest books in real life, they're somewhat conditioned to sign them whenever they're presented with the opportunity. People are simply more likely to sign a guest book than to answer a long, drawn-out survey.

You can make your electronic guest book different by giving visitors to your site the option to answer a few well-targeted survey questions. Because it's supposed to be just a guest book, you don't want to go overboard. A couple of questions (no more than eight), just to help you identify who is visiting your area, however, is not inappropriate.

Warning

Remember that your guests may be paying a per-minute fee, so don't make your online surveys so long and detailed that guests bail out — unless you promise something in return for their time.

Your electronic guest book should be attractively designed so that it looks like a real guest book. Ask visitors to complete the standard questions: name, e-mail address, mailing address, and telephone number. Always put this information at the top of the survey.

This information alone enables you to create a customer database to mail information to them electronically or by traditional mail. In addition, a hidden benefit is that you are building an asset of your company — a customer database that you can lease to other companies for a profit when it gets large enough (in the tens of thousands of names, for example).

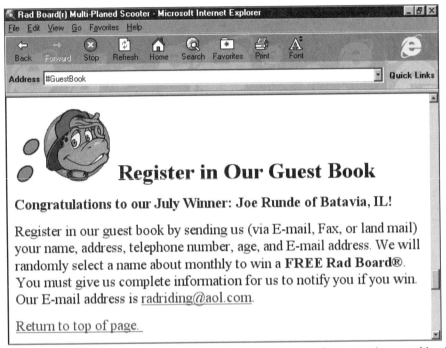

Figure 12-2: Give visitors an incentive — a freebie or at least a chance to win something free — and you have a greater chance that they will sign your electronic guest book.

Tip

Be sure to limit your questions so that no more than eight responses are required from a visitor. If you have too many questions or if you ask open-ended questions, chances are slim that anyone will complete the entire survey. Always be sure to put at the top of the electronic guest book form the questions you most want visitors to complete.

After you get customer feedback, don't just thumb through the results. You have to figure out any gaps between what the customer expected and wanted versus what your company provides and then develop a plan of attack to fix the gap.

Communicate with your customers. Large companies, such as AT&T, may call 2,500 customers per month to get feedback about just one marketing program. Calling customers on the phone in this way may cost a company a small fortune. You can do it online, however, for just a fraction of the cost and get meaningful results in just a fraction of the time.

Becoming a Member of the Family

If you have a Visa or MasterCard, your credit-card company probably considers you a cardholder. How boring. If you have an American Express card, however, you're a member (and "membership has its privileges"). American Express spent boatloads of money on research to reach the conclusion that people would rather be "members" than just "cardholders." It doesn't matter that the relationship between the customer and the credit-card company is identical; it just *feels* better to be a member.

Tip

People like to feel as though they're part of something, as though they *belong*. One way you can create this sense of belonging in your online area is to offer some sort of public message area in which your customers can communicate with each other and with your staff. This technique works especially well if your product or service caters to some sort of niche market; it is ideally suited for virtually any hobby or specialty interest you can think of.

Just like an online survey, of course, a message area can provide you with valuable information. Because it's a public message area, you have the opportunity to, in effect, read the minds of your customers by seeing what they have to say to each other. For example, reading a customer comment that begins with, "Gee, I wish that I had a way to. . ." could lead to a new product for your cyberstore.

The downside to message boards is that they can be a nightmare to manage. Strangely, although people don't really expect a reply to a letter they write to a newspaper editor, they do seem to expect (and I'm not sure why) some sort of response to a message-board posting.

The Komputer Klinic sometimes gets more than 1,000 daily messages on the America Online board. Figure 12-3 shows just one example. Here's how we handle the volume of messages: Members of my staff and I answer as many messages as we can; because we simply cannot respond personally to every person, however, we provide online customers with a way to communicate with either myself or a member of the staff — live and in virtual color through chats too. Live chat sessions are a little trickier to set up, but the hour or so per week that you spend online talking with your customers is worth it.

Be a Winner!

Just as everyone likes to be a member, everyone likes to be a winner. Contests, sweepstakes, giveaways, and games are a good way to introduce new goods and services as well as attract new customers. You have to give out great freebies, of course, but — more important — you also must be sure to cover your butt legally.

Figure 12-3: Message boards and chat rooms are a great way to create two-way online conversations with your customers.

Warning

Court rulings and legislation have been passed recently to limit the use of contests. For starters, you must post the official rules of your contest online and be sure that the contest is legal. I recommend that you consult with a lawyer before launching a contest. She can help you develop the contest rules and make sure that you don't get into any legal hot water.

Spend some time online, and check out current contests. On America Online, use the keyword CONTEST. On the Internet, type **contest** as the search word at Yahoo!, and a bunch of contests are displayed on-screen. Check out what other people are doing. If a company repeats a contest, you know that it is working.

I dropped by The Travel Channel Online (http://www.travelchannel.com) to check out the rules for its monthly photo contest, as shown in Figure 12-4. (I figured that it was a better choice than Andy's Ant Farm contest.) The posted rules for the photo contest include the following:

✦ You must own the rights to the photo you submit! This means that it is *your* photograph!

✦ All photos must be accompanied by a separate entry form.

◆ All photos for the following month's contest must arrive by the 15th of the previous month.

◆ Any photos arriving after the 15th will be submitted for the next month's contest.

◆ All photos become the property of The Travel Channel Online Network and cannot be returned.

◆ All contest winners and entries will be posted on the first day of the month.

◆ All photos become the property of The Travel Channel Online Network and cannot be returned.

◆ The Travel Channel Online Network reserves the right to decline placement of any picture.

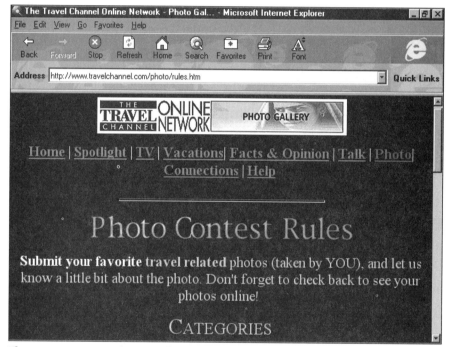

Figure 12-4: Be sure that you always post the rules to your online contests.

I can only imagine some of the photos that must get submitted at this site. As for your contests, I'll say it again: Make sure that your contest is legal before launching it.

It doesn't even matter what the prize is — people just like to know that they have won *something* (personally, I would rather win a million dollars in the lottery than a lucky rabbit's foot). With that in mind, it only makes sense to offer online contests with prizes.

Your online contests can be simple. For example, you might want to enter into a weekly or monthly drawing everyone who signs your electronic guest book. Like everything else you do, your contest should serve the additional purpose of helping to promote your business in some way.

For a prize, you can offer samples of your product or service. Just remember that the prize must have value of its own. If you offer a prize that's useful only if the winner buys something else from you, your contest probably will do your reputation more harm than good.

Tip

Don't be afraid to ask companies to donate contest prizes in exchange for publicity. After all, you have to show a picture of the prize and explain the benefits of the product or service so that entrants know that it's worth their time to try to win. That's publicity and free advertising for the company who donates the prize!

If you want to offer major prizes, such as airfare and hotel accommodations, you have to be patient. You can call airlines and hotels yourself or pay someone else to arrange it all for you.

One company hopes to be the next one-stop shop for vacations. Vacation Celebration, at `http://www.free-vacation.com` on the Web, promises to be "a proven promotional program that can significantly increase the amount of traffic to your Web site and provide you with the name, address, phone number, and e-mail address of potential customers who visit your site." Although the vacation is free to the winner who receives it, *you,* as the giver, pay for it (see Figure 12-5). The price of a vacation depends on the length of the promotion, but the average cost is $95 per month. For this amount, you get to give two adults and three children a three-day, two-night vacation package valued from $500 to $700.

I asked Brent Crabtree, the president of Vacation Celebration, how he makes his money. "We don't make it by charging $95 a month. We make money by selling sponsorships for the vacation." Interesting.

Rarely does the Komputer Klinic not have an online contest in progress. Prizes have ranged in value from $29.99 to more than $500. You might think that I actually bought the prizes. No way!

Tip

Because the Komputer Klinic asks computer companies to donate software programs in exchange for publicity, we get our prizes for free! It's just a matter of reaching the right person at the company you want to donate the prize. That person is — drum roll, please — the guy or gal in charge of public relations or the product's marketing manager.

Target the company you want to donate the prize and explain your contest, the amount of traffic you expect (you may have to stretch it a little), and the great opportunity it is for the company. You may be surprised at the positive response you receive and the freebies that companies will deliver to your door for your online contest.

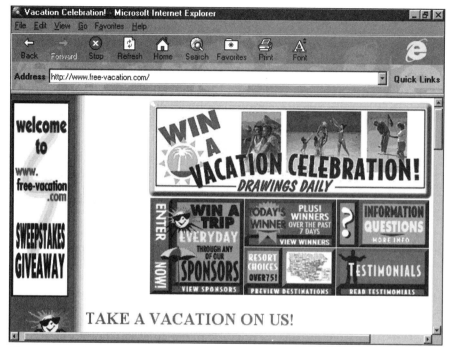

Figure 12-5: The `free-vacation.com` site provides Web sites with promotional resort-vacation getaways — for a price.

In Cyberspace, You Gotta Look Sharp

It may be true that beauty is only skin deep. Unfortunately, the way a person looks often makes the first impression, and a first impression is a lasting impression. That's as true for an online area is it is for anything else. You may have the greatest online business idea in the history of personal computing. That's great! If your site doesn't *look* good, however, people assume that it *isn't* good and move on to your competitors' sites. That's bad.

Looking good in cyberspace presents a unique challenge. When you're producing printed materials, the sky is the limit, graphically speaking. You can make your pictures, illustrations, and other graphical elements as sophisticated and complicated as you want. No matter how colorful and ornate you make your pages, your printing costs stay pretty much the same. You have no reason not to have the best-looking graphics possible.

Although the cost of graphics is no more of a concern in the online arena than for printed pieces, you must address one other issue: *bandwidth,* or the amount of information that can be squeezed over a phone line through a modem at a particular time. For the foreseeable future, you're stuck — most of your customers will access your online area by modem. Even with a 28.8 Kbps modem or higher, complicated graphics can take longer to download than most people are willing to wait. If your customers spend too much time waiting and not enough time doing, they're likely to look elsewhere. Your challenge, then, is to create a visually pleasing site not overburdened by large graphics that clog up the bandwidth. Where do you draw the line?

If you decide to set up shop on a commercial online service, the service provides you with plenty of direction in this area. You don't have much latitude because the online service dictates the size and resolution of your graphics.

On the Web, however, you're on your own. Fear not — Kim Komando here, to help answer the question of how much graphical content is too much and how much is just enough? You should remember two things about graphics on the Web (and online in general):

✦ **Standard screen resolution:** This measurement of how good an image looks is 72 dots per inch (dpi). If you look closely at your monitor, you should see a bunch of dots. Specifically, *dpi* measures the total number of dots squeezed into one square inch. Any graphic or text element is composed of dots (in the same way a Matisse painting is made up of small brush strokes).

Resolution of an image is one of the factors that determines its file size. The higher the resolution, the bigger the file; the bigger the file, the longer it takes for the graphic to pop up on-screen. Don't forget that resolution is both a horizontal and vertical measurement.

A 200 dpi image, therefore, is four times larger than a 100 dpi image (100 vertical dots × 100 horizontal dots = 10,000 dots; 200 vertical dots × 200 horizontal dots = 40,000 dots). By keeping your images at 72 dpi, you ensure that your graphics look as good as possible and that they are as small as possible.

✦ **Bit depth:** This measurement also determines how good a graphic looks on-screen. The largest possible bit depth is 24-bit color (you may have heard it referred to as "millions of colors"). This 24-bit color is considered photorealistic. The higher the bit depth, the larger the image; the larger the image — you know — the longer it takes to show up on a customer's monitor.

Not everyone, however, has a monitor and a graphics card that can display 24-bit color. The lowest common denominator here is 8-bit color, or 256 colors. Unless you have some compelling reason to display images in 24-bit color, you should never go beyond 8-bit color. Depending on the image, you may not even need that much to produce an image with an acceptable appearance. The lower you can make the image's bit depth, the smaller the file is and the faster it downloads to a customer's system.

The other question to answer about Web graphics is which format to use, JPEG or GIF. Because both formats are compressed and therefore load more quickly, either one is ideal for online use. The difference between them is that all GIF files have a maximum bit depth of 8, and all JPEG files are stored as 24-bit images.

Tip

You might think that JPEG files would be larger than GIF files. Not so fast. Because the compression method used in JPEGs is generally more efficient than the one used in GIFs, JPEGs are generally smaller than GIFs. The drawback to JPEGs is that not every available Web browser supports them. If you limit yourself to GIF images, you guarantee one thing — that your customers can use any Web browser to view the files.

One way to make your site attractive without becoming a bandwidth burden is to make sure that your text is formatted attractively, as shown in Figure 12-6. Right now, you don't have much control over the fonts displayed on a Web page because users can set and change the fonts from their browser's settings. You can at least make good use of formatting techniques (such as bold, italics, and headlining) on your Web page, however. Simple fonts, such as Times Roman, Helvetica, Courier, and Arial, are generally the easiest fonts to see on-screen.

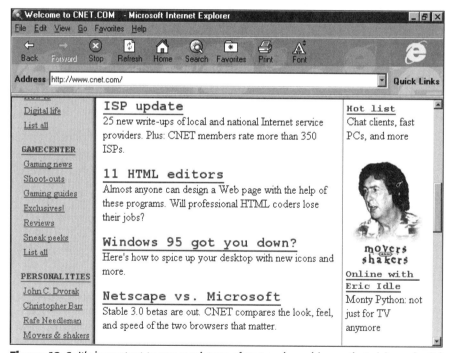

Figure 12-6: It's important to use a mixture of text and graphics so that visitors don't have to wait too long for a Web page to show up on-screen.

Technology is always changing. As I write this book, Adobe and Microsoft are working together on a new font technology called *OpenType,* which supposedly will replace both Type 1 and TrueType fonts (the ones everyone uses now). The reason that this joint effort is important to you and your online shop is that the resulting font format is supposed to be truly universal, even on the Internet. In other words, if Microsoft and Adobe are successful in pulling this project together, you will be able to format your Web pages with specific fonts, just as you would do in your favorite page-layout program.

Tip

Here's the bottom-line rule of thumb for creating pretty pages on the Web: Make the page look as good as possible, but keep the entire thing (all the text and graphics) under 60K or so for your main page, and less for supplemental pages. Most users find this size tolerable, if not desirable. Also, if you use a single large graphic element, try to use that same element on each page rather than use a different one on each page.

The reason for using the same graphical element is that most current images *cache* (temporarily store) images as they are downloaded. The next time a browser needs that image, whether it's for the same page or a different one, the browser reads the image from your hard disk (instead of downloading it again).

I gave the Komputer Klinic Web designers and programmers one more tidbit to follow: The total amount of time any first-time visitor must spend waiting to see any page on the Klinic site must be less than 20 seconds using a 14.4 Kbps modem. If the total amount of time for a screen to appear is less than 20 seconds, however, you get a gold star.

Providing Quality Content

A good-looking online area may make a good first impression, but the quality of the information you present keeps 'em coming back for more. To be successful, you simply must offer top-notch content that gets updated regularly (preferably daily).

The informational content on your site can be broken down into two basic components:

✦ What you have to say

✦ How you choose to say it

What you have to say

Because everyone is pressed for time these days, you don't want to waste a customer's time with useless or unimportant information. As Joe Friday once said, "Just the facts." You don't want to give customers more information than they need. You might end up confusing them, which lowers the chance of making a sale. Worse, you might tick off your customers because of the time you have taken from them.

Your goal is to provide just enough information for a potential customer to make a purchasing decision (see Figure 12-7). If you were selling boxes of crayons online, for example (I realize that crayons may not be a realistic example, but work with me on this), it's useful to tell customers that the box includes 500 different colors. It doesn't add much value, however, to list all 500 colors. That information would only slow down the process.

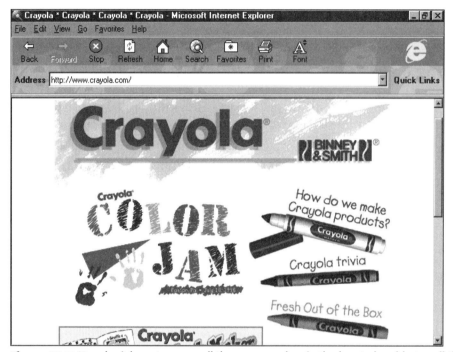

Figure 12-7: You don't have to name all the crayon colors in the box to be able to sell them on the Internet.

The key to saying the right things is to stay focused. You're generally much better off if you can clearly articulate your niche rather than attempt to be all things to all people. Try to put yourself in the shoes of your customers. If you were considering purchasing your product or service, how much information would you really need in order to make a decision to buy?

In the online world, you must remember, of course, that you can also provide value-added information that doesn't relate directly to the purchase of your product. You can also provide, for example, background and historical information about your particular area of expertise.

This value-added information creates in the mind of your customers a sense that you're there to do more than just sell a product, that you truly have their best interests in mind. (You care!) Don't post a bunch of useless information, however, just for the sake of having something there. As with your product information, make sure that your value-added information is truly useful. If the information informs or entertains customers, put it online. Otherwise, trash it.

One last word of advice on the subject of "what you have to say." Avoid too many long-winded phrases and flowery adjectives. Think twice before you use "puff-speak." Rather than say "at this point in time," for example, use the word "now." Here are some more puff-speak examples that drive people nutty:

✦ On the grounds that

✦ As a result of

✦ By virtue of the fact that

✦ In spite of

All these phrases usually can be replaced by just one word: *because.*

Words such as *best, superior, outstanding, unsurpassed,* and other self-promotional, meaningless adjectives should be used sparingly too. These types of words and phrases may sound good when *you* read them, but they don't provide any useful information when *your customer* reads them. After all, would anyone use any negative words to describe their own product?

Tip

Even a person selling pure garbage would use positive-sounding words to describe the product. Again, stick to the facts, and avoid injecting your own wonderful opinions. You can get by with quotes from other people saying how fine, superb, unparalleled, and excellent your products or services are, but be sure to use testimonials from past customers (with their permission, of course) rather than your own.

How you choose to say it

Just as important as what you say is *how* you say it. Online, "saying it" begins with good writing. If you don't have the necessary skills to produce crisp, concise, persuasive, and — most important — grammatically correct copy, find someone who does. It doesn't cost much, and every community has tons of freelance writers. If you need a writer, pick up your local newspaper, and read its columns and stories. When you find one you like, pick up the phone and ask to speak with the reporter who wrote the story you like.

Tip

Newspaper writers generally don't pull down quite the same level of income that a corporate president does. Frankly, many reporters are starving; they write because it's their passion, not for the salary they receive. You may be surprised at the enthusiastic response you get from reporters when you present them with the opportunity to make some extra money creating copy or editing your words. Ask how much they charge, and remember the first rule of negotiation: He who mentions price first loses.

Wages for writing skills follow certain standards, however. You can look them up in the *Writer's Market.* You can find this helpful book, which is updated yearly, at your local library or bookstore.

Your customers expect to deal with a professional organization, and nothing puts a "rank amateur" stamp on your site faster than poorly written copy.

Warning

You may think that your product or service is so amazing and wonderful that customers won't be concerned with such minor issues. If that's the way you think, all I can say is that you're dead wrong. Even one simple typographical error can make your site seem suspect. If you can't spell, customers will think that you also take the quality of your products and services lightly, and they won't buy from you.

Organizing your information

Just as important as writing in the "how you say it" discussion is the organization of your site. Even if you have in place all the other components I have already discussed, you will drive customers away in droves if they get lost in your online area or cannot quickly and easily find what they're looking for.

Sometimes it's tempting for beginners to create a complicated hierarchy of menus and submenus, just because they think that it gives their site more substance. I have news for these people: Your customers aren't looking for sophisticated sites. They're looking for useful information and quality products. Your job is to deliver those two items as simply and efficiently as possible.

Tip

Sometimes, of course, you want to provide large amounts of information. Although you're better off keeping things short, you shouldn't leave out important information just to keep your content within some predefined length. If you do need to deliver some sort of lengthy information, break it up into several articles rather than present one long dissertation. Just think of the people in your life who talk and talk without letting you get a word in edgewise. Makes you want to scream, eh? The same thing happens online; rather than scream, however, users just click and take their credit card to another online area. You generally should limit the information you present on-screen to chunks of 200 lines or fewer.

By limiting the amount of information you present at one time to your customers, you make even the longest documents more manageable, as shown in Figure 12-8. Each info chunk is not only easier to digest but, if you provide a point-and-click index to those other chunks, it's also much easier for your customers to locate exactly the information they want.

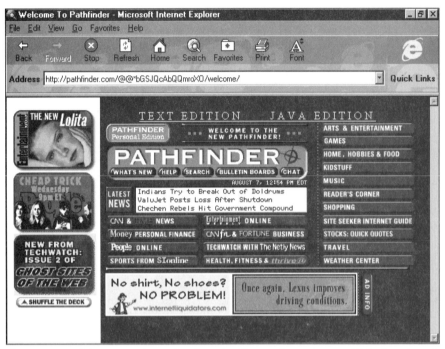

Figure 12-8: Visitors must know just from looking at the areas on a Web site where the point-and-click of a button will land them.

One other key to a well-organized online site is the use of *navigational guides* (those little buttons, arrows, and site maps that enable customers to jump from one spot on your site to another, unrelated area). Again, you have to walk that fine line between providing enough help and providing too much. A well-done navigational aid moves customers from one point to another as easily as possible; an overdone navigational aid only confuses them and convinces them to buy — from someone else!

After customers sign your electronic guest book, for example, give them a break. Rather than display the message "Your request has been submitted" on-screen, send them automatically back to your main screen.

Tip

Put a little toolbar at the bottom of every page. It doesn't have to have (nor should it have) many buttons. The optimum number of buttons on a toolbar is three to six; then users can, for example, return automatically to the page or area they came from, go to your main screen, go to an area toward which you are trying to direct traffic, or go to the hottest area on your site.

Offering Cross-Promotional Opportunities Aplenty

If you could set up the perfect online site, each area of your site would be visited in equal amounts. Customers would want to see every part of your site every time they visit. That never happens, of course, no matter how hard you try and how well your business does. Like it or not, some areas will always be more popular than others. That's not a bad thing. If you adjust accordingly, you can turn it into a good thing. The key is to cross-promote one area in another area.

If you have a question-and-answer message area in which you answer customer questions, for example, you can reference documents from your educational area in your answers. Likewise, in your educational documents, you can (where appropriate) point out the educational value of participating in your message boards.

Tip

Every time a potential customer accesses some sort of "free" information or service on your site, that experience should somehow promote some aspect of your business.

Cross-promotional opportunities don't come just from your site, though. If you're smart and a "people person," it should not be difficult to establish reciprocal-link agreements with other, related, noncompetitive cyberbusinesses. Unless your site is particularly obnoxious or offensive, other businesses are usually more than happy to exchange links with you. Every person who visits the other site, therefore, has the opportunity to check out your site too. It's a win-win situation.

Rather than directly soliciting links, get creative. That's what the Klinic did with its home page in launching the Official Komando Kool Site of the Week award, as shown in Figure 12-9.

Every week, members of the Komputer Klinic staff choose their favorite Internet and online areas. The Klinic sends the winning site an official notification e-mail letter in addition to instructions for placing a graphic (which I personally designed in three minutes) on that site's home page. The graphic is a link back to the Klinic's home page.

Do the math: The Klinic chooses 20 to 30 Kool Sites per week, and there are 52 weeks in a year. In one year, we have added almost 1,500 links to the Klinic's home page! Pretty cool, huh!

Don't think that this sort of thing works only for Web sites. You can use this strategy on the commercial online services too. If you don't believe me, just check out the Komputer Klinic on America Online (we call them "Friends of the Komputer Klinic").

Figure 12-9: The Komputer Klinic gives awards to the best sites on the Internet and gets a link from winners in return.

Keeping Current

I know that you're probably tired of reading about surveys by now because I certainly am, but let me talk about them one more time. Online survey after online survey has shown that the easiest way to drive users away from a Web site or online area is never to change the content they see. You may have the greatest Web page on the entire cyberplanet. Unfortunately, no matter how good it is, if you never update the content, it's old news the second time someone drops in. To keep people coming back to your site, you need a constant stream of new information with which to greet customers on their return visits.

Keeping an online area up-to-date is probably not as easy as you might think. Part of the reason is that you have two different areas of concern. You must be able to distinguish between those two areas and then capitalize on their distinctions.

The first concern is content. Are you out of stock on a particular item? Have you changed the price? Do you have an online event coming up? You owe it to your customers to make sure that they have up-to-the-minute information. Anything less can cost you a sale, alienate customers, or (if it looks as though you falsely represented a product or service) get you into legal trouble.

Tip

Keeping your own information current is only the beginning, however. As an aspiring cyber-entrepreneur, it's also your obligation to stay abreast of current developments in the technology that made your venture possible. Doing business online is a dynamic endeavor. You cannot just set up shop and expect your business to stay the same forever. By continually exploring new technologies and implementing the ones that make sense in your own online areas, you show your customers that you're willing to adapt to their needs and demonstrate that you are committed to the online community.

Remembering Not to Forget the Money

No matter what you do online or how you do it, make sure that you don't lose sight of the fact that you're doing it all for a reason: to make money. There's absolutely nothing wrong with admitting that. It's the reason that the baker bakes, that the shoe salesperson sells shoes, and that the factory worker stands on the assembly line day after day. It's what makes the world go 'round.

What that statement means to your cyberbusiness is that your online area must, above all, give potential customers a way to become actual customers. You must provide them with some way to spend their money. (Now would be a good time to review Chapter 10. It talks about security and online-payment methods.) If you're involved with some sort of business in which you can't actually sell your product online, you must at least provide users with a way to submit serious inquiries to you. I realize that I sound like a broken record, and I can guarantee that I will say this again before you finish this book, but if you can't convince the buying public to part with their cash, it doesn't matter how many other things you do right. Your business will not succeed. Period. That's exactly what I *don't* want to have happen. I want you to succeed. If you remember only one thing from reading this book, please let it be what I have written in this last section.

Part IV

Advertising, Publicity, and Sponsorships

CHAPTER 13

Advertising Your Cyberbusiness

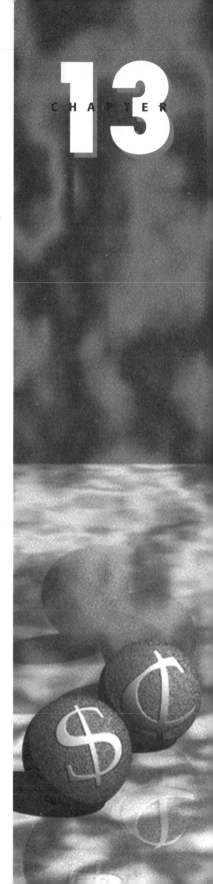

Put on your thinking cap. Which radio format draws the most people who own or use a personal computer: classical, adult contemporary, Top 40, country, news talk, sports talk, urban, New Age, or nostalgia? More than likely, you pictured most people be-bopping to Mariah Carey or the Rolling Stones while surfing online. If you chose any other answer than the news-talk category, you are wrong by a long shot, or at least according to the radio-industry research company The Interep Store.

If you want to advertise your online service business or a computer-related product, buying advertising during a talk-radio show is a good bet. Working down the food chain, buying time on my computer-related network talk-radio show is an even better idea. (It's shameless, I know, but you should acquire the same trait if you want to succeed. Never be afraid to ask for the order.)

Like other aspects of marketing, the process of choosing the best places for your marketing messages involves *demographics,* or knowing whether an audience matches your customer profile. (I'm sure that I have drilled into your head the importance of demographics enough that I shouldn't have to do it again in this chapter.)

Kim's Thoughts on Madison Avenue

Let me start out in this chapter by distinguishing between advertising and publicity. *Advertising,* as I use the term, means making some sort of financial investment (spending money) to put your message directly in the face of potential customers. On the other hand, publicity (which I discuss in Chapter 14) usually costs very little and is a less direct approach than advertising. The purpose of publicity is to get other people, mostly the news media, to do "advertising" for you.

Warning

Don't be fooled. Advertising an online business is a tricky matter. For one thing, although millions of users are online, the total number of users represents only a small fraction of the total population who, for example, watch television or listen to the radio. The traditional advertising media, such as radio and television, *may* not be the best places to advertise your online business. Television and radio advertising can work, but it depends on what you are selling and what you hope to achieve by advertising.

The biggest problem with online advertising is, frankly, that it is still in its infancy. Companies are still experimenting with the best ways to make advertising work as a revenue-generating source. I'm not saying that online advertising doesn't work; there just may be ways no one has thought of yet to make it work better.

The last section in this chapter presents Komando's picks for getting the latest information about online advertising. Don't go there just yet. Read this chapter from start to finish so that you know the lingo and understand the opportunities I mention.

What Works?

Before you continue reading, I present the three main purposes of advertising: Remind, inform, and persuade your customers. (You may remember this stuff from Chapter 12.) Taking things a step further, I am sure that you are wondering what the three purposes have to do with your online advertising. I'm so glad you asked. (I just love one-way conversations.)

When I talk about accomplishing the goal of reminding a customer that you exist, it's just that: From the simplest view, customers have to know that you help populate the world before they can plop down their credit cards to buy your products and services. I am sure that you can pick the AT&T logo from a crowd of logos (see Figure 13-1). Advertising made that possible.

Automobile advertisements are very informative. You hear or read about all their nifty features and financing plans. Although hardly anyone realized for years that Chrysler made up the term "Corinthian leather," it made consumers think that they got more than just "leather." Where do you think the leather came from? A Corinthian cow?

Testimonials from past customers are usually the persuasion factor in advertising (just watch any television shopping channel). You should use testimonials as much as possible. They are effective in making customers trust that the product you deliver is of high quality and value. As a rule, try to use testimonials that match the demographics

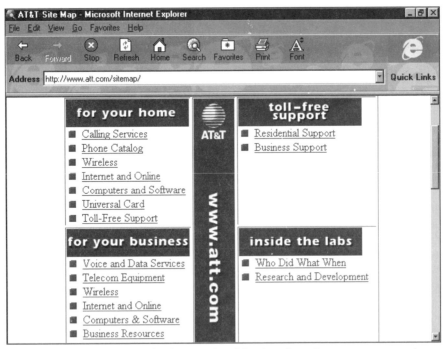

Figure 13-1: One of the goals of AT&T advertising is to keep its company name, image, and diverse product line in front of new and existing customers (in other words, to remind customers that the company exists).

of your audience. If you are selling the book *How to Find Your Soul Mate on the Information Superhighway,* for example, it's pointless to have a retired nun talk about how much the book changed her life.

Even if you have all three advertising goals covered, one of the biggest problems of traditional advertising is that it cannot close a deal or directly get cash out of a consumer's pocket. Because the online environment changes all that, it's what I focus on in this discussion. You can present your message *and* ask for the order. In addition, I am guessing that you are interested in advertising not for the purpose of taking a public stance on a policy (called *advocacy advertising*) but rather for the purpose of *generating additional sales.* My focus in this chapter is the use of advertising to make money. (What a novel thought.)

Note

Again, it's important to remember that no matter where you place advertising, its purpose is *not* to generate additional publicity. The two concepts are complementary, but definitely not equal. (I discuss publicity in the next few chapters of this book.)

Understanding the Components of a Good Advertisement

When you develop an online advertisement, you must consider many issues. Sure, you first must figure out what you are going to sell in the advertisement. Equally as important, however, what is the theme of your message? To help answer that question, think back to the discussion of Maslow's pyramid and Komando's Theory of Buy-Me-Now Needs in Chapter 3. (I would have repeated the entire chapter to save you some time and to save myself from carpal-tunnel syndrome, but the publisher who paid me big bucks to write this book wouldn't let me. So you get to flip back to Chapter 3.)

As a quick review, you can identify the best theme for your message by looking at how the product or service you are selling appeals to your customers. For example, can your product or service save them time or their marriage? Work into your advertisement the answer or common problem (or both) that your product or service solves. Then decide on the tone of the advertisement: Does it evoke fear, humor, greed, or dreams of doing something better within the person who views the message?

Comparing your company to your competition

If you can make either a direct or indirect comparison with your biggest competitor, do it. After all, this technique has worked with long-distance carriers for years, and their increase in revenue proves it. The ever popular Pepsi Challenge is another classic example of comparative advertising, but the same principles also apply in cyberspace (see Figure 13-2).

Consider the answer to these questions before telling the world that you're better than your competition:

+ Do you offer lower prices than your competitors?

+ Do you have a better return policy?

+ Do you guarantee a better turnaround time for your particular service?

+ How do you compare in terms of years of experience?

Favorable answers to any of these questions may serve as the basis for some sort of comparative advertising. Just make sure that you have facts to substantiate your claims or else you may hear from your competitors' lawyers.

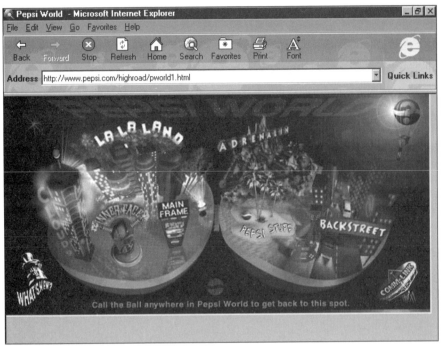

Figure 13-2: The Pepsi-versus-Coke challenge works to increase consumer awareness and sales both inside and outside cyberspace.

Getting someone else to tell your story

Do any celebrities use your product? Celebrity endorsements are a killer way to stimulate sales. You must be careful to use a credible source and to make sure that consumers can easily make a connection between the celebrity and your product.

It has been said, and I wholeheartedly agree, that word of mouth is the best advertising. Think about it. Would you be more likely to go to the car dealer your best friend rants and raves about or to the one with the flashiest television commercial that says, "No bull"? The question is, "How can you get a satisfied customer in Seattle to speak to a potential customer in Orlando?" Easy. Ask them to.

If you have received favorable e-mail from a satisfied customer, you may want to consider quoting that person as a testimonial in one of your advertisements. A testimonial can be a powerful tool if the person you're quoting has a powerful message. Make sure that you don't take any old wishy-washy statement just for the sake of having a testimonial. Your testimonial should drive home your message.

To cover your butt legally, make sure that you get the author's permission before using a testimonial. Many people don't mind being publicly quoted; they liked to be asked first, though. As the advertiser using a quote, make sure that you get written permission in the form of a release. Depending on how you use the quote, you may also have to pay the person for the quote. We pay people one flat dollar.

Coming up with advertising materials

Now I introduce the concept of the hard sell versus the soft sell. A *hard-sell* advertisement gets right to the point and says, in effect, "You need and want this product because. . . ." No beating around the bush. A television example of a hard sell is a commercial for headache medicine in which an actor speaking directly to you and looking as though he hasn't gone to the bathroom for a week explains why it's in your best interest to choose his product. *He* uses it, after all.

A *soft-sell* advertisement gently coaxes you to buy a particular product. To use a television ad as another example, consider an all-American family sitting around the breakfast table, each member perfectly content because Mom has served fresh-squeezed orange juice from Florida. "Wow! Great juice, Mom. I love you!" This advertisement doesn't get in your face, like the actor in the preceding example does. Instead, it implies that if you drink orange juice from Florida, you too will be a happier and healthier person.

Sending the right message is one thing; putting it all together takes talent. Just so that you know what you're getting into, a typical advertisement is made up of five distinct elements:

- ✦ Headline
- ✦ Illustration
- ✦ Body copy
- ✦ Customer ordering method
- ✦ Company logo with your slogan (or company *signature,* as advertisers like to call it)

If the creative side of your brain isn't in high gear, admit it. Get hold of an advertising or design agency that does (preferably, one who also understands the online marketing environment).

I've said it before, and I'll say it again: If you expect to be regarded as a business professional, all your communication devices (advertisements, letters, press releases — whatever) must look and sound professional.

Even if you do hire outside help, however, you're still the one in charge. It's your responsibility to offer some sort of direction to your consultant or advertising agency.

Again, which type of advertising you choose to employ is entirely up to you. As you decide, you should consider the overall personality of your business. If you're selling hunting knives online, a hard-sell approach might be in order. If you're selling custom gift baskets, a soft-sell advertisement might work.

Note

The great thing about creating an online advertisement is that you usually can place the same ad in newspapers or magazines without much work, even if you are placing a print ad in the online environment. And just as soon as the world is racing online with ultrafast modems, television and video advertisements will become common online. (Online marketing is not unlike marketing to people in a country other than your own. Certain rules, customs, and terms are unique to the Internet, and each online service has its own unique personality. Make sure that you observe these rules and customs.) Until that time comes, the following section presents a few ways in which you can advertise your products online now.

Examining Your Options on the Commercial Online Services

If you set up your cybershop on a commercial online service, such as America Online or CompuServe, a number of advertising options are available to you. I have already discussed classified advertising, but you can spend your advertising dollars in many more places. How much you fork over depends on what you are hoping to achieve from your advertisements.

Participating in shopping malls

Examine, for example, the options available to you as a participant in the CompuServe Electronic Mall, as shown in Figure 13-3. I mentioned in Chapter 8 that the basic annual cost of participating in the Electronic Mall is $50,000 plus 2 percent of your annual sales. The advertising opportunities I discuss in this section are in addition to that amount. The bottom line: You had better be selling something damn good.

Every time CompuServe members enter the Electronic Mall, they see a marquee advertising or spotlighting one of the mall merchants. When you consider what you're already paying to be on the Electronic Mall in the first place, marquee advertising seems to be a relatively low-cost add-on. It's similar to deciding whether shelling out another $300 for a CD player for your $60,000 Mercedes Benz is worth it. At the time this book was written, prices for marquee advertising ranged from $2,500 for 12 weeks to $7,500 for a full year.

The only shortcoming of CompuServe's marquee advertising is that you have no guarantee of exactly how often users will see your advertisement. If 10 companies sign up for marquee advertising, your message is displayed to every tenth visitor. If 100 companies sign up, however, your message is displayed to only every hundredth visitor. And the price always stays the same.

Figure 13-3: The CompuServe Electronic Mall offers many advertising avenues. Restrict your participation in this type of advertising until your online business is well established.

CompuServe also distributes a version of its Electronic Mall on CD-ROM. This option enables Mall advertisers to take greater advantage of multimedia presentations that would be too large to offer over a modem connection. If you participate in the CompuServe CD Storefront program, you can incorporate a variety of multimedia elements (music, video, and animation, for example) into your advertising.

The minimum cost of CD Storefront participation is $5,000 plus 2 percent of any sales. That price may not seem all that bad. Just keep in mind that this amount is *in addition to* the amount for a standard storefront in the regular Electronic Mall. My advice: Reserve your participation in this type of advertising until your online business is well established.

Buying ads in magazines

Many commercial online services also send their members a monthly printed magazine. In addition to providing members with important information about the service, these magazines also give online merchants the opportunity to do print advertising for a precisely targeted market.

Rates aren't cheap, of course. You can tell just by looking at who buys the full-page advertisements in these magazines. Flipping through a recent issue of *CompuServe* magazine, for example, I noticed advertisements for Columbia House, United Airlines, and Mercury automobiles, just to name a few. Even the minimum listed rate for a simple classified ad is $1,000.

Including information with your advertising

Advertisements aren't just a means to flash your product and toll-free number on a customer's screen. It's often better to tie your message in with some information. On America Online, for example, MGM/UA was a regular addition to the Entertainment section of Parent Soup (keyword PARENT SOUP), as shown in Figure 13-4. MGM recommended a weekly Friday Night Video for families. Polaroid has had an entire area in Parent Soup dedicated to building children's self-esteem through picture-taking.

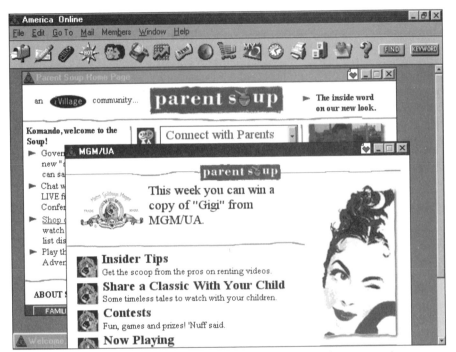

Figure 13-4: Providing information consumers can use is another way to give your advertising message the attention it deserves. Parent Soup is loaded with tips and provides MGM-sponsored Friday Night Video recommendations.

As you have learned already, menus on the commercial online services are normally managed and run by the company that provides the information in the area, not by the commercial online service. My employees and I run the Komputer Klinic, for example, on America Online and the Microsoft Network. Think of a commercial online service as the owner of the building and each menu on the service as a tenant. The tenants decorate their area with their own sponsors.

If you are interested in advertising within a particular area that is not the main marketplace or mall on a commercial online service offering, drop the forum manager an e-mail message. You can usually find the person's name and e-mail address in the "About" section of the area. Forum advertising prices range from a few dollars to hundreds or even thousands of dollars a day. It's all in the traffic.

Paying by the number of people who see your ad

Generally, online advertising takes into account the "traffic" (the hits, or visits) and then another important factor: what's seen and what's clicked. Here's what I mean. Just because you place your advertisement within another company's forum or online service area, you have no guarantee that everyone who enters the area will see the ad. Be sure (this is a biggie) that you have a way to track the number of people who click a button to find out more about you.

An online service obviously has no way to forecast exactly how many people will click a button to see and (you hope!) act on your message. The company should, at the very least, be able to give you an educated guess. In addition, ask to speak with some past advertisers on the service so that you know what you're likely to get for your money.

You must evaluate each advertising opportunity on its own capability to generate income. If your business is so strong that it warrants being on a commercial online service in the first place, chances are that opportunities like the ones I just described are worth exploring.

Advertising on the Internet

Web sites that are extremely popular with the average cyberconsumer have something you want — potential customers — and they know it. These days, it's not uncommon for these sites to sell advertising space to almost anyone who wants it, including you. This type of advertising is especially popular on the various search engines, such as Yahoo! and InfoSeek.

A typical Web advertisement works somewhat like the CompuServe marquee advertising I mentioned earlier in this chapter. Joe or Jane User accesses a particular home page and sees your advertisement at the top or bottom or somewhere else on the requested page. The great thing about this sort of advertising is that your marquee is also a button linked to your Web site; clicking it takes the potential customer directly to your cyber front door.

I already mentioned Yahoo! and InfoSeek, so let's look at their rates (see Figure 13-5). The rates I mention were current at the time I wrote this book, but are subject to change, of course.

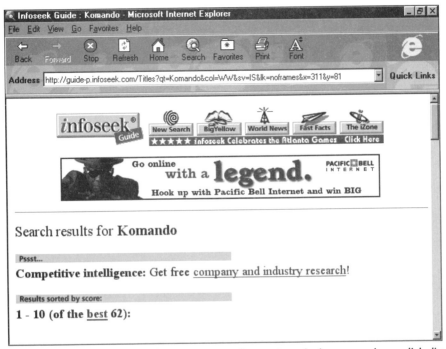

Figure 13-5: Advertising on the Internet usually consists of a banner and one-click direct access to an advertiser's home page (Pacific Bell, in this case).

In most cases, Web advertising is based on the number of hits, or *impressions,* per month. In other words, you pay according to how many users are shown your particular advertisement in a month. By Internet standards, 100,000 impressions per month is a relatively small amount. That many impressions from Yahoo! will cost you anywhere from $2,000 to $5,000, depending on exactly where on Yahoo! your advertising image is displayed. The InfoSeek price tag for that number of impressions is $3,500.

At the other end, consider ten times that amount, or one million impressions. At InfoSeek, it costs $15,000 to reach one million users per month. Over at Yahoo!, that same exposure can cost as much as $50,000, again depending on image placement.

Most of these sites also offer other, specialized advertising opportunities. Yahoo! has a special area called Web Launch, for example, in which new sites can be posted for immediate exposure. The current cost to have your link included on the Web Launch page is $1,000 per week.

Tip

To get current rates and marketing opportunities, drop by the site on which you want to advertise and ask. Just send along your request to info@yahoo.com or info@whatever.com. Mention that you want to spend money — you will get an answer.

Harnessing the Power of E-Mail

E-mail works well for keeping in touch with the family, but you can also use it to promote your advertising campaign by using one of these methods:

✦ Send e-mail en masse to a targeted mailing list.

✦ Send e-mail to any person's e-mail address you can find or buy. This technique, the cyberspace equivalent of junk mail, is frowned on by the Internet community at large. Just as with paper junk mail, however, one truth remains: If it doesn't produce results, advertisers won't waste their money on it.

Warning

It's up to you to decide whether to go this route. If you do, be aware that you risk damaging your reputation with some users. Also be aware that most commercial online services prohibit this sort of activity. The loophole is that the commercial online services have no control over the type of mail that comes over the Internet (yet, anyway).

E-mail offers several advertising advantages. For starters, your message can be deposited in your potential customers' electronic mailbox only seconds after you send it. By using the appropriate mass e-mail list program, you can personalize messages too. If you want to change the text in your e-mail message, you can do it quickly and easily.

You can also match the demographics of the people on an e-mail list with your customers' demographics. A good list is everything; don't do a search for mailing lists on the Internet and pick the first one you see.

To be a smart mailing-list shopper, be sure to do the following:

✦ Check the quality of the list or — at the very least — how recent the list is.

✦ Check the number of times a list has been sold to other people. A list that has been *banged* (that's industry talk for "used") many times is worse than having no list at all.

✦ As a baseline, a good e-mail list that contains the real name, mailing address, and phone number of its "listees" usually costs about $200 for 5,000 to 8,000 names.

Tip

✦ A mailing-list company often provides, at no charge, 100 or so test names. You just have to know to ask for a free sample (and now you do).

When you develop your own mailing list, you have several options. Although I neither endorse nor condemn this method, perhaps the easiest way is to collect e-mail addresses from relevant Usenet newsgroups and listserv mailing lists.

If you're selling online tax advice, for example, you can look for Usenet newsgroups that cater to small-business owners. By identifying potential customers who already have shown some sort of interest in your general field, you can keep your advertising much more targeted.

The other, more acceptable, method of advertising with e-mail is the use of an *auto-responder*. With this method, when someone requests information about a particular product or service of yours, a program running on either your PC or the host system of your commercial online service or Internet service provider sends out an auto-mated response that includes all the necessary information. (This information may be the exact same stuff you used for your mass e-mailing.)

The big difference with an auto-responder is that it is sent only to people who ask for it. You can publicize your auto-responder in your other communication pieces, and you can include a button for it on your site. If at all possible, use an electronic "guest book" at your home page to come up with your e-mail list.

Note

In the real world, direct mail accounts for a little less than 20 percent of total advertising expenditures. It's only a matter of time before that number reaches up and hits the online world. You should keep abreast of the controls being established on junk e-mail. Offline, the not-for-profit Direct Marketing Association (DMA) does this job, and the group is now getting involved in the online world, as shown in Figure 13-6. Drop by the DMA Internet site, at `http://www.the-dma.org/`, for the latest news about e-mail advertising and its regulations.

Gauging Response

Big companies have large amounts of money to spend on advertising and on testing the effectiveness of their ad campaigns. As I advised earlier in this chapter, the only criterion that you — as a small fledgling business or one that advertises strictly for the buck — should use to measure the effectiveness of an advertisement is how much money it makes for you. If you're advertising in several places, how can you tell which advertisement resulted in which sale?

On a commercial online service, the answer is easy. Because you're doing *all* your advertising on one online service, simply observing whether sales increase after you publish your advertisement tells you quickly whether your money was well spent.

Finding out where your sales come from on the Internet is a little trickier. For starters, always make sure that you can access the actual counts. Because this process is entirely electronic and on the Internet, so are the traffic counts. Most online advertis-

Figure 13-6: The DMA is the largest and oldest organization dedicated solely to the evolving area of direct marketing and its everyday issues.

ers have a hidden area that contains the area's traffic; you may have to push forum managers a little to gain access to these areas. If not, ensure that the traffic counts or hits are audited.

Maybe you have placed an advertisement on *both* Yahoo! and InfoSeek. Either of these companies can tell you how many people have accessed your site through your advertisement's link. This information doesn't tell you, however, how many of those accesses resulted in sales. You also might have done some classified advertising in various places. How do you measure results when advertisements are placed in several areas?

Tip

One way is to make a duplicate copy of your main Web page for each place in which you advertise and then use the unique Web address for that particular copy in that particular advertisement. Each of these duplicates can have the same links to all the supplemental pages; only the first page is different. If you link your Yahoo! and InfoSeek advertisements to two different Web addresses, for example, you can determine exactly where customers are coming from as they enter your site, and you can then determine which advertisement is more effective.

Another tracking method is to make a unique "special offer" in each advertisement. That way, when a customer asks for that particular offer, you immediately know which advertisement generated the sale.

If you are unable to price your products or services differently, use promotional codes: For example, you can tell one set of customers that they are "2001" customers and tell another set that they are "2002" customers. You can use this same method with your online order forms; just put the customer code somewhere at the bottom of the form. Along the same lines, you might have a few toll-free-order phone numbers you dedicate to different online sites, but that method can get costly.

The simplest way to track sales and ad results, of course, is simply to ask your customers. On your online order form, simply include a question that asks how the customer heard about your site. The problem with this technique is that many people won't answer this simple question. If you rely on a toll-free-order hotline and ask customers this question, you get a large number of "I don't know" responses.

You also must verify not only that your advertisement is producing results but that it is also producing *positive* results. If you're spending $15,000 a month on an InfoSeek advertisement, you had better make sure that you're making more than $15,000 *in profit* from the sales it generates.

Your online advertisement may be seen by a million people, but if not a single person from that million buys your product, your advertisement is a complete failure. That term may sound harsh, but it's a cold, hard advertising fact.

After you hear it, it seems obvious, but most of the would-be cyber-entrepreneurs I meet seem to miss this most important point: If you're willing to commit advertising dollars to a particular advertising vehicle, that advertisement — in order to be considered a success — must result in more income than it costs. If you don't come to terms with this simple idea, you will get fooled into spending money on "good deals" that aren't good deals at all.

Knowing when a good deal isn't a deal after all

Time and time again, I see business start-ups throw away their money on "bargain" advertising. Stop and think about it, though. Is it smarter to spend $500 on an advertisement that brings in $250 in additional income or to spend $5,000 on an advertisement that brings in $10,000 in additional income?

In the first example, you spend only a tenth of the larger amount on your advertisement, but you sustain a 50 percent *loss* on that advertising investment. In the second example, you spend ten times as much money, but you also *double* your money. If you don't remember anything else from this chapter, remember that you must evaluate every advertising opportunity *solely* on its capability to generate additional income for your business.

Don't get me wrong — even good advertising doesn't always bring immediate results. Sometimes it takes a while for your advertising to catch on. You may have to advertise for two or three consecutive months before you begin to see those positive results. It's up to you to draw the line between waiting for an ad to catch on and throwing good money after bad.

Komando's picks for online advertising information

The commercial online services have special-interest groups and forums dedicated to advertising. The following list presents some online advertising references on the Internet so that you can find more information and keep up with what's happening with advertising online:

✦ ***Advertising Age:*** Read the online version of the advertising-industry magazine (`http://www.adage.com`).

✦ **AdMarket:** Visit this site to learn more about online promotions, advertising agencies, and media opportunities (`http://www.admarket.com`).

✦ **Advertising Law:** The information at this site can help keep your company out of trouble and let you catch up on the latest in rules and regulations (`http://www.webcom.com/~lewrose/home.html`).

✦ **Graphics Artist Guild:** Drop by and get information about advertising design and leads on designers you might hire (`http://www.gag.org`).

✦ **The Graphics Exchange:** Browse a gallery of art samples from members of the exchange (`http://www.gx.com/tgx`).

✦ **Simba:** This site (at `http://www.simbanet.com`) is one of my favorites. It has the latest information and news about online advertising in addition to radio, television, and print opportunities (see Figure 13-7).

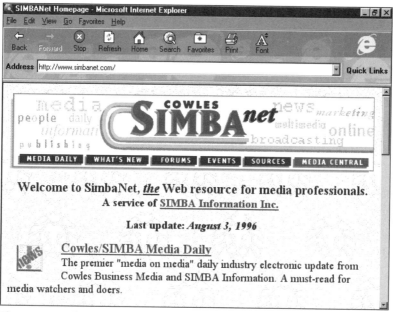

Figure 13-7: The Simba information network provides timely news, analysis, exclusive statistics, and proprietary forecasts on developments in the media and information business.

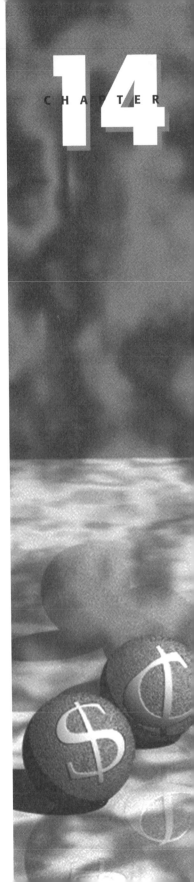

Taking Advantage of Publicity

I was feeling a little harried last week when a good friend called. I never seem to have enough time in a day, and, to make matters worse, I had to turn down the opportunity of a lifetime so that I could finish this chapter: My mother offered me an all-expenses-paid trip to Hawaii. The catch was that the plane, with her on it, was leaving in 24 hours, with or without me.

My friend volunteered a solution. "Kim, if only you would write the book that really explains how you got where you are today, you would be able to *live* on the beach in Hawaii all year 'round," he said. Falling for the bait, I asked, "And what might that book be?" I could just see the smug look on his face over the telephone as he responded, "Why, *The Art of Shameless Self-Promotion,* of course!"

Consider this chapter a preview of a book that may get published someday. My friend's comment has a great deal of truth to it, and, you know, I was rather flattered by it. After all, shameless self-promotion doesn't put a burden on your budget. There's no room for pride when you are publicizing yourself and your company's products and services. When someone turns down an opportunity to write about you, you have to find someone else who will. If you aren't willing to say "I'm great!" how can anyone else believe it?

In Chapter 13, I covered the ins and outs of advertising your cyberbusiness. Although publicity can be important to your success, it offers one distinct advantage over advertising: For the most part, it's free! As you should already know by now, we budding millionaires absolutely love anything that's free *and* that somehow works to our advantage.

Unlike an advertisement in which you essentially get in a customer's face and say, "Buy this now," the purpose of publicity is to make your potential customers, suppliers, stockholders, and the general public aware of your company and what it does.

Publicity is not an island; it must be coordinated with your other cyberbusiness ventures, such as advertising and marketing. Whereas advertising is more concerned with a customer's immediate actions, publicity is more of a long-term strategy. Simply stated, there are hardly any quick responses when you talk about publicity.

You can buy an online, newspaper, magazine, radio, or television advertisement today, and, as long as your check doesn't bounce, you have a guarantee that the ad will be placed. On the other hand, you can send out a press release or take a reporter to lunch today, and the story you provide about your company may not appear for months. It may never appear, in fact. If you learn the fine art of shameless self-promotion, however (I teach you the brushstrokes of that concept in this chapter), you will be steps ahead of your nearest competitor. It worked for me, and it can work for you too.

The Press Release: The Cornerstone of Publicity

The most important weapon in your arsenal of publicity tools is, without a doubt, the press release. Virtually all publicity centers on this one- or two-page document. But what is a press release?

A press release is, in its simplest form, just an informational document you distribute to various media sources (newspapers, magazines, consumer Web sites, radio stations, and television stations, for example) in the hope that these sources will pass along your information to their respective readers, users, listeners, and viewers. You probably would be surprised to know how many news stories start out this way.

Every time you read about new quarter-end losses at Apple Computer, for example, where do you think the information comes from? Do you think that every newspaper and magazine in the country sends a reporter to Cupertino to get the story? No way! At the end of each quarter, most major corporations issue their quarterly results to the public in the form of a press release. A reporter at each publication may write the article that appears in the publication, but all the basic information comes from the press release.

Warning

Press releases are very important to your business. Purely from an image standpoint, they tell reporters that you mean business. (Remember that you may have to send out a handful of releases before you ever get noticed.) Be careful, however: Every release you send had better contain newsworthy material, or (similar to the boy who cried "Wolf!") you may get a bad reputation in the media.

Send out a bunch of garbage, and that great release about your company setting the pace for online sales probably will get trashed. You have to walk a fine line between sending too many releases and not sending enough releases. As a new company or an existing company entering a new business arena, you should have something newsworthy to say every month. (In the following section, I tell you what to say in your releases.)

"But I Don't Have Anything Newsworthy to Say"

My sincerest hope is that you will never have to announce to the public that your company lost billions of dollars in the preceding quarter (unless you made gazillions in the process). Nonetheless, if you think that you don't have anything important to say about your business, perhaps your business isn't that important and you should consider another line of work. I don't mean to sound austere, but think about it: If you are launching a truly worthwhile business, you ought to have plenty of things to tell the world about it.

Here are a few situations that warrant a press release:

✦ **The formation of your business.** Starting up is the single most important event in the history of your company. It's certainly worth letting the world know about it. That you are launching this business indicates that it is something new or unusual, so focus on this event in a news release.

✦ **New products or services.** If you elect to offer a new product or service, you want and need as many people as possible to know about it. A press release not only tells people about your new offering but also lets them know that you're a progressive business interested in staying ahead of the game.

✦ **Promotions and new hires.** Growth is always perceived as a positive sign for a business. One sure sign of growth is the promotion or hiring of an individual to fill some key role that will somehow increase the effectiveness of your operation. Did you hire a new business accounts manager so that you can better meet the needs of your business customers? Those clients should know about your new hire. Have you promoted an employee to the position of customer service director so that you can be more responsive to customer needs? Your customers should know about it. Focus on how new hires and promotions affect your business and your customers.

✦ **New clients.** If you are involved in a business-to-business venture, you should send out a press release every time you land a new client, especially if that client is well known in a particular field. If you set up an online order-ahead system for McDonald's, for example, letting others in that industry know about it may well lead to contracts with Burger King or Wendy's.

✦ **Anniversaries and other milestones.** If you have reached your fifth anniversary, for example, or have earned a million dollars in annual sales for the first time, tell the world. This event lets the public know that you're not just some "flash in the pan" operation — you're in it for the long haul.

✦ **Special sales.** If you plan to offer limited-time special pricing on some of your products, you naturally want to advertise that fact. Just don't forget to send out a press release about your sale. Whether the information appears as an ad or as a news story in the same publication, it reaches the same number of people. The difference, as I said, is that the press release is free.

✦ **Special events.** Are you sponsoring some sort of special event, such as a free seminar? Maybe you plan to attend a major trade show. If so, a press release ensures that as many people as possible know about it.

These are just a few examples of the numerous times that it's appropriate to send out a press release. I hope that the ideas in this list have gotten you thinking. If you're not sure whether a particular situation warrants a press release, send one out anyway. The cost is so low that you have nothing to lose. Just don't issue release after release only for the sake of sending one. Make sure that each release can stand on its own merit.

Determining the Purpose of a Press Release

Before you begin to write a press release, you must be clear in your own mind about exactly why you're writing it. You can't just spray a bunch of disjointed information at the media and expect them to use it. You have to not only provide good information but also *make a point.* Your press release must have some other purpose than just to say, "Look at us! We're terrific!"

All press releases can be divided into three primary categories:

✦ **The backgrounder:** Builds a foundation for your standing in the business community. A good example of a backgrounder piece is the one you write to announce the formation of your company. A backgrounder provides some sort of overview information about your company, its people, your goals, a particular area in which you are involved, and what you are doing differently from your nearest competitor.

✦ **The announcement:** The most common type of press release. As its name implies, this type of press release "announces" to the world some important event or situation. Special events, awards, recent hires and promotions, new products or services, and new clients all qualify for announcement press releases.

✦ **The follow-up:** A reminder about earlier information. Remember that press release you wrote to announce your upcoming free online seminar? Was the seminar a success? Now that it's over, you should send out a press release detailing just how fabulous it was. That way, you're likely to get even more publicity the next time around.

Press releases also have one cousin worth mentioning at this point: the feature article. If you are an expert in your particular field and you can write well, an editor may agree to publish an article of yours with your byline attached to it. In other words, your name and a brief biographical blurb are printed with the article.

The key to writing a feature article is to remember that it cannot directly promote your business. Suppose that you develop World Wide Web home pages. You might convince an editor to accept an article called "Ten Steps for Building a Better Web Page," in which you provide useful information to readers and establish yourself as an expert in your field. The thinking behind this strategy is that a certain number of people who try to build their own Web page will find the task too daunting and turn to you, an expert, for help.

On the other hand, never in a million years would an editor accept an article called "Why You Should Hire Me to Build Your Perfect Web Page." The primary goal of your article must be to serve the reader, not the writer.

For years I wrote anything I could for free — newspaper articles, magazine stories, and scripts. Granted, it didn't directly help pay my bills because no cash changed hands. Rather than receive a payment check, I opted to have something resembling the following information and byline published with my articles:

Copyright ©1996 The Komando Corporation. All rights reserved.

Kim Komando, a TV host and syndicated talk-radio host, is the founder of the Komputer Klinic on America Online (keyword KOMANDO), on the Internet (http://www.komando.com), and on the Microsoft Network (go KOMANDO) and is the author of *1,001 Komputer Answers* and *CyberBuck$: Making Money Online,* both published by IDG Books Worldwide, Inc. You can send Kim e-mail at komando@komando.com. To order any of Kim's training products or to get your free catalog of Komando products, call 1-800-KOMANDO.

Remember that a byline is really an advertisement, even though you don't pay a dime for it. Better yet, because readers are reading something you personally wrote, you gain credibility.

Notice the copyright symbol in the first line of my byline. Whenever possible, keep all copyrights to your works. You can then sell or barter an article you write for one publication to a different publication. Don't be afraid to distribute the same article to more than one newspaper or magazine (people do it all the time). *Just don't sell your articles to competing publications.*

The last sentence in any byline is the most important: It lists the phone number readers can call to buy your products or services. Your byline may not be as long as mine, but even if your article appears only within an online publication, make sure that your byline includes a phone number customers can call. Some people, still reluctant to order anything online, are more comfortable picking up the telephone.

As you build your writing portfolio, you can work for a byline *and* advertisements. Heck, maybe you can do it now. Just ask — the worst a publisher can do is turn you down.

Suppose that you write an article and you want more than just a few sentences in your byline. You also want an advertisement to appear in the publication. You can usually get a one-third-page advertisement in exchange for a 700-word article. (I have traded one column for a $30,000 ad!) It's not that my writing is worth that much (at least in the publisher's mind) — you just have to "make him an offer he can't refuse."

Negotiate with the publisher, and specify that you will accept having the ad run on a *space-available* basis (your ad is run when the publisher has available space). If the space isn't available one month, that's cool — just make sure that the publisher finds room for your ad at least once per quarter per submitted article it publishes.

Considering that a 700-word article can pay as little as $70 or as much as $700, a $30,000 trade is darned good. Now you have to ensure that your ad brings in at least some sales. If you are touting the convenience of ordering home medical supplies online, for example, cutting a deal with *Runner's Magazine* doesn't make much sense. You get the point. To reap as much success as possible, match the publication's audience with your customer profile. (I discuss the general subject of writing in more detail in Chapter 15.)

Understanding the Mechanics of a Good Press Release

Every press release ever written (or at least every press release that didn't end up in the trash can or recycle bin) has followed essentially the same format, as shown in Figure 14-1.

After you understand the components of a good press release, you are steps ahead of any competitor who doesn't. I know — I get tons of unsolicited e-mail messages that say one thing: "Please tell your audience about us." Sorry — if it looks like a story and not a bona fide press release, into the intergalactic bit bucket it goes. As a member of the media who has worked for years to establish my credibility, I cannot afford to report anything that's even borderline shady. And many of my peers operate on the same principle.

Because you are doing business in cyberspace, you should distribute as many press releases *electronically* as possible. Nonetheless, you probably will have to send out some of them on paper. The reason I bring up this subject now is that the formatting requirements for paper and electronic releases are a little different from each other. In this section, I distinguish between the two.

Your printed press releases should be double-spaced, just like the reports you wrote in high school. Electronic press releases, on the other hand, have no such requirement. In the electronic version, however, rather than indent to indicate a new paragraph, you should include an extra hard return.

FOR IMMEDIATE RELEASE

Press Contact:

Joe Smith, The Komando Corporation
Phone: 602-970-1207 / Fax: 602-970-1208
E-mail: komando@komando.com

USA Today Picks Komando Komputer Klinic As Hot Site

Scottsdale, AZ (June 5, 1996) — The Kim Komando Komputer Klinic is honored to be chosen as a Hot Site by USA Today Online (www.usatoday.com). The Komputer Klinic was also recognized in the Thursday, June 6 newspaper edition of USA Today, in its "New and Notable" column, which features the best of the week's daily Hot Sites.

"We look for sites that are interesting, useful, and entertaining," said Sam Meddis, the technology editor for USA Today, explaining why the Komputer Klinic was chosen as a Hot Site. Every day, Mr. Meddis searches for Web pages that appeal to the wide variety of Web surfers who read USA Today online and offline.

"The tips are cool, and I like the style of the Komputer Klinic Web site," Meddis said. He is confident that people surfing the USA Today Cool Sites will enjoy the Komputer Klinic's attractive style and informative tips concerning computing problems.

"We are excited to receive this honor from such a respected newspaper and online resource," said Kim Komando, the owner of Komando Corporation. "Our staff has worked hard to create a Web site (www.komando.com) that offers the latest in computer expertise while also being easy to understand and navigate."

The Komputer Klinic's Hot Site listing on USA Today Online can be found at http://167.8.29.8/life/cyber/ch0603.htm.

Kim Komando shares her computer expertise with a wide audience through a syndicated newspaper column, various feature magazine stories and books, a syndicated talk-radio show, a television computer show, training CD-ROMs, multimedia titles, and online services. Komando's upcoming book is titled CyberBuck$: Making Money and Komando's best-seller, 1,001 Komputer Answers, was just reprinted again and is now available throughout the world under foreign translation and distribution rights.

Based on The Nation's Newspaper, USA Today Online is one of the most extensive free sites on the Web. It features more than 25,000 pages of up-to-the-minute news, sports, five-day weather forecasts for 750 cities, stock quotes, and three-dimensional graphics — available 24 hours a day, seven days a week. Special features include comprehensive coverage of the Atlanta Olympic Games, unsurpassed coverage of college sports, and extensive guides for worldwide travel. More than 250,000 readers visit the site daily.

Figure 14-1: A standard (but outstanding) press release.

Creating the Ideal Press Release

The following list describes the elements of the ideal press release (starting at the top):

◆ **Company name and address:** On printed press releases, your company letter-head provides this important information. On an electronic release, you can just type the information (include phone and fax numbers and an e-mail address) single-spaced at the top of the release.

◆ **Name of the contact person and the person's phone number:** Even if the contact person is you, and even if the phone number is the same as the one you just typed in the company information section, make sure that you include this information. If an editor wants to contact your company, this line is the first place in which she looks for the information.

◆ **Current date and the phrase "FOR IMMEDIATE RELEASE" in all capital letters:** In some cases, a company might want its information released at a later date. This line lets an editor know that this information is timely *now*.

◆ **Proposed headline:** As likely as not, a publication will choose some other headline than the one you propose. If nothing else, however, your headline lets the editor know immediately what the press release is about. Your headline, therefore, should be as brief, yet as descriptive, as possible.

◆ **Body:** Do you remember how you learned to write a book report in school? You begin with some sort of summary statement, and then you provide relevant information, usually three or more points, that support your statement. Finally, you close with a recap of the information you presented.

When it comes to press releases, forget everything you learned in school.

When you submit your press releases, you are competing with a zillion other press releases on an editor's desk. You *must,* therefore, open with a bang. The standard press release format calls for placing the most important information at the beginning of the release and then including other facts in descending order of importance. Visually, you can think of this format as an upside-down pyramid.

◆ **Standard company blurb:** This single paragraph summarizes what your company does, where it's located, and other information. Although a publication seldom uses this information, it's a good idea to have it there, just in case.

◆ **Ending characters:** End your press release with one of three sets of characters centered on the page:

# # #

- 30 -

END

Equally important (if not more so) as getting the press release format right is including good content. I touched on this subject briefly in the "Body" entry in the preceding list. Make sure that you put the most important information at the beginning of your release and the least important information at the end.

Tip

Another common press release technique is to quote someone relevant to the press release immediately after you provide that first important bit of information. A quote gives your press release a sense of authority and implies that the press release consists of more than just its author's perspective. If your press release not only talks about your company but also includes news about another company, get two quotes: one from the other company and one from yours.

Finally, most editors have little tolerance for poorly written press releases. If you think that your writing skills aren't up to snuff, hire someone to do the writing for you: It's money well spent. You don't have to hire a high-priced public relations firm; your next-door neighbor may have a flair for writing. Chances are that a person you're already acquainted with will be more than happy to write your press releases for $25 to $50 a pop. (Who knows? You may even find someone willing to work for beer.)

If you're new to the press release bandwagon, go surfing online and read other companies' press releases to get an idea of what to put in your release. Almost all large corporations with a site on the Internet have a special area that contains only their press releases. Search the Internet for releases distributed by your competitors.

Warning

Searching the Internet for the phrase *press release* yields thousands of results. Make sure that you fine-tune your search phrase.

Here are a few World Wide Web sites with press releases for you to check out:

✦ **PR Newswire:** In this holding bin of press releases, you can search by company name to find a particular release (`http://www.prnewswire.com`).

✦ **Microsoft:** Be sure to look at the backgrounders while you're hunting here (`http://www.microsoft.com/corpinfo/pr.htm`).

✦ **Lego:** We all loved them as kids (`http://www.LEGO.com/`).

✦ **White House:** Get the official news directly from the executive branch (`http://sunsite.unc.edu/white-house/white-house.html`). Figure 14-2 shows a press release that welcomes you to the White House.

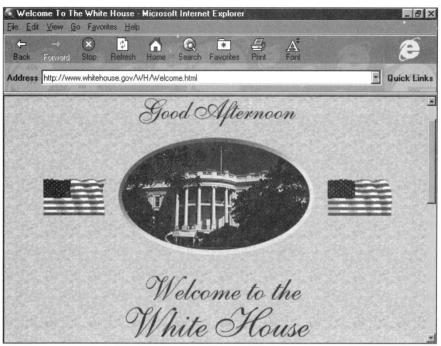

Figure 14-2: Press releases are important to any business. Even the President of the United States must issue press releases that follow a standard format.

Distributing a Press Release

As I mentioned earlier in this chapter, you can distribute your press releases in two ways: electronically and good ol' snail mail. Because you are doing business in cyberspace, you obviously want to distribute your press releases electronically whenever possible. For starters, it's quicker and much cheaper. The first step in this entire process is to determine exactly to whom you want to send your press releases (this process isn't all that difficult).

Warning

You may be wondering why I didn't mention how to send your press releases by fax. It's a bad idea, for several reasons. The primary reason is a legal one: In an attempt to end the upsurge of "junk faxes," some states have made it illegal to send a fax to a person or company with whom you have not established a previous business relationship. (As a member of the media, I know that I'm not the only one who gets somewhat annoyed when a company ties up a fax line with a press release.) For example, if you have never contacted a reporter before sending your press release in a fax, the reporter may be unlikely to press charges, but you may be setting yourself up for legal trouble. Just be sure to ask before you send a fax.

Knowing who should receive your press releases

Here's a list of outlets you should add to your press-release mailing list:

✦ All local newspapers

✦ Any local or regional magazines that cater to your target market

✦ All national magazines that cater to your target market

✦ Any electronic magazines (both Web-based and e-mail-based) that cater to your target market

✦ Any local or national trade groups that cater to your target market

The most important part is identifying the particular person within each organization to whom you should direct your press releases. Having a real-life name can only enhance your chances of getting your press release through to the right person. Otherwise, it might end up on the desk of someone else who doesn't give a hoot about you or your business.

Tip

If an organization has an online presence, you should explore it thoroughly. You probably can find the information you need there. If no online site exists (your local newspaper may not be online yet, for example) or the information you need isn't there, a simple phone call should clear up the matter. Just explain what your business does, and ask for the name of the appropriate person to receive your press releases.

Many editors and reporters often put their e-mail address at the end of their columns or stories. Begin collecting in a database any of these addresses you come across and also keep a collection of Internet sites that list e-mail addresses. One of these sites is http://www.reporters.net/ (see Figure 14-3). On the commercial online services, simply perform a search using the word *reporter* in the member directory. The names and e-mail addresses will pop up on-screen. Killer.

Warning

Just because a particular editor or other newsperson has an e-mail address doesn't necessarily mean that she wants to receive press releases that way. Some editors claim that e-mail press releases clutter up their inboxes and that they would rather receive them by U.S. mail. Other editors prefer e-mail press releases because they don't have to be retyped. Make sure that you know the preference of each person on your list.

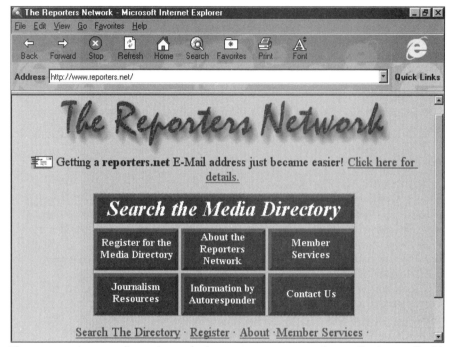

Figure 14-3: Internet directories make it easy to get a reporter's or editor's e-mail address.

Some insider tips

If it turns out that all your media contacts prefer e-mail press releases, you're lucky. More likely, however, you will have some in both categories. In either case, the mechanics of distribution are pretty simple.

Any decent e-mail package enables you to create groups of recipients. For your e-mail press releases, simply create a group that includes the e-mail addresses of all your media contacts. That way, you have to generate only one e-mail message in order to distribute your press release to all those people.

Tip

Check your e-mail program and make sure that it provides a way to create a list of addresses. This list makes things easy for you because you can simply send mail to one list rather than to every person individually. Another benefit is just as important: By mailing to a list, when members of the media receive your release, all they see in the To: section of the address is "presslist" or something similar, not the e-mail address of everyone else who received the release.

Rather than work with a list, my company uses a mass e-mail system that has been set up so that every member of the media who's on the list to receive a press release gets a *blind carbon copy* (the recipients of the message don't know who else has also received a copy). Depending on which e-mail program you use, making a blind carbon copy can be as simple as putting the recipient's e-mail address in parentheses. Then, because recipients see only their individual e-mail address, they aren't aware that they were part of a mass press-release mailing. This strategy may seem a little sneaky, but there's a perfectly logical reason for using it: If members of the media know that a press release they receive has also been sent out to a large number of other people, they may not want to cover the story because they usually try to be the first to report something "juicy." Think about all the times a television anchorperson has reported a story as "exclusive," and you get my point.

Tip

As a general rule, never distribute your press releases as e-mail attachments. Always include the entire press release in the body of your message. The reason is that some e-mail addresses on your list may include people with accounts on the commercial online services, such as CompuServe and America Online. Although you can send simple e-mail messages to people on all these different services, e-mail attachments often don't make it through the system. Because the Infobahn can be bumpy at times, recipients sometimes receive a bunch of jumbled characters — not a legible press release. Editors and other journalists who receive e-mail attachments have to spend time downloading and then opening the files. Who has the time? No one.

Sending press releases through the U.S. Postal Service involves a little more work than sending them electronically. First, you should enter recipients' names and addresses in a database program that can print labels. Then, whenever you have a press release to send out, you can print a set of mailing labels and the appropriate number of press release copies. Grab an envelope, stuff and label it, add postage, and it's ready to go.

Warning

You can send out press releases as often as you want. Generally speaking, the more, the better. You should never, under any circumstances, however, send two separate press releases in the same envelope or as part of the same e-mail message. Doing so diminishes the apparent importance of each one. Worse, someone might assume that you accidentally sent two copies of the same release and ignore one of them. To take this admonition a step further, I suggest that you wait at least two to five days before you send a subsequent press release. Even if you send releases separately on the same day, someone might mistakenly assume that they're duplicates. By putting the space of a few days between your press releases, you ensure that each one gets the full attention it deserves.

Storing Online Press-Release Archives

You can distribute your press releases in one more place: on your own Web site. When you set up an online area, you want three basic groups of people to visit your site:

✦ Existing customers

✦ Potential customers

✦ Media people (a group often overlooked by inexperienced entrepreneurs)

Tip

As the old saying goes, "Any press is good press." The more you can do, therefore, to accommodate press people and attract them to your site, the better off you are. The easiest way to attract them is to include a button to go to a Press Releases page. This button gives media people immediate access to any information, past or present, that they may want or need about your company.

You don't have to make available every single press release you have ever written, but keeping the past six months' worth (or even a year's worth) isn't a bad idea. The most important thing is that you get new press releases online immediately. As I mentioned in Chapter 12, timely information is one of the most valuable assets for your online area.

Putting Search Engines and Index Sites to Use

Although press releases are important, they aren't the only way to get out the word about your business. In cyberspace, you have a unique opportunity to get more coverage, in the form of various search engines and index sites on the Internet, such as Yahoo! and Magellan.

The first way to take advantage of these search sites is to submit a simple listing. If your business is listed on Yahoo!, for example, every time a person does a search for your type of business, your name appears on the "hit" list. Don't forget that *free* is one important element of good publicity. In terms of publicity (not to be confused with advertising), therefore, make sure that you go for only a free listing.

Many search sites also encourage users to suggest other Web sites to be featured in some special way. Search sites prosper in part because they keep their visitors supplied with an endless list of new and exciting featured sites. It generally doesn't cost anything to make a suggestion — or to have your site chosen as a featured site. If your Web site is featured by one of the search sites, you most likely will be allowed to use your logo to indicate this distinction.

The Web version of my Komputer Klinic does exactly that. To ensure consistency, we submit — to everyone and anyone online — a canned blurb about our site. You should develop the same type of blurb for your online area. Here's mine.

The Komputer Klinic was founded by TV host, syndicated talk-radio host, syndicated newspaper columnist, contributing magazine editor, and author Kim Komando. Here, Kim and her comrades have free answers to computer questions, give tips, tricks, and secrets, and more, with one goal: We make computers easy! Our home page is `http://www.komando.com`.

A Word about Usenet Newsgroups

In addition to Web pages and e-mail on the Internet, you may come across an entirely different area, called *Usenet newsgroups* (also called *Usenet, newsgroups,* or just *news*). Think of a newsgroup as a big bulletin board to which people can tack pieces of paper. Just as you might place your business card on the bulletin board at a local supermarket, you can do the same with electronic messages in the Internet newsgroups (see Figure 14-4). Newsgroups are sorted into broad topics, or *domains,* that enable you to take part in communities of people who are interested in specific topics. The domain name is on the left side of a newsgroup name.

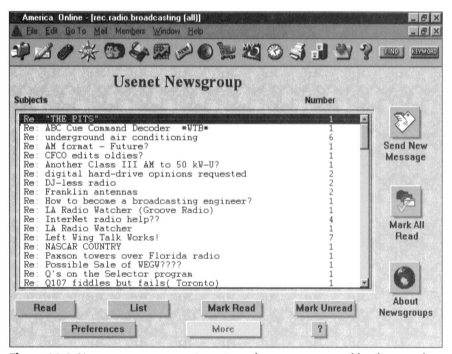

Figure 14-4: Newsgroups are a great way to exchange messages with other people about a specific topic. You can access newsgroups by using any commercial online service or Internet browser.

Some common domains are described in this list:

- ✦ **alt:** Anything goes
- ✦ **comp:** Computer-related topics
- ✦ **misc:** Miscellaneous topics
- ✦ **news:** News about the Usenet and related programs
- ✦ **rec:** Recreational activities
- ✦ **sci:** Scientific topics
- ✦ **soc:** Social issues
- ✦ **talk:** Controversial cultural and social issues

Like the Internet, the newsgroups area is freewheeling and without many constraints. The `alt` domain, in fact, has practically no restrictions.

On the opposite side of the `alt` domain spectrum are moderated newsgroups. Any message posted to a moderated newsgroup is first sent for approval to the *moderator,* or the person who oversees the discussion. The moderator not only decides whether the message is appropriate but also edits the message (if necessary).

With about 20,000 newsgroups and more from which to choose, it's tempting for cyber-entrepreneurs to begin posting little promotional messages on every single one of them. Let me tell you, this practice, called *spamming,* does more harm than good. It's considered extremely poor netiquette (Internet manners) to post any commercial message in a newsgroup in which this type of message isn't explicitly welcome.

With such a large number of newsgroups, of course, a few are bound to accept commercial messages. If you find some newsgroups appropriate to your message, by all means, post away. Participate intelligently in newsgroups composed of members of your target audience, and include in your signature your business name, address, and URL. Then make sure that those newsgroups are the only ones in which you post messages. You can run a great business for 20 years, but spam just once, and they'll call you a spammer forever (see Figure 14-5).

Engaging in Online, Real-Time Chats

Another way to promote yourself and, by extension, your business is in online, real-time chat sessions. A chat session is basically a question-and-answer conference you hold with whichever online users happen to drop in. Whatever you type on-screen is

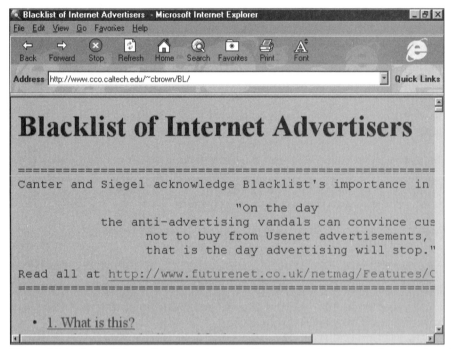

Figure 14-5: Some lists on the Internet contain the names of people and companies who spam. Make sure that *your* name doesn't appear on these lists.

displayed instantly to people in your online audience. For example, I regularly host just such an event on America Online. To be a host on an online service, simply ask the forum manager of the area in which you are offering your services. You can find the manager's e-mail address in the About section of the area.

On the Internet, you can set up your own Internet Relay Chat (IRC) channel. As in a chat on an online service, people using IRC type messages to each other, and these messages appear on-screen instantaneously. (Almost instantaneously — if a message has to go to the other side of the world, it takes a few more seconds, of course.)

Believe it or not, at any hour of the day (even as you read this sentence), hundreds, if not thousands, of people all over the world are banging out messages to each other.

Many people can chat at the same time about the same subject, and discussion topics vary as much as the participants do. Some discussions are conducted on a regular basis, and some are held almost nonstop. Each subject or discussion group is referred to as a *channel*.

Tip

To set up an IRC for your company, ask your Internet provider or a local college computer geek for some help. The process is somewhat complicated, and — unless you wear a bona fide pocket protector — you don't want to handle the technical side. Focus on your real goal: publicity and making money.

When you host an online chat, you can tap in to your audience *and* it's a fun time.

And now, guess what you get to do in celebration of such an event? That's right! Issue a press release — you get to go to the next chapter!

Before you continue, though, haul out the Vision for a Mission book you created in Chapter 4. List all the ways in which you can publicize your business and the steps you must take to get the job done. Do it now, while all those ideas about spreading the word about your company and your products or services are fresh in your mind. This is no time to be lazy. Your livelihood is depending on it. I want you to be a success — it's important to me. After all, I did give up a free trip to Hawaii to write this chapter for you. It's the least you can do for me.

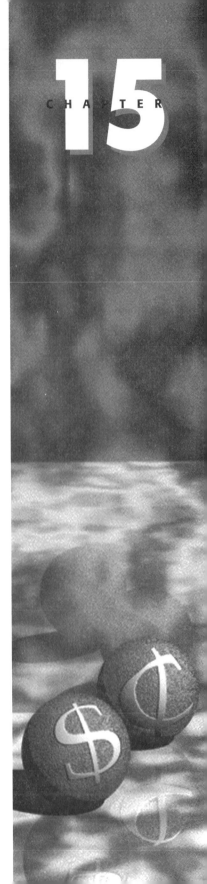

Promoting Your Online Business Offline

No matter how many customers visit your virtual storefront, every single one of them has a life outside of cyberspace (with the possible exceptions of Sandra Bullock's character in *The Net* and, of course, me). That means that the real world provides many opportunities to promote your cyberbusiness, some of which I have already discussed (see Chapters 13 and 14). In this chapter, I give you a few more ideas to keep you busy, each of which is Komando-tested and -approved.

Finding the Hidden Expert Within

I have to believe that because you're starting a cyberbusiness, you have some sort of expertise in your chosen field — no matter what that field is. Other, less experienced people in your field or outside your realm of expertise more than likely can benefit from your valuable knowledge.

What I'm leading up to in this discussion makes most people cringe, but it's a powerful promotional tool: public speaking. If you can't bring yourself to stand up in front of a room full of strangers and take a few minutes to impart your personal words of wisdom, you're not alone. If you can, however, you give yourself a strategic advantage.

Note

Who says that talk is cheap or that you have to talk for free? Public speaking is a $75-billion-a-year industry, and perhaps you can get a slice of it. Experienced public speakers can make $25,000 per speech, and even newbies can easily earn $500 per appearance. Not bad for a few hours of work, eh? That information alone should be enough to get you over your fear.

It has worked for me. I was shaking the first time I stood up in front of a group of people. And, you know what? The first network talk-radio show I did (broadcast in Chicago) scared the daylights out of me, until I remembered something: I knew more about my area of expertise than anyone in that audience did.

Developing the confidence you need

You *must* develop confidence, and that process takes time. If you have the will and are just a little short on public-speaking skills and confidence, I suggest that you get in touch with an organization called Toastmasters International. The sole purpose of this group, which has local chapters all around the country, is to promote personal growth through public speaking. It's an organization for novices and experienced veterans alike.

You can take the low-tech approach of looking in your phone book for the local Toastmasters chapter. Or you can just point your Web browser to http:// www.toastmasters.org, which is the home page for Toastmasters International, as shown in Figure 15-1. This site has, in addition to important information about membership and benefits, a comprehensive listing of local chapters around the world. Finding one near you is just a point-and-click away.

You might be surprised to find out that Toastmasters also has many specialty clubs, such as Le Gourmet Toastmasters, of Costa Mesa, California. You can find it at http://www.oac.uci.edu/indiv/bhudack/toastmst/Le-Gourmet.html on the Web (see Figure 15-2). This group meets at a different gourmet restaurant each month. (Maybe a little good food can drive away that fear of public speaking.)

If you're into Usenet newsgroups, you can also check alt.org.toastmasters for some ongoing discussion.

If you can't find any information about Toastmasters on the Net, you're just not looking.

Maybe you want to hone your public-speaking skills, but you don't want to join a club. And maybe you want to do it without even leaving your computer chair. You're in luck. The University of Kansas offers a Web site called Virtual Presentation Assistant, as shown in Figure 15-3. It's at a complete online tutorial for public speakers (at http://www.ukans.edu/cwis/units/coms2/vpa/vpa.htm).

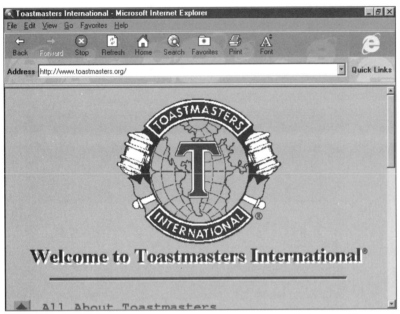

Figure 15-1: Toastmasters International provides the tools that enable people to develop pubic-speaking skills. In Toastmasters, you learn by doing — by speaking to groups.

Figure 15-2: Some Toastmasters groups focus on specific themes. At Le Gourmet Toastmasters Club, all speeches are about food or the entertainment industry.

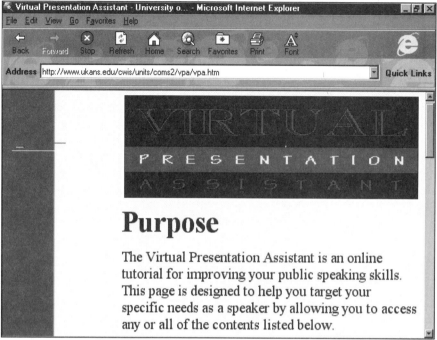

Figure 15-3: You can improve your public-speaking skills online by using the Virtual Presentation Assistant.

Major topics in the tutorial can help you learn how to accomplish these tasks:

✦ Determine the purpose of your talk

✦ Choose a topic

✦ Research your topic

✦ Analyze your audience

✦ Support your points

✦ Outline your points

✦ Use visual aids effectively

✦ Present your speech

You can take a class at a local college or university too.

Lining up speaking engagements

After you have honed your public-speaking skills, how do you find speaking engagements to help develop your style and confidence? You have a couple of options.

First, you can contact local trade and business groups that cater to your particular field or industry. Networking groups are also a good place to begin. These groups usually have regular meetings that often feature a guest speaker. That guest speaker can be you! Just contact the organization and let someone know that you are available to speak about a particular topic. It's often a challenge to find qualified speakers, and the organization may be receptive to your call. You never know unless you ask.

After you have found these organizations, you should also consider joining them as a member and getting involved in some way. Most trade organizations are always looking for volunteers to handle all sorts of tasks (publicity, printing, and special-event planning, for example) and generally give special recognition to volunteers. This strategy is a great way to keep your name in front of the public all year round.

Not sure where to look for these groups? One good place is the business section of the local newspaper or any other area business publications. You're likely to find a calendar of events that lists various groups and their meeting times. You can attend one of the meetings before you offer to speak so that you know exactly what to expect.

Many major metropolitan areas have a speakers' bureau, which is an agency that exists simply to match qualified applicants with organizations that need a speaker on some particular topic. You have to pay, of course, to register with a speakers' bureau; that's one of the ways in which these groups support themselves. If a bureau can get you good engagements, however, it may be worth the expense.

Maybe you're wondering whether any "virtual" speakers' bureaus are on the Net. Of course, there are! Did you expect anything less?

Point your Web browser to `http://www.publicspeaker.com`, for example. Public Speaker bills itself as *the* Internet source for public speakers (see Figure 15-4). It's easy to get yourself listed on this site, but it's definitely not free. Depending on the listing style you want, a listing costs anywhere from $120 to more than $1,000 a year.

Other similar Web sites include the ones in this list:

✦ The Speakers' Bureau: `http://www.mcanet.com/speakers.html`

✦ The Jocularity Speakers' Bureau: `http://www.jocularity.com/sbureau.html`

✦ Walters International Speakers' Bureau: `http://www.walters-intl.com/bureauhome.html`

✦ World Class Speakers: `http://www.speak.com`

✦ American Program Bureau: `http://www.apb-speakers.com`

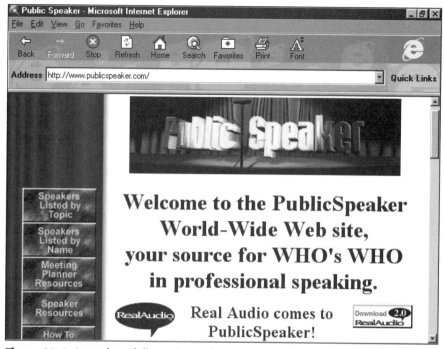

Figure 15-4: A number of directories and resources on the Internet are dedicated to putting speakers together with meeting planners.

Making money for talking about your area of expertise

In addition to promoting your business, increasing your public-speaking skills has another benefit to you (which I mentioned earlier in this chapter): money! As you become more experienced, your services will most likely be in greater demand. Organizations may begin to offer you money — cold, hard cash — just to come speak to them for awhile. Top speakers can make from $1,000 to $25,000, *plus expenses,* such as travel and lodging in five-star hotels.

When I started out in this business, I didn't get paid for my public-speaking engagements. Eventually, some were free and some were paid. Just recently, I established a policy specifying that, except for charitable organizations, I no longer do unpaid speaking engagements. In addition to promoting my various business ventures, my public speaking has turned into a steady income stream.

Almost as important as the time you spend giving a speech is the time you spend afterward with your audience. Don't cut out through the back door the moment you're finished. Instead, stick around and talk with audience members. Hold an informal question-and-answer session, pass out a few business cards, and maybe make a few new contacts.

Let's face it: Anyone can be trained to give a speech. When you meet your audience members face-to-face, however, they know that your words are coming from the real you — that they're not some rehearsed piece you may or may not have written yourself. This is your chance to make an impression.

Tip

You have to remember one more thing about being an expert. As your business grows, you become an expert in not only your original field of expertise but also the area of doing business online. This topic will be a hot one for years to come, so make sure that you include it in your list of possible topics.

Using the Tools of the Trade

People have been doing public speaking probably since man figured out his first word. In this information age, you have at your disposal a variety of high-tech presentation tools guaranteed to make your gig as a public speaker easier and more effective. I'm talking about your computer, of course, and all the various presentation devices you can attach to it.

First, let me cover the software-presentation tools. You have plenty to choose from out there, but two of the most popular presentation packages are Microsoft PowerPoint and Adobe Persuasion (see Figure 15-5). Both programs offer a variety of functions to simplify the presentation process. You can make individual "slides" that you can print as transparencies, as real slides, or on paper handouts or create a disk-based slide show you can send to others. One of the most powerful means of presentation is to present information directly from a computer. Using your desktop PC, you can also include such features as audio and video clips.

Presentation applications can also help you create attendee handouts with multiple slide images on each page, which produces a much smaller handout that's easier to manage. You can also prepare detailed speaker notes so that you never get on-stage with that blank gaze that says "I forgot" (the goldfish look!) on your face.

As I just mentioned, making a presentation from your PC or laptop computer is the most versatile way to go. Unless you want everyone huddled around your monitor, all trying to see one screen, you need some extra equipment to project your presentation on a screen or wall. You have two basic choices: an LCD panel or a data projector.

An LCD panel looks sort of like a monitor screen with no back to it. It lays across a standard overhead projector and plugs in to your computer the same way a monitor does. Your presentation is then displayed on the panel. The light from the overhead projector passes through the panel and projects the whole thing in living color.

On the other hand, you don't need an overhead projector if you have a data projector (an all-in-one unit). You simply plug in the projector to your PC in the same way as you would plug in a monitor and then blast your presentation onto the screen. A data projector generally gives you a larger, crisper image than does an LCD panel.

Figure 15-5: Microsoft PowerPoint, much like Adobe Persuasion, is an essential software program for public speakers.

The bad news about all this projector talk is that a top-of-the-line LCD panel or data projector costs several thousand dollars. The good news is that, in a larger city, you probably can find a couple of places that rent them.

I recently gave a speech at a home improvement convention (you know — the shows that bring out the best in renovations, sliding doors, doghouses, and pools). I was there to talk about the impact of personal computers and the Internet in the home.

I had arranged with the convention organizers to give my presentation using PowerPoint. I sent them by e-mail a 20MB file, including slides, sound, animations, and video clips. The organizers called and verified that they had received the file and that it was working. Not one to take chances — I have been around computers for too long — I hauled my trusty desktop computer with me to the convention hall (which, luckily, was local).

Good thing. The convention organizers couldn't open the file because they didn't have enough RAM (a type of memory) on the computer at the convention hall. They had tested my file only on the computers at their office. Gee, thanks.

Next, someone lugged my desktop computer up to the podium, and it worked like a charm. It worked so well that, as my computer system was being set up, everyone in the audience saw the entire content of my hard disk: My file manager was shown open and in full view on the 24-foot screen.

I have a habit of giving my files names such as Network Television Contract That I Would Never Sign in My Life, Network Television Contract That I Did Sign, AT&T Deal I Want Really Badly, Letter to My Friends at the IRS, and — you get the point. All eyes in the audience had an in-depth look into my professional and personal life just by looking at the files on my PC. Talk about embarrassing.

I seized the moment, grabbed the laser pointer, and said, "Let's get started by allowing me to tell you a little about our company." I then pointed to each file as I explained how each one was related to my business. How's that for an opener? The moral of the story: Whenever you depend on technology, you have to be flexible.

Being an Expert: Part II

In addition to finding public-speaking opportunities, you (as the subject-matter expert — or SME, in media lingo) may get many opportunities to be interviewed by the media. Every time you can get quoted somewhere — anywhere — you're doing your business a favor. This strategy garners publicity for your business and establishes more credibility for you as a true expert.

Again, the question of how to find and identify these opportunities arises. And again, the best line of attack is to take the direct approach. Contact the appropriate editors at related trade and consumer publications as well as local newspapers, and let them know that you are available for interviewing on a particular topic. To find editors' names, go to a publication's Web page.

Identifying legitimate sources is often a challenge for media people; assuming that you target the right publication and editor, that editor may be happy to receive your call.

Tip

If you're considering television or radio interviews, you should usually make your pitch to the producers of those shows. These people direct the focus of the shows and guide the hosts and their questions. Sometimes, however, a local newscaster may take an interest in your story and your business, but only if he finds in them some interesting human-interest element. For example, are you a single, working mother who started up her cyberbusiness on the side and who has her eight children helping out by answering e-mail? Probably not, but you get the picture.

When you're contacting members of the media, don't forget that increasingly more newspapers, television stations, and radio stations have their own Web sites. These sites usually include e-mail addresses of key employees. A Web site is an ideal way for you to make contact.

To get an idea of what to expect from these Web sites, search for local radio and television sites on the commercial online services and on the Internet or check out these examples:

✦ Charleston.Net (`http://www.charleston.net`): A Web site sponsored by the *Post and Courier,* a newspaper in Charleston, South Carolina (which, incidentally, carries my column), as shown in Figure 15-6

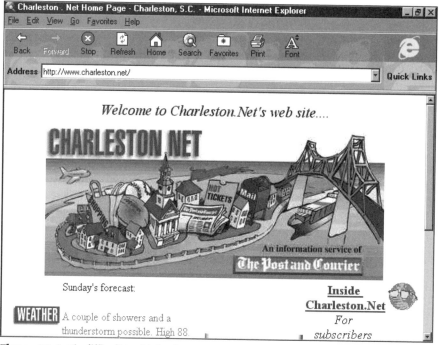

Figure 15-6: It's difficult to think of a newspaper that's not online. Use these sites to help spread the word about your expertise.

✦ KLTY-FM Dallas (`http://www.klty.com`): One of the largest Christian radio stations in the country

✦ KLAS-TV Las Vegas (`http://www.infi.net/vegas/online`): A television station in Las Vegas, Nevada (be sure to check out its "Ultimate Guide to Las Vegas Internet Addresses")

✦ WTIC-AM Hartford in Connecticut (`http://www.wtic.com`): A great talk-radio station

It pays, of course, to do your homework ahead of time. Before you approach media people, you may want to consider learning a little about their industry. The best way is to read their industry trade publications. You could go to all the trouble of tracking down these publications in your local library, but why do you think we have the Web, anyway? Many publications have their own Web sites, and finding out what they have to say is only a mouse click away.

Here are a couple to get you started:

✦ Broadcasting & Cable (`http://www.broadcastingcable.com`): A trade publication for television-station and cable-system operators

✦ R&R on the Web (`http://www.rronline.com`): The Web site for *R&R* magazine, a leading trade publication for the radio and recording industries (see Figure 15-7)

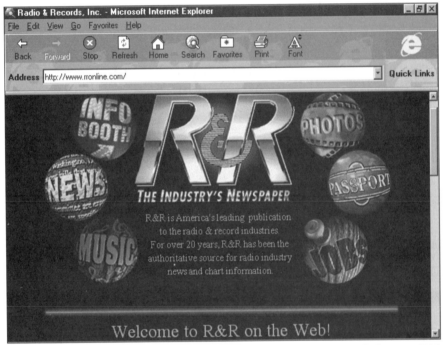

Figure 15-7: Learning about the broadcasting industry is as easy as pointing your Web browser to the right sites.

Another option is to have yourself listed in *The Radio and TV Interview Report,* a directory of people who are available for radio interviews. For a couple of hundred dollars, you can have your name and area of expertise listed in this periodic publication. When a representative of a radio station wants to interview someone about a particular topic, that person can look in the directory — and maybe choose you! This directory is published by Bradley Communications (call 800-989-1400). Unfortunately, it doesn't have a Web site — yet.

Unless you really are having a space alien's baby, it's not likely that you will be paid for an interview. Nonetheless, the additional exposure is well worth the few minutes it takes. Interviews go quickly, but be sure to give out your toll-free number and online address more than a few times! Here's a rule of thumb: A person has to hear a phone number three times before deciding to call.

Being an Expert: Part III

Another way to show your expertise to the world is by writing about it, in either consumer magazines or trade publications. (I mentioned this subject briefly in Chapter 14.) A benefit of writing is that, after your article is published, you have copies that you can distribute and use over and over again. In most cases, you can even post the articles on your Web page and cite the magazine in which they originally appeared.

So how do you get started with this whole writing thing? You begin where any writer begins, with the current edition of *Writer's Market* (published by Writer's Digest Books; Cincinnati). This annual book is the freelance writers' Bible. It lists hundreds of consumer magazines, trade publications, and even book publishers that might be interested in your writing. Best of all, the trade and consumer listings are organized by category, which makes it easy to find just the right publication for your field.

In one sense, writing is much like public speaking. When you first get started, you may get little or no pay for your efforts. Your only payment is the publicity your article generates. As you become more well known, your writing becomes more valuable in the marketplace, and you get paid more and more to do it.

Warning

Like many other fields, freelance writing has its own rules of etiquette. If you don't familiarize yourself with them ahead of time, you won't get far. The best place to begin is in the front section of the *Writer's Market;* it has plenty of information about the rules of the road. Make sure that you know what you're doing before you get started.

Disappointed that you're not the world's greatest writer? It's not necessarily a problem. That's why God invented ghostwriters. *Ghostwriters* are professional writers who, for a fee (of course), will write an article for you and allow you to put your name on it. This practice may seem a little strange at first, but it's a common one among America's top executives. Many Fortune 500 companies even have full-time employees whose only job is to write articles and speeches for its executives.

The biggest obstacle is, naturally, price. After you find a "ghost" who you believe can do the job, you have to ask yourself one simple question: "Is the publicity I get from this article worth the expense of the ghostwriter?" If you're getting paid for the article, you can just pass along the payment to the ghostwriter. Simple. If you're not getting paid, on the other hand, you have to consider this question more carefully.

Living Life in the Real World

Let me remind you that, because we all exist in the real, physical world, you never know which of the people you encounter in your everyday life are potential customers in cyberspace. All your business communications, therefore, should draw attention to your online presence. This advice may sound obvious for a new cyberbusiness, but it may not be so obvious for an existing business that's simply opening a cyberbranch.

Check your business cards, stationery, print advertisements — in short, every single piece of printed material you have. Do they include both your e-mail and Web addresses? If not, you may want to explore the cost of having these materials reprinted so that they include this important information.

When people telephone your office, you naturally want to help them out as quickly and courteously as you can. At some time, however, you inevitably have to put people on hold. Sure, you can let callers listen to some local radio station or canned music while they're on hold, but why not take this opportunity to tell callers about your business?

At my company, we try not to leave people on hold for more than 30 seconds, but when it's unavoidable, callers get to hear all about the exciting stuff we're working on. Rather than have a bland voice say, "Thanks for holding," make your message meaningful, and use it as a way to increase your sales as well as your credibility.

Here's what you might hear if you call my office and are put on hold:

✦ "Get fast, easy, instant answers to your computer questions from America's favorite expert, Kim Komando. The *Orlando Sentinel* said that Komando's book 'is unquestionably the best how-to book for personal computing.' 'There is scarcely a topic that isn't covered,' said the *Chicago Tribune*. Order your autographed copy of *1,001 Komputer Answers* today!"

✦ "*Information Week* calls Kim Komando 'a one-person PC industry.' Whether seen on television, in newspapers, in magazines, on America Online, the Microsoft Network, or the Internet or heard on network radio, you can turn to Kim Komando and our staff with confidence."

✦ "The Komando Corporation has helped millions of people just like you over the years to become computer-savvy with our complete line of training systems, video programming, software, books, CD-ROMs, and much more. We make computers easy, but don't just take our word for it — find out for yourself."

The beautiful thing about "music on hold" is that it doesn't cost a great deal of money. It also makes your business sound professional and, well, large (like a *FORTUNE* company). WestStar Digital Audio produced my company's music on hold, and it can do yours too (for a few hundred dollars). For more information, call 602-912-9458.

Tip

You have to surround your customers with sales information. To return to radio or television advertising for a moment, make sure that you include your electronic information there too. In 1995, Motorola began displaying its Web address at the bottom of every television advertisement it runs. Now, virtually every major corporation on the planet includes its Web address in its TV commercials. I even noticed a Web address at the bottom of a Wal-Mart commercial the other night (see Figure 15-8).

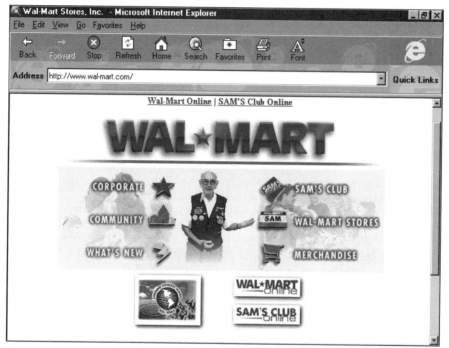

Figure 15-8: Wal-Mart spreads the word about its Web page within its TV advertising, direct-mail catalogs, print advertisements, and even inside its stores.

It doesn't cost anything to include your Web page address, and it can only benefit your business. Your commercial should (you hope!) spark a genuine interest in viewers. Giving them your Web address provides them with a way to follow up and obtain additional information, all from the comfort of their own computer chair.

Another way to spread your name around is by having it listed in as many appropriate directories as you can find. Hundreds and hundreds of directories are published every year, ranging from your college or high school alumni directory to international trade directories. The more of these directories in which you are listed, the more chances you have to make the world familiar with your name.

One great source for directories is the book *Directories in Print,* published annually by Gale Research (see Figure 15-9). You can order it directly from the Gale Research Web site, at `http://www.thomson.com/gale/gale.html`.

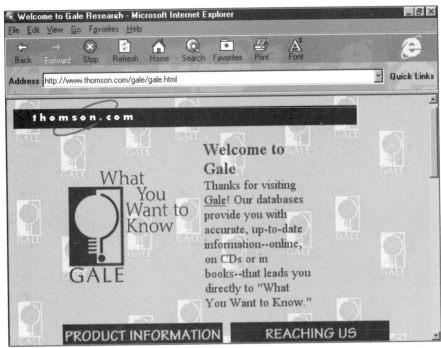

Figure 15-9: The more directories in which you are listed, the more chances you have to make the world familiar with your name. To help, Gale Research publishes *Directories in Print.*

Bringing Current Customers into Cyberspace

If you have a traditional business and you want to open a second location on the other side of town, you want to make a big deal out of it. You want as much publicity as possible for the grand opening, and you surely want to let your existing customers know about the availability of your new location.

Tip

In this sense, expanding your current business into cyberspace is no different. As I mentioned at the beginning of this chapter, you never know which of the people you encounter in your everyday life are potential customers for your online business. If you have an existing customer list for your current business, I suggest that you do some sort of direct mailing to let your customers know about your new cyber-location. If you have another mailing you regularly send out, such as monthly statements, you can simply include your announcement. (This technique saves you plenty in postage costs.)

Here's the bottom line on publicity: Everyone you meet is a potential customer. Maybe they simply don't realize it yet, but it's your job to let them know. Telling them through targeted acts of publicity is a sure way to success.

Part V

Keeping the Lines of Communication Open

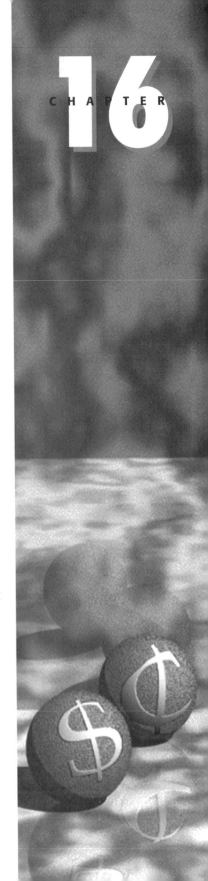

Data-Based Marketing that Keeps on Selling

I knew that I was in trouble when a friend called and began her conversation with, "I met your soul mate last night, and he wants to have dinner with you." From the way she described him, I was about to meet a man who is built like a Greek god, who carries the likes of Donald Trump's financial statement, and who doesn't have a matched set of emotional baggage. Maybe it's me, but I kept thinking, "Okay, so what's wrong with him?"

I swore off blind dates a long time ago.

Even though someone tells you how wonderful a person is, you just never know until you gaze into that person's eyes. If the person hits a few of your hot buttons, a blind date may indeed turn out to be, at the very least, an enjoyable evening. When you think about it, a date is nothing other than a sale. You have to have the right look, say the right things, be the right person. You know what I mean.

When you're selling products or services online, how can you hit your customers' hot buttons without really knowing what those buttons are? The answer is easy: Database marketing.

The concept of database marketing might sound so intimidating that you may believe that only someone with a Harvard MBA knows what it means and how to make money with it.

Wrong. Database marketing is easy to understand and put into practice. At the risk of offending marketing gurus who write encyclopedia-size books about the subject, let me present the official, no-hype Komando premise of database-marketing. Don't worry — you have to be able to grasp only two ideas.

Realizing that Existing Customers Offer Tremendous Opportunities

First, it's easier and cheaper to sell something to an *existing* customer than to generate a new customer. Think about it in your everyday life. Do you do most, if not all, of your grocery shopping at one particular market? Do you shop there because the market is convenient or clean or simply because you never know for sure how much money you have in the bank and your favorite market will accept your personal check without a guarantee card?

Now consider what I would have to do to make you agree to shop elsewhere. Would lower prices make you drive another block, or should I offer triple coupons? Okay, I'll even help you out by carrying your groceries.

Online, you probably tap in to the same resources repeatedly. Want to search for a topic on the Internet? Rather than try different sites every time, I'll bet that you regularly stop by Yahoo!, Lycos, AltaVista, or another familiar search engine. You read the same publications online that you read by the pool, right?

Note

Because we humans are predictable and because habits are hard to break, many marketing campaigns (for everything from long-distance service to soft drinks) are designed to make customers switch their allegiance from one company to another. If you can sell an existing customer more products or services, however, you don't have to invest the time and money involved in convincing a potential cash-bearing customer to give your company a shot.

Because existing customers already know the quality of your products or services, they feel comfortable making a purchase from you (assuming that you "did right" by the customer in the first place). By selling to a current customer again, you achieve two objectives:

✦ Reduce the cost per order

✦ Increase the profit per order

See? Easy stuff.

Letting the Least Buy the Most: The 80-20 Rule

The other fundamental concept of database-marketing is also simple. This concept centers around the belief that a large percentage of sales (about 80 percent of any result) comes from a relatively small percentage of customers (roughly 20 percent). This concept may sound like doom and gloom because you're depending on a small number of customers to pay the bills, but it's the truth.

In most companies, 80 percent of total sales are made to 20 percent of their customers. A company's remaining 20 percent of sales are made to the remaining 80 percent of its customers. Your job is to exploit that 80 percent potential and to be confident that the 20 percent will follow.

As an online marketer, you must court your customers. You must know what to present to your customers that will turn them on (strictly from a sales perspective, of course). Your challenge lies in being able to do it without the benefit of a face-to-face encounter.

Having your customers tell you all you need to know

The most cost-effective form of marketing to court your customers is probably database marketing. To help you understand this term, take those words apart. *Data* is information about your customers, and you *base* your *marketing* efforts on what you already know about those customers.

Tip

You simply use *all* the information you gather about your current customers and potential customers to develop a strategic marketing plan. I'm talking about the online and offline information you have collected from surveys, guest books, customer-satisfaction forms, contest entries, suggestion boxes, and demographic research.

Suppose that you have developed a whiz-bang software product which runs only on Windows 95. Suppose also that you have come up with some sort of marketing and promotional campaign that will cost $1 for every potential customer you reach. Finally, assume that you have identified 20,000 potential customers and that you know from your research that only 4,000 of them use Windows 95. It's the 80-20 rule in action: Eighty percent of your sales will come from 20 percent of your customers.

For the sake of simplicity, assume that every Windows 95 user who sees your marketing materials will buy your product on the spot just because it's so amazing. Maybe instead of selling a software product, you're selling a living, breathing, corn-chip-eating Microsoft technician who sits by your customer's side day after day to fix any PC burps. (That *would* be amazing.)

If you don't gather any detailed information about the 20,000 people in this example, you have to market to every single one of those 20,000 people, or 100 percent of your potential customer base: Print your materials; design your online area; send out any supporting propaganda; answer inquiries; take customer calls. You would have to utilize every tool in your marketing bandwagon to close sales on a population the size of a small sports arena, and that would cost you a considerable chunk of change, or $20,000.

But what if you know exactly which of those 20,000 customers uses Windows 95? You can then market to only those users, get just as many sales, and save yourself $16,000. This example is overly simplified, but you get the idea. Database marketing enables you to get absolutely the most bang for your buck.

Helping customers benefit from database marketing

Database marketing also benefits your customers. The more you know about them, the more you can tailor your products to address their specific needs.

Suppose that your wonderful software product is some sort of contact-management program. If you know, for example, that a few hundred people on your list are real-estate professionals, perhaps you can modify your program to meet their special contact needs. You might add specific fields that real-estate brokers and agents find helpful, such as anticipated date of home purchase, whether buyers are prequalified for loans, and buyers' dream-home parameters. Potential customers may jump at the chance to buy a contact manager created specifically for real-estate professionals, whereas they may not give a generic contact manager a second glance (see Figure 16-1).

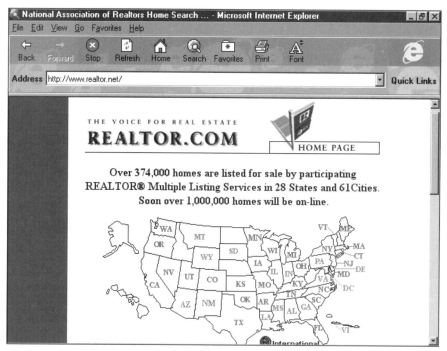

Figure 16-1: Rather than market a program to everyone, you can probably sell more of your product if you tailor it toward a specific audience.

Database marketing enables you to more accurately anticipate your customers' needs and adapt your marketing strategy to meet those needs. Your cyberbusiness then has a better chance of success because you're not "all over the board." You spend your money and time marketing to only those customers who are most likely to buy your product or service.

Examining the Database-Marketing Cycle

Like any other form of successful marketing, database marketing is a continuing cycle of analysis, planning, and implementation, as shown in Figure 16-2. As you begin to formulate your strategy, you have to remember that these three steps are equally important.

Analysis is simply the process of looking at your raw information and determining exactly what it *means*. Well-organized information (which you can get directly from your customers) is the foundation of a database-marketing plan,. Although your analysis must be thorough and detailed, the information you're analyzing should be manageable. The end result of your analysis should be a determination of exactly which customers are likely to be receptive to exactly which products and services you offer.

Figure 16-2: Like a gear in a piece of machinery, the database marketing cycle keeps turning as your business grows.

In the *planning* stage, you decide exactly which action to take as a result of your analysis. Whereas your analysis answers the *who* question, your purpose in planning is to figure out *how*. This process is no different from the development of any other marketing plan, except that your focus now is on exactly who comprises your audience.

The third stage, obviously, is implementation, or putting your plan into action. Wait — you're not finished. After you have taken action, you have to look at the result of your plan and see what you did right and what you did wrong. In other words, you simply return to the analysis stage. First, however, you have to get your data ducks lined up, which I describe in the next section.

Gathering Information for Database Marketing

Before you run off to develop a database-marketing strategy, you need, of course, a database of information to work with. Ideally, you collect this information for free. (I touched on this subject in Chapter 4, but this section presents more fodder for you to consider.)

Registration cards

In Chapter 4, I used the example of a software-registration card as a tool for gathering customer information. Every time you buy new software, a registration card is included in the product package. The only information the software company truly needs is your name and address and the product's serial number. Have you ever seen a registration card, however, that doesn't ask all sorts of other questions? I haven't — not even at my own company!

Self-addressed, stamped registration cards are included in all the Komputer Klinic's PC learning products, and the responses on the cards tell us a great deal about our customers. These extra questions help us gather demographic information we can then use for additional database marketing.

Ever fill out a free subscription card for a magazine? From free issues of popular computer magazines to the more obscure publications, such as *Water World* ("serving the municipal water and wastewater industry"), your one-stop shop for free subscription cards is at `http://yotta.com/magazine/free.htm` on the World Wide Web. This site has examples of different magazine-subscription forms.

Let's look at the free online-subscription form for one of my favorites, *CleanRooms* ("a monthly magazine serving the various industries employing contamination control and ultrapure materials and process technologies").

The subscription form has standard questions, such as "What's your mailing address?" It also has other questions, including "Which category best describes your company's primary manufacturing concern at this location (components or end product)?" and "Which category best describes your primary job function?" The form asks many more questions that are obviously not necessary in order to slap a mailing label on a magazine (see Figure 16-3). The company that created this card is gathering information for potential advertisers and is target-marketing its audience by either e-mail or regular snail mail.

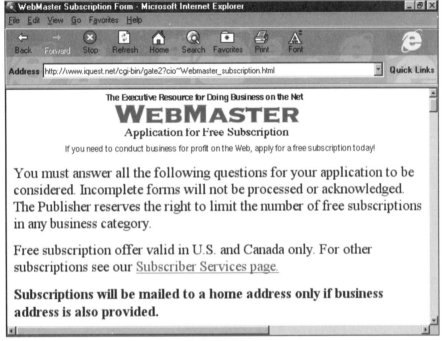

Figure 16-3: Free magazine-subscription cards always ask many more questions than are necessary to mail the publication.

Tip

The bottom line about information gathering is that most people are willing to complete forms but not to offer personal information (if you consider "personal" information to be the type of CD-ROM drive you own), unless they have some sort of additional incentive. Simply stated, you must give people something in exchange for the time they spend giving you the information you want.

Most people register their software products so that they can get free technical support and any other benefits that go along with registered ownership. In filling out a registration card, many people figure, "Why not just go ahead and answer all the questions?" I can guarantee that if the Komputer Klinic provided one card for registration and another for personal information, it would never receive a single personal-information card.

This message is also reinforced within Komputer Klinic products. The Klinic's training CD-ROMs, for example, include a special reminder at the end of the lessons it presents:

> And if you want to be notified automatically of upgrades and future products as well as get special savings offered *only* to our loyal customers, register your purchase with The Komando Corporation. Plus, as our special thank you, you'll also be automatically subscribed to our *free* weekly electronic newsletter, full of tips, tricks, and secrets designed to keep you up-to-date. So if you have not registered yet, pause the audio now and follow the instructions under "Registering with Komando." Or complete the registration card included with your purchase and mail it in. Heck, we even pay the postage. Keep in touch with us so that we can keep in touch with you!

The president of a large software company recently told me that his company's registration rate was only 5 percent. In contrast, the Komputer Klinic gets approximately a 70 percent return rate on registrations. I think that the Klinic's free electronic newsletter is the clincher. Consider giving away something in exchange for registration information. This highly flexible idea can easily be adapted for any business (see Figure 16-4).

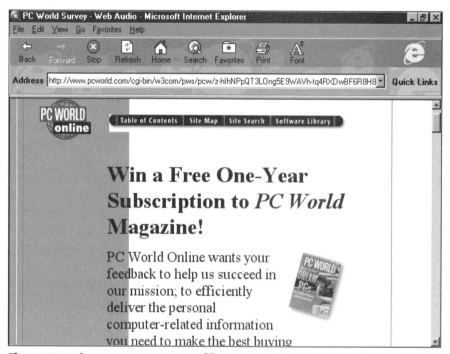

Figure 16-4: If you want customers to fill out your online surveys, you have to give them something for free.

Online surveys

Another way to collect information is by taking an online survey. You have to be careful with surveys, though. A fine line exists between "gathering information so that we can serve you better" and "getting as much personal information as possible so that we can sell you tons of stuff." If your survey gives the impression of the latter rather than the former, you won't get many responses, and you may even end up hurting your business. Even if you can put together an acceptable survey, some people simply won't participate in them.

The good news is that posting an interactive survey on your online area or Web site is relatively inexpensive. In other words, you have no reason *not* to have one. Even if only half the people who visit your site take the time to complete a survey, you still get plenty of valuable information that you wouldn't get otherwise. Just remember to rotate your surveys periodically so that people don't see the same one every time. Surveys that are "stale" (like *anything* online that's stale) can be a turn-off to users.

Tip

To get more customers to respond to your surveys, put your surveys in the form of a contest. You simply host a "free" drawing for some sort of prize and include your marketing questions on the entry form.

Because people like to receive free stuff and because they like to be "winners," even the offer of a free T-shirt may be enough to pull in some extra responses. The more valuable the prize, of course, the bigger your response. If you offer a brand-new Cadillac in your free drawing, I can assure you that you will collect more marketing information than you could possibly use in 20 cyberbusinesses (and I can also assure you that mine will be one of the first entries you receive).

Paying for information

After you have thousands of customers, you can use all sorts of different techniques to gather all sorts of marketing information. When you're just getting started, on the other hand, you usually don't have many customers from whom to draw information. If you're intent on doing database marketing from the beginning, when you have no sales and no customer data, virtually your only option is to buy the information from someone else.

Remember those software-registration cards? They usually say something like "Check here if you *don't* want us to share information about you." As I said, these companies don't really *share* anything — they just sell your information if you let them. They don't typically sell it directly to another retailer or manufacturer, however. Instead, they sell it to a company that specializes in brokering this type of information. These companies can then combine information from several sources to create one monster database.

Warning

The important thing to remember is that these types of services aren't cheap. Depending on how specialized the information, how recent the database, and how many names in the database, you can end up spending thousands of dollars. And limitations sometimes exist on how long or for what purpose you can use the information. If you buy a database and it pays off, great! If it doesn't do what you expect, however, you can waste plenty of money.

In many ways, the manner in which you build your customer database is limited only by your own ingenuity. If you think that your online products or services are perfect for companies that are members of a local Better Business Bureau, buy those names. Contact your local Better Business Bureau, and ask the cost and use policies for its member database. Or point your Web browser to `http://www.bbb.org` to get that information and much more (see Figure 16-5).

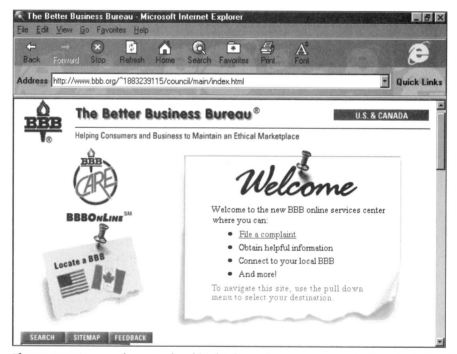

Figure 16-5: You can buy membership databases from many organizations, including the Better Business Bureau.

Now it's time to exercise your brain cells. If your online product for sports enthusiasts is a natural for anyone who reads a sports-related magazine, what should you do? You guessed it — contact the magazine to lease its subscriber database. If you want to tap a particular company's database (known in marketing lingo as *leasing*), just ask. The worst that can happen is that someone will tell you "No." If you get a "Yes," however, you're steps ahead of the game.

Tip

As with any other business, look for a database source that has been in business for a few years and that has a respectable client list. You must consider obvious issues, such as price, but you also have to ask about past uses of the names (how many times they have been leased already) and average response rates. Will you receive just addresses, or more, such as age, income level, hobbies, and interests? Are you paying just for mailing labels that are perfect for one-time use, or will you get a database file you can search and use repeatedly with your PC?

On America Online, use the keyword Simba to check out the Direct NewsLine area (see Figure 16-6). This area provides a daily update on the direct-marketing industry and available databases. The following sampling of databases was listed on the eventful day I wrote this chapter (note that the cost in U.S. dollars is for 1,000 names and that *M* is the Roman numeral for 1,000):

✦ American Baby Grandparents: 174,352 active grandparents @ $75/M

✦ Aspen Wellness 7-Day Diet: 40,000 program buyers @ $85/M

✦ SkyMall Catalog Ride-Along: 30M August @ $60/M

✦ Ziff-Davis International Database: 85,446 unduplicated subscribers @ $250/M

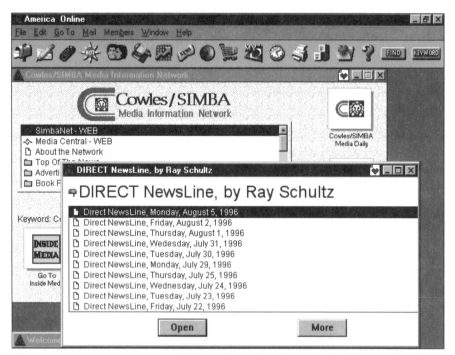

Figure 16-6: Direct Newsline publishes information about mailing lists available for lease.

Companies that sell databases, such as the ones in this list, are on the commercial services and on the Web. Use your favorite search engine with keywords such as *database* and *sales*. I don't want to promote any particular company, so I'll let you find them yourself. (Don't whine — it's the least you can do for me because today is my birthday, and I'm working. True story.)

Knowing What Else You Need

Now that you have all this wonderful customer data, you obviously need a place in which to store it all. That storage place is a file you create in a database program. The file is called a *database,* or customer information file.

In general terms, a database is just a list of something; that something can be your customers, friends, enemies, VCR tapes, or every item in your home or office. Your phone book is a list, or database, of all the people who live near you and the places where you can spend money. The difference between a list and a database is flexibility. You can use a list only in its original form (alphabetical, for example). With a database, however, you can sort and present information based on any combination of its elements (zip code, age, and business, for example).

The technoids who create software programs couldn't just leave things simple and call the program that helps you manage lists a "list program" — that would make life too easy. They had to call it a "database program." In technical terms, a database is a collection of information on a computer. Think about this the next time you look at your address book. You can put it in your computer and call it an "address database." Everyone should own one.

The big deal about a database program is that you can quickly find that one piece of information you want. Want to know which customers bought from you in the past six months? No problem. How about finding all the customers who bought something recently and who live in a certain zip code and have the first name Herbert? No problem. Get the point? Good.

Choosing the Right Database Program

Exactly which database program you use isn't nearly as important as making sure that you can *use* it to its fullest extent. You may want to invest in a full-blown database program, such as Claris FileMaker Pro or Microsoft Access, both of which offer excellent help to get you started.

On the other hand, you may be able to get the ball rolling with one of the simple database programs that come in an "ensemble" package, such as ClarisWorks or Microsoft Works. Again, the important thing is that you choose a program you're comfortable with and that enables you to manipulate and extract your valuable information as easily as possible.

Note

You may be tempted to set up your customer information file in a spreadsheet program, such as Excel or Lotus 1-2-3. You may be able to get by with a spreadsheet program, but I recommend against it. That's not really what these programs were designed for, and sooner or later you will want to do something with that information that your spreadsheet just can't handle.

"But How Do I Really Do It?"

I would love to be able to give you step-by-step instructions for designing a sophisticated database in which to house your customer information file, but that information is simply beyond the scope of this book. In this section, however, I give you some ideas to help you get started.

Suppose that one of your customers, Wanna Bea Admiral, who bought a $1,000 painting from you online, lives at 1234 Main Street, Anytown, Arizona 85003.

In your customer database, all the information about Wanna (or any other customer) is called a *record*. A *field* is an area in your database that holds specific information from each customer record.

Here's the information for each field in Wanna's record in your database:

Field	Information You Enter
First Name	Wanna
Middle Name	Bea
Last Name	Admiral
Purchase Price	$1,000
Street Address	1234 Main Street
City	Anytown
State	AZ
Zip or Postal Code	85003

You can also put other fields in your database, such as E-Mail Address, Credit-Card Number, Telephone Number, Fax Number, and Notes.

The important thing is to split all the information about a record, or about one particular customer, into as many fields as you can without having so many parts that it becomes overwhelming. For example, your customer database may consist of these fields:

✦ Mr./Mrs./Ms.

✦ First Name

✦ Middle Initial

✦ Last Name

✦ Company Name

✦ Address

✦ City

✦ State

✦ Zip/Postal Code

✦ Telephone Number

✦ Piece of Art Purchased

✦ Purchase Date

✦ Purchase Amount

When you put all the fields together and enter information in them, you create a record. If 100 customers are entered in your customer database, you have 100 records. (And if you have sold 100 paintings online at $1,000 apiece, I'm in the wrong business.)

To help you avoid mistakes, most database programs enable you to place restrictions on what you enter in a field. *Character fields* accept anything you want to put in them: letters, numbers, symbols, or a combination plate that contains a little of everything. Character fields usually contain a customer's name, address, city, state, Zip/postal code, and telephone number.

Guess which type of information numeric fields in a database contain? Yes — we have a winner. You can enter only numbers into *numeric fields.* Use a numeric field when you plan to use a number in formulas or for calculations. The purchase amount or outstanding balance should be set up as a numeric field. In some databases, you have to leave an empty slot, called a *calculated field,* for the result of a calculation on the numbers in the database. You never enter information directly into this field. An example of a calculated field is the purchase amount plus the sales tax.

You use another field format, a *date field,* when you work with time-sensitive information, such as the number of days a payment is past due or the number of days between receiving and shipping an order. You can usually set the date format to look any way you want (25-12-97 or December 25, 1997, for example).

Another handy field type you shouldn't overlook is the *logical field,* such as Yes/No and True/False. The Komputer Klinic uses a logical field in its customer-satisfaction surveys.

Note fields (or *memo fields*) resemble little "sticky notes" you can use to enter specific information in individual records in a database.

Tip

Before you sit down at your computer to design your database, pull out a sample invoice, your customer phone book, and any other traditional paper-based item you use now. Look at it carefully, and pay attention to the spots on which you have to enter information to complete your form or entry.

List on paper all customer-information fields you want to be able to save and then search through with your computer. After you complete the list, leave it alone for a day or so. Show it to the people who will use your database, and ask for their suggestions. Then go through the list one last time and use your chosen software program to design your database. This procedure limits the changes you have to make to the design later.

Finding Online Help with Setting up a Database

Now let me offer some online resources to help you along the database design way.

For starters, point your Web browser to `http://www.ins.at/gmaier/main.htm`, the Database-Marketing Web site. Compiled by a variety of marketing professionals, this site offers a relatively comprehensive online tutorial that covers every imaginable aspect of database marketing. You can even get your individual questions about database marketing answered *for free* (at least at the time I wrote this book). A notice on this site, however, says that the free service isn't likely to continue indefinitely. Bummer.

If your database-marketing strategy includes a direct-mail campaign, you don't want to miss the online tutorial at `http://www.g1.com/present/reducost/sld001.htm` (see Figure 16-7).

Brought to you by Group 1 Software, this interactive workshop is called "Reducing Direct Mail Costs: A Working Checklist and Tutorial." It has 35 sections that cover a variety of topics, including the ones in this list:

✦ What to expect in this tutorial

✦ Don't cost-cut to excess

✦ How do we measure cost?

✦ Materials: A sample mail package

✦ Combining pieces

✦ Classes of mail

✦ What is required for postal discounts?

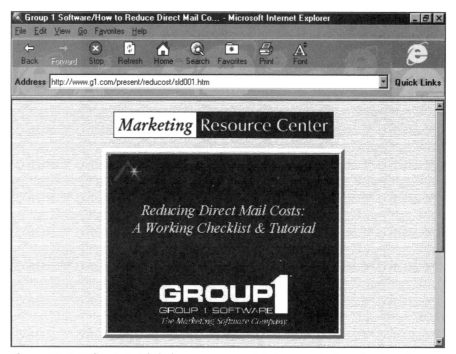

Figure 16-7: Online tutorials help you put your database-marketing plan in action.

✦ Address correction and standardization (coding)

✦ Why are bad addresses so expensive?

If you want help in developing your database-marketing system, check with a company called Database Connection, at `http://www.dbconnection.com`. Its Market Builder system "provides the tools needed to increase sales by leveraging your customer and prospect foundation." This networkable system, designed using Microsoft Access, consists of these four components:

✦ **Query Builder:** Centralizes the inquiry process

✦ **Campaign Builder:** Provides the power of a marketing agency

✦ **Survey Builder:** Provides the capabilities of a survey service bureau

✦ **Territory Builder:** Manages your sales force

If you're wondering exactly how to reach all those potential cybercustomers, take a look at the Interactive Publishing Alert, at `http://www.netcreations.com/ipa/adindex`. This site has a Search database of Web sites and online areas around the world that accept advertising. You enter specific criteria (such as how much you want to spend, the type of site or area you're looking for, and the minimum number of hits you're willing to accept), and in seconds IPA presents you with a hot-linked (one-click access) list of sites and areas, complete with current rate information.

Another great online resource for database-marketing information as well as information about all sorts of other marketing and advertising techniques is the Sharrow Marketing and Advertising Resource Center. You can find it on the World Wide Web at http://www.dnai.com/~sharrow/enter.html, as shown in Figure 16-8.

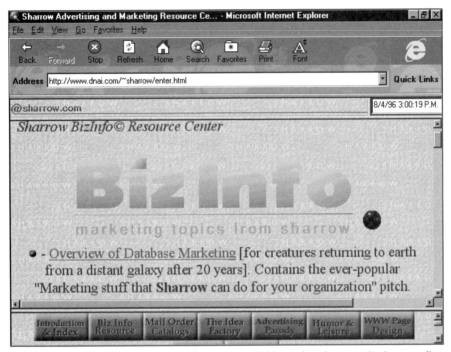

Figure 16-8: Among the many good reports available at the Sharrow site is an audit to assess your current customer database.

This site has plenty of information, but you can point your trusty Web browser to http://www.dnai.com/~sharrow/db_mktg.html to go directly to the database-marketing section.

Timing Is Everything

Like most information these days, the facts and figures in your customer information file have a limited lifespan. If you market any type of computer-related products, consider how often you change and upgrade your own computer system; that means that at least some of the information you have about your customers' systems will probably be outdated within six months or a year. Obviously, a customer's age changes every year. Assuming that your customers are a fairly bright lot, their income should change every year too.

The point I'm trying to make is that you cannot just set up a customer information file in some hot database program and expect that information to keep your business going for the rest of its life. It all goes back to the cycle of analysis, planning, and implementation I mentioned earlier in this chapter (refer to Figure 16-2). Part of that cycle *must* involve keeping your customer-information file as current as possible. In the long run, having bad information can be worse than having no information.

One way to keep your records updated is to ask your customers to do the updating for you. You can simply send them an e-mail message stating that, to ensure that you can give every customer the individualized attention she deserves, you want to verify that you have current information. Then just present some sort of report that reflects the information you have about them.

Again, many customers need extra incentive to make it worth their while to provide you with updated information. Remember that even something small will probably do the trick. I don't recommend a contest as an incentive in this case, however. Instead, make sure that *every* person who responds gets something for his effort. After all, your customers have already spent their money with you and have already given you the original information. It's not unreasonable on their part to expect a little something for their trouble.

To Sell or Not to Sell

After you put together a substantial customer information file on thousands of people (each of whom you know is just dying to spend more money), the little cash register in your head might go "Cha-ching!" Why not become one of the *sellers* of marketing databases rather than one of the buyers?

Warning

When people disclose personal information to you, they usually expect you to hold that information in confidence, unless you tell them otherwise *beforehand*. I'll use the example of the software-registration card one more time; specifically, the box labeled "Check here if you don't want your information shared with anyone else." If you provide the check box on the card and a customer doesn't check it, he gives you *implicit* permission to share his information.

On the flip side, if the registration card doesn't even have a box to check, it isn't logical or ethical for you to *assume* that it's okay to share a customer's information. If you sell the information anyway, a customer can't do much about it. Over time, however, you probably will get a reputation for being a little sleazy in that area, and that practice can ultimately affect your sales.

Tip

If you're giving serious thought to someday selling the data in your customer information file, you have to begin planning now. Let the people who are giving you the information know that you may later "share" it with another company. Like any good company, add to your electronic form a box that says "Check here if you don't want your information shared." Most important, if customers do check that box, make darned sure that you abide by their wishes.

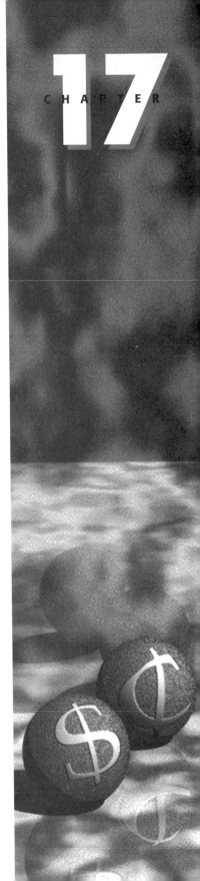

Maintaining Customer Contact and Building Loyalty

Potty training a toddler. Getting your spouse to change the empty roll of toilet paper. Balancing your checkbook. Having a great blind date. Putting your kids through college. These are a few examples of life's major accomplishments.

On the flip side, getting someone to buy something from you one time is no big deal. Even a New York City street vendor peddling a fake Rolex can do that. The trick is in getting the same customers to return again and again in order to spend more and more of their dollars. Repeat customers are the best way to achieve your goal of maintaining a low cost per order, which translates into higher profits. Customer loyalty is unquestionably the greatest asset a business can have. Many service-oriented businesses, such as advertising agencies, are eventually sold, in fact, based primarily on who comprises their list of loyal clients.

No matter which kind of business you're in, out in cyberspace or over on Main Street, a key component to building customer loyalty is to keep open a continuous line of communication between you and your customers. This principle is nothing new. In our personal lives, lost communication sends many relationships looking for help from divorce attorneys. In business, it is equally as important to maintain constant contact with customers, or else you may lose them too.

Good communication involves more than just sending a message, however. Regardless of whether you send a message online or offline, an effective message must accomplish three important goals:

✦ It must get the attention of the person who receives it.

✦ The person who receives the message must be easily able to understand it.

✦ It must spark a need to act on something.

As an aspiring cyber-entrepreneur, you're especially lucky because communication is what being online is all about. Survey after survey has shown that people get online to meet, to learn, and to be entertained, which is perhaps the reason for so many "virtual affairs." People feel more comfortable telling their deepest secrets to a person sitting on the other end of a computer screen than they do face-to-face or in real life. To see intimate conversations taking place among total strangers, drop in to an online chat room late some night.

Tapping in to the minds of online customers and making your brand name a part of their everyday life is easy. From the simplest online marketing example, because you have e-mail addresses for your customers, you can reach every single one of them (or at least their electronic mailboxes) in a matter of seconds.

Whether your online venture is engaging in business-to-business marketing or relying on individual consumers for revenues, you must maintain constant contact with your customers. For starters, you should seriously consider adding an electronic newsletter to your marketing communications bandwagon. It's a super way to achieve that goal of "in-your-face" marketing.

Getting the Scoop on Electronic Newsletters

One of the fastest, easiest, and potentially most effective ways to stay in touch with your existing customers is to publish a periodic electronic newsletter. (I think that every cyberbusiness should have one.)

Don't get all bent out of shape about adding another project to your plate. I realize that you have a great deal to do in order to launch your cyberbusiness, and an electronic newsletter will occupy some of your valuable time. How much of your time it takes, however, depends on how frequently you publish it (weekly, monthly, or quarterly). If you start from scratch every week, drafting and sending a weekly newsletter, for example, you're probably spending too much time on your newsletter and not enough on your business.

Here's the inside scoop on the weekly electronic newsletter the Komputer Klinic sends out to almost 100,000 e-mail addresses. Distributing a weekly electronic newsletter is no big deal for my company. The newsletter contains a new column I write for not only the newsletter but also the newspaper syndicates that distribute my column.

I write the column and get paid for it by the newspapers that print it. The only real expense I incur is the hour or so it takes for an intern to format the newsletter and send out a mass e-mailing. In hard dollars, it costs about $10 to distribute the electronic newsletter. Not bad for a direct-mail piece, eh? You would spend at least $30,000 in postage alone to send a traditional mailer to 100,000 customers.

Getting the timing down

If you don't have the luxury of using new weekly material that already exists, you may think that distributing an electronic newsletter once every four months or so is a good time line. Not so. If you sent out your newsletter only quarterly, you're probably not keeping your customers current enough with what's happening in your business. Even if the information is up-to-date and timely, your customers probably will forget about your company and its superior products or services long before you publish the next edition.

In my humble opinion (or IMHO, in e-mail jargon), your best bet is a monthly newsletter. The timespan is infrequent enough that you're not wasting your life toiling over your electronic newsletter, yet it's frequent enough that your customers are kept abreast of your company's news and your company name is regularly put in front of their faces.

Presenting the right information

After you decide how frequently to publish your electronic newsletter, what should you put in it?

Note

That's a good question. The most important thing to remember is that your newsletter is *not* one giant advertisement. You're not just handing out an online flyer. The purpose of your newsletter (or any newsletter, for that matter) is to give readers some sort of useful information about your industry or area of expertise. If the only thing your newsletter does is attempt to sell your products or services, customers will treat it just as they treat any other junk e-mail: Your newsletter will end up in a Deleted Mail folder faster than you can say "Publisher's Clearing House." If sales hype is all you plan to publish, why waste your time? In the long run, publishing a newsletter that consists of only hype can hurt your reputation and cost you sales.

An offline business helps illustrate what I mean. Every month, a Southern California membership warehouse named Fedco mails out to its members a multipage circular that tells about the numerous sales and specials it has available that month. Throughout the pages of the Fedco circular, however, are a dozen or so stories about California history, points of interest, and famous people. Fedco pays professional writers to write these articles for one simple reason: People who might otherwise toss the Fedco advertisement in the trash instead take the time to look it over and read the articles. If someone who's reading an article happens to notice an interesting lawn mower or pair of running shoes on the opposite page, it's all the better for Fedco. In your newsletter, you must take the approach of providing value to readers.

Here's a short list of components you should include in every electronic newsletter, regardless of your type of business:

◆ **Notice of specials and sales:** Yes, I told you to be sure that your newsletter isn't a giant advertisement for your company's products or services. I don't mean, however, that you're supposed to avoid marketing altogether. After all, the people who read your newsletter have bought from you before, and (assuming that you did your job properly) they probably will buy from you again. Sale information, therefore, is useful: Most customers will appreciate hearing about ways to save money on something they may already want.

◆ **News bits:** *USA Today* was the first major publication to figure out that most Americans, bombarded almost nonstop by the flow of information, like to receive news and other information in small, meaningful chunks. The news section of your newsletter can include news about your business (for example, a new Pentium Pro to better serve your customers, more 800 numbers for greater phone access, or the hiring of a new director of sales and marketing) and relevant news about your industry (for example, improved government census information that's available online, new research proving that bicyclists who wear helmets have a lower risk of injury, or an increase in champagne sales since Kim Komando finished writing her *CyberBuck$* book).

If you include news snippets about your industry, be sure to get the proper permissions to reprint the information.

Remember that the average reader of your newsletter may not have the same understanding of the topic as you. I'm not suggesting that you write "down" to your customers; just write in a conversational style, and make sure that anyone, computer literate or not, can easily understand the final copy. Your goal is to write on a fifth- to eighth-grade level. (Most printed newspapers follow this rule too.)

◆ **How-to or "tips and tricks" column:** As in the Fedco example I just mentioned, remember that it's free, useful information that adds value to your electronic newsletter. If you can provide articles that tell people how to make better use of their time and other resources, they not only read your newsletter but also look forward to receiving it again because it has value that directly influences their life.

Cosco, another discount warehouse, sends out a direct-mail flyer. Each issue, usually placed in the middle of the computer ads, carries a column written by Bill Gates that *The New York Times* carries too. I'm not sure that this idea is a good one, though. I believe that Cosco would do better with another angle on its computer column, perhaps with a more consumer-oriented focus. Mr. Gates focuses on the future, whereas I write about ways in which consumers can use technology *today.* (If you work for Cosco, I would appreciate it if you would voice my sentiments to the powers that be.)

You can put plenty of other elements in your newsletter, but this list should give you a good start. Just remember to add a small dose of creativity. No one will want to read your newsletter if it looks like the same old thing everyone else publishes or if it contains prose that only your mother would love.

Now is a good time to pull out your Vision for a Mission book (refer to Chapter 4). Make a list of all the information you want to (and can) put in your newsletter. Create a working table of contents. Try to limit the amount of material you personally have to write. Tap in to the resources of people around you who may want to help out for the sake of publicity. After all, you can offer the writer of the piece a byline that includes his name, company name, and even telephone number. It doesn't hurt to ask — the worst a writer can do is turn you down or offer an alternative (an article he has already written for another publication, for example). My company gets calls from aspiring millionaires, nonprofit groups, and even Fortune 500 companies who want a Kim Komando column for their publication. I usually send them a column, as long as they acknowledge my copyright. Documented nonprofit organizations can use the columns for free.

Making your information visually pleasing

After you know that you want to produce a monthly newsletter and you have a good idea of what you want to put in it, the biggest issue that remains is choosing the format of the newsletter. In much the same way as you have several options for the style that best suits your fashion palette, you can format your newsletter in one of several ways:

✦ As a text-based document

✦ As a separate page on your Web site or online area

✦ As an Adobe Acrobat PDF file

In this section, I help you figure out which option you should use in your newsletter.

Text-based documents

One option you have is to create a strictly text-based document that you send out as e-mail. Here are some advantages of this type of newsletter:

✦ It's easy to produce.

✦ The file size is small (even with a large newsletter).

✦ You can easily distribute it as the body of an e-mail message.

✦ You can reach all your customers in one fell swoop by using a mass-mailing e-mail program or mailing list (which I describe later in this chapter).

Text-based newsletters also have some disadvantages:

✦ They're not especially pleasant to look at — just a bunch of plain text on-screen. (If you go this route, you can't add even the simplest graphics.)

✦ Readers have no easy means of navigation unless they have some sort of special text-viewing utility. If a particular article is at the end of the newsletter, they can't just click a button to jump to it. Instead, they must keep scrolling down until they find the article they want.

Note

Luckily, as commercial online services grow, so does their number of features. Like many services, America Online enables you to add color, change font size, add boldface and italics, and put hot links in your e-mail. Use these features, which are a big stride for electronic-text-based newsletters, in your e-mail, but remember: If you format your newsletter using the AOL e-mail tools and send your e-mail from AOL to a customer with an Internet account — poof! — the formatting disappears. Usually, only members of the service from which the e-mail originated can see the formatting.

Your Web site or online area

Another option is to post your newsletter as a separate page on your Web site or online area. This method offers a couple of advantages:

✦ You have some control over the formatting (how the thing looks), and you can add graphics and other elements.

✦ If you post your electronic newsletter for the world to see, you don't have to worry about distribution — it's just *there*.

The second benefit can work to your disadvantage, though. If your newsletter is just sitting there among the millions and millions of Web pages, you have absolutely no way to guarantee that a single customer will give it a second look. If you post your newsletter on your Web site or online area, you're creating some extra work in that you have to spend some time generating interest in your newsletter and getting people to find it and read it.

Adobe Acrobat PDF file

If you create your newsletter as an Adobe Acrobat PDF file, two separate software components come into play. First, a program you use at your end turns any file created in any program into a viewable, portable format. As long as the person at the other end has the Acrobat viewer, she can view the pages in your document just as you created them — fonts, artwork, and everything.

By using Acrobat, you can create a stylized newsletter in a program such as Quark Xpress or Adobe PageMaker and rest assured that people around the world can see it exactly the way you created it. After your newsletter is finished, you can post it as a downloadable file on your Web site or online area, or you can send it to customers as an e-mail attachment.

Warning

You're asking for trouble if you send e-mail attachments to a commercial online service from outside that service and vice versa. Because the file must travel over the Infobahn, it's likely to hit a few potholes before it hits a recipient's electronic mailbox. For example, certain file size limitations (usually 32K) exist on e-mail attachments that go from the Internet to AOL (check with your particular service). The commercial services are working hard to fix this limitation and may even have a solution by the time you read this book.

The benefits of using Acrobat for your electronic newsletters are numerous. You can create an electronic newsletter that has all the advanced design elements of a printed piece. Because Acrobat viewers are available for Windows, DOS, and the Mac, virtually all the computing public is covered. In addition, so that people can view PDF files directly online, Adobe and other companies are working to create an Acrobat plug-in for popular Web browsers.

The biggest problem with using Acrobat is that it requires users to have the appropriate viewer program. You can give away these programs with your newsletter, but many users are reluctant to install another program on their system, especially just to read a newsletter. Another problem is that if your post your PDF newsletter as a downloadable file on your site, you have the same distribution problems as in the technique I just described (posting your newsletter at your Web site): You have to make an effort to get people there to download it. If you decide to e-mail the PDF file, you're stuck with the file size limitations I just mentioned.

To keep up-to-date with Acrobat developments and to get the Acrobat viewer for free, point your Web browser to the Adobe home page, at `http://www.adobe.com` (see Figure 17-1). If you choose to use Acrobat to format your newsletter, you need the software program that's available from most computer retailers, mail-order catalogs, and online computer malls. The viewer is free, but the program that enables you to create the newsletter is not.

Choosing the best format for your newsletter

Because it's clear that none of these methods of electronic newsletter publishing is perfect, which one should you choose? My personal recommendation is to go with the e-mailed, text-only newsletter. It may not be pretty, but the entire purpose of your newsletter is to deliver valuable information, not a work of art. In addition, you know that every single person in your customer information file will have at least some exposure to your newsletter. Even if customers see the file only long enough to delete it, at least they have seen it.

Get 'em hooked on your newsletter. It's a great way to keep your company name in front of your customers and develop customer loyalty and trust. Loyal customers then will feel more comfortable spending money at your cyberstore. After the process of distributing your newsletter is running smoothly, you may want to consider adding more to your online communications mix. The good news is that you put FAQs (the subject I cover in the following section) in only one place: your online area.

Figure 17-1: Adobe Acrobat products are cross-platform tools for electronic publishing; you can create, view, and navigate documents in electronic form, print them, or distribute them electronically to others.

Just the FAQs

If you're tired of answering the same questions from a number of customers, you will love the FAQ (pronounced "fak," as in "attack") as a means of communication. In Chapter 9, I briefly mentioned the idea of creating a company FAQ, or Frequently Asked Questions file. Now it's time to dig in to some FAQ specifics.

The whole idea of a FAQ is to put information about your company into a logical question-and-answer format. Assuming that you have done a good job of creating your FAQ and that people actually read it, this type of document helps you to avoid having to repeatedly answer the same questions from your customers. A FAQ is an extremely cost-effective means of providing customer service.

To get your FAQ going, try to remember which questions people ask you more than a few times a day or week. Or just make up some questions about your company and then answer them. Any existing company literature you have is a good place to begin. If not, try to put yourself in the shoes of your customers. Consider their level of knowledge, and then try to figure out what they probably don't know but should.

Only you can say exactly what is appropriate to put in your FAQ, based on whatever field you're in (see Figure 17-2). At minimum, cover the who, what, where, when, and how of your cyberbusiness. It's okay to have some marketing lingo in a FAQ, as long as it isn't all advertising hype.

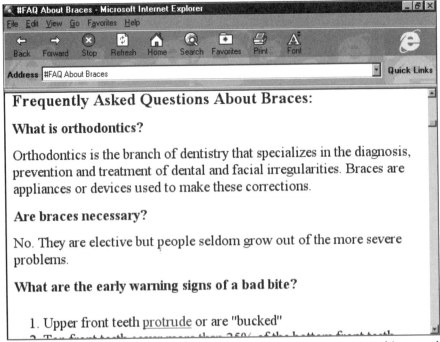

Figure 17-2: It's hard to come up with a Web site that can't use a FAQ. In this example, an online orthodontist answers many patients' questions about braces.

My company's FAQ covers specifics about the operations of the Komputer Klinic. The topics covered include the live broadcast of our shows, how to order products, whom to call for technical support and customer service, how to subscribe to our electronic newsletter, and more.

Like anything else in your cyberbusiness, your FAQ should grow and change. It's relatively easy: Just keep an eye on which types of questions are coming from your customers. If your customers repeatedly ask you a particular question, just add the question and the appropriate answer to your FAQ. It's that simple.

Tip

I suggest that you make your FAQ available online as both a viewable document and a downloadable file. Some people want a document to pop up online so that they can get all the information immediately. Others appreciate the opportunity to read it later, when they're offline. You have no reason not to accommodate both these groups. You are, after all, a customer-service-oriented company, right?

Venturing into Usenet Newsgroups

Warning

Tens of thousands of Usenet newsgroups are on the Internet, each one devoted to a unique topic. With all the available groups — and, consequently, all those people — in one place, you might be tempted to post a small, unassuming advertisement in each newsgroup. *Don't do it!* If you engage in this practice, known among Internet people as *spamming,* you are considered the lowest of the low.

To illustrate this point, let me tell you about a friend of mine. My friend owns a business that specializes in what he calls "information packaging and distribution" (Web-page development, along with some other stuff). A few weeks ago, he got the idea of promoting his business by offering a free service to the Internet community. The concept of this service, called the Super Daily Vocabulary Builder, is that after you sign up, you receive a new vocabulary word by e-mail each business day.

This idea doesn't sound bad. My friend was faced with the problem, however, of getting the word out about his new service. He figured that because he was offering a free service with no strings attached, people wouldn't mind much if he posted his announcement all over the Usenet.

Wrong! Unfortunately, he did just that: He posted his little announcement in hundreds of newsgroups. In one weekend, he received about 300 angry responses "flaming" him for posting his announcement in inappropriate newsgroups. The responses ranged from polite ("Please don't do this anymore") to vulgar profanity (use your imagination!) to downright violent ("I hope that you get hit by a truck and die slowly and painfully").

Internet users didn't limit their actions to direct complaints. My friend's ISP (Internet service provider) received more than 200 complaints, many of them demanding that my friend's account be canceled immediately. One fellow sent him a lengthy e-mail complaint — 100 times — and another sent him more than 5MB of junk data, both actions designed simply to harass my friend and bog down his e-mail. In cyberspace, they take no prisoners.

All this may seem a little childish to you, but it is simply the way of the Internet world. People take their newsgroups seriously. If you don't know the rules of the jungle, you had better just stay out. For more information about this topic, take a look at these Web sites:

✦ 101 Ways to Be Obnoxious on Usenet (`http://www.indirect.com/user/steiners/usenet.html`)

✦ The "Stop Spam" Page (`http://www.iac.co.jp/~issho/stop-spam.html`, as shown in Figure 17-3)

✦ The Spam FAQ (`http://ddi.digital.net/~gandalf/spamfaq.html`)

✦ NASS (Netters Against Spam Spewers) (`http://www.newwave.net/~beavis/nass/nass.html`)

✦ What Is Usenet? (`http://www.tezcat.com/~abbyfg/faq/what-is-usenet.html`)

Figure 17-3: Spamming is a serious etiquette offense on the Internet.

Incidentally, in my friend's case, it wasn't all bad news. That first weekend, he also received more than 2,000 sign-ups for his Super Daily Vocabulary Builder. The emotional impact of all those flames, however, took a toll on him, and he has sworn off spamming for good. He now promotes his free vocabulary-building service only on his Web site (which, in case you're interested, is at `http://www.info-wave.com/sdin`).

Introducing Mailing Lists, Listservs, and Majordomos

What makes the Internet such a powerful medium is that the services it can carry are limited only by the imagination of its users. Internet mailing lists are another example of a simple yet powerful and time-saving service you can use to your advantage. *Listserv* and *Majordomo* are two other terms you might hear associated with these mailing lists; they're just two UNIX-based software packages used to administer these mailing lists (see Figure 17-4).

Figure 17-4: L-Soft International, Inc., develops and licenses the original (Eric Thomas's) LISTSERV software, the first popular software program written to manage electronic mailing lists.

How exactly do you use a mailing list? You can use a mailing list in one of two ways:

✦ To act as a manager for a discussion group (the most common use)

✦ To automate the process of distributing your message to a large group

Suppose that the subscribers to a particular mailing list have signed up to actively participate in a conversation. All these members are given a central e-mail address to which they can send their comments. After a message hits that address, it is automatically redistributed to everyone else on the mailing list. In this way, participants can engage in an open, active discussion carried out entirely through e-mail.

Note

The one problem with this setup is that if several hundred members are on the mailing list, you can end up getting several hundred e-mail messages every day from people on the list. To help control this problem, most lists offer a *digest* option in which all the messages for a given day are compiled into one giant e-mail message and then forwarded to you as a single message. In the long run, this technique saves plenty of download time and makes it much easier to skim through the messages to find the ones that interest you.

The other great thing about Internet mailing lists is that the entire process, including subscribing and unsubscribing, is totally automated. Each mailing-list software program works a little differently; the normal process to subscribe, however, is simply to send an e-mail message to the specified address with the word *subscribe* and the name of the list as the body of the message. The software at the other end reads the information in your message and automatically signs you up. In no time at all, you begin receiving messages.

Warning

As with Usenet newsgroups, thousands of mailing lists are out there, and their members don't care much for spamming. Sending an off-topic or commercial message is a sure way to get yourself into the same kind of trouble as my friend did with the newsgroups.

On some mailing lists, of course, your message might be appropriate. The question is, how do you find these lists? It's simple! Just point your Web browser to `http://www.liszt.com/`. The Liszt site offers a searchable (by category and name) directory of more than 50,000 mailing lists, as shown in Figure 17-5.

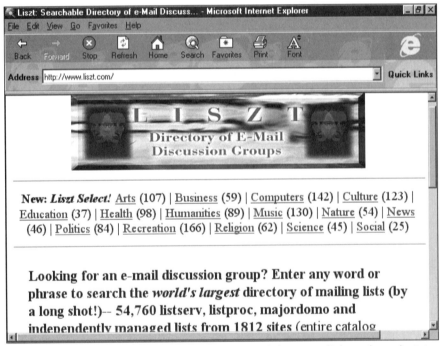

Figure 17-5: Liszt is a mailing-list octopus; it spreads its arms all throughout the Internet and compiles the results from your searches into a single directory.

Even if you can't post a commercial message on a particular mailing list, joining one that relates to your field still has some benefits. First, it can help you to gather valuable information about your potential customers, the type of information that may find a nice home in your customer information file. Joining it enables you to "get inside their heads," so to speak. In addition, there's nothing wrong with engaging in some sort of discussion in which you happen to mention your business — as long as it pertains to the conversation. Your signature line can be an advertisement, as long as it's short. Here's my signature line:

> The Komando Corporation makes computers easy!
> The Komputer Klinic on the Web: `http://www.komando.com`
> The Komputer Klinic on America Online: keyword KOMANDO
> The Komputer Klinic on MSN: go KOMANDO
> To order any of our computer training systems, call 1-800-KOMANDO

Suppose that you discover that no mailing list covers your particular field. Why not host one? Your local ISP probably already has all the software in place to manage your mailing list. Because the computer does everything with not much human interaction, your service provider shouldn't charge much, if anything, to manage it for you. Creating a mailing list can be a good promotional vehicle that helps to establish you as a leader in your field. Just be sure to put your home-page address in your signature line.

As I mentioned earlier in this chapter, you can use mailing-list software to manage the distribution of e-mail to a large audience. When you're just starting out, you're lucky to have a couple of hundred names on your internal mailing list. It shouldn't be too difficult, therefore, to distribute your product announcements and electronic newsletters from your own PC.

As times goes by, however, and the names on your client list number in the thousands, managing your e-mail distribution can turn into a nightmare. At that point, just call your local ISP and ask the folks there to handle the mailing-list distribution for you. After you turn your list over to them, all you have to do is send your message by e-mail to one single address at the ISP, and its software automatically forwards it to everyone on your list. What could be simpler?

Understanding the Ins and Outs of E-Mail

Because many of the marketing and sales techniques I have discussed involve e-mail in some manner, now is a good time to take a closer and more detailed look at the entire e-mail phenomenon and what it all means.

As a pure marketing tool, here are some of e-mail's strong points:

✦ **It's extremely fast.** You can blast an e-mail message across the country or around the world in a matter of seconds. Short of a personal phone call or video conference, in fact (both of which cost substantially more), it's the quickest known way to deliver information.

✦ **It's extremely cheap.** If you look at all the different uses you get from your online account and how many e-mail messages pass through your mailbox in a month, you will probably find that each individual e-mail message costs just pennies (or nothing!) to send. That's right — you can get free e-mail from companies such as Juno and Freemark. The catch is that each message contains an advertisement. Which other methods of communication do you know of that enable you to communicate with your customers for free?

✦ **It's likely to be read.** Unless your message looks and reads like a blatant advertisement, most people will take the time to open it and see what it's all about. You gain a powerful advantage over people who do bulk mailing through the U.S. Postal Service. (I don't know about you, but 99 percent of my junk mail hits the round file before it ever gets opened.)

Does e-mail have a downside?

The biggest problem with e-mail marketing seems to lie in keeping your e-mail address list current. Now more than ever, people are much more likely to change their e-mail address than their postal address. With more and more companies competing for your online membership, people are more tempted to bounce from one free offer to another. Try CompuServe for 30 days for free, and then cancel and give an America Online trial membership a whirl. Then you can move on to the next service. Trying out all available services is smart shopping on the part of consumers because they can easily decide which one best meets their needs. It doesn't help you much, though.

As I said earlier, you don't want your message to come off looking like junk mail. People don't like junk mail in their postal mailboxes, and they seem to like it even less in their virtual mailboxes. The truth is that no matter how hard you try, someone will look at your mailing as junk mail. That's just life.

As an example, the Komputer Klinic does not blindly send out its free electronic newsletter — users must request that it be sent to them. To subscribe, you have to fill out a form on America Online, the Microsoft Network, or the Internet. Or you can simply send e-mail to `KlinicNews@aol.com` with the word *subscribe* in it. Nonetheless, in each mass mailing, a certain percentage of people write back to accuse us of mailing something to them without their permission. Go figure.

One more e-mail drawback (as I discussed earlier in this chapter, in the section "Making your information visually pleasing") is the way it looks. I would bet that someday someone will develop an e-mail standard that facilitates highly stylized messages. In the meantime, however, we're all stuck with e-mail ugliness. But it's cheap.

Looking at the Good, the Bad, and the Ugly

The process of formatting e-mail is a fine art. Exactly how *do* you keep your e-mail messages from looking like junk mail? I can better answer this question with a couple of examples:

SUBJECT: AMAZING, NEW PRODUCT YOU CAN'T LIVE WITHOUT

This is your lucky day, my friend! You have been chosen as one of the select few who have received this message and, with it, the opportunity to purchase the all-new Electronic Super Wonder Widget at the incredibly low factory-direct price of $29.95. If you respond before midnight tonight, we will include the Electronic Super Mini Widget at no additional cost. This $17.95 value is absolutely free!

Now consider this message:

SUBJECT: A message from XYZ Company

Dear Valued Customer,

We're happy to announce that we have signed an exclusive contract to sell the Electronic Super Wonder Widget, a product you may have already heard of. Through this arrangement, we can offer this unique product for only $29.95. We have been so impressed by this product that we will include, for free, an Electronic Super Mini Widget — a $17.95 value — just to get you to try it. As with all our products, of course, your satisfaction is 100 percent guaranteed.

Which message did *you* like better? Which one do you think is more likely to hit your computer's Recycle Bin in a heartbeat? Both messages say pretty much the same thing, but the tone in each one is dramatically different.

Tip

Keep in mind that online users are generally more educated and more (for lack of a better word) sophisticated than the average person on the street. The advertising message that works for the *National Enquirer* crowd will probably flop for the online crowd. (I am not insinuating that the *National Enquirer* crowd has below-average intelligence. Heck, even I have a subscription because I find great stories for my radio show in it. Online, however, the key is subtlety.)

Dealing with E-Mail Terrorism

One of the Internet's strengths is also one of its weaknesses: All its millions of users can remain relatively anonymous. A certain small percentage of users believe, unfortunately, that this anonymity gives them a license to act like complete jerks at the slightest provocation. (Remember some of the responses my friend received from newsgroups?)

Sooner or later, you probably will make someone angry about something you did online. Your action may be something minor, but, as I just said, the anonymity of the Net gives some loonies a perfect opportunity to overreact.

An Internet *flame* is a nasty letter of complaint. Depending on who sent the flame and what the complaint is about, you're likely to see all sorts of words and suggestions that may make you blush. That part is unfortunate. The good news, however, is that, regardless of the content of a flame, it is just a harmless piece of e-mail.

A mail bomb is another story. No, nothing explodes. Remember the newsgroup guy who sent my friend a hundred e-mail complaints? That was a mail bomb, albeit a small one. (That one was probably a mail grenade.) A *mail bomb* is simply a flood of messages to someone's electronic mailbox. The number of messages is so large that it becomes an extreme nuisance to (and sometimes even an unreasonable burden on) the system on which the e-mail account resides. If you get mail-bombed, contact your ISP or online service as soon as possible.

Remember how easy it is to sign up for an Internet mailing list? And remember that about 50,000 mailing lists exist? If you really tick someone off who's savvy enough to pull it off, that person can conceivably subscribe you to hundreds of mailing lists, resulting in potentially thousands of e-mail messages being sent to you every day. This problem is not an easy one to handle. You face the option of either unsubscribing to each list individually or cutting your losses and changing your e-mail address. Before you do anything, though, contact your ISP or online service for assistance.

Tip

Just remember to try not to make anyone on the Internet mad at you and to keep an eye out for any suspicious e-mail activity so that you can nip it in the bud.

Responding to Inquiries, Complaints, and Compliments

Except for actual orders, any e-mail messages you receive from your customers probably fall into one of these three categories:

✦ Inquiries

✦ Complaints

✦ Compliments

Although each type of message requires somewhat different handling, they have one thing in common: If one person said it, someone else probably will say the same thing. You can then put related messages in the FAQ you post on your Web site.

After you begin responding to customer e-mail, you should archive your responses in a FAQ so that you can add them to your FAQ as well as recycle them later when a similar situation arises. Archiving saves you plenty of time and trouble and ensures that you handle customer-service matters with some consistency.

The key to using a "canned response" is to make sure that it doesn't look like one. Everyone likes personalized service, and some folks may be offended by an overtly canned message. In other words, rather than open a message with the phrase "Dear valued customer," use the individual customer's name, such as "Dear Fred" or "Dear Mr. Flintstone." Then your customers know that you're writing your messages specifically to them.

You can use a canned e-mail response as long as you make clear from the get-go that you're doing so. Here's the beginning of a letter my Komputer Klinic sends in response to e-mail messages sent by listeners of my radio show:

> Hi!
>
> First, a big thanks for listening to my network talk-radio show, Kim Komando's Komputer Klinic. It's really cool that you do, and I appreciate it. This is a form letter. Don't get all excited. I like to be up-front — life is too short for otherwise.
>
> Now before you get upset and think, "Jeez . . . I got a form letter," relax. This form letter is just our way of letting you know that we received your question and that we will send you the answer in a personal reply as soon as possible! We're running less than a week's turnaround on responding to questions (just so you know). Sure hope your question wasn't along the lines of "They are turning off my electricity, and my modem will be repossessed in two days." You will have to call the show then.
>
> But take this form letter as a way to get some insider tips and answers to commonly asked questions.

Answering customer questions

For the most part, inquiries are simple to handle. You can usually just pull a response directly from your FAQ. If you do, make sure that you tell customers where you got your answers so that they know to check there first the next time they have a question.

Warning

Be careful, though. You don't want to sound as though you're saying, "Next time, check the FAQ, you idiot." Instead, say something like, "For your convenience, answers to many of the most commonly asked questions are available in our FAQ. To look at it yourself, all you have to do is. . . ."

Handling customer complaints

Complaints put you at a disadvantage from the beginning. Because people are already dissatisfied with *something,* your challenge is to bring them back into the fold, so to speak.

Remember that old saying "The customer is always right"? It's as true in cyberspace as it is anywhere else. The quickest way to make a complaint situation worse is to take the defensive. The quickest way to smooth things over, on the other hand, is to agree that a customer has a legitimate complaint.

Don't get me wrong. Although someone might complain about a particular policy, you don't have to change the way you do things for just one customer. Complaints from several people might indicate that your policy is a bad one. In this case, you want to let customers know that you understand *why* they feel the way they do. Then explain *why* your policy is the way it is. Close by telling customers that, although you must adhere to your policy, you're still interested in keeping their business.

Tip

If a complaint arose over a *misunderstanding* about one of your policies, you may want to consider waiving the policy just one time. Just make sure that your customer knows that it's a one-time deal, and then consider rewording the policy.

Accepting and acknowledging compliments

Compliments are the easiest e-mail messages to handle because they always consist of good news. Just be sure to do two things:

✦ Send the customer a note of thanks. You may even want to consider offering a token of your appreciation, such as a special discount or small piece of merchandise.

✦ Reprint on your testimonial page a quote from the customer's complimentary e-mail message. (If you don't yet have an online area full of praise from your customers, now is the time to think about it.) When you reprint a compliment, make sure to get the customer's permission first. Because the compliment was sent as a personal message to you, the customer may not care to have it posted for the entire world to see. The last thing you want to do is turn a positive situation like this one into a negative one.

Building Loyalty after the Sale

Much like any kind of business you can think of, building loyalty in cyberspace often comes from the little things you do to make customers feel appreciated. You should have an auto-responder set up, for example, to thank your customers for every order they place. This way, when customers submit electronic orders, an e-mail message is automatically sent out to thank them.

If you get lots of repeat business, you may want to consider awarding customers discount points or something similar (your frequent-flyer program, so to speak).

The number of ways in which you can show appreciation for your customers is limited only by your imagination. Think about the places you like to shop and why you shop there. Many of the things that keep you coming back to a particular shop can most likely be translated into a cyberspace equivalent.

Tip

You can learn a great deal from your competitors too. Drop by their online areas to see the ways in which they keep in constant contact with their customers. If possible, spend a few bucks and buy something from them. Make occasional complaints so that you can experience for yourself how they handle them. (I often do this myself.)

Tip

You can learn much from shopping your competitors' online sites, not only about their operations but also about your own. If you ever call a competitor's order line, especially in smaller companies, you will be amazed at the amount of inside information you can get from the person who answers the phone. Remember that, as a cyber-entrepreneur, you are in the game to win. Learn as much as you can, but never compromise your ethics or your integrity — that's the surest route to failure.

On a final note, know that e-mail, listservs, Usenet, and much of what you have read about in this chapter are part of the Internet's "old school." They hold to the tradition that the Internet is noncommercial. The World Wide Web, only a few years old, is already blatantly commercial. Compare PBS to an infomercial. What if Ron Popeil started slicing and dicing on a PBS channel? Might outraged viewers flood his 800 number to complain (and block others from ordering)? The same thing applies to e-mail, listservs, and Usenet. It's an entirely different culture. People don't want to spend their computer time (translation: their money) to retrieve your commercials. Imagine junk mail arriving with postage due. It's the same thing.

Part VI

Must-Have Insider Knowledge

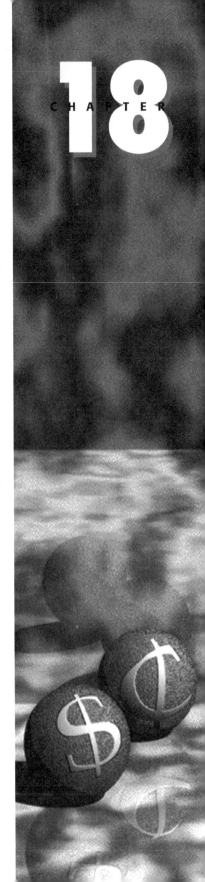

Making the Most of Online Business Resources

I used to have an imaginary friend whose name was Paul Clark, and I was never ashamed to tell business associates about him. "You know, I would love to take advantage of this opportunity now, but first I have to ask Paul, in my office, to do some research." Or maybe I wanted Paul to do a marketing forecast to see whether we were directing "our" efforts toward the right area. When I was starting out in the computer business, I didn't want to let on that I was a one-person show. One day, after a company president had become somewhat leery about the "smallness" of my operation, I happened to look underneath my desk and, as I spotted my PC, *Paul Clark* was born. Paul no longer works for my company, but you can have your own Paul Clark, Paula Clark, or (the Mac version) Mary Ann Clark.

Today it's even easier to appear to be a part of a large organization because your modem is the ultimate key to a gold mine of valuable information to help get your business launched. In this chapter, I've collected of some of the best business resources in cyberspace. This list certainly doesn't even come close to covering every online business resource, but it's a great starting point. One or two of these Web sites may be repeated from other chapters in this book, but I want to make sure that you have the entire list in one place.

Marketing and Demographic Resources

Knowledge is power. As an online entrepreneur, you can easily keep up-to-date with the latest research to better market your customers; most of the information you might need is just a point-and-click away.

The U.S. Census Bureau lookup page
(`http://cedr.lbl.gov/cdrom/doc/lookup_doc.html`)

Retrieve demographic data directly from the archive tapes of the United States Census Bureau. You can perform your search directly from the Census Bureau system or from one of several mirror sites around the country. (A *mirror site* is a duplicate of the original site.) The Census Bureau site has complete instructions for using the system, including several examples of how you can use the data. It also lists a number of independent reviews of the site.

Selected tables, "The Black Population in the United States: March 1994 and 1993"
(`http://www.thuban.com/census/index.html`)

This site contains extensive information derived from the latest census data and has information about the African-American population of the United States. The information, compiled by Claudette Bennet of the Census Bureau, includes information in these categories:

- ✦ General
- ✦ Family
- ✦ Income and employment
- ✦ Education
- ✦ Poverty

Housing and household economic statistics
(`http://www.census.gov/ftp/pub/hhes/www/index.html`)

Another good source from the Census Bureau, the information at this site is available for free for now. The U.S. government plans to shift it gradually to a paid subscription service, however, so take advantage of it while you can. The information at this site is broken down into the following categories:

- ✦ Housing statistics
- ✦ Household economic statistics
- ✦ Health insurance
- ✦ Income and poverty
- ✦ Labor force

✦ Poverty dynamics

✦ Program participation dynamics

✦ Small-area income and poverty estimates

✦ Wealth (I like this one!)

United States Census Bureau home page (http://www.census.gov/)

If you can't find what you're looking from the other Census Bureau pages in this section, check out this site (it's the momma bear), as shown in Figure 18-1.

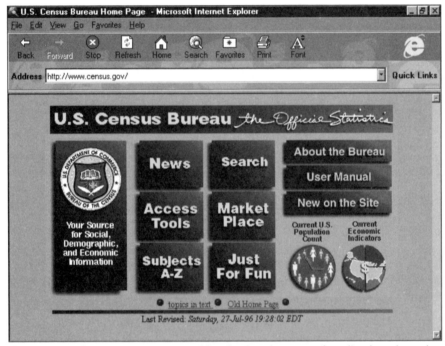

Figure 18-1: The Census Bureau provides timely, relevant, and quality data about the people and economy of the United States.

The advertising and public relations page of Newspage

(http://www.newspage.com/NEWSPAGE/cgi-bin/walk.cgi/NEWSPAGE/info/d17/d6/)

The Newspage is a great source of up-to-the-minute information about marketing, advertising, and promotions. It features full-length news stories that cover these topics:

- ✦ U.S. advertising industry
- ✦ Major advertising agencies
- ✦ Advertising campaigns
- ✦ TV and radio advertising
- ✦ Print media advertising
- ✦ Electronic advertising
- ✦ Promotions and other advertising
- ✦ Market research
- ✦ Interactive kiosks
- ✦ U.S. public relations industry

1st Steps: Marketing and Design Daily (http://www.interbiznet.com/nomad.html)

1st Steps, another daily news site for marketing information, focuses on the design and creative aspects of marketing. Check out this site if you plan to do any of your own design work.

Advertising Age (http://www.adage.com/)

This site is the home page for *Advertising Age* magazine, the nation's leading trade publication for the advertising industry. You can find some excellent information here as well as links to many other noteworthy sites.

Lookup USA (http://www.abii.com/)

If you're in a business-to-business field, you can find some great information at Lookup USA, as shown in Figure 18-2. Look up companies large and small to get contact information and their overall credit ratings. For a fee, you can get more detailed information, but even the free information is excellent.

Marketing on the Internet (http://www.netresource.com/itp/reptoc.html)

At this site, you can get a great tutorial that covers a variety of issues facing Internet marketers (and that supplements the vast knowledge you have gained by reading this book). The tutorial covers various topics:

- ✦ Introduction and rules of distribution
- ✦ Executive summary
- ✦ Description and brief history of the Internet
- ✦ The nuts and bolts of the Net
- ✦ The World Wide Web in brief

✦ Who's out there?

✦ Why market on the Internet?

✦ Internet marketing overview

✦ Retooling your marketing objectives for the Internet

✦ Providing a reason to come to you

✦ Persuading the prospect

✦ Form versus substance: The pretty-pictures trap

✦ Internet marketing trends

✦ Choosing a presence provider

✦ Real-world case studies

✦ The cost

✦ `Netresource.com` (or the current site's sponsor)

✦ Pitfalls and conclusions

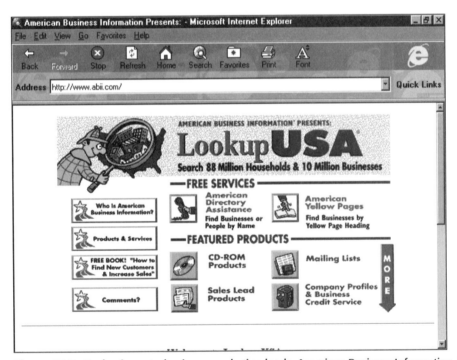

Figure 18-2: For business-to-business marketing leads, American Business Information, Inc., provides information about businesses: address, names of key executives, employee size, sales, credit scores, and more.

The Marketing Resource Center (`http://www.dev-com.com/~cmg/`)

Brought to you by Concept Marketing Group, this site is another great source of free marketing information. If you're wondering what's on this site, the opening blurb says it all: "We are creating this center to provide you with valuable resource material to help your business grow. Articles, marketing tips, statistics, FAQs, and software reviews are just a few of the many resources you will find here. Or click on our EXPOSE link for a listing of promotional sites to make your presence known on the Web." This site claims to be updated weekly.

Web Digest for Marketers (`http://wdfm.com/`)

Web Digest for Marketers is an e-mail-based "biweekly bulletin or executive summary that reports on the latest marketing sites to come onto the Web." Best of all, subscription is free. This list shows some of the topics at this site:

✦ Financial

✦ Retail

✦ Travel

✦ Direct response

✦ Fortune 500 companies

✦ Internet marketing tools

AdMarket (`http://www.admarket.com/`)

AdMarket is more of a gigantic links site than an informational site, as shown in Figure 18-3. Its links (which cover marketing, media, advertising, and public-relations content on the World Wide Web), however, are extensive and good. This site is well worth checking out.

Thayer Morgan's home page (`http://www2.pcix.com/~thayer/MainServices.html`)

This site offers a number of free resources, including a subscription to a free marketing newsletter. Mr. Morgan also provides a free, no-obligation review of your current marketing strategy and a number of free online reports, including the ones in this list:

✦ Why your marketing may not be working

✦ Learning the five steps to a successful direct-marketing campaign

✦ Profiting from space and classified ads

✦ Using the Web as a viable marketing tool

✦ Understanding the elements of effective sales literature

✦ Determining whether you need a marketing consultant

Figure 18-3: AdMarket is the gateway to marketing, media, advertising, and public-relations content on the World Wide Web.

World Wide Web marketing resource locator
(http://www.tippecanoe.com/actserch.htm)

ActivMedia and Tippecanoe's site is designed to help you find just the marketing help you need. You answer a questionnaire that describes your needs, and the system automatically returns a list of qualified consultants.

Proxima (http://www.proxima.com/)

I stumbled on this marketing-and-design company when I took a Proxima-designed poll for the *USA Today* weekend edition. Proxima, Inc., has a long list of links to clients, including *USA Today,* 1-800-MUSICNOW, and the Universal Press Syndicate (the home of such names as *Doonesbury,* Dear Abby, *FoxTrot, Calvin & Hobbes, Bizarro, Cathy, Garfield,* and *For Better or Worse*). Proxima has developed more than 80 World Wide Web sites for corporations whose annual revenues exceed $100 billion (see Figure 18-4).

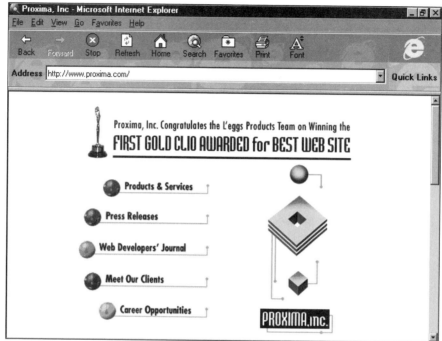

Figure 18-4: The Proxima *Web Developer's Journal* site features news, tips, and editorials.

Business-Management Resources

Keeping in touch with the latest research is important, and so is running your company. For help with the day-to-day operations of your future Fortune 500 company, look no farther than your computer monitor.

U.S. Small Business Administration (http://www.sbaonline.sba.gov/)

The best place to begin looking for management resources is the U.S. Small Business Administration (SBA). The SBA was created in 1953 as an independent agency of the federal government to aid, counsel, assist, and protect the interests of small-business concerns. The major content on this site is divided into the three equally important areas of starting, financing, and expanding your business, (see Figure 18-5). This site also has links to the SBA FTP and Gopher servers in addition to a library of shareware programs for running your business.

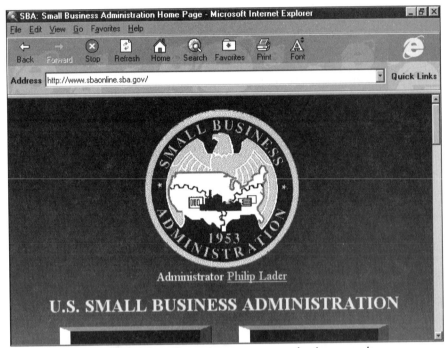

Figure 18-5: Now the SBA is online to better serve your business needs.

The Internet Business Center (http://tsunami.tig.com/cgi-bin/genobject/ibcindex)

The Internet Business Center claims to be "a one-stop shop for business information on the Internet." Take a look for yourself — you won't be disappointed. This site has simply too many resources to list here.

Business Resource Center (http://www.kciLink.com/brc/)

The Business Resource Center is another good business site. Its content is broken down into the following topics:

✦ Getting started

✦ Marketing department

✦ Management center

✦ Financing guide

The Integrity Center, Inc., tutorial on pre-employment screening
(http://www.integctr.com/Tutorial.html)

When you get ready to hire employees in your company, you may want to consider preemployment screening. If so, check out this site first (see Figure 18-6); it covers the following topics:

✦ What is important to my company?

✦ How do I suffer direct loss?

✦ How do I suffer indirect loss?

✦ How do I select personnel intelligently and reduce loss?

✦ What is knowing governance?

✦ What is negligent hiring?

✦ What is negligent retention?

✦ Discrimination versus accuracy

✦ Drawing the line

✦ What are some screening pitfalls?

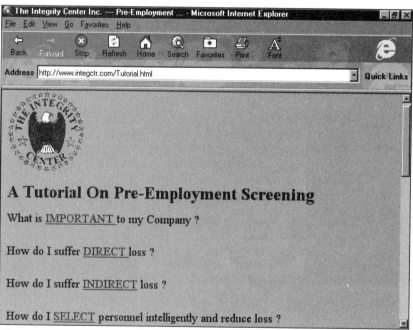

Figure 18-6: Hiring the best people for your company is a tough job, but this online tutorial can help you make the right decisions.

Edmonds Training & Consulting (http://www.coaching.com/edmonds/)

Edmonds is another business consultant with another free newsletter (the Internet has tons!).

Strictly Business! (http://www.uni.com/)

This site, loaded with plenty of free information about management and marketing, offers two free newsletters and plenty of links.

The Computer Solutions Bureau (http://www.computerinfo.com/)

If you enjoy being able to compare various computers and peripherals at trade shows but don't want to drive around the country looking for them, this is the site to browse. The Computer Solutions Bureau bills itself as an online computer trade show (you have to register, but it's free).

The Smart Business Supersite (http://www.smartbiz.com/)

The Smart Business Supersite was designed with one clear mission: to be the single most important source of high-quality, how-to business information on the Net. The Supersite carries plenty of advertising, but it still has some good, free resources, including management tips and a careers section, as shown in Figure 18-7.

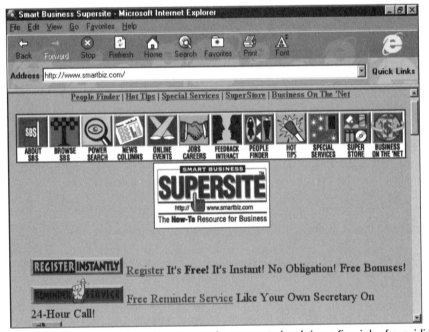

Figure 18-7: The Smart Business Supersite seems to be doing a fine job of providing high-quality business information on the Net.

For a direct link to more resources on the Internet for advertising and marketing, point your Web browser to `http://www.yahoo.com/Business_and_Economy/Marketing/`.

Financial and Economic Resources

You don't have to be a financial whiz to run a company. But you do have to manage operating expenses, keep tight controls on where your money goes and how it comes in, and watch for economic indicators that may influence your business.

Area Development Department business cost comparison
(`http://www.webcom.com/njida/pseg/buscost.html`)

If you're wondering how your labor costs, taxes, and other expenses stack up against foreign companies, visit this page. You can download a free interactive program that calculates the information you enter about operating expenses and compares your costs with costs in three major U.S. cities and in the United Kingdom and Germany.

Electronic Card Systems (`http://www.ecsworldwide.com/`)

ECS is a specialist in "card not present" transactions for merchants of all sizes, including start-ups. You don't get any free resources on this page, but be sure to check out "Merchant Guidelines — Things you should know before you sign up with any credit-card processor." Depending on your operation, this page could come in handy (see Figure 18-8).

NetCat home page (`http://www.dynamicweb.com/`)

NetCat, another product page, should be of particular interest to online marketers. Rather than go to all the time, trouble, and expense of developing your own catalog system, check out this Internet-based catalog ordering and quotation system.

RonTek Enterprises tips page (`http://www.rontek.com/tips.html`)

This page is load with free tips about Internet-based commerce, including how to handle online credit-card transactions, set up a low-cost Internet presence, and a variety of other topics.

Mutual Fund Investors Resource Center (`http://www.fundmaster.com/`)

If you're thinking about mutual funds on the Internet, this is the place to go. Through its online ordering system, you can request a free prospectus, account application, and information from more than 75 mutual-fund families.

Commercial Finance Online (`http://www.cfonline.com/`)

The Commercial Finance Association is the trade group for commercial finance companies, factories, banks, and other financing agencies engaged in the asset-based financial-services industry on an international, national, regional, and local basis (see Figure 18-9).

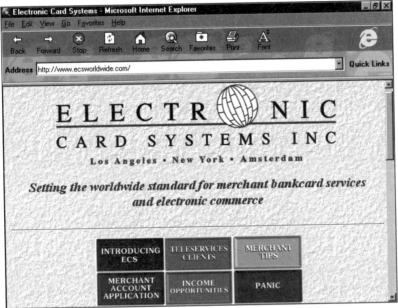

Figure 18-8: Electronic Card Systems sets up bank-card accounts for merchants of all sizes.

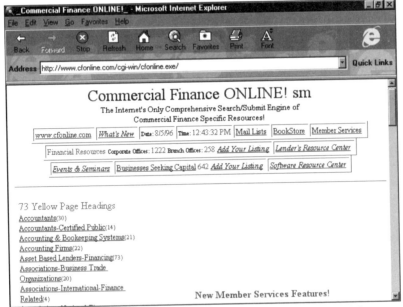

Figure 18-9: This comprehensive directory of Internet-based financial resources has it all, from accountants to venture capital and from attorneys to shareware. Don't miss this one.

Welcome to the Finance Learning Center (http://financelearningcenter.com/)

If you want to brush up on your knowledge of finance, take a look at this page. The Finance Learning Center offers a variety of online and disk-based learning opportunities. They aren't free, but they aren't that expensive either.

The New York Institute of Finance Bookstore
(http://nestegg.iddis.com/nyifcat/nyifhome.html)

Perhaps school isn't your thing, but you want to read up on some financial topics. If so, point your browser to this site; it offers the following product categories:

- ◆ Books
- ◆ Independent study
- ◆ Computer-based training
- ◆ CFA and NASD exam preparation

Ben Franklin Technology Center (http://www.libertynet.org/~bftc/)

This site won't appeal to everyone, but if you happen to live in Pennsylvania *and* are involved in a high-tech start-up, check out this site for financing assistance.

Digital Technology Partners (http://www.dtpnet.com/)

Digital Technology Partners says that it is "the first venture capital firm focused exclusively on the Internet and interactive media." If you're looking for financing, this might be a good place to begin.

MoneyHunter (http://www.moneyhunter.com/index.htm)

This sponsor-supported site helps entrepreneurs connect with venture capitalists. Plenty of financing information is available, and (best of all), because of the sponsorships, all MoneyHunter services are free.

The FinanceHub (http://www.FinanceHub.com/welcomef.html)

The FinanceHub offers links to hundreds of financing sources.

Price Waterhouse LLP national venture capital survey (http://www.pw.com/vc/)

The folks at this site do a quarterly study of the investments of more than 1,000 venture-capital firms throughout the United States. It analyzes investments from numerous areas, including software, hardware and peripherals, semiconductors and equipment, and biotechnology and medical instrumentation (see Figure 18-10). You can view the data at this site according to a number of different sorting criteria.

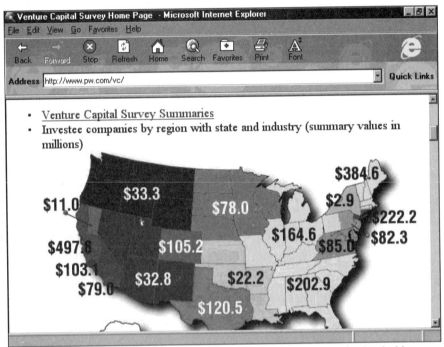

Figure 18-10: If you think that your company has the right stuff to be funded by venture capitalists, check out the updated surveys at the Price Waterhouse site.

Venture Capital World on the Internet (http://www.ccpartner.se/)

Venture Capital World is another site that seeks to match entrepreneurs with investors. It includes a searchable database of projects seeking investments (add yours to the database!). If you're looking for something to invest in, look up the project that interests you.

Career and Employment Resources

Putting together a good team to help run your company into the heavens, not into the ground, is hard work. Luckily, many resources on the Internet are available to help you, whether you're looking to hire or to be hired.

The World Wide Freelance Directory (http://www.cvp.com/freelance/)

This directory is a comprehensive listing of independent consultants and firms from many different areas of expertise. Some of the categories include programmers, HTML editors, graphic artists, documentation writers, and management consultants. Best of all, you can have yourself added to the directory for free.

The ConsultantSee Network (http://www.consultnet.com/)

The purpose of this directory is to enable hiring managers to choose from an exceptional pool of talented professionals. Managers don't pay to use the directory, but a three-month listing costs $35.

Encompass (http://www.well.com/user/careerc/)

The Encompass site promotes a career-development technique called *career crafting*. You can find some free stuff here, including a page called "Ten Tips to Avoid: Common Mistakes Made in Careers" and free, live Internet career seminars.

The Monster Board (http://www.monster.com)

The Monster Board is the Web-based cyberoffice for TMP Worldwide, an international recruiting and employment agency. This site has tens of thousands of job listings in addition to career information and an area in which you can post your résumé.

Hotjobs Online Technology Employment Center (http://www.hotjobs.com)

At the Hotjobs site, you can post your job listings and résumés. It specializes in Fortune 500 and other high-profile companies and focuses on computer careers.

Best Jobs (http://www.bestjobsusa.com/)

Best Jobs was named an "Outstanding Job Resources Site" by the JobHunt: On-Line Job Meta-List. It has job listings, valuable career information, and free résumé postings.

America's Job Bank (http://www.ajb.dni.us/)

America's Job Bank, another source for job listings and career information, makes good use of Web-authoring features such as tables (see Figure 18-11).

Federal Jobs Digest (http://www.jobsfed.com/fedjob4.html)

If you're interested in federal jobs, you can find a couple thousand of them listed here. Jobs are divided into these categories:

- ✦ Administration and management
- ✦ Engineering
- ✦ Law enforcement
- ✦ Science and math
- ✦ Social science and legal
- ✦ Computer
- ✦ Accounting, auditing, and budgeting
- ✦ Medical
- ✦ Secretarial and clerical
- ✦ Trade and postal

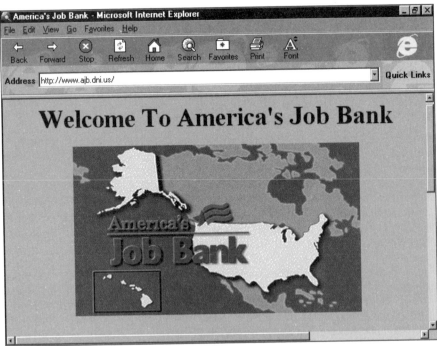

Figure 18-11: America's Job Bank is a service of the U.S. Department of Labor and your state's public employment service agency.

The Business Job Finder (http://www.cob.ohio-state.edu/dept/fin/osujobs.htm)

Provided for free by Ohio State University, this page helps you identify the business field that's right for you.

The Consultant Job Finder (http://www.cob.ohio-state.edu/~fin/jobs/consult.htm)

Similar to the Business Job Finder, this Ohio State site helps answer many questions about becoming a consultant and whether it's the right job for you.

ZD Net Jobs Database (http://www.zdnet.com/zdi/jobs/jobs.html)

The Jobs Database is another job-listing and résumé-posting site. What makes this one interesting is that it's sponsored by the computer publishing giant Ziff-Davis. Because this site is part of the ZDNet site, it may mean higher visibility for you.

E-Span (http://www.espan.com/)

E-Span is another comprehensive job-listing and career-management site.

What about the Online Services?

The Internet isn't the only place to look online for business resources, of course. In this section, I describe what you can find on some of the larger online services.

Cruising CompuServe

CompuServe, the oldest of the major online services, has long been considered *the* choice for businesspeople, and for good reason. Although most other services seem to target the consumer market, CompuServe continues to market itself as primarily a business tool. Its content reflects this focus.

Click your mouse on the Professional icon on the service's opening screen, and you're off to an expanse of useful information. You can access a number of special-interest areas, including aviation, business management, data processing, media services, engineering, and entrepreneurial and small business.

The entrepreneur/small business area is particularly interesting. It offers access to more than 15 related services, including several forums in which you can "discuss" various issues with other CompuServe members who share a common interest. Pick up some advertising tips, for example, in the PR and Marketing forum. Find answers to your legal questions in the Legal forum. Or, if you're involved in overseas trading, check out the International Trade forum. If your home doubles as your office, you don't want to miss the Working from Home forum. Most CompuServe forums have software libraries in which you can find useful programs to download.

If you're thinking of starting a new business, don't overlook the Entrepreneur's Small Business Square. In addition to its own forum, this area offers a database of more than 1,500 franchise and business opportunities. In the Small Business Emporium, you can purchase guide and software packages that provide everything you need to start up any of a number of businesses.

Looking for online publications? CompuServe offers *Fortune* magazine and *IndustryWeek Interactive* in addition to a database of U.S. government publications. You can also find Hoover's Company Database, a business demographics service, and a number of services related to finance and investing.

Accessing information on America Online

America Online, on the other hand, is much easier to navigate, and it has incredible resources to help give your business a competitive edge. The center of the AOL business offering is its Small Business Resource (keyword YOUR BUSINESS), as shown in Figure 18-12. This area offers assistance in such topics as exporting, finance, computing, sales, and marketing from organizations such as the U.S. Small Business

Administration, the U.S. Postal Service, *Inc.* magazine, the Legal Information Network, and too many other groups to mention. Use the keyword INDUSTRIES to tap in to specific business sector chats, message boards, and more.

You can get real-time, personalized help for your small business during daily AOL lunchtime chats. Past topics include "How to price a service-related business," "Running a newsletter business," and "Increase sales and income by enhancing communication with your clients." I stopped by a few chats; it's a great way to pick up some tips while eating your peanut-butter-and-jelly sandwich.

Figure 18-12: The Your Business area on America Online is a valuable resource for new enterprises.

Like CompuServe, AOL has an extensive Business News section. You can get industry news listed by industry, international news listed by country, or business news from other sources, such as *The New York Times* and the Cowles/Simba Media Information Network.

If you have an AOL account, spend a few minutes setting up your personalized news profile (keyword News Profiles). After you type certain phrases or topics that interest you, news that matches your criteria is automatically sent to your electronic mailbox.

This technique is a super way to keep up with a particular industry in addition to your competitor's announcements. Best of all, unlike other services that charge for this type of feature, customized news delivery is free on America Online.

Perusing Prodigy

Prodigy offers perhaps the most extensive means to network with other business people, on what Prodigy calls bulletin boards (or BBs, for short). Much like a local bulletin-board system you might dial up, each BB has several different message areas.

The Your Business BB has almost 30 different message areas, including Great Ideas/ Startup, International Business, Legal and Government Matters, and Real Estate Network. You can probably find two or three message areas relevant to your business.

Prodigy also offers some unique business-information services. For example, the personal-news service Headsup will (for $29.95 per month) scan hundreds of articles daily, looking for as many as ten topics you specify. A listing of the articles related to your topics is automatically sent to Prodigy via e-mail or fax. If you aren't sure whether this service is for you, you can try it out for free for one month.

The NEXIS Advisor contains thousands of business-related articles you can skim by topic. You can download individual articles for less than $2 apiece.

You see, as long as you have your trusty modem, you never have to go it alone, with or without Paul Clark.

Copyrights and Other Legalities

Cyberspace has been hailed as an outstanding way to move vast amounts of information from point to point and from person to person. By now, after reading most of this book, you know that it's true. Because of the online phenomenon and the great accessibility of information, you have, at least to some extent, more power at your fingertips than some of the greatest rulers in history. Power often brings its share of problems, of course (bigger problems than becoming egocentric).

Millions of people who are new to the "information game" are now carelessly cruising the information superhighway. They steal what they want when they want it and put it wherever they want to put it. Many people don't have the slightest clue about the rules and regulations that govern the exchange of *all* information, electronic or otherwise. Furthermore, some people have a clue but don't care.

It's not that absolutely no controls exist to protect your rights. We have copyright laws, after all. Many online enthusiasts don't know the first thing about copyright law or how it affects them. Others are so caught up in the online hysteria that they think that copyright laws should be abolished. This last part is bad news if you are the author of any intellectual property. If you aren't an author now, you surely will be as you develop your online area.

When people infringe on your copyrights, their actions either cost you money or make money for themselves based on your efforts. It's easy to see that either case isn't fair. You must do whatever you can to prevent others from infringing on your copyrights, and, in turn, make sure that you don't infringe on anyone else's copyright.

Understanding the Basics of Copyright Law

Copyrights refer to the bundle of exclusive rights the law provides for the author of any work of art or literature or any work that provides information, such as a book, magazine article, or FAQ. The copyright laws (which apply equally to digital and printed works) give you the right to

✦ Distribute the work

✦ Reproduce the work

✦ Create *adaptive,* or *derivative,* works, which are new works based on but not identical to the original work

✦ In the case of artistic work, perform or display that work

Note

Many people mistakenly believe that in order for a work to be legally copyrighted, it must be registered with the U.S. Copyright Office. Wrong! The truth is that your work becomes protected under copyright law the moment you create it. As I have typed each word in this book, it has become protected by copyright law. As you draft each original work for your online area, you own the copyright. In the case of employees, under most state law, you own their works unless an agreement to the contrary is in place.

Maybe you're wondering exactly how long a copyright lasts. The short answer is "a long time." The long answer is that it all depends on when the work was created. Because the copyright laws were revised in 1976, the date of publication is important. For works created and published before 1978, the copyright lasts for 75 years from the date of publication. If the work was created during that time but not published, the copyright expires December 31, 2002. These dates obviously don't affect your online work, but they may be important if you decide to use some other work that was published during this period.

For works published in 1978 or later, the copyright lasts for the life of the author plus 50 years, *as long as the author is a live person.* If the legal author is a company or other organization, the copyright lasts for 75 years after publication or 100 years after creation, whichever comes first.

What Do You Mean "As Long as the Author Is a Live Person?"

What the heck is the phrase "as long as the author is a live person" supposed to mean? How can an author not be a live person? The answer is that the legal definition of an "author" is not exactly the same as the standard definition you or I might give.

An entity can become an author, in the legal sense of the word, in one of four ways:

✦ You can independently author a work. If you write the Great American Novel, for example, you are considered the legal author of that work and you own all copyrights until you sell all or part of them to a publisher.

✦ If you collaborate on your novel with one or more people, your group is collectively considered the author.

✦ If an employee writes a particular work on behalf of his employer, the employer is considered the author of the work.

✦ If an independent contractor writes a particular work under a work-for-hire agreement for a company, the company is considered the author of the work. If I develop a brochure for my company, for example, whether someone on staff writes the copy or a freelance copywriter writes it, my company is considered the author for copyright purposes.

Despite these laws, I don't take chances with freelance writers or artists. I have each person or firm sign an agreement that includes (among other things) the text shown in Figure 19-1. I am showing you these paragraphs only for discussion purposes; they do not constitute a whole and complete work-for-hire agreement. You must consult an attorney to draw up a complete agreement.

Don't take chances and think that the money you might spend on an attorney to cover your copyright butt is not worth it. The last thing you want is for someone to write or design something that makes millions for you and not have an agreement in place. Trust me — the person who did the design or work will eventually want a cut of the pie, unless you have him sign a work-for-hire agreement that covers you legally.

Handling Copyright Notices and Registration

Back to copyright law. If copyright law protects you from the moment you create something, why bother putting copyright notices on everything and registering your work with the U.S. Copyright Office?

To give notice to the world about when a work was created and who owns the copyright, you place in your work a copyright symbol (©) or the word *Copyright* usually followed by the year of copyright and the name of the copyright owner.

Tip

Establishing a copyright is especially important in the online world. So much information is available in the public domain of cyberspace that you must be sure to distinguish your work. If you fail to put a copyright notice on your digital work, someone may mistakenly assume that it's in the public domain and "borrow" it without your permission. Adding a copyright notice lets people know that you own the copyright and that they cannot use your work unless they get your permission.

Assignment of Rights: You hereby grant and assign exclusively to Komando Korporation all your copyright and all other rights throughout the world, in all forms and media, whether now or hereafter known, for the entire duration of such rights and any renewals and extensions thereof for all Works you create for Komando Korporation. All original artistic works accepted by Komando Korporation are considered Work-for-Hire for Komando Korporation under the United States Copyright Law. You are an independent contractor and not an employee of Komando Korporation. You represent that each of the Works you create is your original work and that it does not infringe on anyone else's copyright or any other rights. You assign to Komando Korporation all rights to the Works throughout the world, including claim to copyright.

Representations and Warrantees: You agree to the following:

i.) Each Work in total will be original and previously unpublished.

ii.) You will not publish, distribute, or otherwise exploit any Work, in full or in part, in final, preliminary, or modified form, or authorize the foregoing, in any media prior to, concurrent with, or — except as specifically provided within this agreement — subsequent to its acceptance by Komando Korporation.

iii.) You will be the sole author or designer of each Work except as otherwise agreed to by Komando Korporation, your execution and delivery of this agreement will not violate any contractual or other obligation, and you have the right to enter into this agreement and to grant and assign all the rights granted and assigned in this Agreement.

iv.) No contribution will be false and defamatory or falsely disparage any product, service, or company or violate or infringe any right of privacy, copyright, or any other rights of any third party or any applicable law.

Compensation: As total and complete compensation for your Works created under this Agreement, you shall receive $ _____.00 in U.S. dollars. You shall receive no royalties or any other compensation from Komando from the sale or use of any of the Works.

Figure 19-1: A sample work-for-hire agreement.

When you drop by most Web pages and online areas, you see a notice (normally at the bottom of the page) similar to the one shown in Figure 19-2. This type of notice is all you need, but a little more protection of your rights never hurts.

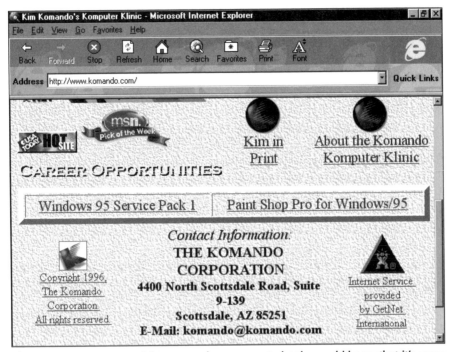

Figure 19-2: Post a copyright on your home page to let the world know that it's yours.

If you click the copyright notice link on my company's page, you see text similar to Figure 19-3. Because the document is long (blame it on the lawyers), it shows only some important paragraphs. Feel free to adapt it for your online business use, but be sure to have your attorney look it over for accuracy and viability for your own cyberbusiness.

Before I return to the issue of copyrights, let me tell you just one reason that the Terms of Use shown in Figure 19-3 include even more paragraphs than are shown here. About three years ago, I received an e-mail message from a man who took the Klinic's advice about fixing a computer problem. He claimed that a member of my staff did not tell him the total time it would take to fix the problem. I could tell from his e-mail messages that he was setting up my company for a legal dispute. The e-mail messages explained that he used his computer primarily for business and that it was out of commission for three full days while he fixed the problem. He usually makes $500 a day in his consulting business, or so he claimed.

Terms of Use

Please read this document very carefully. This important document contains the rules of Kim Komando's Komputer Klinic that you agree to.

First, use your best judgment in evaluating all information contained in or opinions expressed in Kim Komando's Komputer Klinic. You should be no less careful in your evaluation of such information and opinions on Kim Komando's Komputer Klinic as you are in everyday life. You expressly agree that your use of Kim Komando's Komputer Klinic is solely at your own risk and is subject to all applicable local, state, national, and international laws and regulations. Kim Komando's Komputer Klinic and its owners are not liable for the improper use or the distribution of the information made available through this service. The opinions expressed within Kim Komando's Komputer Klinic are solely those of the person or entity named as the author.

Kim Komando's Komputer Klinic makes no representations about the suitability of the information contained in the documents and related graphics published on Kim Komando's Komputer Klinic for any purpose. All such documents and related graphics are provided "as is" without warranty of any kind. Kim Komando's Komputer Klinic hereby disclaims all warranties and conditions with regard to this information, including all implied warranties and conditions of merchantability, fitness for a particular purpose, and non-infringement.

In no event shall Kim Komando's Komputer Klinic be liable for any special, indirect, or consequential damages or any damages whatsoever resulting from loss of use, data, or profits, whether in an action of contract, negligence, or other tortious action, arising out of or in connection with the use or performance of information available from Kim Komando's Komputer Klinic. The documents and related graphics published on this server may include technical inaccuracies or typographical errors. Changes are periodically added to the information herein. Kim Komando's Komputer Klinic may at any time make improvements and/or changes in the product(s) and/or the program(s) described herein.

All Content is protected by copyright pursuant to U.S., international conventions, and other copyright laws as a collective work and/or compilation, and Kim Komando's Komputer Klinic owns a copyright in the selection, coordination, arrangement, and enhancement of such Content.

Permission to use, copy, and distribute documents and related graphics available from Kim Komando's Komputer Klinic is granted, provided that (1) the below copyright notice appears in all copies and that both the copyright notice and this permission notice appear, (2) use of documents and related graphics available from Kim Komando's Komputer Klinic is for informational and non-commercial purposes only, (3) no documents or related graphics available from Kim Komando's Komputer Klinic are modified in any way, and (4) no graphics available from Kim Komando's Komputer Klinic are used, copied, or distributed separate from accompanying text.

Any rights not expressly granted herein are reserved by Kim Komando's Komputer Klinic. Any software that is downloaded should always be virus-checked by the user of Kim Komando's Komputer Klinic.

You may upload to Kim Komando's Komputer Klinic's software files and message boards or otherwise transmit on or through Kim Komando's Komputer Klinic only Content that is not subject to any copyright or other proprietary rights protection (collectively, "Public Domain Content") or Content in respect of which the holder of any copyright, trademark, or other proprietary rights ("Rights") has given express authorization for distribution on Kim Komando's Komputer Klinic without any restriction whatsoever, and in respect of which any moral rights of any person or entity have been completely and irrevocably waived. Any copyright Content submitted with the consent of a copyright owner other than you should contain a phrase such as "Copyright owned by [name of the owner]; Used by Permission." The unauthorized submission of copyright or Content which is otherwise subject of any third-party Rights constitutes a breach of the Kim Komando's Komputer Klinic rules and may also render you liable to the holder of such rights. Remember that you, not Kim Komando's Komputer Klinic or its affiliates or independent contractors, are exclusively responsible for any liability resulting from infringement of Rights arising from such submission or transmission.

By submitting Content to any "Public Area" (Public Areas are those areas of Kim Komando's Komputer Klinic that are generally accessible to other persons, such as public chat rooms, message boards, and file uploads), you are deemed automatically to grant — and/or warrant that the holder of any Rights or Moral Rights in such Content has completely and effectively waived all such Moral Rights and expressly, validly, and irrevocably granted to you the right to grant — Kim Komando's Komputer Klinic the royalty-free, perpetual, irrevocable, non-exclusive right (including any moral rights) and license to use, reproduce, modify, adapt, publish, translate, create derivative works from, distribute, perform, and display the Content (in whole or part) worldwide and/or to incorporate it in other works in any form, media, or technology now known or hereafter developed for the full term of any Rights that may exist in such Content.

You also permit any person to access, view, store, and reproduce the Content for personal use. Subject to the foregoing, the owner of Content placed on Kim Komando's Komputer Klinic retains any and all rights that may exist in such Content.

Kim Komando's Komputer Klinic, Komando, and other names of Komando products refer-enced herein are service marks, trademarks, or registered trademarks of Kim Komando's Komputer Klinic or its owners. All other product and company names mentioned herein are the trademarks of their respective owners. Note that all company trademarks, service marks, etc. are generally not indicated in online text messages but are acknowledged and recognized by Kim Komando's Komputer Klinic.

(continued)

Komputer Klinic, posted on Kim Komando's Komputer Klinic, or sent to someone identified as a representative of Kim Komando's Komputer Klinic is at all times the exclusive property of Kim Komando's Komputer Klinic.

Upon request of Kim Komando's Komputer Klinic, you agree to defend, indemnify, and hold harmless Kim Komando's Komputer Klinic, its affiliated companies, licensees, and others from all liabilities, claims, and expenses, including without limitation reasonable attorney's fees. Should any part of the Kim Komando's Komputer Klinic rules be held invalid or unenforceable, that portion shall be construed consistent with applicable law as nearly as possible to reflect the original intentions of the parties and the remaining portions remain in full force and effect. These rules shall be governed by the laws of the State of Arizona, and you and Kim Komando's Komputer Klinic each submit to the exclusive jurisdiction of the courts in Maricopa County, Arizona.

Figure 19-3: A sample copyright notice.

For his lost time and alleged damages, this guy wanted me to send him a check for $5,000 to cover his damages! I told him to contact my lawyer. It ended up that he didn't have a case primarily because he had agreed to the Klinic's terms of use when he tapped in to my online area. I'm sure that some lawyers will dispute the point that a terms-of-use agreement protects the developers and owners of Internet sites. Just watch the barrage of attorneys who show up to speak to victims' families after any major catastrophe. Rather than make money the old-fashioned way, by earning it, many people will abuse the system to extort money from you.

I hope that you never have to sue anyone for infringing on your copyrights. If you do, however, registration with the U.S. Copyright Office may play an important role in making your case. Suppose that you create some sort of work and a competitor steals and uses that work. If you haven't registered your work, the case can boil down to a matter of your word versus the other person's. If you have registered your work with the U.S. Copyright Office, on the other hand, the validity of your claim is quite clear.

If your works are creative in nature (screenplays and works of fiction, for example), you can register them at various creative registries and achieve the same basic effect as though you had registered with the U.S. Copyright Office. The important thing is that you have some independent, third-party record of your copyright.

Knowing What Copyrights Don't Cover

Rather than try to list all the things that copyrights cover, it's easier to look at what they *don't* cover — it's a short list.

For starters, copyrights do not cover facts and ideas — only the words you use to express those facts and ideas. It's a fact, for example, that George Washington was the first President of the United States. No one can hold a copyright to that fact. If you write a biography of George Washington that includes this fact, however, you own the copyright to your book as a whole. Even though facts cannot be copyrighted, a unique *collection* of facts can be copyrighted as long as that collection is the result of some creative effort.

This rule of copyright explains why, for example, a book of *Star Trek* trivia can be copyrighted. It also explains why the courts ruled, in a landmark decision, that your local telephone company's white pages cannot be copyrighted. In this case, the courts ruled that an alphabetical organization of name and telephone numbers did not meet the definition of a creative work and could not, therefore, be protected.

Note

It's important to know exactly what is considered a *fact* in the eyes of the law. Because a recipe, for example, is considered a fact, you cannot copyright a recipe. On the other hand, you can copyright a specific collection of recipes organized into a cookbook.

On the digital front, you cannot copyright a mathematical equation. Think about what would happen if someone held a copyright to 2+2=4 or some other common equation. Because a computer program is, on the other hand, ultimately just a *collection* of mathematical equations and expressions, a computer program can (as we all know) indeed be copyrighted.

Working in the Public Domain

Copyright law also does not apply to any work considered to be in the public domain. As with public-domain software, anyone and everyone can freely use this type of work. An author may have intentionally given up her rights to a public-domain work, such as a commentary posted on the Internet with a notice from the author releasing that commentary into the public domain.

Any work whose copyright has expired is also considered to be in the public domain. Based on the time limits I discussed earlier in this chapter, you know that anything authored more than 75 years ago is considered to be in the public domain (including, for example, most classical music, the works of the Greek philosophers, and any writings by early U.S. Presidents).

One more type of work is considered to be in the public domain immediately after it is published: any work authored and published by the government. You can borrow from IRS booklets, federal election materials, and other government publications as freely as you want.

In some limited instances, someone may be able legally to use your copyrighted work without your permission. The purpose of this *fair use* concept is to allow for a free flow of information for educational purposes. If the local college professor wants to use a quote from *CyberBuck$* to illustrate a point in his online commerce course, he can do so without my permission or the permission of IDG Books Worldwide, Inc.

On the other hand, any fair use cannot diminish the value of a copyrighted work. The college professor in the preceding example could not, for example, reproduce this entire book and distribute it to his class. He would essentially be giving each student a free copy of my book, and I would lose out on any potential sales to that group of students.

Three general areas are considered fair use and therefore require no permission for use from the copyright owner:

✦ Criticism and comment: If someone writes a review of this book, she can quote a few passages to illustrate a point.

✦ News reporting: If a reporter discovers something in this book that he deems newsworthy, he has the right to report on it.

✦ Research and education: As in the preceding example, a professor could quote from this book for instructional purposes.

Using Someone Else's Work

Warning

If you plan to use someone else's copyrighted work for your financial benefit, you must get their permission — plain and simple. You can never, ever, simply assume that it's okay to use a work because your use of it isn't that big of a deal.

To illustrate the assumption of public-domain fallacy, did you know that the traditional "Happy Birthday" song is a copyrighted work? This fact has no bearing, of course, on being able to sing it at your child's birthday party. Every time that song is sung in a movie, however, it's done so with the permission of the copyright owner.

Pooh on Winnie-the-Pooh

If you think that your use of a copyrighted work is no big deal, just consider Winnie-the-Pooh. Like any other celebrity, Winnie-the-Pooh has his fans, even out in cyberspace (see Figure 19-4). Just as all sorts of fan sites have proliferated on the World Wide Web, so did Winnie-the-Pooh sites. Many of these sites included, unfortunately, scans of copyrighted Pooh artwork.

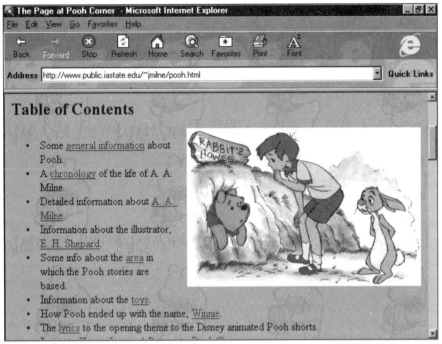

Figure 19-4: Many Winnie-the-Pooh fan-club sites violate copyright laws.

The people who published these Web sites certainly didn't intend to break the law; they just wanted to honor the object of their admiration. Regardless of their intent, however, they did break the law. When the owners of the copyrights for these works got wind of it, they legally forced the site owners to remove the copyrighted works from their sites. It may seem to be no big deal to display these works (and you may even believe that the copyright owners were just being mean), but, believe me, the first time you find a copyrighted work of yours on someone else's Web page, you begin to think differently.

"I didn't know" just doesn't cut it

I want to make you aware of one more copyright case. A while back, *Playboy* magazine sued the operator of an electronic BBS because the BBS included scans of copyrighted pictures from the magazine in addition to the logo for the Playboy bunny. The BBS operators argued that they didn't even realize that the material was posted on their BBS. Incredible as it may seem, however, the courts upheld the idea that specific knowledge of the infringement isn't necessarily required in order to establish liability. In other words, in this case, ignorance was not bliss; the BBS operators were found guilty of the infringement.

"Royalty-free" doesn't give you free reign

In this digital age, you have to also make sure that you don't get confused between the public domain and the purchase of specific rights to a work. I'm sure that you have seen advertisements for "royalty free" CD-ROM collections of clip art, sounds, and animations. When you buy that type of CD-ROM, you are actually buying specific, non-exclusive rights as defined in the disc's packaging.

Your purchase of the CD-ROM *does not* constitute the release of the work into the public domain. In other words, you have the right to use the contents of the CD in whatever way the packaging describes. Your next-door neighbor, however, has no right to use the disc you purchased. In terms of copyrights, that would be similar to giving your neighbor pirated copies of your software.

Freeware and shareware

You can also find plenty of clip art, images, and other graphics files online. America Online alone has thousands and thousands of these types of files. Just because they're there, seemingly free for the taking, you still cannot assume that they're part of the public domain. Like any other type of software you find on AOL, these files are identified as either shareware or freeware. Although any file identified as freeware is considered part of the public domain, any designation as shareware indicates that the author has retained some or all rights and that you most likely will have to pay for any commercial use of the file.

Out on the Internet, it's not always easy to know whether a file you download is freeware or shareware. Depending on where you visit, freeware may or may not be distinguished from shareware. In this case, you have to make sure that you read the entire copyright notice that comes with any file you download. If a file has no copyright notice, your safest bet is to assume that it *is* protected by copyright law. Because you presumably can't find out who the copyright holder is in these cases, you should avoid using the file altogether.

Note

At some point you may want to use some copyrighted material that hasn't necessarily been offered for use. Suppose that you're selling The Beatles memorabilia online and that you want a segment of "I Am the Walrus" to play for every person who visits your Web site. You first must track down the owner of the copyright (maybe it's the record company, maybe it's Paul McCartney, maybe it's Michael Jackson — who knows?). Whoever the author is, you must find that person and obtain explicit written permission for your use of the material. That it was "too difficult" to find the proper copyright owner and obtain permission is no legal defense for infringing on someone else's copyright.

Here's the bottom line: If the entire success of your business depends on using someone else's copyrighted material, you must make some major adjustments to your business plan. No copyrighted work can be so important to your business that it's worth risking a lawsuit for copyright infringement. If you make a mistake in this area, let it be that you were too careful rather than not careful enough.

A Few Words about Electronic Databases

Earlier in this chapter, I mentioned that although individual facts are not protected under copyright law, specific collections of facts are protected by these laws. Considering the proliferation of online databases, I want to make sure that you understand exactly how copyright law applies to this particular medium.

Like any other collection, an online database is covered by copyright law. You also must look at the contents of the database, however, to determine whether copyright law also covers each individual item in the database. An online database of football statistics, for example, would be protected by copyright law, but each individual statistic is not protected.

Many computer magazines, on the other hand, have their own Web sites. If you visit one of these sites, you're likely to find a searchable database of previously published articles that have been electronically archived and that are available for viewing and downloading.

Don't be fooled. Every single article in that database has just as much protection under copyright law as it did when it was first published in the magazine.

Protecting Your Copyrights

I have talked plenty about dealing with other people's copyrights and protecting yourself from copyright-infringement lawsuits. What I haven't talked much about is protecting the rights of your copyrighted work.

As I mentioned earlier in this chapter, you should always place, at minimum, a copyright notice on any of your protected works. The notice doesn't necessarily have to be conspicuous, but it must be visible. In the case of an online article, FAQ, or other text document, you're probably better off placing it at the beginning of the work rather than at the end. This placement ensures that everyone who looks at the article sees the copyright notice, regardless of whether they read the entire document.

Only you can decide whether to register your work with the U.S. Copyright Office. Some paperwork is involved, in addition to a cost. It's up to you to place some sort of dollar value on your work and decide whether the cost and effort of registration are worth your while.

Both these measures are preventive ones, of course, but what do you do if you discover that someone has already infringed on your copyright?

The first thing to remember is not to get excited. In most cases, the infringement is both unintentional and relatively harmless. Unless you can determine that you have truly suffered a financial loss due to the infringement, your best bet is to advise the other party (politely!) that he has infringed on your copyright and should cease use of the work immediately. This notice usually does the trick.

If the other party doesn't comply with your request in a timely manner, however, or if you can determine that you have already sustained a financial loss (remember that the other party's financial gain often can be considered your financial loss) as a result of the infringement, it's time to see an attorney.

My only advice at this point is to seek an attorney who specializes in copyright and intellectual-property laws. As with medicine, you're usually better off with someone who specializes in your problem than with a general practitioner.

Seeking Out Online Copyright Resources

To keep up-to-date in the area of online copyright rulings, point your Web browser in these directions:

✦ Copyright Clearance Center (`http://www.copyright.com/`): The Copyright Clearance Center, Inc. (CCC) is a not-for-profit organization that provides copyright news and a pay service to identify copyright holders.

✦ Information Law Alert (`http://infolawalert.com/`): Drop by and get your free sample issue that covers copyright issues in a digital environment.

✦ The Copyright Website (`http://www.benedict.com/`): This site provides real-world, practical, and relevant copyright information of interest to (in their words) "infonauts, Net surfers, Web spinners, content providers, musicians, appropriationists, activists, infringers, outlaws, and law-abiding citizens."

✦ U.S. Copyright Office (`http://lcweb.loc.gov/copyright/`): This official government site, shown in Figure 19-5, contains oodles of information and links to copyright-related sites, including ASCAP (American Society of Composers, Authors, and Publishers); The Authors Registry; BSA (Business Software Alliance); BMI (Broadcast Music Incorporated); Copyright & Intellectual Property Forum (CNI-Copyright); MPLC (Motion Picture Licensing Corporation); National Writers Union; SPA (Software Publishers Association), and many more!

Applying Trademarks

Whereas copyright law protects works of the author, *trademark* law protects names, titles, short slogans, and logo designs.

For example, the name Microsoft belongs to, obviously, Microsoft Corporation. This ownership interest in the name is covered by trademark laws. These same laws also protect Microsoft, however, in the use of its slogan "Where do you want to go today?" Although the slogan isn't protected by copyright law, if you tried to use it in your online business, the Microsoft corps of trademark attorneys would be all over you like nerds at a computer clearance sale.

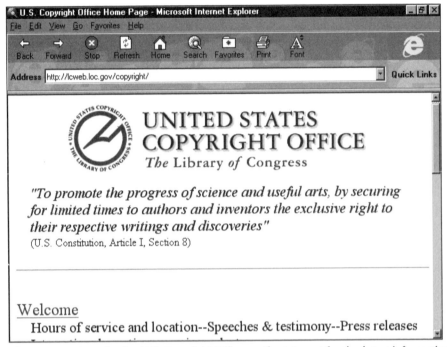

Figure 19-5: Drop by the U.S. Copyright Office on the Internet for the latest information about copyright laws.

As I just mentioned, trademark law also applies to logo designs. For years, Intel (the giant manufacturer of computer chips such as the ever-popular Pentium) has used as its logo the phrase *Intel Inside* inside a "swooshy"-looking circle, as shown in Figure 19-6. A few years ago, an Intel competitor designed a logo that consisted the word *Ditto* inside the same swooshy circle. This company apparently figured that it was safe because it used different wording in its logo. Intel didn't agree; it filed an infringement complaint based on trademark law.

I don't recall now whether the courts decided the case or whether a settlement was reached out of court. The result, though, was that the company no longer uses that logo.

Protecting Your Product Names

Trademarks don't apply just to names of companies. They apply also to product names, an area in which things sometimes get tricky. Rollerblade, for example, is a specific brand of inline roller skates. It not uncommon, however, for people (even journalists who should know better) to use the term "rollerblades" in generic references to inline skates.

Figure 19-6: You would be in sorry shape if you tried to use the Intel Inside logo on your products. (Just ask one company that did.)

The world is full of similar examples. Kleenex is a registered trademark for a brand of tissue, for example, and Jell-O is a registered trademark for a brand of flavored gelatin.

When a term is trademarked, you can't use it for your own products; also, in any reference you make to a trademarked name, you must refer to the name correctly. If you're writing for whatever reason about a mishap in your kitchen, for example, you cannot write "I slipped on my rollerblades and spilled my Jell-O, so I had to clean up the mess with a Kleenex." You would have to write something like this instead: "I slipped on my Rollerblade brand inline skates and spilled my Jell-O brand gelatin, so I had to clean up the mess with a Kleenex-brand tissue." You could also just use the simple version: "I slipped on my skates and spilled my dessert, so I had to clean up the mess with a tissue."

If you happen to write the sentence incorrectly, as in the preceding example, you probably would just receive a letter of warning from each trademark owner. If you use one of those names for your own product, however, you're in for a major (losing) legal battle.

No matter how original you think your product name is, someone, somewhere, has probably already thought of it and registered it with the U.S. Patent and Trademark Office. Before you make a final decision about your company or product name, you have to do some research.

Fortunately, trademark research isn't that difficult. You can do trademark research online in a number of places, including on CompuServe and a couple of different Web sites. The only drawback is that most trademark directories, even on CompuServe, charge a fee for their service.

At the Easy On-line Trademark Search and Registration site (`http://pomo.nbn.com/home/tm/`), for example, you pay $250 to search the first trademark and then $50 for each additional mark (see Figure 19-7). While I was writing this chapter, the folks that run this site were having a sale: "As a special promotion this week, your fifth search is *free!*" Oh, boy.

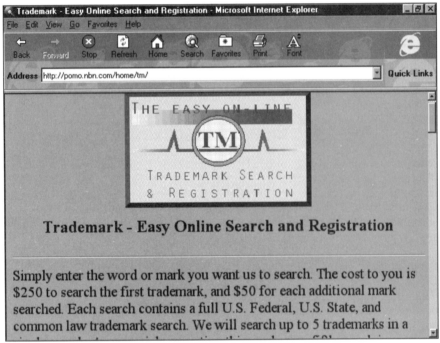

Figure 19-7: Before spending money researching trademarks online, check out one of the online libraries. Most of them have the information you need, and, best of all, they're usually free.

Fortunately, virtually every major public library has trademark records at least on microfiche, and many now have the information on CD-ROMs that you can access from dedicated PCs at the library. You get all the benefits of online trademark research with none of the cost.

Trademarks are similar to copyrights in that registration isn't required for protection under the law. Like copyrights, however, trademark notices and registration can be important preventive measures to help you protect your intellectual property.

Protecting Your Inventions with Patents

Now let's look briefly at the other half of the U.S. Patent and Trademark Office. Whereas copyright law basically protects your written work, a *patent* protects your inventions from being copied.

Key differences exist, however. First, protection under patent law is not automatically granted. You must apply for a patent, and it must be granted by the Patent and Trademark Office. Just because you have applied for a patent doesn't mean that one will be granted to you.

Tip

To qualify for a patent, your invention must be both unique and not obvious. If your invention doesn't meet both these requirements, your application for a patent is rejected. For this reason, patent applications can take many years to process, as the Patent and Trademark Office attempts to verify the unique, non-obvious nature of your invention. Despite its length, this process is the only way to protect your inventions.

In the past couple of years, a number of patent cases have made headlines in the computer industry. A while back, Compton's NewMedia was granted a patent for a multimedia search routine. This application created an uproar with other companies in the industry who claimed that the routine was by no means unique. As far as I know, this case hasn't yet been settled. If Compton wins, it will be able to charge a fee to anyone who wants to use that technology.

Failing initially to enforce your patent does not necessarily relinquish your rights. In the past couple of years, Unisys has decided to begin enforcing the patent on its popular GIF graphics-file format. (This format is often assumed to be in the public domain.) Likewise, IBM has opted to enforce its patent for Object Linking and Embedding (OLE), a technology most people think that Microsoft invented.

One area in which patents differ widely from copyrights is in duration. A patent is good for 17 years from the date of issuance. Period. After that, anyone who wants to can use or duplicate an invention without permission.

To learn more, drop by the U.S. Patent and Trademark Office, the official government site (http://www.uspto.gov/), on the Internet (see Figure 19-8).

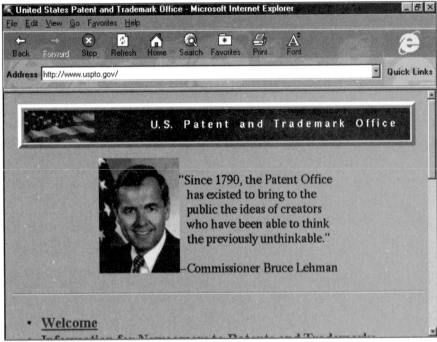

Figure 19-8: The U.S. Patent and Trademark Office is a great source of information.

The Bottom Line

Everything I've said in this chapter boils down to two important rules:

✦ Don't mess with anyone else's intellectual property.

✦ Don't let anyone mess with your intellectual property.

✦ Don't be your own lawyer when it comes to copyrights, trademarks, and patents.

(I threw that last one in there just to make sure that you're awake.)

Spreading Your Safety Net and Managing the Criminal Element

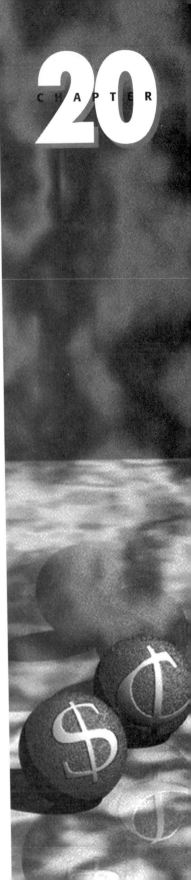

I hopped on the Komputer Klinic Webmaster's computer a few weekends ago just to download a few files I needed so that I wouldn't "hang" my system. As I looked on his computer for the folder that contains the Klinic sign-on software, I saw a few red flags: files that would make your Mom blush.

I opened the files and felt betrayed to see that they were exactly what I had expected. As I looked more closely at what else was on this guy's computer, I found games with time stamps recorded during the mid-afternoon, when he was supposed to be working. I checked his Web browser cache directory and found pages named Dirty Dukes and Virtual Dancers — names that had nothing to do with Komputer Klinic business (helping people with their computers).

I had had some other problems with this employee, but I had blamed myself for being too busy to manage him. I had even met with him at least three or four times a day, and I can assure you that it's not as though he had tons of spare time to mess around.

First thing Monday morning, I called him into my office. I showed him hard copies of what I had found. I explained that his actions were in violation of his employment agreement and were a misappropriation of company funds. I had no choice but to terminate him, effective immediately. He stood up, shook my hand, and said, "Kim, it was a pleasure working for you. I have one question for you, however: How can it be a misappropriation of company funds to use my computer to play games during business hours when I sometimes work on the weekends and don't tell you?"

Because I liked the guy, I gave him a few lessons about employee–employer respon-sibilities. I told him that he should learn a lesson from his experience with the Komputer Klinic and take it with him somewhere else. I hope that he did.

In Chapter 10, I talk a great deal about security, most of it related to online transactions and protecting yourself from crackers and hackers. Although your online transactions represent a valuable asset, both in terms of the dollars you have now and the dollars you hope to earn, they definitely are not your only security concern.

Tip

Think of your business as a mighty fortress. (I realize that this analogy may sound corny, but work with me here.) If you spend all your time protecting the front gate, one of your enemies is likely to slip in through the back gate. If you don't take appro-priate measures, one of your own subjects may get the idea that it's okay to take a little of your money and share a little of your wealth.

Protecting the future of your online business means protecting its operations now.

Protecting Yourself from Unscrupulous Employees: An Inside Job

A security program for any business, cyber or otherwise, must begin at home. You hire each and every one of your employees because you think that they can do a good job *and* because you trust them. The overwhelming majority of the people you hire will probably never betray that trust, but the proverbial bad apple is always lurking somewhere.

Warning

One thing you don't want to do in your workplace is to create an air of mistrust. If you act in such a way that employees think that you don't trust anyone or if you institute security measures that make it seem that way, your employees may become hostile and try to pull something just to "get even" with you.

The trick is to make your security measures appear to be standard procedures that no one thinks about much, other than to make sure that they're followed (procedures designed for "the other guy" or for employees who haven't been hired yet). Although you must take security measures seriously, don't make a big deal out of them with your employees, other than to make sure that everyone knows about and fully understands them.

In most businesses, and especially in cyberbusinesses, your ideas can be one of your most valuable assets. From the corner appliance store to major corporations, the history of business is littered with examples of employees who stole their employer's ideas to strike out on their own. As you learned in Chapter 19, however, copyright and similar laws don't cover ideas — only their specific expression.

Making Employees Sign on the Dotted Line

How can you protect yourself against actions like these? First, make sure that every new employee signs an employment contract or policy statement that includes a nondisclosure agreement. You might even want to include a non-compete covenant. Most people think of a contract as having a specific duration; in other words, a contract that binds both parties for a year, for example.

That's not what I'm talking about. An employment contract, agreement, or policy statement doesn't have to have a specific duration. It must only spell out exactly what you expect from each employee in terms of performance and behavior.

An important part of an employment contract is a *nondisclosure agreement*. This clause in a contract specifically prohibits employees from stealing any of your ideas and using them for their own benefit. The wording in your nondisclosure agreement should be as specific as possible.

Here are some things you should include in a nondisclosure agreement:

✦ First and foremost, any trade secrets you have developed

✦ Any unique methods you have developed that help you automate your business

✦ An exclusive client list, if you have one

✦ Any special technique that helps you cut costs

✦ Any information employees have access to that could be harmful if it fell into the wrong hands

You have a right to protect anything that gives you a unique advantage over your competition.

Research-and-development efforts you may have under way also represent a distinct advantage. Your nondisclosure agreement should also protect you from these sorts of leaks.

Tip

A nondisclosure agreement should cover anything you wouldn't want your competitors to know about.

In addition to signing a nondisclosure agreement, every employee of the Komputer Klinic signs a computing-policy statement. Feel free to adapt my nondisclosure agreement for your online business use (see Figure 20-1), but be sure to have your attorney look it over first for accuracy and viability for your cyberbusiness.

Nondisclosure Agreement

THIS AGREEMENT (the "Agreement") is made between The Komando Corporation and Peak Interactive, Inc. ("Companies" or the "Employer") and _____ ("Employee") and entered into on _____,19__.

For all purposes in this Agreement, the following definitions shall apply:

"Business Endeavors" shall mean any and all documentation, business know-how, and information related to Kim Komando and/or the Companies' Business Endeavors and any and all improvements, modifications, and enhancements, whether or not patentable, whether or not copyrightable, as provided to Employee during the relationship with the Companies, where the Companies do not disclose directly or publicly any and all documentation, business know-how, and information as relates to the Business Endeavors.

"Trade Secrets" shall mean any and all documentation, business know-how, and information relating to the past, present, or future business of the Companies, whether or not patentable, whether or not copyrightable, as provided to Employee during the relationship with the Companies, where the Companies do not disclose directly any and all documentation, business know-how, and information as relates to the Trade Secrets, or any plans thereof, or relating to the past, present, or future business of a third party or plans thereof that are disclosed to the Companies.

"Confidential Information" means nonpublic information that the Companies designate as being confidential or that, under the circumstances surrounding disclosure, ought to be treated as confidential. "Confidential Information" includes, without limitation, information relating to, released or unreleased, the Companies' software or hardware products, the marketing or promotion of any of the Companies' products, customer lists, the Companies' business policies or practices, and information received from others that the Companies are obligated to treat as confidential. Confidential Information disclosed to Employee is covered by this Agreement.

"Confidential Materials" shall mean all tangible and intangible materials containing Business Endeavors, Trade Secrets, and Confidential Information, including without limitation written or printed documents and computer disks or tapes, whether machine- or user-readable.

Based on the above, the parties hereby agree as follows:

Employee acknowledges that the Confidential Materials are the sole and exclusive property of the Companies. Employee shall surrender possession of any and all such Confidential Materials to the Companies upon any suspension or termination of the relationship with the

Companies. If, after said suspension or termination, Employee becomes aware of any Confidential Materials in possession, Employee shall immediately surrender the possession thereof to the Companies.

Employee may not reverse-engineer, decompile, or disassemble any Confidential Materials, including any software developed by either itself or another company as disclosed to Employee.

Employee recognizes that Companies' Confidential Materials are valuable, special, and unique assets of the Companies. Employee agrees that the Employee will not at any time or in any manner, either directly or indirectly, divulge, disclose, or communicate in any manner any Information to any third party without the prior written consent of the Employer. Employee will protect the Information and treat it as strictly confidential. A violation by Employee of this paragraph shall be a material violation of this Agreement.

The obligations created by this Agreement shall survive the expiration or termination of this Agreement. Employee agrees that any breach of the covenants set forth in this Agreement would cause Employer irreparable harm, that measuring the damages from such breach would be impracticable, and that money damages therefore would be an inadequate remedy for any such breach. Accordingly, Employee agrees that if he or she breaches any covenant in this Agreement, Employer shall be entitled, in addition to and without limiting any other remedies it may have, to injunctions or other appropriate orders to restrain any such breach without showing or proving any actual or monetary damage.

If it appears that Employee has disclosed (or has threatened to disclose) Confidential Materials in violation of this Agreement, Employer shall be entitled to an injunction to restrain Employee from disclosing, in whole or in part, such Confidential Materials or from providing any services to any party to whom such Information has been disclosed or may be disclosed. Employer shall not be prohibited by this provision from pursuing other remedies, including a claim for losses and damages.

The confidentiality provisions of this Agreement shall remain in full force and effect for a five-year period after the voluntary or involuntary termination of Employee's employment.

Recognizing that the various items of Confidential Materials are special and unique assets of the Companies, Employee agrees and covenants that for a period of three years following the termination of this Agreement, whether such termination is voluntary or involuntary, Employee will not directly or indirectly engage in any business competitive with the Companies. Directly or indirectly engaging in any competitive business includes, but is not limited to, (i) engaging in a business as owner, partner, or agent (ii) becoming an employee of any third party that is engaged in such business (iii) becoming interested directly or indirectly in any such business or (iv) soliciting any customer of Employer for the benefit of a third party that is engaged in such business.

(continued)

The Companies understand that Employee may possess proprietary information of third parties and may have ongoing obligations to such parties with respect thereto. The Companies especially require that Employee shall honor such ongoing obligations to such third parties and shall not use for the benefit of the Companies or disclose to the Companies any such proprietary information. Employee warrants or represents that he or she has the ability to enter into this Agreement and perform all obligations thereunder and that there are no restrictions or obligations to third parties that will in any way detract from or affect his or her performance thereunder.

In the event that any provision of this day Agreement is determined to be invalid and/or unenforceable by a final decision of a court of competent jurisdiction, it shall not affect the remainder of the Agreement, which shall survive and remain in full force and effect. Any dispute that arises thereunder shall be resolved by arbitration pursuant to the rules of the American Arbitration Association or the rules of the State of Arizona.

In the event that any litigation or arbitration is commenced to enforce any of the provisions of this Agreement, the prevailing party of said litigation shall be entitled to all costs thereof, including reasonable attorney's fees. This Agreement shall be governed by and interpreted in accordance with the laws of the State of Arizona, County of Maricopa.

AGREED to the date first written above, the parties sign in agreement.

Kim Komando
President, The Komando Corporation
President, Peak Interactive, Inc.

_____
Signature

and

Employee:

_____
Name

_____
Signature

Figure 20-1: A standard nondisclosure agreement.

Sharing Passwords and Codes to Keep Costs Down

Passwords, either for online systems or just the security system on your front door, can represent a real problem. I know of plenty of companies in which employees are allowed to share passwords. Sometimes everyone in the entire company uses the same password to enter the building. Or maybe just everyone from the accounting department uses the same system password.

It's good to have this level of trust in your employees, and you may go a lifetime without any problems. It takes only one security breach, however, to make you think twice about these types of policies.

The problem is that enhanced security usually means better (more expensive) systems and additional procedures. Stop and think for a moment about what you stand to lose from even one security breach. Put in those terms, the extra expense and effort is probably well worth it.

Tip

My bottom-line rule for passwords is this: Make sure that every employee has his or her own password, and make the sharing of passwords prohibited under the terms of your employment agreement or computing-policy statement. Just to play it safe, require your employees to change their system passwords periodically (every 30 days, for example). If your system can force employees to change their passwords at set intervals, that's all the better.

I'm not foolish enough to think that every single reader of this book will follow this advice. If you do want to cut corners and have shared passwords, you must change your passwords *at least* every time an employee leaves your company, especially if that employee was terminated involuntarily. Nothing can foul things up like a disgruntled ex-employee going ballistic on your computer system.

Granting Access to Employees Who Really Need It

The great thing about computerized security systems is that it's usually easy (if you know what you're doing) to control who has access to what. Because your marketing people don't need access to the same information as your accounting people, you should adjust their system privileges accordingly. The key is to make sure that no one has access to more information than necessary. If they do, it can lead to both intentional and unintentional actions that are equally disastrous. It's better to start off too restrictive and have to add more privileges later.

If all your systems are in-house, including your Web server, it's all handled by your trusted system administrator. If your cyberstore is housed on a commercial online service or ISP host system, the service can handle most security issues. Either way, you must keep the person responsible for handling access changes constantly informed of what's going on within your organization.

No matter where your cyberstore resides (on your system, on an ISP system, or on a commercial online service), the most critical access privilege is probably the ability to modify your online content.

Warning

Especially with Web pages (on which everyone and his uncle these days seems to be an HTML expert), employees face plenty of temptation to log on and make their own little tweaks that they're positive will greatly enhance your system without causing even the smallest problem. The old adage "Too many cooks spoil the soup" is extremely true in this area. You have much more at stake than a pot of soup, however. A foul-up in your online area can end up costing you a great deal of money.

Although you want to encourage employee suggestions and make your employees feel as though they're contributing to the success of your organization, security is one area in which you must draw the line. In my opinion, only two people in your organization — you and your system administrator — should have direct access to your online content. If you're your own system administrator, that narrows the field. Your online content is just too important to handle any other way.

Handling E-Mail Matters on a Shoestring

When you're first getting started, you may not need any sort of formal internal e-mail system. Even years down the road, you may not need such a thing. Even though my company, for example, has been going strong for many years, it's still relatively small in terms of number of employees. Sometimes, however, I do have to communicate with employees while they're at home. Also, I like to take advantage of the "virtual office" concept. Some of the people who work for me are spread out all over the country.

What all these people have in common is that I have given them all America Online accounts, which enables me to use AOL as my own intracompany e-mail system. This way, I have easy access to my employees, and they have easy access to me — no matter where we are. In addition, I don't have to worry about such issues as e-mail attachment incompatibility across multiple online systems.

Another good thing about AOL is that I can set up five users on one master account (or five e-mail accounts for the price of one). The only drawback is that only one of the five can be logged on at any particular time (surprisingly, not much of a problem so far).

Warning

One potential problem exists, however. Although I make it clear to each employee that it is expressly prohibited, the chance always exists that someone will go into some sex chat room or other inappropriate area. I don't tell any of my employees how to live their lives, but when they log on with a Komando sign-on, they're representing the Komputer Klinic, and it's *my* image that their actions can damage (that's a headache I just don't need).

Figure 20-2 shows part of my company's computing policy, which every one of my employees signs. Feel free to use this policy agreement if you want, but first make sure that your attorney approves it.

```
                        Computing Policy
```

Section 1: General online policy

After you receive an online account to be used to access the network and computer systems on that network, including both our internal network and any external network, such as the Internet and commercial online services, you are solely responsible for all actions taken while using that online account. Therefore:

Applying for an online account under false pretenses is a punishable disciplinary offense.

Sharing your online account with any other person is prohibited. In the result that you do share your online account with another person, you are solely responsible for the actions that other person appropriates.

Deletion, examination, copying, or modification of files and/or data belonging to other users without their prior consent is prohibited.

Use of facilities and/or services for commercial purposes is prohibited.

Use of facilities and/or services for entertainment purposes is prohibited.

Use of facilities and/or services for immoral or unethical purposes is prohibited.

Use of facilities and/or services for any online chat purposes is prohibited.

Any unauthorized, deliberate action that damages or disrupts a computing system, alters its normal performance, or causes it to malfunction is a violation regardless of system location or time duration.

Removal of *any* company property without expressed consent from the company's office manager is prohibited.

Section 2: Electronic-mail policy

Whenever you send electronic mail, your name and online account are included in each mail message. You are responsible for all electronic mail originating from your online account. Therefore:

Forgery (or attempted forgery) of electronic-mail messages is prohibited.

Attempts to read, delete, copy, or modify the electronic mail of other users are prohibited.

Attempts at sending harassing, obscene, and/or other threatening e-mail to another user is prohibited.

(continued)

Attempts at sending unsolicited junk mail, "for-profit" messages, or chain letters is prohibited.

Section 3: Network security

As a user of the network, you may be allowed to access other networks (and/or the computer systems attached to those networks). Therefore:

The use of systems and/or networks in attempts to gain unauthorized access to remote systems is prohibited.

The use of systems and/or networks to connect to other systems, in evasion of the physical limitations of the remote or local system, is prohibited.

Decryption of system or user passwords is prohibited.

The copying of system files is prohibited.

The copying of copyrighted materials, such as third-party software, without the express written permission of the owner or the proper license, is prohibited.

Intentional attempts to "crash" network systems or programs are punishable disciplinary offenses.

Any attempts to secure a higher level of privilege on network systems are punishable disciplinary offenses.

The willful introduction of computer "viruses" or other disruptive or destructive programs into the organization network or into external networks is prohibited.

Your signature below indicates that you thoroughly understand and accept these policies as grounds for your employment:

Signature	Date	Online Account

Figure 20-2: Make sure that your employees know what's acceptable when they sign on using a company account and resources.

Warning

I have just one more word to the wise about e-mail: Be careful of what you say. Watch humor and your language carefully. One person's joke is another person's grounds for a lawsuit. Many people tend to think that e-mail is as secure and private as a personal conversation, but that's just not the case.

Even deleting a message is no surefire way to keep someone else from reading it. Thanks to such things as daily backups and the undelete features on current systems, long forgotten e-mails can come back to haunt you. These capabilities have given rise, in fact, to a cottage industry of cyberdetectives who specialize in retrieving this type of data.

Tip

Here's a simple rule of thumb to follow if you're trying to decide whether some bit of information is appropriate for e-mail: If you want to say something that you wouldn't put on a written memo to become part of a permanently archived file, you probably shouldn't say it in an e-mail message either. If something is that important or confidential, your best bet is to pick up the phone or meet that person face-to-face.

Figuring Out Whether You Really Can Get Rich Quick

In this chapter, I have talked mostly about protecting your company from internal elements. You certainly cannot overlook the nasty people outside your organization, however, who would happily fleece you of your hard-earned money. Perhaps the best place to begin this part of the discussion is with the proverbial "get rich quick" scheme.

The way this type of scam evolves with the development of technology is amazing. The old, low-tech days saw the proliferation of "get rich quick by stuffing envelopes" scams. I remember the time when answering machines first began catching on. Suddenly the world was full of "get rich quick with your answering machine" scams. The dawn of desktop publishing gave rise to "get rich quick by publishing your own information" scams. As soon as 900 numbers appeared on the scene, scores of companies were willing to tell you how to get rich quick with your own 900 number — for a price. And don't forget the mid-1980s, when dozens of different real-estate gurus offered to tell you how to become a tycoon with no money, no credit, and no brains. With all the current Internet hype, of course, you run into the inevitable "get rich online" schemes.

The lure of easy money certainly has a strong appeal. Stop and think about it for just a minute. Suppose that there really was a way to "make $24,000 in 24 hours." And suppose that you knew this fantastic secret. Would it make more sense for you to use this secret yourself or for you to try to sell it to me for $25?

Note

That these people are trying to make their fortunes by selling an idea rather than using it themselves is proof positive that the idea itself is of little value. Every cyber-entrepreneur's dream is to follow Bill Gates down the road to success, but it can't happen overnight. Bill Gates got where he is today by working his butt off for many, many years and always staying dedicated to his vision. The unfortunate truth for all you would-be instant millionaires is that the only way to get rich quick on the Internet is by selling other people "get rich quick on the Internet" packages.

Preventing Credit-Card Fraud

Credit-card fraud is another security issue. You have to watch out for people who attempt to use bogus credit-card numbers to purchase your goods and services. In a traditional storefront, you have the opportunity to at least check the signature on the back (with some financial institutions, you can also check the picture on the front) to the person presenting the card. In your cyberstorefront, you have no such opportunity.

The first rule of accepting credit cards may sound obvious: Don't fulfill any orders until the credit-card payment is authorized. As you're starting out, you may have to complete this process manually, but you must follow through with it nonetheless. I have talked to a number of otherwise smart businesspeople who sold merchandise at computer trade shows but didn't spend the extra money for a phone line to authorize credit-card transactions. To save a few bucks, they accepted transactions offline and keyed them in "back at the shop." One guy got burned for a $3,000 computer system.

Warning

Because things happen so quickly in cyberspace, of course, it's often easy for criminals to grab credit cards and try to use them before they're reported as stolen. Also, because criminals have to steal only the credit-card numbers (not the actual cards) for their dirty online deeds, they may be able to use the cards without the cardholders even knowing that the numbers have been "lifted."

One good way to substantially reduce online credit-card fraud is to implement some sort of offline address-verification program for new customers and then ship only to that address on all future transactions. You can verify both postal and e-mail addresses so that this concept works equally well for merchandise you deliver either online or offline. This way, even if someone tries to dupe you with a bogus card, he can't. In the worst-case scenario, you ship merchandise to a legitimate customer who, in all likelihood, will simply return it promptly.

If you process credit cards electronically, check with your merchant account (the company that set you up to take credit-card orders). My company's account, for example, now cross-references the shipping address with the credit-card billing address. If the addresses are different, the order is flagged as invalid.

Additional Tips for Password Protection

Earlier in this chapter, I talked about administering a password program for your employees. What I didn't mention were methods that individuals can use to protect their own passwords. These guidelines apply whether you're the sole employee in your business or you have 100 people working for you.

The first method is simply not to give out your password to other people. This advice may sound so obvious that you're laughing right now, but — believe me — it happens, and to people as smart as you and I are.

Here's an example. Every so often, some idiot on America Online gets this brilliant, "original" idea. You open your mailbox and discover a message from some official-sounding screen name, such as PassAdmin. The message informs you that, because of some sort of unintentional corruption in the AOL database, you must tell this person your password as a means of authenticating your account. It all sounds very official and, on the surface, very believable.

It's all baloney, of course. If there were really a problem with your password, you wouldn't be able to log on to the system in the first place. Yet people fall for this type of scam. AOL periodically sends messages to remind members that no one from the service will *ever,* under any circumstances, ask for their password.

If you don't give out your password voluntarily, some people simply try to guess it. The first and simplest rule in creating your password is not to make it obvious. If your name is Bob, for example, you would have to be an idiot to make your password "bob." Most security experts agree, however, that you should go one step beyond non-obvious and *not* use a regular, English word for your password. For all intents and purposes, using a seemingly random jumble of letters makes guessing your password a tough task.

Tip

Avoid using your name, birthdate, or some other obvious information in your password. A good password is between six and ten characters long and includes both letters of the alphabet and numbers or punctuation marks. This type of password is more difficult to guess, but it is also more difficult to remember. If security is an issue, never write your password down on a piece of paper and leave it in or around your desk.

To force users to adhere to this additional level of security, I have even heard of some ISPs who run automated programs that attempt to guess their customers' passwords by using standard, English words. If the program is successful, the ISP sends the customer an e-mail notice advising that it's time to change the password.

Tip

Despite all this advice, some people will undoubtedly use real words for their pass-words simply because they're easier to remember. Fortunately, some online pass-words are case-sensitive: You can alter a password by changing the case of some of the letters. If you want to use "pizza" for your password, for example, because it's your favorite food and therefore easy to remember, make it "piZzA." Even if someone guesses "pizza," it doesn't match up.

The other generally accepted password-security measure, which I mentioned earlier in this chapter, is to change your password regularly. This way, even if some evildoer does manage to figure out your password, it is of value for only a limited time. Naturally, the protection benefits you until the next time you change your pass-word, but it's still a good idea to use in conjunction with the other measures I have mentioned in this section.

Paper: The Final Defense

Any decent computer system has some sort of audit trail built in. That is, it has some way to keep a record of everything that happens on that system for later review. This audit trail should monitor every action, by recording what was done, when it was done, where it was done, and who did it. Although all this information starts out in digital form, it is commonly printed on paper (or committed to microfilm) for archiving purposes (hence, the term *paper trail*).

I can't overstate the importance of an accurate paper trail. Without exception, every major case of computer crime (including the apprehension a couple of years ago of master cracker Kevin Mitnick) was solved by carefully analyzing the invaded system's audit trail.

Just knowing that you have a good audit trail in place may be enough to scare off some people. If a paper trail doesn't scare them off, it may be the only means authorities have of tracking down and prosecuting cybercriminals after a crime has been committed.

Searching Out Internet Resources

After talking about all the ways in which you can get ripped off in cyberspace, it may seem strange to say that the Internet also has terrific resources to help you prevent security breaches. For more information, check out these valuable resources:

✦ **Electronic Frontier Foundation:** A nonprofit civil liberties organization working in the public interest to protect privacy, free expression, and access to public resources and information in new media (http://www.eff.org/)

✦ **HR Headquarters:** A complete online service for human-resources information and policies (http://www.hrhq.com/)

✦ **Yahoo!:** The one place to see a complete listing of security-related sites (http://www.yahoo.com/Computers_and_Internet/Security_and_Encryption/)

✦ **National Computer Security Association:** Provides key services to three principal constituencies: end users of digital technologies, computer and communications industry product developers and vendors, and computer and information security experts (http://www.ncsa.com/).

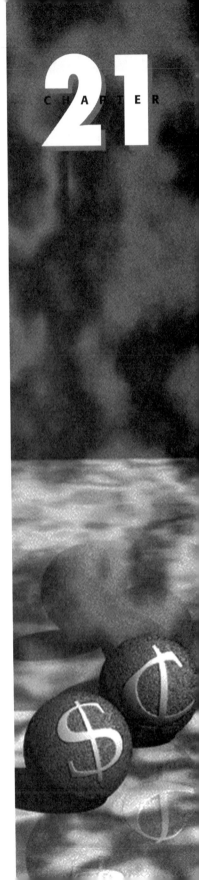

Looking Forward

By now you're probably wondering where the entire area of online and Internet business will progress from here. If I have done my job in this book, you should have at least a good idea about the answer to this question. The one thing to remember about any cyberbusiness, no matter what it is that you are selling, is that it's very different from any type of traditional business.

To use an extremely low-tech example, I would bet that shoe-repair professionals today do more or less the same things in more or less the same ways that shoe-repair professionals did them 10 years ago — or 50 years ago, for that matter.

I can tell you with a higher degree of certainty, however, that every single successful online business is doing things differently today (at least to some extent) from the way they did them only one year ago. When you're online, you're a part of cutting-edge technology. Technology changes so quickly that you're faced with either changing with it or being left behind.

With that in mind, I want to comment in this chapter on some of the trends and issues that I believe will affect your online business in the months and years to come.

Internet Appliances

For such a simple idea, Internet appliances have certainly created a great deal of controversy and hype. In case you're not familiar with the term, an *Internet appliance* is a device that connects to your television and enables you to access the Internet without having to use a real PC.

The reason that Internet appliances are such a hot topic is that this model of computing threatens the income of some of the biggest players in personal computing. Appliances make it possible for consumers to use little if any hard disk space and to have no system applications. Basic computer applications (word processing, database, and contact management, for example) reside on whichever host system subscribers use.

To type a letter, you launch the appropriate application from the host system in much the same way as local-area network users now use networked applications. When you finish, you can print the letter on your printer. If you want to save it, however, you save it on the host system in a directory reserved for only your files.

The biggest names in the computer industry, in both hardware and software, derive much of their profit from the traditional desktop model of personal computing. A user has a fully loaded PC on her desk, packed with RAM, a big hard disk, and a half-dozen or so applications purchased at a retail outlet. If the online community begins to shift toward a computing model in which people buy "wimpy" systems and no software, it's easy to see what will happen to some of those big companies' profits.

In my opinion, the use of Internet appliances can mean only positive things for a cyberbusiness. I for one would never buy a so-called Internet appliance. Few people I know would be likely to buy one either. The truth is that I'm a technologically savvy person, and so are my friends. And so are you.

Here's my point. You may get excited to hear how many millions of people are online. They represent only a small portion of the overall population, however. Millions and millions of people out in the world don't know "diddly" about computers and aren't willing to spend $2,000 or more to find out about them.

On the other hand, if you tell these technologically inexperienced people that they can jump into this Internet thing for about $300 — using their dear old television to boot — you will generate a great deal of interest.

The way I see it, Internet appliances have no chance of replacing stand-alone desktop computers, as least not until every single one of us has a supersonic-fast T1 line coming into our living room. The technologically savvy among us (and those who aspire to be) will continue to buy personal computers. An entirely new segment of the population, however (people with less interest and less money) will take the Internet-appliance road to the information superhighway.

The bottom line is that you will end up with many more millions of potential customers than you have now. You may never buy an Internet appliance, but what if your next-door neighbor buys one and uses it to connect to your site and buy your products? Who are you to complain? As long as more people get online, you don't have to concern yourself with how they get there.

Smart Cards

A high degree of uncertainty exists about which of the many current online payment options will evolve into the industry standard. If I had to make a guess, I would say that the answer is "none of them." I predict that, before anything ever gets decided, smart cards will arrive on the scene and take over as the payment method of choice, both online and off.

To understand the concept of smart cards, you have to understand that they represent only a particular use of microchip technology. They can be used for all sorts of applications, from credit cards to medical IDs. What makes smart cards so exciting is that each one carries its own microchip that can handle several hundred times the information a magnetic-stripe card can handle.

With all this additional capability, a smart card can hold and manage several different applications. For example, you can store your credit card, ATM card, and frequent-shopper card from a local department store on one smart card that's the exact size of your current credit cards.

The smart-card application that generates the most excitement, however, is *stored value.* This application is intended as a direct replacement for cash, in what are called *micropayments,* loosely defined as the payment for any product less than $20. You go to your bank's ATM, just as you do now, but rather than withdraw physical cash, the ATM "loads" your smart card with digital cash. When you go to a store and buy something, this digital cash is transferred directly from your card to the merchant. Smart cards are exciting news for online businesses.

You already know that credit cards in some form are now the logical choice for online payments. Credit cards are impractical for micropayments, however, especially in the range of $10 or less. The reason is that credit-card processing is expensive, primarily because of the live, online link required to process payments.

When you go to the store to pay for something with your credit card, the store must establish a communications link with a credit-card authorization center to make sure that the card is good. The concept of stored value eliminates the need for this link. The "digital cash" just moves from your card to the merchant with no third-party authentication.

The exciting thing about stored value is that this type of transaction costs less to handle than even cash transactions do. It has been estimated that the process of handling cash (counting it, taking it to the bank, dealing with employees who pocket a few dollars here and there) costs American businesses between 5 and 7 percent of their cash receipts. Stored-value smart cards eliminated most of these expenses. (Just imagine what a 5 to 7 percent increase in your profits would mean.)

You can see that traditional merchants have a financial incentive to want to implement stored-value technology. For this reason, you're likely to see increasingly more modems and PCs that are capable of using this same payment method for online commerce.

Because of the cost involved in accepting credit-card payments, 50-cent and $2 items just aren't practical for current online sales. After stored-value cards become popular, however, you will be able to sell items for a nickel and still make a profit. This method is especially beneficial to your online company if you're selling information products directly because you won't lose money after you pay those credit-card processing fees. To understand why, read on.

Commercial Online Services

In this chapter, I have told you about Internet appliances that will get millions of new users online and stored-value cards that will make it economically feasible to accept micropayments online. For the commercial online services, this news is good news.

Some people think that the Internet means doom for companies such as America Online and CompuServe. On the contrary, these companies are best positioned to exploit the Internet and shape its future.

Think about it. The commercial online services have already developed substantial, rich online content. How difficult can it be to migrate that content to the World Wide Web?

Two things will change for the online services. The first is competition. One reason that the current market for online services has remained small compared with the entire population is the investment — in both time and money — required to get one up and running. The Apple eWorld service, for example, didn't even make it to its second birthday. And whatever Microsoft eventually makes out of the Microsoft Network will be dramatically different from the initial MSN concept.

Because you can now start up a Web-based online "service" for a fraction of what it cost to start AOL, however, increasingly more subscription Web sites will be created, especially ones that cater to a particular niche or area of specialization. A large number of new services won't last, but I'm sure that at least a few worthwhile ones will.

Lower start-up costs and increased competition will lead to another change in the way online services conduct their business: the way they handle pricing. With two or three online services from which to choose, it's not exceedingly difficult to decide how you want to spend your $10 a month. When you can choose from several good sites, however, get to them all through a single modem connection, and then jump back and forth between them, your choices become much more difficult.

No matter how good the content on any particular service, no one wants to subscribe to 20 different services at $10 a pop. I believe that the currently popular flat-fee pricing structure will give way to more of a "pay as you go" approach. Rather than pay $10 a month to AOL, for example, subscribers may pay $1 a month for a basic membership. Then, when they access a particular area, such as the AOL Daily News section, it may set them back another quarter.

With this type of pricing structure, subscribers will be able to get only the features they want from all the different services without putting themselves in the poorhouse. More important, your cyberbusiness customers will be able to realize these same benefits, which makes the online environment that much more attractive.

Bandwidth

Every time I download a file in five minutes that would have taken me more than an hour with my first 2400 bps modem, I am truly amazed. When I consider that I'll be able to download that same file in less than a minute with an ISDN connection, I am even more amazed. I believe that ISDN technology and, more realistically, data-cable modems (I discuss them in more detail later in this chapter) represent the next great leap in consumer bandwidth.

To some extent, it's already happening. In California, for example, Pacific Bell already has in place a home ISDN program. In 1996, Pacific Bell began offering this service with direct Internet access. (This is hot stuff!)

High-speed transmission (five times faster than a 28.8 Kbps modem) isn't the only thing ISDN offers, however. Because an ISDN line is a digital line, it can carry voice, data, and fax transmission over the same line — and at the same time!

ISDN is an expensive area to get into right now. The modems it requires cost about three times as much as the average 28.8 Kbps modem. Service setup from a phone company is a little pricey too. And ISDN connections to ISPs (Internet service providers) generally cost more than standard dial-in connections. Like any other market product, however, connection prices will drop as their popularity increases.

All this increased speed will create a much more enjoyable online experience for your cyberbusiness customers. Faster speeds will also enable you to create much richer multimedia content for your cyberstore. Suppose for a moment that the average cybersurfer is willing to wait 20 seconds for a particular event. If ISDN is five times faster than any current capability, you will be able to stuff five times as much data into those 20-second downloads.

In short, ISDN will enable you to explore the use of audio, video, and animations on your online area like never before. Assuming that you make wise use of the extra bandwidth, you can only enhance your sales effort. And that, my friend, means more

Look for T1 lines to become more viable for businesses and consumers as costs come down. These superfast lines will enable a 10MB file to be transmitted in less than ten seconds!

Cable Modems

Maybe cable modems will happen, and maybe they won't. As far as I'm concerned, the jury is still out on this one, at least for the next year or so.

Cable modems are already available, and they have been for years. If you're wondering why they haven't caught on with consumers, the answer in general terms is that when two separate industries try to join forces for a common end, it's usually a slow go.

On one side of the issue is the cable industry, whose only business (and, therefore, only area of expertise) is to deliver television programming. On the other side is the computer industry, whose expertise is, obviously, in computers.

Each one of these industries has its own generally accepted "rules of play," its own dynamics, and its own philosophies and points of view. They're just plain different from each other. To understand what I mean, try to picture Fidel Castro and the President of the United States sitting down together to try to come up with the perfect form of government.

I think that it would be fantastic if cable modems would catch on with consumers. These modems would blow ISDN lines out the door. Heck, for that matter, they would blow T1 lines out the door. I'm just a little skeptical about whether all the parties involved in this venture will be able to establish a meeting of the minds, so to speak.

Online Banking

All across the country, banks and credit unions (both large and small) are making the leap into cyberspace, by offering real-time, Internet-based banking services. Although these services may not have a direct effect on your business, I believe that they will have an indirect positive effect.

Think about it for a minute. The security of Internet-based financial transactions is still a hot topic. Even though consumers' fears are largely unfounded, people are still hesitant to engage in online commerce. As a small online merchant, you can tell them until you're blue in the face that they have nothing to worry about. On the other hand, if Bank of America, Citibank, and Chase Manhattan come along and claim that there's nothing to worry about, people will probably listen.

People obviously trust their financial institutions. If they didn't, they wouldn't store their money there. By offering Internet-based banking services, financial institutions are legitimizing the idea of online commerce. More trust means that more people are willing to spend more of their money online. And that means, of course, more money in your pocket.

Information as a Product

I mentioned the concept of selling information a little earlier in this chapter. It sort of resembles the idea of "If I could get just $1 from every person." If you can sell small amounts of information for small amounts of money to large numbers of people, you stand to make large amounts of money. If you still haven't decided on a particular type of online business, this area is one that you should explore. I believe that it will turn out to be one of the largest growth industries in the history of online commerce.

The great part is that, because so much information is available, the possibilities are endless. As an exercise, take a walk through your favorite bookstore and look at all the different book subjects. Each one of these areas represents a special interest that carries with it a need for special information. If you can find a special-interest area that's demographically likely to have a high percentage of online users, you just may make a killing by providing the information those people need or want.

In Closing

One of my good friends claims that he had always wished that he had been born during the golden age of the Industrial Revolution. At one point in his life, he longed to have experienced the excitement and increased entrepreneurial spirit which dominated that era. My friend had wanted to be in on the ground floor as business (as society as a whole, in fact) began moving in a new, uncharted direction.

My friend doesn't feel this way anymore. He realizes that he is now in the midst of exactly what he had longed for earlier in his life — except that the current situation is even better. He doesn't need to invest a fortune to build factories and pay hundreds of employees to make his fortune. Everything he needs is at his fingertips, only a few keystrokes away.

I hope that you feel the same excitement I do about doing business in cyberspace. It has been compared to the Industrial Revolution and the California Gold Rush and even to Jed Clampett's striking oil. In my opinion, however, the potential for cyberspace businesses is better than all these things.

I cannot think of any time in history when the future has held so much potential for so many people. Maybe you have some doubts now, but I know that if you truly apply yourself, you can achieve all the success you deserve. I have tried to make this book as useful as possible for you. With all the different ideas I have presented, you probably won't be able to use them all. Even keeping track of all the ones you do use may be a big job. My parting advice is to make a checklist of all the tips in this book that you feel are appropriate for your cyberbusiness.

This checklist and your Vision for a Mission book can act as your to-do list as you put together your virtual business. That way, you won't forget anything important. Good luck with all your future endeavors. Please feel free to visit me and all the Komandos from the Komputer Klinic:

- **On the Internet:** http://www.komando.com
- **On America Online:** Keyword KOMANDO
- **On the Microsoft Network:** Go command KOMANDO

Good luck, and may all your online dreams come true!

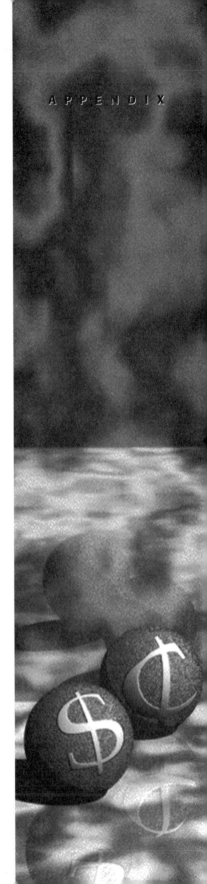

Installing the CyberBuck$ CD-ROM

I know that it seems incredible, but, included in the price of this tome of online marketing knowledge, you also received a CD-ROM loaded with great stuff. (If you somehow haven't noticed, the publisher packaged a CD-ROM inside the back cover of this book.) A CD-ROM holds about 640MB of information; this one is filled with as many bytes as possible to make sure that you get your money's worth.

To use the *CyberBuck$* CD-ROM, you need the items in this list:

✦ A 486-based computer or better

✦ Windows 3.1 or Windows 95

✦ At least 8MB of RAM

✦ A CD-ROM drive

Setting Up the CyberBuck$ CD-ROM

It's easy to use the *CyberBuck$* CD-ROM, but first you have to tell your computer how to use it.

You have to know which drive letter your computer calls the CD-ROM drive (on most computers, it's drive D). If you're not sure which letter represents your CD-ROM drive, here's the easiest way to find out: If you're using Windows 3.1, open File Manager from the Main program group; if you use Windows 95, click the Start button, the Programs folder, and then the Windows Explorer option. Either way, the drive letters for your hard disk drive, floppy disk drive, and — bingo — your CD-ROM drive are displayed. Look for the icon that looks like an ordinary CD you play in your stereo. The letter next to the CD-ROM drive icon is the drive letter for your CD-ROM drive.

Installing the *CyberBuck$* CD-ROM is easy:

1. Start Windows 3.1 or Windows 95. Make sure that all other applications are closed.

2. Remove the CD-ROM from the back cover of this book.

   Sharp objects and CD-ROMs don't play together well, so forgo your inclination to use a knife or a can opener to remove the CD-ROM from the packet (you might damage the disc). Instead, use your thumbnail or grab hold of the little flap that covers the disc and pull the flap up and then off.

3. Place the CD-ROM into your computer's CD-ROM drive.

4. From File Manager, choose File⇨Run from the menu bar or, from Explorer, click the Start button and then Run. In the Run dialog box, type the following line (where D: represents the drive letter of your CD-ROM drive) and click OK:

   D:\SETUP

After the *CyberBuck$* CD-ROM is installed on your computer, a CyberBuck$ program group or folder appears on your Windows desktop. To use the information on the CD-ROM, place it in your CD-ROM drive and then, from the CyberBuck$ program group or folder, double-click the CyberBuck$ program icon.

After the CD-ROM is loaded, a collection of icons is displayed that contains the other software programs and special offers you get to take advantage of just because you bought this book. Click on an icon to start that program (you may have to be patient until something happens). When you want to exit from a program on the CD-ROM, you can usually press Alt+F4 to get out quickly.

CyberBuck$ for Your On-Screen Reading Pleasure

Because the text for this entire book is on the *CyberBuck$* CD-ROM, you can search for a particular topic and have it appear on your computer screen faster than you can say, "I want money!" You can even read this book page-by-page on your computer screen if you want (just don't read it that way while you're in the bathroom!).

To use the electronic version of this book, first place the *CyberBuck$* CD-ROM in the CD-ROM drive on your computer. From the CyberBuck$ program group or folder on your Windows desktop, double-click the CyberBuck$ program icon, and then choose the CyberBuck$ icon from the CyberBuck$ menu.

AT&T WorldNet℠ Service Sign-on Software

A world of possibilities. . . .

With AT&T WorldNet℠ Service, a world of possibilities awaits you. Discover new ways to stay in touch with the people, ideas, and information that are important to you at home and at work.

Make travel reservations at any time of the day or night. Access the facts you need in order to make key decisions. Pursue business opportunities on the AT&T Business Network. Explore new investment options. Play games. Research academic subjects. Stay abreast of current events. Participate in online newsgroups. Purchase merchandise from leading retailers. Send e-mail.

All you need is a computer with a mouse, a modem, a phone line, and the software enclosed on the *CyberBuck$* CD-ROM. AT&T has taken care of the rest.

If you can point and click, you're there

Finding the information you want on the Internet with AT&T WorldNet Service is easier than you ever imagined it could be. That's because AT&T WorldNet Service integrates a specially customized version of the popular Netscape Navigator™ software with advanced Internet directories and search engines. The result is an Internet service that sets a new standard for ease of use — virtually everywhere you want to go is a point-and-click away.

Choose the plan that's right for you

If you're an AT&T Long Distance residential customer signing up in 1996, you can experience this exciting, new service for five free hours a month for one full year. Beyond your five free hours, you are charged only $2.50 for each additional hour. Just use the service for a minimum of one hour per month. If you intend to use AT&T WorldNet Service for more than five hours a month, consider choosing the plan with unlimited hours for $19.95 per month.

The five free hours are limited to one AT&T WorldNet Account per residential billed telephone presubscribed to AT&T for "1+ area code + number" long-distance dialing. Unlimited usage offers are limited to one logon per account at any time. Other terms and conditions apply. Prices quoted are current as of 4/22/96 and are subject to modification by AT&T at any time. Local, long-distance, or 800-number access charges and additional access charges and/or taxes that may be imposed on subscribers or on AT&T WorldNet Service will apply to all usage.

If you're not an AT&T Long Distance residential customer, you can still benefit from AT&T quality and reliability by starting with the plan that offers three hours each month and a low monthly fee of $4.95. Under this plan, you are charged $2.50 for each additional hour, or AT&T WorldNet Service can provide you with unlimited online access for $24.95 per month. It's entirely up to you.

If you're not currently an AT&T Long Distance Customer but would like to become one, please call 800-431-0800, ext. 21624.

AT&T WorldNet Service minimum system requirements

To run AT&T WorldNet Service, you need:

+ An IBM-compatible personal computer with a 386 processor or better

+ Microsoft Windows 3.1*x* or Windows 95

+ 8MB RAM (16MB or more recommended)

+ 11MB of free hard disk space

+ 14.4 Kbps (or faster) modem (28.8 Kbps is recommended)

We're with you every step of the way, 24 hours a day, seven days a week

Nothing is more important to AT&T than making sure that your Internet experience is a truly enriching and satisfying one. That's why AT&T's highly trained customer service representatives are available to answer your questions and offer assistance whenever you need it — 24 hours a day, seven days a week. To reach AT&T WorldNet Customer Care, call 1-800-400-1447.

Installation tips and instructions

+ If you have other Web browsers, please consider uninstalling them according to the vendor's instructions.

+ At the end of installation, you may be asked to restart Windows®. Don't attempt the registration process until you have done so.

+ If you are experiencing modem problems trying to dial out, try different modem selections, such as Hayes Compatible. If you still have problems, please call Customer Care at 800-400-1447.

+ If you are installing AT&T WorldNet Service on a PC with local-area networking, please contact your LAN administrator for setup instructions.

✦ Follow the initial online prompts and/or start-up instructions given to you by the vendor product you purchased. These instructions tell you how to start the installation of the AT&T WorldNet Service Software.

✦ Follow the on-screen instructions to install AT&T WorldNet Service Software on your computer.

When you have finished installing the software, you may be prompted to restart your computer. Do so when prompted.

Safeguarding your online purchases

By registering and continuing to charge your AT&T WorldNet Service to your AT&T Universal Card, you enjoy peace of mind whenever you shop the Internet. If your account is compromised on the Net, you aren't liable for any online transactions charged to your AT&T Universal Card by a person who is not an authorized user.

Today cardmembers may be liable for the first $50 of charges made by a person who is not an authorized user, which will not be imposed under this program as long as the cardmember notifies AT&T Universal Card of the loss within 24 hours and other-wise complies with the Cardmember Agreement. Refer to Cardmember Agreement for definition of "authorized user."

Setting up your WorldNet account

If you have not set up the *CyberBuck$* CD-ROM on your computer, follow the setup instructions in the section "Setting Up the *CyberBuck$* CD-ROM," at the beginning of this appendix. To set up your AT&T WorldNet Service Account, place the *CyberBuck$* CD-ROM in your computer's CD-ROM drive and then, from the CyberBuck$ program group or folder on your Windows desktop, double-click the CyberBuck$ program icon.

From the *CyberBuck$* CD-ROM main menu, double-click either the AT&T WorldNet Service icon for Windows 3.1 (if you are a Windows 3.1 user) or the AT&T WorldNet Service icon for Windows 95 (if you are a Windows 95 user). The AT&T WorldNet Service program group or folder appears on your Windows desktop.

1. Double-click the WorldNet Registration icon.

2. Follow the on-screen instructions and complete all the stages of registration.

After all the stages have been completed, you are prompted to dial in to the network to complete the registration process. Make sure that your modem and phone line are not in use.

Registering with AT&T WorldNet Service

After you have connected with the AT&T WorldNet online registration service, you are presented with a series of screens that confirm billing information and prompt you for additional account setup data.

The following is a list of registration tips and comments that will help you during the registration process:

✦ Use registration code **LHSQIM631** if you are an AT&T Long Distance Customer. Use registration code **LHSQIM632** if you use another long-distance carrier.

✦ AT&T advises that you use all lowercase letters when assigning an e-mail ID and security code because they are easier to remember.

✦ Choose a special security code that you will use to verify who you are when you call Customer Care.

✦ If you make a mistake and exit the registration process prematurely, all you have to do is click on "Create New Account." Do not click on "Edit Existing Account."

✦ When choosing your local-access telephone number, you are given several options. Please choose the one nearest to you. Please note that calling a number within your area does not guarantee that the call is free.

Connecting to AT&T WorldNet Service

When you have finished registering with AT&T WorldNet Service, you are ready to make online connections:

1. Make sure that your modem and phone line are available.

2. Double-click the AT&T WorldNet Service icon.

Follow these steps whenever you wish to connect to AT&T WorldNet Service.

©1996 AT&T Corp. All Rights Reserved. AT&T WorldNet is a service name of AT&T Corp. Netscape Navigator logos, Netscape Navigator, and Netscape are trademarks of Netscape Communications Corporation. Microsoft is a registered trademark and Windows is a registered trademark of Microsoft Corporation.

America Online Free Trial Membership

You have read all about the marketing opportunities on America Online in this book, and now you can try the service for free! All you have to do is double-click the America Online icon from the CyberBuck$ main menu and follow the installation instructions. You see the special certificate you need in order to take advantage of the free AOL trial membership packaged with the CD-ROM in the back of this book.

Minimum system requirements

To use the America Online membership kit on the *CyberBuck$* CD-ROM to sign on to America Online for Windows, you need the items in this list:

✦ A 486-based computer or higher

✦ Windows 3.1 or Windows 95

✦ 8MB of RAM

✦ 15MB of hard disk space

✦ 14.4 Kbps or faster modem

✦ An active phone line

Becoming a member

If you have not set up the *CyberBuck$* CD-ROM on your computer, follow the setup instructions in the section "Setting Up the *CyberBuck$* CD-ROM," at the beginning of this appendix. To use the information on the *CyberBuck$* CD-ROM, place it in your CD-ROM drive. From the CyberBuck$ program group or folder on your Windows desktop, double-click the CyberBuck$ program icon. From the CyberBuck$ menu, double-click the America Online icon to install the AOL software and follow the instructions on your screen.

When the installation is complete, double-click the America Online icon. Then follow the on-screen instructions, which include a one-time registration process. You are asked to choose a screen name and password to use during future sessions on the service. You are also asked to enter your billing information, which the company uses when your free trial membership ends.

If you have any trouble setting up the AOL software, call 1-800-827-6364.

When you see the Welcome window, your registration is complete and you are online. Have fun. Oh, and be sure to drop me an e-mail note (my e-mail screen name is KOMANDO) to announce your arrival.

Using keywords

Keywords are shortcuts you type to move quickly between America Online areas. You can access keywords in one of three ways:

✦ Choose Go To Keyword from the menu bar.

✦ Press Ctrl+K.

✦ Click the Keyword icon on the toolbar.

After the Keyword screen is displayed, simply type a keyword and press Enter. The keywords in Table A-1 can help you get started.

Table A-1	Some Helpful AOL Keywords
Keyword	*Area or Service*
KOMANDO	Kim Komando's Komputer Klinic
DISCOVER	AOL overview
SUPPORT	Members' Online Support
DIRECTORY OF SERVICES	Directory of services
FILE SEARCH	Search software libraries
NEWS	News and finance
STOCKS	Stock quotes/portfolio
PEOPLE CONNECTION	People Connection
ENTERTAINMENT	Games and Entertainment
TRAVEL	Travel and Shopping

For a complete list of keywords on America Online, choose Go To Keyword from the menu bar and click the Keyword List button.

Signing up for your trial membership

Your AOL trial membership begins the day you first sign on to the service; it expires after 30 days. During this 30-day trial period, your membership gives you these benefits:

✦ Free sign-up

✦ Free first month's membership

✦ Fifteen free hours of connect-time (you must use them within 30 days of your first sign-on)

After your trial time has ended, you don't have to do anything else to become a member; you are charged a monthly membership fee after the first month ends. When you go through the registration process, you choose a billing option. For example, you may ask America Online to automatically charge your Visa, MasterCard, Discover, or American Express card. Or you may have your charges deducted from your checking account.

For information about how to cancel your membership, choose Go To Keyword from the menu bar and type **Cancel** or call the America Online toll-free number (800-827-6364). You must cancel within 30 days of your initial connection to avoid being charged your first monthly fee. Your membership continues on a month-to-month basis until you cancel.

Your use of the America Online software constitutes your acceptance of the America Online terms of service, available online in the free Members' Online Support department. Please read the terms to get important information and conditions of your membership. America Online, Inc., reserves the right to change the terms of service, membership fees, and online charges at any time after giving notice to members.

Note

Use of America Online requires a major credit card or checking account. Users outside the 48 contiguous United States may have to pay a communications surcharge, even during the trial period. Limit one free trial per individual.

Building Your Free Home Page at the Komputer Klinic

Over the years, the award-winning Kim Komando's Komputer Klinic has become one of the premier sites on the Internet (see Figure A-1). You can use the Klinic's success to help build your own success. How? By purchasing this book, you are entitled to receive a free home page and get your own little piece of cyberspace. It makes perfect sense. Now that you know the online marketing ropes, my goal is to help you become your own publisher on the Internet with easy-to-use tools.

Here are some of the benefits of having a home page at the Komputer Klinic:

✦ You can create your own home page on the World Wide Web to showcase your company as well as distribute text, graphics, or sound files to your friends and associates.

✦ You receive tools to create your own page on the World Wide Web. You can create a page with text in addition to photos, graphics, or sound by using a simple form. You don't have to know a thing about the computer language called HTML (Hyper Text Markup Language). The Komputer Klinic has eliminated the need to learn how to read HTML — all you have to do is fill in a form.

✦ The Komputer Klinic gives each person who has purchased *CyberBuck$* as much as 2MB of hard disk space. You can store image files for use in your Web pages, or you can make files and documents available to your friends and co-workers.

✦ If you are an experienced user and do know how to use HTML, you can create a page on your own computer by using HTML editing software and then upload your page to the disk space available to you, for free, in the Komputer Klinic.

Figure A-1: You can have your own little piece of cyberspace for free at the Komputer Klinic home page.

> ✦ After you have your home page set up at the Komputer Klinic, be sure to check out the area that describes how to put your products in the official *CyberBuck$* online shopping mall.

Tip

The *CyberBuck$* CD-ROM in the back of this book contains the secret code you need in order to access the area within the Komputer Klinic where you can get your free Web page. To see that information now, follow the CD-ROM installation instructions and then double-click the Free Home Page icon. It's that easy.

Wait — There's More!

After you have the *CyberBuck$* CD-ROM set up on your computer, you can use the on-screen menu options to take advantage of other goodies that IDG Books Worldwide, Inc., and I have put together especially for you!

SurfWatch

SurfWatch lets parents, teachers, and employers block from their computers any unwanted sexually explicit and other material from the Internet, without restricting the access rights of other Internet users. The software removes no material from the Internet; it simply blocks the material from any computer or local network on which the software is installed. SurfWatch screens Internet newsgroups, World Wide Web, FTP, Gopher, chat, and other services. Double-click the SurfWatch icon from the *CyberBuck$* CD-ROM menu to see a special pricing offer for people who buy this book, or call 800-566-2636 for more information.

iMALL, Inc.

Double-click the iMALL icon from the *CyberBuck$* CD-ROM main menu to preview one of the most popular and talked-about malls on the Internet. Boasting more than 6 million hits per month, iMALL has demonstrated the unlimited possibilities of growing sales on the Internet. iMALL's electronic-mall format has a strong presence on the Internet (http://www.imall.com). To learn more, double-click the iMALL icon from the *CyberBuck$* CD-ROM menu.

Network Music

Network Music is one of the nation's largest producers of music, sound effects, and production elements for the broadcast, commercial, and audiovisual industries. Presentation Audio is a breakthrough CD-ROM audio library that brings professional-quality music and sound effects to the desktop for users of popular presentation products. Each volume in the five-volume library includes 30 music beds in 60-second, 30-second, and tag versions; 100 sound effects; and 100 production elements, chosen around a specific theme. These volumes are available in the library:

- ◆ Business/Office
- ◆ Pop Culture
- ◆ High Tech/Electronics
- ◆ Environments/Atmospheres
- ◆ Comedy/Animation

For a sampling of the company's products, double-click the Network Music icon from the *CyberBuck$* CD-ROM main menu. You can also visit the Network Music home page, at http://www.networkmusic.com.

TuneUp.com

Just as car owners have come to rely on the convenience of quick-change oil shops, customers who sign up for TuneUp.com subscriptions can periodically stop by to get a quick tune-up for their PC. With a subscription to TuneUp.com, you can also use other value-added services on the Web site, including the ones in this list:

- ✦ Tips from Kim Komando
- ✦ Printer driver updates
- ✦ Computer-parts purchasing
- ✦ Software demos
- ✦ Free Ziff-Davis trial subscriptions
- ✦ Advertisement banners with special offers

After you preview TuneUp.com on the *CyberBuck$* CD-ROM, you can get even more information from its home page, at (http://www.tuneup.com).

Innovative Quality Software

Innovative Quality Software stands alone in the PC digital-audio industry with first-class products and service. The award-winning Software Audio Workshop product line has been expanded to include SAW, SAW Plus, SAW Classic, and a line of FX modules. Innovative Quality Software continues to meet the needs of a cutting-edge industry that demands quality, performance, and value. For more information about Innovative Quality Software after you use the company's demo on the *CyberBuck$* CD-ROM, visit its home page, at http://www.iqsoft.com.

Æxpert, Inc.

Æxpert, Inc. is a computer-technology company dedicated to the design, development, and sale of tools used to simplify and improve the investment process. Æxpert offers intelligent investment tools for use by individuals, financial advisors, institutions, and financial-service companies. For more information about Æxpert, Inc., after you use the company's demo on the *CyberBuck$* CD-ROM, visit its home page, at http://www.aexpert.com. (If you get an error message when you first start this program, just exit from the main Komando screen and start over.)

Interactive Marketing Communications

Interactive Marketing Communications, a Softbank Interactive Marketing company, is dedicated to providing leaders and innovators in the marketing, brand, and advertising industries with the most up-to-date information and resources. It provides these resources through its events, such as Camp Internet and IM Conferences, its *Interactive Marketing* magazine, and its Web site (http://www.imcweb.com).

Updates to This Book

The dynamic nature of the Internet makes it impossible to ensure that every Internet address in this book will be accurate at the time you read it. The Komputer Klinic on the Internet has a special section to help you keep up-to-date (point your Web browser to `http://www.komando.com/cyberbucks`). Be sure to check out this area often. Besides, since you have learned about marketing on the Web, it's a natural for you to use the Web's vast resources to expand your new knowledge.

Index

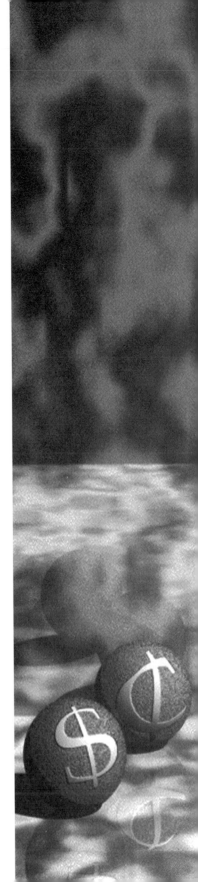

✦ **E** ✦

✦ H ✦

✦ I ✦

NOTES

NOTES

DUMMIES PRESS™

The Internet For Macs® For Dummies® 2nd Edition	by Charles Seiter	ISBN: 1-56884-371-2	$19.99 USA/$26.99 Canada
The Internet For Macs® For Dummies® Starter Kit	by Charles Seiter	ISBN: 1-56884-244-9	$29.99 USA/$39.99 Canada
The Internet For Macs® For Dummies® Starter Kit Bestseller Edition	by Charles Seiter	ISBN: 1-56884-245-7	$39.99 USA/$54.99 Canada
The Internet For Windows® For Dummies® Starter Kit	by John R. Levine & Margaret Levine Young	ISBN: 1-56884-237-6	$34.99 USA/$44.99 Canada
The Internet For Windows® For Dummies® Starter Kit, Bestseller Edition	by John R. Levine & Margaret Levine Young	ISBN: 1-56884-246-5	$39.99 USA/$54.99 Canada

MACINTOSH

Mac® Programming For Dummies®	by Dan Parks Sydow	ISBN: 1-56884-173-6	$19.95 USA/$26.95 Canada
Macintosh® System 7.5 For Dummies®	by Bob LeVitus	ISBN: 1-56884-197-3	$19.95 USA/$26.95 Canada
MORE Macs® For Dummies®	by David Pogue	ISBN: 1-56884-087-X	$19.95 USA/$26.95 Canada
PageMaker 5 For Macs® For Dummies®	by Galen Gruman & Deke McClelland	ISBN: 1-56884-178-7	$19.95 USA/$26.95 Canada
QuarkXPress 3.3 For Dummies®	by Galen Gruman & Barbara Assadi	ISBN: 1-56884-217-1	$19.99 USA/$26.95 Canada
Upgrading and Fixing Macs® For Dummies®	by Kearney Rietmann & Frank Higgins	ISBN: 1-56884-189-2	$19.95 USA/$26.95 Canada

MULTIMEDIA

Multimedia & CD-ROMs For Dummies® 2nd Edition	by Andy Rathbone	ISBN: 1-56884-907-9	$19.99 USA/$26.99 Canada
Multimedia & CD-ROMs For Dummies® Interactive Multimedia Value Pack, 2nd Edition	by Andy Rathbone	ISBN: 1-56884-909-5	$29.99 USA/$39.99 Canada

OPERATING SYSTEMS:

DOS

MORE DOS For Dummies®	by Dan Gookin	ISBN: 1-56884-046-2	$19.95 USA/$26.95 Canada
OS/2® Warp For Dummies® 2nd Edition	by Andy Rathbone	ISBN: 1-56884-205-8	$19.95 USA/$26.99 Canada

UNIX

MORE UNIX® For Dummies®	by John R. Levine & Margaret Levine Young	ISBN: 1-56884-361-5	$19.99 USA/$26.95 Canada
UNIX® For Dummies®	by John R. Levine & Margaret Levine Young	ISBN: 1-878058-58-4	$19.95 USA/$26.95 Canada

WINDOWS

MORE Windows® For Dummies® 2nd Edition	by Andy Rathbone	ISBN: 1-56884-048-9	$19.95 USA/$26.95 Canada
Windows® 95 For Dummies®	by Andy Rathbone	ISBN: 1-56884-240-6	$19.99 USA/$26.99 Canada

PCS/HARDWARE

Illustrated Computer Dictionary For Dummies® 2nd Edition	by Dan Gookin & Wallace Wang	ISBN: 1-56884-218-X	$12.95 USA/$16.95 Canada
Upgrading and Fixing PCs For Dummies® 2nd Edition	by Andy Rathbone	ISBN: 1-56884-903-6	$19.99 USA/$26.99 Canada

PRESENTATION/AUTOCAD

AutoCAD For Dummies®	by Bud Smith	ISBN: 1-56884-191-4	$19.95 USA/$26.95 Canada
PowerPoint 4 For Windows® For Dummies®	by Doug Lowe	ISBN: 1-56884-161-2	$16.99 USA/$22.99 Canada

PROGRAMMING

Borland C++ For Dummies®	by Michael Hyman	ISBN: 1-56884-162-0	$19.95 USA/$26.95 Canada
C For Dummies® Volume 1	by Dan Gookin	ISBN: 1-878058-78-9	$19.95 USA/$26.95 Canada
C++ For Dummies®	by Stephen R. Davis	ISBN: 1-56884-163-9	$19.95 USA/$26.95 Canada
Delphi Programming For Dummies®	by Neil Rubenking	ISBN: 1-56884-200-7	$19.99 USA/$26.99 Canada
Mac® Programming For Dummies®	by Dan Parks Sydow	ISBN: 1-56884-173-6	$19.95 USA/$26.95 Canada
PowerBuilder 4 Programming For Dummies®	by Ted Coombs & Jason Coombs	ISBN: 1-56884-325-9	$19.99 USA/$26.99 Canada
QBasic Programming For Dummies®	by Douglas Hergert	ISBN: 1-56884-093-4	$19.95 USA/$26.95 Canada
Visual Basic 3 For Dummies®	by Wallace Wang	ISBN: 1-56884-076-4	$19.95 USA/$26.95 Canada
Visual Basic "X" For Dummies®	by Wallace Wang	ISBN: 1-56884-230-9	$19.99 USA/$26.99 Canada
Visual C++ 2 For Dummies®	by Michael Hyman & Bob Arnson	ISBN: 1-56884-328-3	$19.99 USA/$26.99 Canada
Windows® 95 Programming For Dummies®	by S. Randy Davis	ISBN: 1-56884-327-5	$19.99 USA/$26.99 Canada

SPREADSHEET

1-2-3 For Dummies®	by Greg Harvey	ISBN: 1-878058-60-6	$16.95 USA/$22.95 Canada
1-2-3 For Windows® 5 For Dummies® 2nd Edition	by John Walkenbach	ISBN: 1-56884-216-3	$16.95 USA/$22.95 Canada
Excel 5 For Macs® For Dummies®	by Greg Harvey	ISBN: 1-56884-186-8	$19.95 USA/$26.95 Canada
Excel For Dummies® 2nd Edition	by Greg Harvey	ISBN: 1-56884-050-0	$16.95 USA/$22.95 Canada
MORE 1-2-3 For DOS For Dummies®	by John Weingarten	ISBN: 1-56884-224-4	$19.99 USA/$26.99 Canada
MORE Excel 5 For Windows® For Dummies®	by Greg Harvey	ISBN: 1-56884-207-4	$19.95 USA/$26.95 Canada
Quattro Pro 6 For Windows® For Dummies®	by John Walkenbach	ISBN: 1-56884-174-4	$19.95 USA/$26.95 Canada
Quattro Pro For DOS For Dummies®	by John Walkenbach	ISBN: 1-56884-023-3	$16.95 USA/$22.95 Canada

UTILITIES

Norton Utilities 8 For Dummies®	by Beth Slick	ISBN: 1-56884-166-3	$19.95 USA/$26.95 Canada

VCRS/CAMCORDERS

VCRs & Camcorders For Dummies™	by Gordon McComb & Andy Rathbone	ISBN: 1-56884-229-5	$14.99 USA/$20.99 Canada

WORD PROCESSING

Ami Pro For Dummies®	by Jim Meade	ISBN: 1-56884-049-7	$19.95 USA/$26.95 Canada
MORE Word For Windows® 6 For Dummies®	by Doug Lowe	ISBN: 1-56884-165-5	$19.95 USA/$26.95 Canada
MORE WordPerfect® 6 For Windows® For Dummies®	by Margaret Levine Young & David C. Kay	ISBN: 1-56884-206-6	$19.95 USA/$26.95 Canada
MORE WordPerfect® 6 For DOS For Dummies®	by Wallace Wang, edited by Dan Gookin	ISBN: 1-56884-047-0	$19.95 USA/$26.95 Canada
Word 6 For Macs® For Dummies®	by Dan Gookin	ISBN: 1-56884-190-6	$19.95 USA/$26.95 Canada
Word For Windows® 6 For Dummies®	by Dan Gookin	ISBN: 1-56884-075-6	$16.95 USA/$22.95 Canada
Word For Windows® For Dummies®	by Dan Gookin & Ray Werner	ISBN: 1-878058-86-X	$16.95 USA/$22.95 Canada
WordPerfect® 6 For DOS For Dummies®	by Dan Gookin	ISBN: 1-878058-77-0	$16.95 USA/$22.95 Canada
WordPerfect® 6.1 For Windows® For Dummies® 2nd Edition	by Margaret Levine Young & David Kay	ISBN: 1-56884-243-0	$16.95 USA/$22.95 Canada
WordPerfect® For Dummies®	by Dan Gookin	ISBN: 1-878058-52-5	$16.95 USA/$22.95 Canada

Fun, Fast, & Cheap!™

NEW!

The Internet For Macs® For Dummies® Quick Reference

by Charles Seiter

ISBN:1-56884-967-2
$9.99 USA/$12.99 Canada

NEW!

Windows® 95 For Dummies® Quick Reference

by Greg Harvey

ISBN: 1-56884-964-8
$9.99 USA/$12.99 Canada

SUPER STAR

Photoshop 3 For Macs® For Dummies® Quick Reference

by Deke McClelland

ISBN: 1-56884-968-0
$9.99 USA/$12.99 Canada

SUPER STAR

WordPerfect® For DOS For Dummies® Quick Reference

by Greg Harvey

ISBN: 1-56884-009-8
$8.95 USA/$12.95 Canada

Title	Author	ISBN	Price
DATABASE			
Access 2 For Dummies® Quick Reference	by Stuart J. Stuple	ISBN: 1-56884-167-1	$8.95 USA/$11.95 Canada
dBASE 5 For DOS For Dummies® Quick Reference	by Barrie Sosinsky	ISBN: 1-56884-954-0	$9.99 USA/$12.99 Canada
dBASE 5 For Windows® For Dummies® Quick Reference	by Stuart J. Stuple	ISBN: 1-56884-953-2	$9.99 USA/$12.99 Canada
Paradox 5 For Windows® For Dummies® Quick Reference	by Scott Palmer	ISBN: 1-56884-960-5	$9.99 USA/$12.99 Canada
DESKTOP PUBLISHING/ILLUSTRATION/GRAPHICS			
CorelDRAW! 5 For Dummies® Quick Reference	by Raymond E. Werner	ISBN: 1-56884-952-4	$9.99 USA/$12.99 Canada
Harvard Graphics For Windows® For Dummies® Quick Reference	by Raymond E. Werner	ISBN: 1-56884-962-1	$9.99 USA/$12.99 Canada
Photoshop 3 For Macs® For Dummies® Quick Reference	by Deke McClelland	ISBN: 1-56884-968-0	$9.99 USA/$12.99 Canada
FINANCE/PERSONAL FINANCE			
Quicken 4 For Windows® For Dummies® Quick Reference	by Stephen L. Nelson	ISBN: 1-56884-950-8	$9.95 USA/$12.95 Canada
GROUPWARE/INTEGRATED			
Microsoft® Office 4 For Windows® For Dummies® Quick Reference	by Doug Lowe	ISBN: 1-56884-958-3	$9.99 USA/$12.99 Canada
Microsoft® Works 3 For Windows® For Dummies® Quick Reference	by Michael Partington	ISBN: 1-56884-959-1	$9.99 USA/$12.99 Canada
INTERNET/COMMUNICATIONS/NETWORKING			
The Internet For Dummies® Quick Reference	by John R. Levine & Margaret Levine Young	ISBN: 1-56884-168-X	$8.95 USA/$11.95 Canada
MACINTOSH			
Macintosh® System 7.5 For Dummies® Quick Reference	by Stuart J. Stuple	ISBN: 1-56884-956-7	$9.99 USA/$12.99 Canada
OPERATING SYSTEMS:			
DOS			
DOS For Dummies® Quick Reference	by Greg Harvey	ISBN: 1-56884-007-1	$8.95 USA/$11.95 Canada
UNIX			
UNIX® For Dummies® Quick Reference	by John R. Levine & Margaret Levine Young	ISBN: 1-56884-094-2	$8.95 USA/$11.95 Canada
WINDOWS			
Windows® 3.1 For Dummies® Quick Reference, 2nd Edition	by Greg Harvey	ISBN: 1-56884-951-6	$8.95 USA/$11.95 Canada
PCs/HARDWARE			
Memory Management For Dummies® Quick Reference	by Doug Lowe	ISBN: 1-56884-362-3	$9.99 USA/$12.99 Canada
PRESENTATION/AUTOCAD			
AutoCAD For Dummies® Quick Reference	by Ellen Finkelstein	ISBN: 1-56884-198-1	$9.95 USA/$12.95 Canada
SPREADSHEET			
1-2-3 For Dummies® Quick Reference	by John Walkenbach	ISBN: 1-56884-027-6	$8.95 USA/$11.95 Canada
1-2-3 For Windows® 5 For Dummies® Quick Reference	by John Walkenbach	ISBN: 1-56884-957-5	$9.95 USA/$12.95 Canada
Excel For Windows® For Dummies® Quick Reference, 2nd Edition	by John Walkenbach	ISBN: 1-56884-096-9	$8.95 USA/$11.95 Canada
Quattro Pro 6 For Windows® For Dummies® Quick Reference	by Stuart J. Stuple	ISBN: 1-56884-172-8	$9.95 USA/$12.95 Canada
WORD PROCESSING			
Word For Windows® 6 For Dummies® Quick Reference	by George Lynch	ISBN: 1-56884-095-0	$8.95 USA/$11.95 Canada
Word For Windows® For Dummies® Quick Reference	by George Lynch	ISBN: 1-56884-029-2	$8.95 USA/$11.95 Canada
WordPerfect® 6.1 For Windows® For Dummies® Quick Reference, 2nd Edition	by Greg Harvey	ISBN: 1-56884-966-4	$9.99 USA/$12.99/Canada

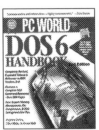

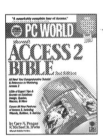

Macworld® Mac® & Power Mac SECRETS™, 2nd Edition
by David Pogue & Joseph Schorr

This is the definitive Mac reference for those who want to become power users! Includes three disks with 9MB of software!

ISBN: 1-56884-175-2
$39.95 USA/$54.95 Canada

Includes 3 disks chock full of software.

Macworld® Mac® FAQs™
by David Pogue

Written by the hottest Macintosh author around, David Pogue, *Macworld Mac FAQs* gives users the ultimate Mac reference. Hundreds of Mac questions and answers side-by-side, right at your fingertips, and organized into six easy-to-reference sections with lots of sidebars and diagrams.

ISBN: 1-56884-480-8
$19.99 USA/$26.99 Canada

Macworld® System 7.5 Bible, 3rd Edition
by Lon Poole

ISBN: 1-56884-098-5
$29.95 USA/$39.95 Canada

Macworld® ClarisWorks 3.0 Companion, 3rd Edition
by Steven A. Schwartz

ISBN: 1-56884-481-6
$24.99 USA/$34.99 Canada

Macworld® Complete Mac® Handbook Plus Interactive CD, 3rd Edition
by Jim Heid

ISBN: 1-56884-192-2
$39.95 USA/$54.95 Canada

Includes an interactive CD-ROM.

Macworld® Ultimate Mac® CD-ROM
by Jim Heid

ISBN: 1-56884-477-8
$19.99 USA/$26.99 Canada

CD-ROM includes version 2.0 of QuickTime, and over 65 MB of the best shareware, freeware, fonts, sounds, and more!

Macworld® Networking Bible, 2nd Edition
by Dave Kosiur & Joel M. Snyder

ISBN: 1-56884-194-9
$29.95 USA/$39.95 Canada

Macworld® Photoshop 3 Bible, 2nd Edition
by Deke McClelland

ISBN: 1-56884-158-2
$39.95 USA/$54.95 Canada

Includes stunning CD-ROM with add-ons, digitized photos and more.

Macworld® Photoshop 2.5 Bible
by Deke McClelland

ISBN: 1-56884-022-5
$29.95 USA/$39.95 Canada

Macworld® FreeHand 4 Bible
by Deke McClelland

ISBN: 1-56884-170-1
$29.95 USA/$39.95 Canada

Macworld® Illustrator 5.0/5.5 Bible
by Ted Alspach

ISBN: 1-56884-097-7
$39.95 USA/$54.95 Canada

Includes CD-ROM with QuickTime tutorials.

Order Center: **(800) 762-2974** *(8 a.m.–6 p.m., EST, weekdays)*

Quantity	ISBN	Title	Price	Total

Shipping & Handling Charges

	Description	First book	Each additional book	Total
Domestic	Normal	$4.50	$1.50	$
	Two Day Air	$8.50	$2.50	$
	Overnight	$18.00	$3.00	$
International	Surface	$8.00	$8.00	$
	Airmail	$16.00	$16.00	$
	DHL Air	$17.00	$17.00	$

*For large quantities call for shipping & handling charges.
**Prices are subject to change without notice.

Ship to:

Name _____

Company _____

Address _____

City/State/Zip _____

Daytime Phone _____

Payment: ☐ Check to IDG Books Worldwide (US Funds Only)

        ☐ VISA   ☐ MasterCard   ☐ American Express

Card # _____ Expires _____

Signature _____

Subtotal _____

CA residents add
applicable sales tax _____

IN, MA, and MD
residents add
5% sales tax _____

IL residents add
6.25% sales tax_____

RI residents add
7% sales tax_____

TX residents add
8.25% sales tax_____

Shipping_____

Total _____

Please send this order form to:
IDG Books Worldwide, Inc.
Attn: Order Entry Dept.
7260 Shadeland Station, Suite 100
Indianapolis, IN 46256

Allow up to 3 weeks for delivery.
Thank you!

IDG BOOKS WORLDWIDE, INC.
END-USER LICENSE AGREEMENT

Read This. You should carefully read these terms and conditions before opening the software packet(s) included with this book ("Book"). This is a license agreement ("Agreement") between you and IDG Books Worldwide, Inc. ("IDGB"). By opening the accompanying software packet(s), you acknowledge that you have read and accept the following terms and conditions. If you do not agree and do not want to be bound by such terms and conditions, promptly return the Book and the unopened software packet(s) to the place you obtained them for a full refund.

License Grant. IDGB grants to you (either an individual or entity) a nonexclusive license to use one copy of the enclosed software program(s) (collectively, the "Software") solely for your own personal or business purposes on a single computer (whether a standard computer or a workstation component of a multiuser network). The Software is in use on a computer when it is loaded into temporary memory (that is, RAM) or installed into permanent memory (for example, hard disk, CD-ROM, or other storage device). IDGB reserves all rights not expressly granted herein.

Ownership. IDGB is the owner of all right, title, and interest, including copyright, in and to the compilation of the Software recorded on the disk(s)/CD-ROM. Copyright to the individual programs on the disk(s)/CD-ROM is owned by the author or other authorized copyright owner of each program. Ownership of the Software and all proprietary rights relating thereto remain with IDGB and its licensors.

Restrictions On Use and Transfer.

You may only (i) make one copy of the Software for backup or archival purposes, or (ii) transfer the Software to a single hard disk, provided that you keep the original for backup or archival purposes. You may not (i) rent or lease the Software, (ii) copy or reproduce the Software through a LAN or other network system or through any computer subscriber system or bulletin-board system, or (iii) modify, adapt, or create derivative works based on the Software.

You may not reverse engineer, decompile, or disassemble the Software. You may transfer the Software and user documentation on a permanent basis, provided that the transferee agrees to accept the terms and conditions of this Agreement and you retain no copies. If the Software is an update or has been updated, any transfer must include the most recent update and all prior versions.

Restrictions on Use of Individual Programs. You must follow the individual requirements and restrictions detailed for each individual program. These limitations are contained in the individual license agreements recorded on the disk(s)/CD-ROM. These restrictions include a requirement that after using the program for the period of time specified in its text, the user must pay a registration fee or discontinue use. By opening the Software packet(s), you will be agreeing to abide by the licenses and restrictions for these individual programs. None of the material on this disk(s) or listed in this Book may ever be distributed, in original or modified form, for commercial purposes.

Limited Warranty.

IDGB warrants that the Software and disk(s)/CD-ROM are free from defects in materials and workmanship under normal use for a period of sixty (60) days from the date of purchase of this Book. If IDGB receives notification within the warranty period of defects in materials or workmanship, IDGB will replace the defective disk(s)/CD-ROM.

IDGB AND THE AUTHOR OF THE BOOK DISCLAIM ALL OTHER WARRANTIES, EXPRESS OR IMPLIED, INCLUDING WITHOUT LIMITATION IMPLIED WARRANTIES OF MERCHANTABILITY AND FITNESS FOR A PARTICULAR PURPOSE, WITH RESPECT TO THE SOFTWARE, THE PROGRAMS, THE SOURCE CODE CONTAINED THEREIN, AND/OR THE TECHNIQUES DESCRIBED IN THIS BOOK. IDGB DOES NOT WARRANT THAT THE FUNCTIONS CONTAINED IN THE SOFTWARE WILL MEET YOUR REQUIREMENTS OR THAT THE OPERATION OF THE SOFTWARE WILL BE ERROR FREE.

This limited warranty gives you specific legal rights, and you may have other rights which vary from jurisdiction to jurisdiction.

Remedies.

IDGB's entire liability and your exclusive remedy for defects in materials and workmanship shall be limited to replacement of the Software, which is returned to IDGB at the address set forth below with a copy of your receipt. This Limited Warranty is void if failure of the Software has resulted from accident, abuse, or misapplication. Any replacement Software will be warranted for the remainder of the original warranty period or thirty (30) days, whichever is longer.

In no event shall IDGB or the author be liable for any damages whatsoever (including without limitation damages for loss of business profits, business interruption, loss of business information, or any other pecuniary loss) arising out of the use of or inability to use the Book or the Software, even if IDGB has been advised of the possibility of such damages.

Because some jurisdictions do not allow the exclusion or limitation of liability for consequential or incidental damages, the above limitation or exclusion may not apply to you.

U.S. Government Restricted Rights. Use, duplication, or disclosure of the Software by the U.S. Government is subject to restrictions stated in paragraph (c) (1) (ii) of the Rights in Technical Data and Computer Software clause of DFARS 252.227-7013, and in subparagraphs (a) through (d) of the Commercial Computer—Restricted Rights clause at FAR 52.227-19, and in similar clauses in the NASA FAR supplement, when applicable.

General. This Agreement constitutes the entire understanding of the parties and revokes and supersedes all prior agreements, oral or written, between them and may not be modified or amended except in a writing signed by both parties hereto which specifically refers to this Agreement. This Agreement shall take precedence over any other documents that may be in conflict herewith. If any one or more provisions contained in this Agreement are held by any court or tribunal to be invalid, illegal, or otherwise unenforceable, each and every other provision shall remain in full force and effect.

Installation Instructions

This book's appendix, "Installing the *CyberBuck$* CD-ROM," gives specific installation instructions for the CD-ROM included in the back of this book.